Lecture Notes in Computer Science 12857

More information about this subseries at http://www.springer.com/series/7408

Stefan Biffl · Elena Navarro ·
Welf Löwe · Marjan Sirjani ·
Raffaela Mirandola · Danny Weyns (Eds.)

Software Architecture

15th European Conference, ECSA 2021
Virtual Event, Sweden, September 13–17, 2021
Proceedings

 Springer

Editors
Stefan Biffl (iD)
Institute of Information Systems Engineering
Technische Universität Wien
Vienna, Austria

Welf Löwe (iD)
Department of Computer Science
Linnaeus University
Växjö, Sweden

Raffaela Mirandola (iD)
Politecnico di Milano
Milano, Italy

Elena Navarro (iD)
University of Castilla-La Mancha
Albacete, Spain

Marjan Sirjani (iD)
Design and Engineering
Mälardalen University
Västerås, Sweden

Danny Weyns (iD)
KU Leuven
Leuven, Belgium

Linnaeus University
Växjö, Sweden

ISSN 0302-9743   ISSN 1611-3349 (electronic)
Lecture Notes in Computer Science
ISBN 978-3-030-86043-1   ISBN 978-3-030-86044-8 (eBook)
https://doi.org/10.1007/978-3-030-86044-8

LNCS Sublibrary: SL2 – Programming and Software Engineering

This Springer imprint is published by the registered company Springer Nature Switzerland AG
The registered company address is: Gewerbestrasse 11, 6330 Cham, Switzerland

Preface

The European Conference on Software Architecture (ECSA) is the premier European conference that provides researchers and practitioners with a platform to present and discuss the most recent, innovative, and significant findings and experiences in the field of software architecture research and practice.

This 15th edition of ECSA focused on the role of software architecture in the next generation of software-enabled systems that aim at addressing societal challenges, such as health, climate, sustainability, mobility, diversity, and future production. These challenges raise questions such as how can software architecture contribute to building and sustaining systems of the future? What automation, tools, and techniques do software architects and engineers need in order to ensure architectures developed are adaptable, evolvable, verifiable, and meet their quality and functional requirements?

Due to the ongoing COVID-19 pandemic, this edition of ECSA was held virtually during September 13–17, 2021, with participating researchers and practitioners from all over the world. The core technical program included a main research track, three keynote talks, and an industry track. Moreover, ECSA 2021 offered a doctoral symposium track with its own keynote, a diversity, equity and inclusion track with its own keynote and a tool and demos track. ECSA 2021 also encompassed six workshops on diverse topics related to the software architecture discipline, such as erosion and consistency, formal approaches for advanced computing, etc. Lastly, ECSA 2021 featured a journal-first track partnering with the Journal of Software and Systems and the IEEE Software Magazine. A selection of revised and extended contributions from all these other tracks are included in the companion proceedings, published in another Springer volume.

For the main research track, ECSA 2021 received 58 submissions in the two main categories: full and short research papers. Based on the recommendations of the Program Committee, we accepted 11 papers as full papers and 5 additional papers as short papers. Hence, the acceptance rate for full research papers was 19% for ECSA 2021. For the industrial track, we received 10 submissions and accepted 5 of them. The conference attracted papers (co-)authored by researchers, practitioners, and academics from 23 countries (Australia, Austria, Belgium, Brazil, Colombia, Czech Republic, Finland, France, Germany, India, Italy, Japan, the Netherlands, New Zealand, Norway, Poland, Portugal, Spain, Sweden, Switzerland, Turkey, UK, and USA).

The main ECSA program had three keynotes. Edward Lee from Berkeley (USA), author of textbooks on embedded systems, digital communications, and, more recently, on philosophical and social implications of technology, talked about "Determinism" in engineering and science. Eoin Woods from Endava (UK), former editor of the IEEE Software "Pragmatic Architect" column and co-author of the well-known software architecture book "Software Systems Architecture", talked about "Software Architecture for a Digital Age". Mats Gejnevall of Minnovate (Sweden), who is widely known thanks to his work with the Open Group enhancing The Open Group Architecture Framework (TOGAF), talked about "Enterprise Architecture in an Agile World."

We are grateful to the members of the Program Committee for their valuable and timely reviews. Their efforts formed the basis for a high-quality technical program for ECSA 2021. We would like to thank the members of the Organizing Committee for successfully organizing the event with several tracks, as well as the workshop organizers, who made significant contributions to this year's successful event.

We thank our sponsor Springer for funding the best paper award of ECSA 2021 and supporting us with publishing the proceedings in the Lecture Notes in Computer Science series. Finally, we thank the authors of all the ECSA 2021 submissions and the attendees of the conference for their participation.

The preparation and organization of ECSA 2021 took place during an unprecedented time in our history, a pandemic situation that has affected us all over the world. We thank the support of the software architecture community that, despite this dramatic situation, continued with advancing the field of software architecture through their scientific submissions to ECSA, while staying flexible as the Organizing Committee had to organize an all-online conference.

September 2021

Stefan Biffl
Elena Navarro
Welf Löwe
Marjan Sirjani
Raffaela Mirandolla
Danny Weyns

Organization

General Chairs

Raffaela Mirandola   Politecnico di Milano, Italy
Danny Weyns   KU Leuven, Belgium, and Linnaeus University,
Sweden

Steering Committee

Muhammad Ali Babar   The University of Adelaide, Australia
Paris Avgeriou   University of Groningen, The Netherlands
Stefan Biffl   Technische Universität Wien, Austria
Tomas Bures   Charles University in Prague, Czech Republic
Ivica Crnkovic   Chalmers University of Technology, Sweden
Rogério de Lemos   University of Kent, UK
Laurence Duchien   University of Lille, France
Carlos E. Cuesta Rey   Juan Carlos University, Spain
David Garlan   Carnegie Mellon University, USA
Paola Inverardi   University of L'Aquila, Italy
Patricia Lago Vrije   Universiteit Amsterdam, The Netherlands
Antónia Lopes   University of Lisbon, Portugal
Ivano Malavolta   Vrije Universiteit Amsterdam, The Netherlands
Raffaela Mirandola   Politecnico di Milano, Italy
Henry Muccini   University of L'Aquila, Italy
Elena Navarro   University of Castilla-La Mancha, Spain
Flavio Oquendo (Chair)   IRISA, University of South Brittany, France
Ipek Ozkaya   Carnegie Mellon University, USA
Jennifer Pérez   Technical University of Madrid, Spain
Bedir Tekinerdogan   Wageningen University, The Netherlands
Danny Weyns   KU Leuven, Belgium, and Linnaeus University,
Sweden
Uwe Zdun   University of Vienna, Austria

Research Track

Program Scientific Co-chairs

Elena Navarro   University of Castilla-La Mancha, Spain
Stefan Biffl   Technische Universität Wien, Austria

Program Committee

Francesca Arcelli Fontana	University of Milano-Bicocca, Italy
Jesper Andersson	Linnaeus University, Sweden
Pablo Oliveira Antonino	Fraunhofer Institute for Experimental Software Engineering, Germany
Paris Avgeriou	University of Groningen, The Netherlands
M. Ali Babar	University of Adelaide, Australia
Rami Bahsoon	University of Birmingham, UK
Luciano Baresi	Politecnico di Milano, Italy
Thais Batista	Federal University of Rio Grande do Norte, Brazil
Steffen Becker	University of Stuttgart, Germany
Amel Bennaceur	The Open University, UK
Alexandre Bergel	University of Chile, Chile
Javier Berrocal	University of Extremadura, Spain
Barbora Buhnova	Masaryk University, Czech Republic
Tomas Bures	Charles University, Czech Republic
Javier Cámara	University of York, UK
Carlos Canal	Universidad de Málaga, Spain
Rafael Capilla	Universidad Rey Juan Carlos, Spain
Jan Carlson	Malardalen University, Sweden
Dario Correal	Los Andes University, Colombia
Vittorio Cortellessa	University of L'Aquila, Italy
Ivica Crnkovic	Chalmers University of Technology, Sweden
Carlos Cuesta	Universidad Rey Juan Carlos, Spain
Rogerio De Lemos	University of Kent, UK
Elisabetta Di Nitto	Politecnico di Milano, Italy
Andres Diaz Pace	UNICEN University, Argentina
Ada Diaconescu	Paris Saclay University, France
Khalil Drira	LAAS-CNRS, France
Laurence Duchien	University of Lille, France
Alexander Egyed	Johannes Kepler University of Linz, Austria
Neil Ernst	University of Victoria, Canada
George Fairbanks	Google, USA
Matthias Galster	University of Canterbury, New Zealand
Joshua Garcia	University of California, Irvine, USA
David Garlan	Carnegie Mellon University, USA
Ilias Gerostathopoulos	TU Munich, Germany
Carlo Ghezzi	Politecnico di Milano, Italy
Maayan Goldstein	Nokia Bell Labs, Israel
Paul Grünbacher	Johannes Kepler University of Linz, Austria
Petr Hnetynka	Charles University in Prague, Czech Republic
Paola Inverardi	University of L'Aquila, Italy
Jasmin Jahic	University of Cambridge, UK
Pooyan Jamshidi	University of South Carolina, USA
Wouter Joosen	Katholieke Universiteit Leuven, Belgium

Rick Kazman   Carnegie Mellon University, USA
Anne Koziolek   Karlsruhe Institute of Technology, Germany
Heiko Koziolek   ABB Corporate Research, Germany
Philippe Kruchten   University of British Columbia, Canada
Patricia Lago   Vrije Universiteit Amsterdam, The Netherlands
Nuno Laranjerio   University of Coimbra, Portugal
Valentina Lenarduzzi   Tampere University, Finland
Nicole Levy   CNAM, France
Grace Lewis   Carnegie Mellon Software Engineering Institute, USA
Anna Liu   Amazon, Australia
Antónia Lopes   University of Lisbon, Portugal
Kristina Lundquist   Malardalen University, Sweden
Ivano Malavolta   Vrije Universiteit Amsterdam, The Netherlands
Sam Malek   University of California, Irvine, USA
Tomi Männistö   University of Helsinki, Finland
Antonio Martini   University of Oslo, Norway
Nenad Medvidovic   University of California, Irvine, USA
Nabor das Chagas   Mendonça Universidade de Fortaleza, Brazil
Marija Mikic   Google, USA
Tommi Mikkonen   University of Helsinki, Finland
Mehdi Mirakhorli   Rochester Institute of Technology, USA
Marina Mongiello   Politecnico di Bari, Italy
Gabriel Moreno   Carnegie Mellon Software Engineering Institute, USA
Henry Muccini   University of L'Aquila, Italy
Juan Manuel Murillo   University of Extremadura, Spain
Angelika Musil   Technical University of Vienna, Austria
Jürgen Musil   Technical University of Vienna, Austria
Elisa Yumi Nakagawa   University of São Paulo, Brazil
Flavio Oquendo   Université Bretagne Sud, France
Ipek Ozkaya   Carnegie Mellon University, USA
Claus Pahl   Free University of Bozen-Bolzano, Italy
Liliana Pasquale   University College Dublin and LERO, Ireland
Cesare Pautasso   USI Lugano, Switzerland
Patrizio Pelliccione   Chalmers University of Technology, Sweden
Jennifer Perez   Universidad Politécnica de Madrid, Spain
Claudia Raibulet   University of Milano-Bicocca, Italy
Maryam Razavian   Eindhoven University of Technology, The Netherlands
Ralf Reussner   Karlsruhe Institute of Technology, Germany
Matthias Riebisch   University of Hamburg, Germany
Patrizia Scandurra   University of Bergamo, Italy
Bradley Schmerl   Carnegie Mellon University, USA
Romina Spalazzese   Malmö University, Sweden
Girish Suryanarayana   Siemens Corporate Technology, India
Bedir Tekinerdogan   Wageningen University, The Netherlands
Chouki Tibermacine   University of Montpellier, France
Catia Trubiani   Gran Sasso Science Institute, Italy

Dimitri Van Landuyt	Katholieke Universiteit Leuven, Belgium
Rainer Weinreich	Johannes Kepler University Linz, Austria
Xiwei Xu	School of Computer Science and Engineering, Australia
Uwe Zdun	University of Vienna, Austria
Liming Zhu	The University of New South Wales, Australia
Olaf Zimmermann	Hochschule für Technik Rapperswill (HSR FHO), Switzerland

Additional Reviewers

Pietro Braione	Darius Sas
Kousar Aslam	Aaron Matthews
Ryan Wagner	Héctor Cadavid
Arda Unal	Christelle Urtado
Andrei Furda	Mirko Stocker
Sumaya Almanee	Anfel Selmadji
Abir Hossen	Sandro Speth

Industrial Track

Program Committee Co-chairs

Marjan Sirjani	Malardalen University, Sweden
Welf Löwe	Linnaeus University, Sweden

Program Committee

Daniele Spinosi	Micron Technology, Italy
Mirco Franzago	University of L'Aquila, Italy
Thomas Kurpick	Trusted Shops GmbH, Germany
Heiko Koziolek	ABB Corporate Research, Germany
Olaf Zimmermann	University of Applied Sciences of Eastern Switzerland, Switzerland
Eoin Woods	Artechra, UK
Darko Durisic	Volvo Car Corporation, Sweden
Henry Muccini	University of L'Aquila, Italy
Zeljko Obrenovic	Adevinta, The Netherlands
Federico Ciccozzi	Mälardalen University, Sweden
Xabier Larrucea	Tecnalia, Spain
Andrei Furda	Queensland University of Technology, Australia
Daniel Lübke	Leibniz Universität Hannover, Germany
Johannes Wettinger	Bosch, Germany

Additional Reviewers

Alessi Bucaioni
Maryam Bagheri

Organizing Committee

Workshop and Tutorial Co-chairs

Patrizia Scandurra   University of Bergamo, Italy
Matthias Galster   University of Canterbury, New Zealand

Tools and Demos Co-chairs

Romina Spalazzese   Malmö University, Sweden
Ilias Gerostathopoulos   Vrije Universiteit Amsterdam, Netherlands

DE&I Co-chairs

Ingrid Nunes   Universidade Federal do Rio Grande do Sul, Brazil
Thomas Vogel   Humboldt-Universität zu Berlin, Germany

Doctoral Symposium Co-chairs

Genaina Rodrigues   University of Brasilia, Brazil
Radu Calinescu   University of York, UK

Journal First Chair

Tomi Männistö   University of Helsinki, Finland

Proceedings Chair

Robert Heinrich   Karlsruhe Institute of Technology, Germany

Publicity Co-chairs

Aurora Macias   University of Castilla-La Mancha, Spain
Jürgen Musil   Technische Universität Wien, Austria

Local Chair

Diana Unander   Linnaeus University, Sweden

Virtualization Co-chairs

Mauro Caporuscio   Linnaeus University, Sweden
Romain Christian Herault Linnaeus University, Sweden

Web Chair

Mirko D'Angelo   Ericsson Research, Sweden

Abstracts of Keynotes

Determinism

Edward Lee ⓘ

University of California at Berkeley, Berkeley, CA, 94720, USA
eal@berkeley.edu

Abstract. Uncontrolled and unintended nondeterminism has been a persistent problem for concurrent, parallel, and distributed software. Recent trends have improved the situation by replacing threads and remote procedure calls with publish-and-subscribe busses, actors, and service-oriented architectures, but even these admit nondeterminism and make building deterministic programs difficult. One approach is to abandon determinism, recognizing that software has to handle unpredictable events, communication networks with varying reliability and latencies, unpredictable execution times, and hardware and software failures. In this talk, I will argue to the contrary, that determinism becomes even more valuable in unpredictable environments. Among its many benefits, determinism enables systematic testing, shifts complexity from application logic to infrastructure, enables fault detection, facilitates composability, and more. The key is to understand that determinism is a property of models, not of physical realizations. In engineering, our primary goal is to coerce the physical world to match our models. In contrast, in science, the primary goal is to coerce the models to match the physical world. In this talk, I will examine what we mean by "determinism" in engineering, science, and a bit in philosophy. Whether a model is deterministic or not depends on how one defines the inputs and behavior of the model. I will conclude by outlining a practical deterministic model well suited for concurrent, parallel, and distributed software. I will describe a realization of this model in a coordination language called Lingua Franca.

Keywords: Concurrency · Distributed Systems · Determinism

Biography. Edward A. Lee has been working on embedded software systems for 40 years. After studying and working at Yale, MIT, and Bell Labs, he landed at Berkeley, where he is now Professor of the Graduate School in EECS. His research is focused on cyber-physical systems. He is the lead author of the open-source software system Ptolemy II, author of textbooks on embedded systems and digital communications, and has recently been writing books on philosophical and social implications of technology. His current research is focused on a polyglot coordination language for distributed real-time systems called Lingua Franca that combines features of discrete-event modeling, synchronous languages, and actors.

Software Architecture for a Digital Age

Eoin Woods (iD)

Endava, 125 Old Broad Street, London, EC2N 1AR, UK
eoin.woods@endava.com

Abstract. The COVID-19 pandemic has increased the pace of digitisation of many areas of our lives, but this is a process that has been underway for some years. We really are living in a "digital age" where many companies outside the traditional technology area, such as John Deere and GE, are building intelligent, connected digital "platforms" for their customers or their entire industry segments. Building these platforms is a very different process to building traditional enterprise applications and has to accommodate constant change, constant learning based on rapid feedback from the operational use of the platform. So software architecture needs to change too, in order to meet the challenges of building intelligent, connected platforms that are constantly in use. In this talk I will explain the challenges that software architects face in the era of digital platform development, the techniques that we are using today to meet those challenges and suggest how I think software architecture will evolve further as a result of the experience we are gaining.

Keywords: Software architecture · Continuous architecture · Digital platforms · Digital transformation

Biography. Eoin Woods is the CTO of Endava, a technology company that delivers projects in the areas of digital, agile and automation. Prior to joining Endava, Eoin has worked in the software engineering industry for 20 years developing system software products and complex applications in the capital markets domain. His main technical interests are software architecture, distributed systems and computer security. He is a former editor of the IEEE Software "Pragmatic Architect" column, co-author of the well-known software architecture book "Software Systems Architecture" and was the recipient of the 2018 Linda M. Northrup Award for Software Architecture, awarded by the SEI at Carnegie Mellon University.

Enterprise Architecture in an Agile World

Mats Gejnevall

mInnovate AB, Växjö, Sweden
mats@minnovate.se

Abstract. There is an ongoing demand for the size and timescale of architectures to become ever shorter. This in turn is resulting in a tendency for enterprises to skip the development of architectures, which in turn is resulting in some high-profile IT failures because of the unanticipated consequences of what appeared to be minor changes. Enterprise Architecture recognizes the need to recursively break down the architecture into more granular levels that can be architected following an Agile approach. Partitioning the architecture work is key for Agile delivery and implies the definition of creating increments based on the enterprise priorities. These smaller pieces, that cover a specific area of the organization, can then be more easily specified and implemented following an agile approach. Enterprises have adapted the agile concepts for the business development for the same reasons and are evolving their business in increments. That has to match with creating architectures and solutions in agile ways. Since the American Department of Defense (DoD) is allowing agile acquisition of solutions, there is a need to ensure that these solutions will deliver the value that is expected. Enterprise Architecture will be one of the important building blocks in that process.

Keywords: Enterprise architecture · Agile · Iterative

Biography. Mats is working with business development using enterprise architecture as one of the methods. Working environment is often sectors like Government, Telco, Supply Chain and Defence either transforming them to Enterprise Architecture work practices or leading and performing enterprise architecture work as both a business and IT architect. The last 15 years Mats has been involved with the Open Group enhancing The Open Group Architecture Framework (TOGAF) and creating related guides. Lately Mats has been involved in creating guides on how enterprise architects could use agile practices. Frequently, he has the pleasure of teaching architecture methods and being a speaker at international conferences on Enterprise Architecture.

Contents

Architectures for Reconfigurable and Self-Adaptive Systems

Dynamic Updates of Virtual PLCs Deployed as Kubernetes Microservices

Heiko Koziolek[1]([✉])(iD), Andreas Burger[1], P. P. Abdulla[2], Julius Rückert[1](iD),
Shardul Sonar[1], and Pablo Rodriguez[1]

[1] ABB Research Germany, Ladenburg, Germany
heiko.koziolek@de.abb.com
[2] ABB Research India, Bangalore, India

Abstract. Industrial control systems (e.g. programmable logic controllers, PLC or distributed control systems, DCS) cyclically execute control algorithms to automated production processes. Nowadays, for many applications their deployment is moving from dedicated embedded controllers into more flexible container environments, thus becoming "Virtual PLCs". It is difficult to update such containerized Virtual PLCs during runtime by switching to a newer instance, which requires transferring internal state. Former research has only proposed dynamic update approaches for single embedded controllers, while other work introduced special Kubernetes (K8s) state replication approaches, which did not support cyclic real-time applications. We propose a dynamic update mechanism for Virtual PLCs deployed as K8s microservices. This approach is based on a purpose-built K8s Operator and allows control application updates without halting the production processes. Our experimental validation shows that the approach can support the internal state transfer of large industrial control applications (100.000 state variables) within only 15% of the available cycle slack time. Therefore, the approach creates vast opportunities for updating applications on-the-fly and migrating them between nodes in a cloud-native fashion.

Keywords: Software architecture · PLC programs · Kubernetes ·
Docker · Microservices · Kubernetes Operator · Performance
evaluation · Stateful applications · Dynamic software updates · OPC UA

1 Introduction

PLCs and DCSs are at the heart of many industrial production processes, such as power generation, mining, chemical production, or paper production [6]. The DCS is market size is at 13.4 BUSD in 2020 and expected to grow significantly in the next few years [3]. PLCs and DCSs receive telemetry data from sensors and cyclically run control algorithms that produce output signals for various actuators, such as motors, pumps, mixers, reactors, heat exchangers, etc. This typically relies on embedded controllers running on purpose-built hardware for high reliability.

© Springer Nature Switzerland AG 2021
S. Biffl et al. (Eds.): ECSA 2021, LNCS 12857, pp. 3–19, 2021.
https://doi.org/10.1007/978-3-030-86044-8_1

However, in recent years, more and more automation customers are starting to adopt server-hosted PLC programs running in container frameworks, due to their reduced costs and easier application management.

Updating PLC/DCS programs shall ideally not require a production stop, which can incur high costs for the associated machinery and processes. Patching PLC runtimes or applications is therefore undesired and only rarely done. Container orchestration (e.g., Kubernetes) allows switching to an updated virtual runtime or application in another container "on-the-fly", by transferring the signal input subscriptions and output publications. However, the newly started runtime or program need to work with the same internal state (i.e. a set of variables storing intermediate calculations) as the former runtime. Due to the short execution cycles (e.g., every 100 ms), the required state transfer from container to container needs to be fast, so that the control actuators continuously receive their control signals without interruption.

Researchers have formerly proposed dynamic update approaches for control applications (e.g. [15,19,20]), but these works were limited to single embedded controllers and could not utilize the advanced orchestration concepts of a container systems. Other researchers validated that PLC programs can achieve their real-time behavior if deployed as software containers (e.g. [5,11,15]), but did not investigate updates involving state transfers. Specifically, for container orchestration systems, there are approaches for state replication (e.g., [13,14,18], which however do not involve PLC programs with short execution cycle times.

We propose a novel state-transfer approach for dynamic updates of Virtual PLCs deployed as K8s microservices. The contributions of this paper are 1) a conceptual architecture for a state transfer method that utilizes the capabilities of a container orchestration framework, 2) a procedure for state transfer across network nodes while adhering to industry standards, and 3) a rationalization of the design decisions for the entire architecture. The approach allows to update both PLC programs and runtimes during system execution. A K8s Operator monitors a running PLC engine, starts an updated PLC engine in parallel, issues the internal state transfer, and then switches over the input/output signal handling to the updated engine.

To validate the approach, we have implemented the conceptual architecture exemplary based on open-source components (i.e., OpenPLC, Open62541, Cereal, Kubernetes, Docker). In a series of experiments, we simulated updating large control applications derived from existing power production and mining plants with up to 500K internal state variables. For an application with 100K state variables the approach was able to transfer the internal state in less than 15 ms, which is significantly lower than the required cycle time. This validates that the approach can update large running applications as desired.

This paper is structured as follows: Sect. 2 provide an introduction to PLC and DCS controllers, as well as containers and the communication framework OPC UA. Section 3 analyzed related work. Section 4 presents the conceptual architecture and the rationale for the design decisions. Section 5 describes the prototypical implementation and testbed, before Sect. 6 explains the experimental results. Finally, Sect. 7 lists assumptions and limitations underlying the approach.

2   Background

PLCs and DCS controllers are used to automate industrial processes, such as power, paper, or chemical production, as well as mining applications or steel plants [6]. Such controllers often rely on real-time operating systems, such as Embedded Linux, FreeRTOS, or VxWorks. A set of five different programming languages for these controllers was standardized as IEC 61131-3 in the early 1990th, including function block diagrams, structured text, and ladder logic [6]. IEC 61131-3 control runtimes execute algorithms such as 'PID controllers', cyclically, usually with cycle times between 10 and 1000 ms. For safety-critical applications such controllers feature redundant processing units with special purpose hardware failover mechanisms. So-called SoftPLCs (e.g., controller runtimes deployed on workstations or servers) are today mostly used in development and testing. However, a growing market of server-deployed Virtual PLCs is expected thanks to the constantly increasing computing capabilities.

Containers (e.g., LXC, Docker) provide an operating-system-level virtualization layer for Linux processes using namespace isolation and resource limitation with cgroups [7]. They can be used to package applications with their required libraries and are a preferred deployment target for microservices. Applications with many containers can be managed with a container orchestration engine, such as Kubernetes. Stateless microservices in Kubernetes are preferred, since they can be easily horizontally scaled-up to support workloads of large internet applications. Virtual PLCs are stateful services, which are also supported by Kubernetes. Usually they have comparably constant workload and do not require horizontal scaling. Industry analysts speculate that software containers will replace embedded software to a large extent in the future, since they significantly improve managing and updating services in an efficient and less error-prone manner [4].

OPC UA provides a middleware and information modeling for industrial applications [10]. It is designed for monitoring industrial devices from workstations, but was lately extended to also support fast, deterministic controller-to-field device communication [2]. OPC UA includes a client/server protocol on top of TCP/IP, as well as a publish/subscribe mechanism on top of UDP. OPC UA address spaces may hold both configuration and sensor data. The Open Process Automation Forum [12] has identified OPC UA as the core communication mechanism in future open and interoperable industrial control systems. Controllers and certain field devices shall be equipped with OPC UA clients and servers, while legacy field buses shall be integrated via OPC UA gateways.

3   Related Work

Numerous authors have surveyed the field of **dynamic software updating**, which includes many approaches in the last 20 years [1,16]. Specifically, for real-time systems, Wahler et al. [20] proposed a component framework and update algorithm based on shared memory transfer. In experiments the framework was able to transfer a 4000 byte internal state of a cyclically executing control program below a 5 ms deadline. Later, they extended the work to allow iterative state synchronization over multiple execution cycles [19]. Their mechanism provides more flexibility but can lead to a never terminating state transfer in case of large or very volatile states. Prenzel et al. [15] discussed dynamic updates of IEC 61499 applications but did not transfer internal variables in their experiments. None of these works assumed a container deployment or state transfer across different nodes.

Another line of research is concerned with the deployment of **Virtual PLCs in container environments**, which shall offer more flexibility for updating and portability [4]. Moga et al. [11] compared virtual machines and containers as deployment targets for industrial applications. They ran the microbenchmark 'cyclictest' inside a Docker container on an Intel Xeon E5 and found that the jitter introduced by Docker was below 20 ms, therefore negligible for most industrial applications. Goldschmidt et al. [5] proposed different use cases for containerized Virtual PLCs, among them dynamic updating. They also executed 'cyclictest' inside a Docker container on a Raspberry PI 2 and showed that the average overhead was below 100 ms. Sollfrank et al. [17] deployed a PID controller based on Simulink C-code in Docker onto a Raspberry PI 4 and concluded that it can meet soft real-time requirements, since the container overhead was below 150 ms. These works were mostly concerned with characterizing the overhead introduced by Linux containers, but did not investigate dynamic updates in detail.

Outside the industrial automation domain, researchers have proposed approaches for **state replication in container orchestration engines**. Netto et al. [13] introduced the DORADO protocol to order requests in Kubernetes that are saved to shared memory (i.e., etc.d) and can be exchanged between container replicas. In experiments, they showed that this increases latency and lead to a leveling out throughput but can tolerate container failures. This work assumes a continuous state transfer between redundant replicas, instead of a one-shot transfer to an updated application. Vayghan et al. [18] introduced a State Controller for Kubernetes that can replicate internal state between containers to enable fail-over scenarios. State is stored into a persistent volume and a standby container can take over serving clients in case of the primary container failing. Experiments with a video streaming application, where the transferred state was the client current streaming position, showed that the approach could reduce the service outage time significantly. Oh et al. [14] proposed a checkpoint-based stateful container migration approach in Kubernetes. None of these works is concerned with cyclically executing control applications that need to adhere to short deadlines.

4   State-Transfer Approach

This section describes the architecture of our proposed state-transfer approach. First, a simple example explains the required internal state transfer in more detail, followed by a description of the static architecture. The dynamic procedure of the state transfer follows next, before the section concludes with a discussion of the included architecture decision points, alternatives, and rational for the made decisions.

4.1 Example

Figure 1 depicts a typical control program in IEC 61131-3 Structured Text (i.e., Pascal-like syntax) from the industrial domain. The function block FT_PIWL refers to a proportional integral (PI) controller with dynamic anti wind-up (WL). It can for example be used to regulate the filling level in a tank or the pressure in a pipe. The program cyclically computes its outputs Y based on the internal state variables t_last and in_last, e.g., every 100 ms. Its actual execution runtime is usually well below the cycle time, e.g., below 5 ms. For a dynamic update of the program, where for example another host node shall take over the execution, these state variables needs to be transferred within the cycle slack time (e.g., 95 ms) in order not to interrupt the underlying production process.

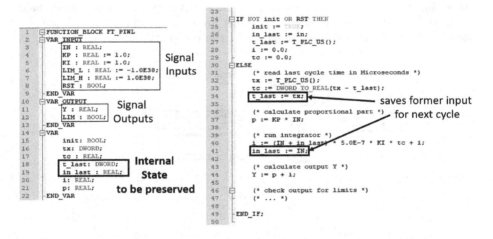

Fig. 1. Example PLC program with internal state to be preserved. The variables t_last and in_last need to be transferred in case the runtime is updated.

Typical control applications in process automation may contain thousands of such state variables, since they regulate thousands of sensors and actuators within a single production plant. During programming, engineers mark specific variables as "retained", indicating that they need to be saved and restored in case a PLC runtime needs to restart. These retained variables are also used by our approach for dynamic updates at runtime.

4.2   Static View

Figure 2 shows a component and deployment view of our state transfer approach. The figure shows a single master node and two worker nodes as a minimal example. In a full-scale system, many worker nodes and redundant masters would be used. The system features a container orchestration engine (e.g., Kubernetes) in order to flexibly deploy and update Virtual PLCs. Today's physical embedded controllers typically need to be shut down, patched, and restarted in case the runtime system needs updates. Figure 2 depicts typical Kubernetes components required on the nodes in light gray (e.g., Kube API server, kubelet, kube-proxy).

Worker 1 contains a **PLC Runtime System** deployed as a "virtual-plc-pod", a K8s custom resource including a container. The custom resource allows the user to parameterize the pod for real-time specifics. This pod can be considered as a microservice of an entire DCS. Preferably, the PLC Runtime System pods are deployed on a Linux node with the PREEMPT_RT kernel patch to achieve soft real-time behavior and minimize jitter in the cycle periods. The PLC Runtime System can execute IEC 61131-3 applications by consuming input signals and sending output values via the OPC UA protocol, to ensure interoperability with IO devices from different vendors. These OPC UA signals are either directly sent by field devices with OPC UA servers or come from field gateways that translate traditional fieldbus protocols or analog signal connections [8]. Such devices are not depicted in the component view for brevity, as

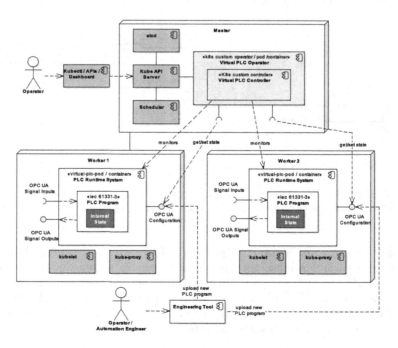

Fig. 2. Virtual PLC state transfer (combined component and deployment diagram)

a single PLC runtime could control hundreds of devices connected via sophisticated network topologies.

An automation engineer can upload a **PLC Program** from an Engineering Tool via the PLC Runtime Systems OPC UA Configuration interface. After start-up, the PLC Program carries **Internal State** in the form of numerous state variables as illustrated in Sect. 4.1. The PLC Runtime System here provides a mechanism to serialize the current values of this Internal State and send it via its OPC UA Configuration interface to any OPC UA client.

Our approach features a custom K8s Operator called **Virtual PLC Operator**. This relies on a standard extension mechanism for K8s[1]. The operator contains a custom K8s controller called **Virtual PLC Controller** that monitors **Virtual-PLC-Pods** and handles their lifecycle via the K8s API as well as their OPC UA configuration interfaces.

The **Virtual PLC Controller** has three options to detect a dynamic update request triggering a state transfer:

1. **Updated PLC program:** The controller can detect if an automation engineer uploaded an updated PLC program via the Engineering Tool. Updated programs often include only minor changes of the internal state structure; thus the internal state of the former program can be largely mapped to the updated program. Newly introduced variables are set to default values, removed variables are discarded.
2. **Updated PLC runtime:** The controller can detect if an operator has pushed a new container image of the **PLC Runtime System** to the container registry. This can be caused by a changed configuration of the runtime system or a new compiled version due to bug fixes or security patches.
3. **Updated host:** The controller can detect if K8s scheduled restarting a PLC Runtime System pod on another node for carrying out maintenance on the former node. For example, the administrator may have selected a node for an operating system update or a hardware replacement.

If such an update request is registered, the **Virtual PLC Controller** follows the procedure depicted in Fig. 3.

4.3 Dynamic View

After detecting and validating the update request (Step 1), the Virtual PLC Controller starts the pod of the PLC Runtime System 2 (Step 2), possibly on a separate node (here: worker 2). The controller connects to both PLC Runtime systems via OPC UA and uploads the desired application to the PLC Runtime System 2. It also connects the OPC UA IO *input* signals to this runtime by setting up according subscriptions, so that it can start executing based on live inputs. *Output* signals will be computed but not published to the field devices, as long as the state transfer has not been executed and the correct execution is verified.

---

[1] https://kubernetes.io/docs/concepts/extend-kubernetes/operator/.

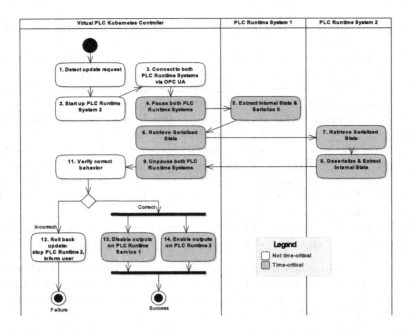

Fig. 3. Dynamic Flow of the state transfer (UML activity diagram)

After this less time-critical initialization, the controller enters a time-critical phase in step 4–9 that needs to complete within the cycle slack time. The controller pauses the execution of both runtimes (Step 4) in order to prevent updates to the internal state. The controller extracts the internal state (e.g., the values of t_last and in_last in Fig. 1) from runtime system 1, which includes serialization to a binary large object (step 5). Via the OPC UA configuration interface and the method `GetState`, the controller retrieves the internal state (step 6) and sends it the runtime system 2 (step 7) using its `RetrieveState` method. This runtime system deserializes and extracts the state, overwriting the corresponding internal state variables (step 8). Finally, the controller resumes both runtime systems, so that they continue executing their control algorithms to compute outputs.

With both engines running, but only runtime 1 publishing output signals to the devices, the controller verifies the correct behavior or runtime 2 by comparing its computed output values to the ones from runtime 1. If runtime 2 produces incorrect values (e.g., by drifting beyond a predefined threshold), the controller rolls back the entire update, stops runtime 2 and informs the user (step 12) of an update failure. If the values are correct and no substantial drift between the values of both runtimes is detected, the controller disables output signal publishing of runtime 1 (step 13) and activates the output signal publishing by runtime 2 (step 14). In this case the update was successful. PLC runtime 1 can be terminated and archived to allow for rollbacks later on.

4.4   Decision Points

The state transfer architecture includes a number of decisions, which we rationalize in the following.

Transfer Mechanism: The transfer mechanism is a core component to enable a reliable, flexible and fast state transfer. As state transfer shall be possible through node/pod boundaries and fit into the open process architecture defined by OPAF, we selected OPC UA as transfer mechanism. OPC UA is purpose-built for industrial applications and provides interoperability as virtual control engines will require to have built-in OPC UA servers. Additionally, by using the already required OPC UA and not exposing additional HTTP, MQTT, or proprietary sockets, the VirtualPLC attack surface is limited. OPC UA can be combined with TSN to provide deterministic real-time communication.

Serialization Mechanism: We decided to transfer the application state as a binary large object (BLOB). A BLOB allows to abstract the internal application memory structure, which is important as the internal memory state structure might be vendor-specific. Hence, using a BLOB instead of structured data, allows to keep the interface of the state transfer service stable for different virtual PLCs. Additionally, it gives the ability to use data compression techniques or encryption.

State Transfer Service as K8s Extension: The state transfer service is a K8s Operator (Virtual PLC Operator) running in an own pod. It should not directly be built into the virtual PLC runtimes, as this would require code duplication in each engine. Ideally, the PLC runtime is not aware of the Virtual PLC Operator and simply exposed the OPC UA interfaces anyhow required by OPAF. Hence, the state transfer is seamlessly integrated in the Kubernetes infrastructure and complexity is hidden from the user by not having a separate interface in the Kubernetes microservice architecture.

Container Virtualization: The state transfer service is designed to be used in a virtualization context by exchanging the application state between different virtual PLCs, deployed as docker container or Kubernetes pods. The architecture and process of the state transfer service can also be used without containers, but this scenario would need an orchestration instance/component which handles the network configuration for the virtual PLC engines and enable the startup and shutdown of those. In general, the K8s system eases the state transfer, the orchestration of virtual control engines and the scheduling significantly.

5   Prototypical Implementation

We prototypically implemented the architecture using open source components. This shall ensure repeatability of the experimental evaluation, which is thus not constrained to commercial software. The concepts behind the architecture also apply to commercial components (Fig. 4).

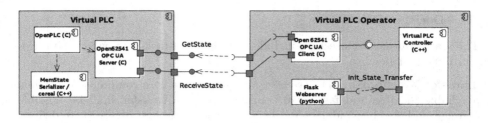

Fig. 4. Prototypical implementation of the state transfer approach

Virtual PLC: We selected OpenPLC[2] as the PLC Runtime System of our prototype. As OpenPLC did not have an integrated OPC UA server to receive and sent signal values, we enhanced the engine by adding an OPC UA server based on the open62541 stack[3]. The OPC UA server was integrated in parallel to the control engine and other components. It shows all variables which are available for the actual running control program as well as the required interface methods for the state transfer. Additionally, we implemented functionality for retrieving the application state out of OpenPLC's internal memory as well as writing back an application state. Therefore, the functionality to pause and resume the entire control engine was introduced and implemented. We also added a new component to OpenPLC, the so called MemState Serializer. This component takes the retrieved application state and serializes it to an array of bytes as well as deserializes it to the necessary internal memory structure. Keeping this component separate from the control engine allows us to exchange the underlying serialization library without touching the main functionality of the Virtual PLC. In the prototypical implementation we used a fast, open source C++ serialization library called Cereal[4].

Virtual PLC Operator: In order to evaluate the proposed state transfer approach, we implemented the state transfer service in C++. The operator contains three main components, a webserver, an OPC UA client and the Virtual PLC Controller. The state transfer service is implemented in C++ by using an open source OPC UA stack, open62541 and a webserver implemented in python, based on Flask[5]. The small webserver allows the user to communicate with the service through a web interface as well as through a REST interface. Two main functions are realized by the integrated Open62541 OPC UA server, a functionality to get an serialized application state from a virtual engine (here called GetState) and another function to send back an serialized application state to a virtual engine (here called ReceiveState).

---

[2] https://www.openplcproject.com/.
[3] https://open62541.org/.
[4] https://uscilab.github.io/cereal/.
[5] https://flask.palletsprojects.com/.

Virtual PLC Controller: The core component of the state transfer takes all necessary inputs from the webserver or the REST interface and starts initiating the state transfer by using the OPC UA client and the required interfaces. The controller receives the serialized application state, which should be transferred from one virtual engine to the other, via the GetState interface and then send it to the receiving engine by using the ReceiveState interface. Hence, this component ensures that all data is transferred properly and the sending and receiving virtual PLCs confirm the successful transfer. In order to guarantee real-time requirements, the controller is implemented as a separate POSIX thread with high real-time priorities. This ensures a deterministic execution of the state transfer, if deployed in a real-time capable operating system.

Software Platform: Finally, the Virtual PLC Operator as well as the Virtual PLC are put into Docker containers and K8s pods. We used the open source StarlingX[6] cloud infrastructure software stack that includes Kubernetes and Docker. StarlingX includes CentOS as Linux OS and nodes can be configured to use a PREEMPT_RT patched kernel for deterministic execution using real-time priorities. However, the results should be similar on other K8s platforms.

Hardware Environment: Our testbed consisted of two master servers ("controllers") in a high availability deployment as well as two worker nodes. All servers were connected using Gigabit Ethernet. Experiments utilized the worker nodes, which were made up of HPE ProLiant DL380 Gen10 Rack Servers with Dual Intel Xenon Silver 4110 CPUs (40 cores) and 256 GB of RAM.

6   Experimental Evaluation

6.1   Test Application Sizing

To make our experimental setting realistic, we reviewed several larger industrial control applications to determine typical cycle times and application sizes.

The control application for one of the largest Liquid Natural Gas (LNG) plants was reviewed by Krause [9] and characterized to comprise of 650.000 variables distributed to 18 different hardware controllers and 10.000 IO devices ($\approx$30.000 variables per controller and 550 IO per individual controller). The cycle time of these controllers was 500 ms.

A different project from the area of mining also used around 500 IO-devices per and almost 200.000 variables in total. Here, the configured cycle time was 250 ms. A third project for a chemical plant had 350 IO-devices per controller and around 100.000 variables in the control programs, while running on a 1000 ms cycle time.

---

[6] https://www.starlingx.io/.

From these applications it becomes clear that the application sizes and cycles times vary from domain to domain. Furthermore, the number of variables may reflect the sophistication of computations needed for a given application. We decided to follow a conservative approach and assume a cycle time of 100 ms for our experiments. In addition, we aimed a state transfer of around 100.000 variables within the cycle slack time. We also assume that all variables are marked as "retained", meaning that they are included in the state transfer, although in practice a much lower number of variables is usually retained. If these conditions are met, then most of the typical industrial application should be compatible with our state transfer approach.

We assume each of the 100.000 variables encoded with 32 bits, thus aiming at a internal state size of around 400 KByte plus metadata. Assuming that the control algorithms need 10% of the cycle time for their computation (i.e., 10 ms), then these 400 KByte need to be transferred in less than 90 ms, resulting in a minimum transfer rate of about 4.5 MByte/sec. Typical RAM, bus, and network bandwidths are far beyond this threshold, so the main bottleneck is expected to be the CPU and possibly the network latency.

6.2   Jitter Characterization

To characterize the real-time properties of our hosts used for running the experiments, we executed the tool 'cyclictest' of the Linux Foundation[7]. It is commonly used to benchmark real-time systems. Cyclictest measures the time between a thread's intended and actual wake-up time, which can include latencies in the hardware or operating system. To simulate meaningful real-time stress conditions, we also used the Linux tool 'stress'[8] as follows:

```
stress -i 40 -c 40 -d 40 --hdd-bytes 20M -m 40 --vm-bytes 10
cyclictest -l100000 -m -Sp99 -i200 -h400 -q >output
```

The tool thus starts as many CPU-intensive and IO-intensive threads as given CPU cores and also uses the hard-disk, resulting in a 100% utilized system. Cyclictest is repeated 100K times with the highest thread priority 99. Figure 5 shows a histogram of the results.

The worst-case latency was 315 ms, which can be compared to other platforms in the OSADL Real-time QA Farm[9]. Since our experiments use cycles times at 100 milliseconds derived from practical application cases, we deem the jitter of our test host node negligible and not interfering with our state measurement experiments.

---

[7] https://wiki.linuxfoundation.org/realtime/documentation/howto/tools/cyclictest/start.

[8] https://manpages.ubuntu.com/manpages/eoan/man1/stress.1.html.

[9] https://www.osadl.org/Latency-plots.latency-plots.0.html.

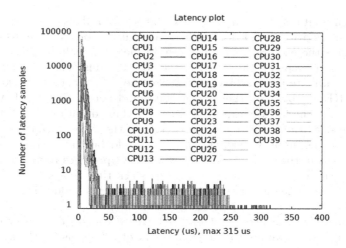

Fig. 5. Cyclictest results (histogram)

6.3   State Transfer Time

To determine the feasibility of transferring a realistic internal state within a cycle slack time of 90 ms, we deployed the prototypical implementation of our dynamic update approach on two worker nodes within our K8s cluster. One OpenPLC runtime ran on the first node, while the Virtual PLC Controller and the second OpenPLC runtime ran on the second node. We uploaded a generated test application with a 100 ms cycle time to the OpenPLC runtime with a varying size of internal state variables. In our experiments, we measured the time for the critical serialization, state transfer, and deserialization (step 5–8 in Fig. 3) from the Virtual PLC Controller.

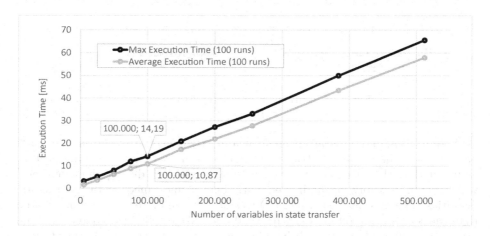

Fig. 6. State transfer times via OPC UA for different number of variables: 100K variables can be transferred in less than 15 ms, well below the cycle slack time of 90 ms.

For each state size from 5000 to 500.000 variables, we executed 100 experiment-runs to account for outliers and distortions in the K8s cluster. Figure 6 shows these aggregated state transfer measure, including both the maximum measured time and the average time for 100 runs. The results show that our dynamic update approach could transfer the internal state of 100.000 variables (400 KByte) between the two runtimes and nodes via OPC UA in 10.87 ms on average. The longest run took 14.19 ms. This duration is well below the target cycle slack time of 90 ms (approx. 16% of the cycle slack time).

Within 90 ms, approx. 600.000 variables could be transferred via network boundaries within the cycle slack time, which thus provides room for very large application. However, not fully utilizing the slack time is a safe way to assure meeting soft real-time guarantees, also under less optimal conditions (e.g., interfering workloads).

To characterize the jitter and find out where the state transfer execution time is spent, we ran an additional experiment of 1000 runs for the state size of 100.000 variables. Figure 7 shows the execution times for the serialization (step 5), the retrieval of the state by the Virtual PLC Controller (step 6), the retrieval of the state by the second OpenPLC runtime (step 7), and the deserialization (step 8).

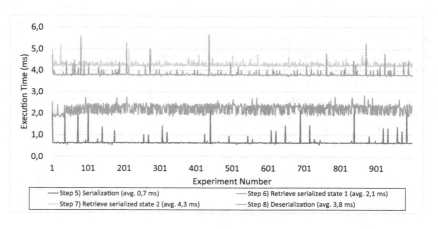

Fig. 7. Execution times for step 5) to step 8)

Serialization and deserialization show a mostly constant execution time with occasional outliers that contribute to the overall state transfer times. It is assumed that the processes may have been preempted during these outliers, which could possibly be addressed with better fine-tuned real-time thread-priorities. The deserialization (step 8) was on average more than 5 times slower than the serialization (step 5), 3.8 ms vs. 0.7 ms. We profiled the code using Valgrind and Callgrind and traced the different times to the external library Cereal used for serialization and deserialization, which is inefficiently implemented for the deserialization of arrays by using string stream-buffers. Other serialization libraries could be tested in this context.

The network transfer times in Fig. 7 are 4.3 ms and 2.1 ms on average. The figure shows that these transfers are much less constant than serialization/deserialization and introduce a additional jitter around one millisecond to the overall state transfer time. This could be attributed to the non-prioritized TCP/IP stacks in the real-time operating system as well as the missing prioritization of network packets in the TCP/IP connection. Using time-sensitive networks (TSN) with appropriate priority classes could be applied to reduce this jitter for even more deterministic state transfer times.

7 Assumptions and Limitations

The following assumptions and limitations are underlying our approach:

- The approach is not applicable and not meant for fast machine control applications in discrete automation requiring sub-millisecond cycle times.
- We used comparably fast server hardware, which currently are often not be available in many smaller production plants, but which is however also required for running non-trivial container workloads in an orchestration system.
- Our experiments included only simulated IO devices, but not real devices communicating with the OpenPLC runtime.
- Our prototypical implementation relied only on open source components. Other OPC UA SDKs, serialization libraries, or PLC runtimes coming from open source or commercial software could potentially achieve better or worse results.
- We restricted the approach to an OPC UA based state transfer. We used client/server communication via TCP/IP in our setup, while pub/sub communication via UDP could be faster. Alternative communication protocols could streamline the state transfer.
- We set all processes in the implementation to the highest real-time thread priorities, which can result in suboptimal jitter.
- The prototypical implementation did not include the verification step 11), which has been shown in other works (e.g., [19], see monitoring component).

Some of these limitations remain conceptual, others could be addressed in future work and additional experiments.

8 Conclusions

We have introduced a novel approach that allows updating industrial control applications at runtime. Automation engineers can much more flexibly change parameters of their control algorithms in order to optimize the automation of many production processes. These algorithmic optimizations are nowadays based on large-scale data analytics and can contribute to major production cost savings. The operators do not need to stop the production processes but can perform the updates on-the-fly, which lowers the barrier to consider updates significantly.

In the Industrial Internet-of-Things (IIoT), more and more sensors, actuators, and controllers are equipped with IP connectivity, requiring continuous security updates. The approach thus also enables updating the PLC runtimes systems to fix bugs and security issues, since the K8s Operator can deploy an updated container image and transfer the state. Furthermore, using the mechanism the Virtual PLC can be moved in a cloud-native fashion between nodes, so that operating systems and container engines can be updated, or hardware can be replaced. This was previously impossible on-the-fly using embedded controllers.

As a next step, we plan to address several of the approach's assumptions, namely testing with other PLC runtimes and using more resource-constrained and thus less costly hardware. The approach could in principle also support fail-over scenarios to provide redundancy, which however require a continuous state transfer. Furthermore, the approach could be extended to optimally select a target node for the updated PLC runtime or to transfer the internal state in smaller chunks to be applicable for special control applications with very low cycle times.

References

1. Ahmed, B.H., Lee, S.P., Su, M.T., Zakari, A.: Dynamic software updating: a systematic mapping study. IET Softw. **14**(5), 468–481 (2020)
2. Burger, A., Koziolek, H., Rückert, J., Platenius-Mohr, M., Stomberg, G.: Bottleneck identification and performance modeling of OPC UA communication models. In: Proceedings of the 2019 ACM/SPEC International Conference on Performance Engineering, pp. 231–242 (2019)
3. Forbes, H., C.D.A.A.G.: Distributed Control Systems Global Market 2017–2022. ARC Market Analysis (2018). https://www.arcweb.com/market-studies/distributed-control-systems
4. Forbes, H.: The end of industrial automation (as we know it), December 2018. https://www.arcweb.com/blog/end-industrial-automation-we-know-it
5. Goldschmidt, T., Hauck-Stattelmann, S., Malakuti, S., Grüner, S.: Container-based architecture for flexible industrial control applications. J. Syst. Architect. **84**, 28–36 (2018)
6. Hollender, M.: Collaborative process automation systems. ISA (2010)
7. Kocher, P.S.: Microservices and Containers. Addison-Wesley Professional (2018)
8. Koziolek, H., Burger, A., Platenius-Mohr, M., Rückert, J., Stomberg, G.: Openpnp: a plug-and-produce architecture for the industrial internet of things. In: 2019 IEEE/ACM 41st International Conference on Software Engineering: Software Engineering in Practice (ICSE-SEIP), pp. 131–140. IEEE (2019)
9. Krause, H.: Virtual commissioning of a large LNG plant with the DCS 800XA by ABB. In: 6th EUROSIM Congress on Modelling and Simulation, Ljubljana, Slovénie (2007)
10. Mahnke, W., Leitner, S.H., Damm, M.: OPC Unified Architecture. Springer, Heidelberg (2009). https://doi.org/10.1007/978-3-540-68899-0

11. Moga, A., Sivanthi, T., Franke, C.: OS-level virtualization for industrial automation systems: are we there yet? In: Proceedings of the 31st Annual ACM Symposium on Applied Computing, pp. 1838–1843 (2016)
12. Montague, J.: OPAF draws nearer to interoperable process control, March 2020. https://www.controlglobal.com/articles/2020/opaf-draws-nearer-to-interoperable-process-control/
13. Netto, H.V., Lung, L.C., Correia, M., Luiz, A.F., de Souza, L.M.S.: State machine replication in containers managed by kubernetes. J. Syst. Architect. **73**, 53–59 (2017)
14. Oh, S., Kim, J.: Stateful container migration employing checkpoint-based restoration for orchestrated container clusters. In: 2018 International Conference on Information and Communication Technology Convergence (ICTC), pp. 25–30. IEEE (2018)
15. Prenzel, L., Provost, J.: Dynamic software updating of IEC 61499 implementation using erlang runtime system. IFAC-PapersOnLine **50**(1), 12416–12421 (2017)
16. Seifzadeh, H., Abolhassani, H., Moshkenani, M.S.: A survey of dynamic software updating. J. Softw. Evol. Process **25**(5), 535–568 (2013)
17. Sollfrank, M., Loch, F., Denteneer, S., Vogel-Heuser, B.: Evaluating docker for lightweight virtualization of distributed and time-sensitive applications in industrial automation. IEEE Trans. Industr. Inf. **17**(5), 3566–3576 (2020)
18. Vayghan, L.A., Saied, M.A., Toeroe, M., Khendek, F.: Microservice based architecture: towards high-availability for stateful applications with kubernetes. In: 2019 IEEE 19th International Conference on Software Quality, Reliability and Security (QRS), pp. 176–185. IEEE (2019)
19. Wahler, M., Oriol, M.: Disruption-free software updates in automation systems. In: Proceedings of the 2014 IEEE Emerging Technology and Factory Automation (ETFA), pp. 1–8. IEEE (2014)
20. Wahler, M., Richter, S., Oriol, M.: Dynamic software updates for real-time systems. In: Proceedings of the 2nd International Workshop on Hot Topics in Software Upgrades, pp. 1–6 (2009)

A Runtime Safety Enforcement Approach by Monitoring and Adaptation

Silvia Bonfanti[1] , Elvinia Riccobene[2] , and Patrizia Scandurra[1(✉)]

[1] University of Bergamo, Bergamo, Italy
{silvia.bonfanti,patrizia.scandurra}@unibg.it
[2] Università degli Studi di Milano, Milan, Italy
elvinia.riccobene@unimi.it

Abstract. The use of models and formal analysis techniques at runtime is fundamental to address safety assurance during the system operational stage, when all relevant uncertainties and unknowns can be resolved. This paper presents a novel approach to runtime safety enforcement of software systems based on the *MAPE-K control loop architecture* for system monitoring and control, and on the *Abstract State Machine* as runtime model representing the enforcement strategy aimed at preserving or eventually restoring safety. The enforcer software is designed as an autonomic manager that wraps around the software system to monitor and manage unsafe system changes using probing and effecting interfaces provided by the system, so realising *grey-box safety enforcement*. The proposed approach is supported by a component framework that is here illustrated by means of a case study in the health-care domain.

Keywords: Safety enforcement · Self-adaptation · MAPE-K · Runtime models · Abstract State Machines@run.time

1 Introduction

Usually a software system can be shown to be safe during the design/development stage by testing, simulation, or formal verification making explicit assumptions about the environment in which the system will execute. However, the safe behaviour of a software system under certain circumstances cannot be completely ascertained at design/development time without deploying it in a real environment. It is fairly well known that it is necessary to deal with the assurance process of software systems also during the operational stage, when all relevant uncertainties and unknowns caused by the close interactions of the system with their users and the environment can be detected and resolved [10,21,28].

A software system can work safely only in certain regions of its state space [2,19]. Some *runtime enforcement* techniques have been used (see [1,15,22], to name a few) to modify the runtime behaviour of a software system, forcing the system to satisfy a set of safety assertions, thus steering the behaviour of the system to stay within its safe regions [16]. Usually, enforcement mechanisms are synthesised

© Springer Nature Switzerland AG 2021
S. Biffl et al. (Eds.): ECSA 2021, LNCS 12857, pp. 20–36, 2021.
https://doi.org/10.1007/978-3-030-86044-8_2

according to a given automata-based formal specification that treats the target system as a black-box by observing mainly the input/output events. A white-box approach that uses a complete knowledge of the system and its external interactions would suffer from problems of scalability and performance. Through probing and effecting interfaces provided by the target system, a grey-box approach that observes specific system's operational changes and then computes safety related compensatory actions would be more effective. However, the adoption of grey-box enforcement mechanisms has not been much explored yet [15].

In contrast to previous black-box approaches that use automata to synthesize safety enforcement mechanisms and perform mainly I/O sanitisation, we propose a novel approach to perform safety enforcement in a gray-box way leveraging the use of software architecture-based self-adaptation [18] and models@run.time [11]. Through probe events (as provided by the probing interface of the managed system, in addition to I/O events) the proposed enforcement mechanism can detect operational changes that might lead to potential safety violations in the short term and proactively actuate an enforcement strategy as dictated by a runtime enforcement model. More precisely, the contribution of this paper is a gray-box enforcement framework based on the feedback control loop model *MAPE-K (Monitor-Analyse-Plan-Execute over a Knowledge base)* [20] to realize the enforcer software as an autonomic manager that wraps around the target system and uses an *Abstract State Machine* (ASM) [9] at runtime (ASM@run.time) [25] as part of the knowledge repository to formally specify and evaluate safety assertions and whether/which reconfiguration actions are required to guarantee compliance with the safety goals. The enforcer therefore steers the correct system behaviour by *adapting* unsafe system changes on the base of the planned enforcement strategy. A preliminary sketch of our approach appeared in [24].

To illustrate our framework, we consider a realistic case-study in the healthcare domain, namely a *Medicine Reminder and Monitoring System* (MRM) for securing patient safety through a software enforcer that remotely controls a smart medicine dispenser.

Differently from conventional runtime verification and monitoring techniques [11] that generally focus on the *oracle problem*, namely assigning verdicts to a system execution for compliance against policies formulated by means of an abstract model (e.g., in terms of temporal logic formulas), runtime enforcement [15] focuses on preventing possible unsafe sequences of events and steering correct system executions, by possibly modifying or avoiding the system execution.

To express safety assertions and enforcement strategies, we here use the ASM formal method, which is supported by analysis tools and techniques, and can be used during the design, development, and operation phases of the assurance process for safety-critical systems [3]. W.r.t. other automaton-based models, (1) ASMs offer the advantage of being easily understandable by practitioners thanks to their *pseudo-code format*, and usable for high-level programming; (2) they offer a precise system specification at any desired *level of abstraction*; (3) they are *executable models*, so they can be co-executed with system low-level implementations [23]. Moreover, ASMs have been already used to provide formal specification of MAPE loops for adaptation concerns [5,6] and for solving interfering adaptation goals [4]. The outcome of the offline formal specification and analysis phase of the enforcement model (i.e., the ASM model) can lead to a re-design of the enforcement strategies if some safety violations and/or goals interferences are discovered [25].

The paper is organized as follows. Section 2 highlights related work. Section 3 presents the MRM running case study and a description of the different scenarios for the safety enforcement experiments that we conducted. Section 4 describes the proposed enforcement approach and its reference architecture, using ASMs as enforcement models. Section 5 provides implementation details of the proposed framework, while Sect. 6 describes how the framework has been instantiated and validated for the MRM system. Finally, Sect. 7 concludes the paper.

2   Related Work

Enforcement mechanisms were initially proposed in the security domain to enforce security and privacy policies [14]. Runtime enforcement was also applied to enforce usage-control policies on mobile devices [26,27]; in [26], for example, a policy enforcement framework based on the concept of *proactive library* is presented and applied to the Android platform using run-time hooking and code injection mechanisms to handle faults caused by bad resource management such as a mobile device. Though this approach to enforce adaptation policies is somehow related to our, it is to be considered also a self-healing solution [15] designed to address a resource-constrained environment.

To assure system safety at runtime, in [13] a robotics programming framework, called SOTER, is presented for implementing and testing high-level reactive robotics software like drone surveillance systems. This framework integrates also a runtime assurance (RTA) system for the use of uncertified components while still providing safety guarantees. Each uncertified component is protected using a RTA module (based on an encoded state machine) that guarantees safety by switching to a safe controller in case of danger. A similar safety enforcement mechanism in the same application domain is presented in [22] to guarantee the safe behaviour of a drone controller.

In [30], a general approach to automatically synthesise enforcer components, called *safety guards*, from a formal specification (a Mealy machine) of safety properties for safety-critical cyber-physical systems is presented. Other similar approaches based on the synthesis of enforcement mechanisms from automaton-based formal specifications of the enforcement strategy are reviewed in [15]. Unlike these synthesis approaches that can be, as any code generation, error-prone and difficult to test, we rely instead on runtime simulation of the safety formal specifications in tandem with the target system. The software enforcer relies on a feedback loop equipped with an enforcement model (an ASM@run.time) that is updated at runtime, when new knowledge about safety changing conditions becomes available; the enforcer uses this model to plan and apply an enforcement strategy (according to the behaviour specified in the ASM@run.time) by adapting the target system. Model-based simulation at runtime has been successfully adopted to enable efficient decision making in self-adaptive systems, usually to assess extra-functional quality properties [29]. Simulation, in general, is less time and resource consuming compared with exhaustive verification techniques, and it is, therefore, particularly advantageous at run-time, when time and resources are often constrained [11].

3 Running Example: The MRM System

The proposed example is inspired by real smart drug systems available on the market and consists of (see Fig. 1) an electronic pill reminder&dispenser (a pill box), a remote control app (e.g., a mobile app running on an Android smartphone) that monitors and controls the pill box (via a local wireless connection, e.g. WiFi or Bluetooth, when the caregiver is in proximity, or via IoT SIM card when the caregiver is away from the patient's home), and an health-care information system on Cloud implementing value-added and persistence services related to a person's health record, treatment and medicine prescriptions inserted by the doctor via a web app. The remote control app is responsible for downloading/uploading patient's information from/to the user's electronic health record on Cloud. The app is also responsible for the correct pill box initialisation once filled and plugged into a home wall outlet, and for dynamically enforcing the pill box re-configuration to ensure the patient safety about medicines intake.

Fig. 1. MRM system: high-level architecture

Initially, the caregiver or the patient through the mobile app downloads a drug file record (e.g., a JSON file) containing all information about the medicines prescribed by the doctor: medicine name, number of doses per day, time schedule, minimum separation (in terms of time) from the medicine M to the interferer N and between the same medicine, and delta time added to the original time schedule to remember the medicine again if a dose is missed. Then, the user has to manually fill the pill box's compartment with the medicines (one medicine type per each compartment) on a daily basis according to the given prescription for the overall treatment duration. Once the medicines have been added into the pill box and the pill box actual configuration has been checked against the prescription via the remote control app, the patient is notified by the pill box when a medicine has to be taken. At the programmed time of a medicine, a notification is sent to the mobile remote control app, an audible alarm of the pill box sounds, a red led, corresponding to the compartment where the medicine to be taken is located, is turned on and the compartment is unlocked. The patient/caregiver has to open and then close the

Table 1. Safety enforcement scenarios

Scenario	Unsafe condition	Enforcement strategy	Enforcement action
MP1	Pill missed	Postpone missed pill without overlapping	Re-schedule pill
MP2	Pill missed	Postpone missed pill with overlapping	Skip current missed pill
LP	Pill taken later	Avoid pills overlapping	Skip next pill if it overlaps

compartment to report to the remote control app that the medicine was effectively taken. If after 10 min from the expected time the medicine is not taken, the red led starts flashing for 10 min further, after which the pill is considered missed by the system.

In case of a missed pill, drug reminder usually notifies the caregiver only. In this example, instead, we assume the remote control app is engineered smarter with a software enforcer that assists patients and caregivers in the medicine intake by re-configuring the pill box automatically. Intuitively, a missed medicine can be re-scheduled later in time, and in case of delayed medicine intake, it must be guaranteed that the next medicines are taken without drug interference. Specifically, the pill box system operates in a safe way for the patient if the following safety assertions are satisfied:

RQ1 [PILL ON TIME]: pills must be taken at the prescription time within a delta time window;
RQ2 [INTERFERING PILLS NEVER OVERLAP]: assumption times of interfering pills must not overlap.

In particular, for illustration purposes, we assume the enforcer automatically re-configures the pill box according to the following *safety enforcement strategies*:

MISSED PILL (MP): A missed pill is re-scheduled by the enforcer by adding the delta time to the original time schedule only if the minimum separation time from the next medicines is observed, otherwise it is definitively missed.
LATE PILL (LP): Since from the scheduled time to the actual time consumption can take up to 20 min, the enforcer checks if the difference between the actual time consumption and the minimum separation from the next medicines is observed. If not, the next pill is skipped.

To exemplify the proposed approach, we consider three safety enforcement scenarios, as reported in Table 1: scenarios MP1 and MP2 capture the two different enforcement strategies in case of a missed pill, while scenario LP refers to a pill taken after the expected time.

4   Safety Enforcement by Monitoring and Adaptation

The safety enforcement approach we propose here is based on the MAPE-K control loop architecture for monitoring and control, and on an ASM as runtime model representing the enforcement strategy for preserving or eventually restoring safety.

Figure 2 shows the architecture of an enforcer software E managing the target system S through a MAPE-K feedback loop in an environment Env. A context $C \subset Env$ of S represents the environmental entities that interact with S and influence its behaviour. During operation, the system perceives parts of C through its input interface (or set of input events) I and reacts accordingly by affecting parts of C through its output interface (or set of output events) O.

Safety-critical actions or relevant state changes of S are monitored by the enforcer (through sensors/probes *Probe* of the system) that can intervene by adapting or modifying the system changes (through effectors/actuators *Effector* of the system). Core to the enforcement process is a runtime model m_S that is part of the knowledge K and used as *enforcement model* for evaluating whether/which reconfiguration actions are required to

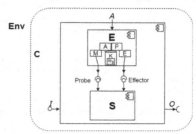

Fig. 2. Safety enforcement by monitoring and adaptation

guarantee safety properties A. Essentially, it is an automaton-based mechanism endowed with an internal memory [16] used by the actual software enforcer to specify the enforcement strategy. The enforcement model m_S is continuously fed up with *Probe* data extracted from the monitored system S about state changes of the system and its context C, and executed at each feedback loop step to analyse whether the safety assertions A continue to be satisfied; whenever this is no longer the case, appropriate system changes are planned and executed by the enforcer. So the enforcer plays the role of autonomic manager of the enforcement process. In order to keep the model in a consistent state and dealing with system change propagation, during the enforcement process the enforcer freezes the overall system computation.

The following sub-sections illustrate how the proposed enforcement approach is realised in practice by exploiting the concept of ASM@run.time to provide an enforcement model in terms of an ASM.

4.1   Abstract State Machines for Specifying Enforcement Models

ASMs [9] are here used to specify the enforcement model. ASMs are an extension of the Finite State Machines. Unstructured control states are replaced by *states* comprising arbitrary complex data (i.e., domains of objects with functions defined on them); state *transitions* are expressed by transition rules describing how the data (state function values saved into *locations*) change from one state to the next. Transition rules have different constructors depending on the update structure they express, e.g., guarded updates (`if-then`, `switch-case`), simultaneous parallel updates (`par`), etc.

An ASM *run* is defined as a finite or infinite sequence of states: starting from an initial state, each state is obtained from the previous one by firing, in parallel,

```
asm safePillbox
import StandardLibrary
import pillbox_sanitiser
signature:
    monitored isPillMissed: Compartment −> Boolean
    monitored pillTakenWithDelay: Compartment −> Boolean
    monitored actual_time_consumption: Compartment −> Seq(Natural)
    out setNewTime: Compartment −> Boolean
    out setOriginalTime: Compartment −> Boolean
    out newTime: Compartment −> Natural
    out skipNextPill: Prod(Compartment,Compartment) −> Boolean
    monitored systemTime: Natural
definitions:
    rule r_enforce = forall $compartment in Compartment do
            par r_pillOnTime[$compartment] r_noOverlapping[$compartment] endpar ...
    main rule r_Main = if state = INIT then r_INIT[] else r_enforce[] endif
default init s0:
    function state = INIT
    function medicine_list = ["fosamax","moment"]
    function amount($medicine in String) = switch($medicine)
                                    case "moment" : 2n
                                    case "fosamax" : 1n endswitch ...
```

Code 1. SafePillbox ASM model

all transition rules and leading to simultaneous (consistent) updates of a number of locations.

Without going into the details that will be presented afterwards, Code 1 reports an excerpt of the ASM *SafePillbox*, which operates as an enforcement model of the MRM system. The section **signature** declares all functions of the model, among which those specifying the model interface with its environment: *monitored* functions are those written by the environment and read by the machine, *out* function are those written by the machine and read by the environment. The **main rule** is, at each state, the starting point of the computation; it, in turns, call all the other transitions rules (e.g., **r_enforce**). The section **default init** defines the initial values for the *controlled* functions, updated by the machine.

Runtime Support. Recently, a runtime simulation engine, **AsmetaS@run.time** [25], has been developed for ASMs within the ASMETA (ASM mETAmodeling) analysis toolset – a set of modelling and V&V tools for the ASM formal method –. It allows handling (including model-roll back capabilities) an ASM model as a living/runtime model to be possibly executed in tandem with a prototype/real system and provides formal support for system properties (i.e., safety) assurance.

4.2   ASMs Operating as Enforcement Models

Let S be the monitored real system and m_S be the enforcement ASM model. Safety violations are captured and compensated at the ASM model level in the following way. The enforcer monitors S by watching its relevant input/output or internal events through the system probes. When a new event occurs that may change the state of S, the enforcer executes the ASM m_S to detect possible safety violations, and it adjusts the system change if necessary.

Safety violations are specified as predicates over ASM state functions, and occur, in a negated form, as *guards* of ASM guarded transition rules representing enforcement operations – here called ASM *enforcement rules* – according to a specific enforcement logic. Safety violation therefore happens when enforcement rules can fire; the output (updates of out locations) of the ASM is used by the enforcer as a prescription/plan for adapting the monitored system S.

```
rule r_noOverlapping($compartment in Compartment)=
    if pillTakenWithDelay($compartment) then
        forall $c2 in next($compartment) do
            if nextPillOverlap($compartment, $c2) then
                skipNextPill($compartment, $c2):= true endif endif
```

Code 2. Enforcement rule for scenario LP

An enforcement rule has the form of a ECA (Event Condition Action) rule:

```
if = ¬(α(e_p)) then
    if = ρ(e_p) then   enforcement plan  endif
endif
```

If $\alpha \in A$ is a safety assumption, the rule fires when an intercepted probing event e_p can violate α, and a *safety repair guard* ρ holds –i.e., $\rho(e_p)$ guarantees the possibility to steer the system to a safe region again –, then suitable enforcement actions (i.e., the *enforcement plan*) are executed.

For example, for the MRM system, considering its enforcement model SafePillbox in Code 1, rule **r_enforce** is executed if the machine is not in its initial state. It, in turn, invokes the two enforcement rules **r_pillOnTime** and **r_noOverlapping** that, for each pill in the compartments, menage the three safety violations scenarios reported in Table 1. For example, Code 2 shows the enforcement rule for scenario LP with unsafe condition *Pill taken later*.

The unsafe condition (i.e., $\neg\alpha$) happens when the guard **pillTakenWithDelay**, which is true on a pill if its **actual_time_consumption** is different from pill's **time_consumption**, holds, violating the safety assumption PILL ON TIME (the boolean value of **pillTakenWithDelay** is provided as probe event, see Sect. 6).

The safety repair guard (i.e., ρ) **nextPillOverlap** holds if, for all next pills, the time distance between the prescription time $t_c(nextPill)$ of the next pill and the actual) consumption time $t_a(currentPill)$ of the taken pill is less than the minimum separation time $minToInterferer(currentPill, nextPill)$ between current pill and next pill, i.e.:

$$(t_c(nextPill) - t_a(currentPill)) \leq minToInterferer(currentPill, nextPill)$$

In case of scenario LP, the enforcer coerces the pillbox to skip the next pill. Details of the enforcement rules **r_noOverlapping** and **r_pillOnTime** managing the two *missed pill* scenarios will be discussed in Sect. 6.

5 Safety Enforcement Framework

The runtime enforcement mechanism presented above must be realised in terms of a suitable software system that can be injected into the target system. The software enforcer is typically designed to act as a proxy which wraps around the system and analyses its external interactions. Although its code may be partially available in the form of a component framework for some core functionalities and the code of the enforcer logic be synthesised automatically by enforcement models (e.g., input/output automata used to specify the particular enforcement strategy), normally the software enforcer is *system-specific* and therefore some manual steps are required to the developers to implement those aspects (such as components for the connection to the managed system) that are abstracted in the enforcement model/framework and that are specific to the target system.

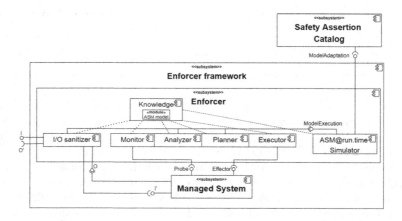

Fig. 3. Enforcement framework architecture.

In this respect, we designed and implemented a Java-based *white-box framework*[1] for common core functionalities that can be conveniently reused by concrete realisation of sets of components to accomplish enforcement tasks for different systems. By exploiting the *Template* design pattern and the *Factory* design pattern, the concrete components have an inheritance relationship with the framework's components[2]. We also combined the MAPE-K control loop style with the *Safety Assertion Enforcer* pattern [17] for shaping the enforcer subsystem.

Figure 3 shows a high-level overview of the enforcement framework architecture. The current prototype framework supports shell-like software applications (in any language) as managed systems and local pipes as first communication means to connect the enforcer software with them. The component I/O

---

[1] The framework is available within the ASMETA GitHub repository https://github. com/asmeta/asmeta/tree/master/code/experimental/asmeta.enforcer.

[2] The concrete component classes implement the basic abstract methods and override the hook methods of the framework's abstract classes to add specific behaviours.

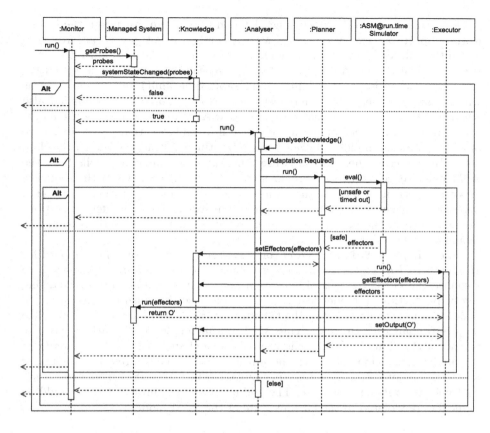

Fig. 4. Enforcer's operation *runFeedBackLoop()*

sanitizer is responsible for exchanging I/O values with the Managed System trough a bidirectional pipeline.

The Enforcer subsystem adopts the MAPE-K control structure and exploits a pull-based interaction to regularly request new data to the probes of the managed system; this approach is also used for the effectors. A MAPE-K control loop is continuously executed to assure the system safety requirements at runtime. The Analyser and Planner components are supported by the ASM@run.time Simulator that can run simulations of ASMs during operation. The UML sequence diagram in Fig. 4 details the safety enforcement by monitoring and adaptation executed by the Enforcer operation *runFeedBackLoop()*, and, therefore, the MAPE-K components interactions to enact the appropriate enforcement strategy as suggested by the ASM model run by the ASM@run.time Simulator.

Note that to avoid deadlock/huge delay in the system execution, the framework supports an execution mode with a configurable timeout, according to which the enforcer does not wait indefinitely for the simulator to finish the ASM run. Specifically, if the ASM model (for some reason) runs too long, its execution times out (according to a specific configurable time limit) and control returns without applying any enforcement strategy. None enforcement is applied also when the ASM model terminates with an UNSAFE verdict, meaning the model execution is in an error/corrupt state due to invariant violations or the existence of logic errors at model level not foreseen/verified during the model development. In this case, the ASM@run.time Simulator automatically rolls back the ASM model execution to its previous state (this is not shown in the sequence diagram, since it is part of the logic of the simulator's operation *eval*), and, depending on the specific reason, online adjustments of the safety assertions (as explained in the next paragraph) or offline model repairs actions would be required.

The subsystem Safety Assertion Catalog realises a sort of dashboard for *Human-Model-Interplay* (both in a graphical and in a command-line way) to visualise the current status of execution and to enact commands for changing safety properties at model level. For this purpose, it consumes the interface ModelAdaptation provided by the ASMs@run.time Simulator. In order to make on-the-fly changes of the underlying ASM runtime model consistently, a separate thread of the simulator (different from the model simulation thread) manages the model adaptation only when the status of the simulation reaches a *quiescent state*, i.e. no enforcement activity is going on. Then, the ASM model execution continues from its current state. The adding of a safety invariant that would be immediately violated in the current state of the ASM model is forbidden.

6 Runtime Safety Enforcement at Work

This section illustrates the instantiation of the proposed framework and the implementation and validation of the enforcement strategies for the MRM system.

6.1 Instantiation of the Enforcement Framework

Figure 5 outlines the instantiation of the enforcement framework shown in Fig. 3 as subsystem of the overall distributed MRM system, which includes also the pill box embedded system. In this example, the Enforcer subsystem runs in a mobile remote control app. We validated the framework using a Java-based simulated version of the pill box, since a realistic pill box device was not available. The Pillbox simulation software, has been obtained by reusing and extending with probes/effectors a previous simulated version of the pillbox, whose abstract behaviour was designed by using ASMs and then prototyped in the Arduino [7] by automatically synthesizing correct-by-design code from the ASM model [8].

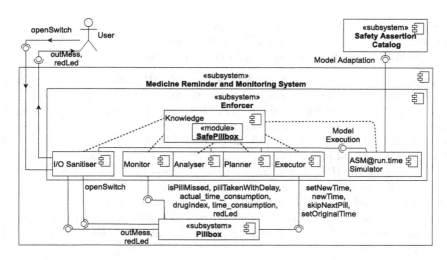

Fig. 5. MRM enforcement framework

The I/O interface of the `Pillbox` subsystem with the user (see the list of events shown beside the interface symbols in Fig. 5) consists of the input signal `openSwitch` for open/close compartment actions received from the user, and of an output message `outMess` and the `redLed` state of each compartment sent as outputs to the user. The `I/O Sanitiser` component within the `Enforcer` subsystem works as *delegator*, which updates the location `openSwitch` of the `Knowledge` component with the value received from the user, and provides outputs `outMess` and `redLed` to the user.

The module `SafePillbox` within the `Knowledge` is the ASM model (see Code 1) used as enforcement model to produce the configuration actions that must be automatically undertaken by the enforcer on the pillbox to preserve safety. The enforcement strategy is formally represented by means of the ASM enforcement rules `r_pillOnTime` and `r_noOverlapping`.

The enforcer monitors the pillbox through the following set of probes:

- `time_consumption`: instant of time in which the medicine must be taken;
- `redLed`: status (on/off/blinking) of the red led for each compartment;
- `drugIndex`: index of the medicine that must be taken;
- `actual_time_consumption`: time in which the medicine has been taken;
- `isPillMissed`: true if current pill has been missed;
- `pillTakenWithDelay`: true if `actual_time_consumption` is different from `time_consumption`.

In case safety assertion are violated, the enforcer affects the monitored system by setting the following effectors:

- `setNewTime`: it indicates if the pill time consumption must be rescheduled;

- `newTime`: it sets the new time consumption;
- `setOriginalTime`: it indicates if the pill cannot be rescheduled;
- `skipNextPill`: it indicates if the pill must be skipped.

Code 3 reports the enforcement rule for the scenario MP1 when the pill is missed (`isPillMissed`) and the enforcer postpones its assumption by delta time: $(t_c(nextPill) - (t_c(currentPill) + \Delta(currentPill)) \geq minToInterfer(currentPill, nextPill)$ where $t_c(nextPill)$ is the time consumption of the next pill; $t_c(currentPill)$ is the time consumption of the current pill; $\Delta(currentPill)$ is the time delay of current pill w.r.t. the consumption time the pill should have been taken; *minToInterfer(currentPill, nextPill)* is the minimum separation time between current pill and next pill (the condition must occur for all next pills). A similar rule (already seen in Code 3) addresses the scenario MP2 when the missed pill is skipped since it cannot be rescheduled. The enforcer coerces the pillbox to skip the current pill by means of the effector `setOriginalTime`. In case of scenario LP, predicate details are explained in Sect. 4.2.

6.2   Validation of Enforcement Strategies

We here show the application[3] of the proposed safety enforcement mechanism by monitoring and adaptation of the pill box device to address the three enforcement scenarios reported in Table 1. Figure 6 shows the mobile control app execution for scenario MP1, where the enforcer intervenes to preserve the pill box safety in case of a missed pill. The time is simulated by setting it in the text box. The `SafePillbox` module is initialised with probes values to get the initial state of the pill box. Red leds are all off; two medicines are in the pill box: moment and fosamax; the fosamax must be taken at 5:50 a.m. while moment at 01:00 p.m. and 07:00 p.m. (in the code, times are defined in minutes from midnight instead of hours:minutes); and all pills have to be taken (none is skipped).

```
rule r_pillOnTime($compartment in Compartment)=
% MP1 scenario
    if isPillMissed($compartment) then
        if rescheduleNotOverlap($compartment) then
            par
                setNewTime ($compartment, drugIndex($compartment)):= true
                newTime ($compartment, drugIndex($compartment)):= at(time_consumption(
                    $compartment),drugIndex($compartment))+deltaDelay(name($compartment
                    ))
            endpar endif
% MP2 scenario
    if isPillMissed($compartment) then
        if rescheduleOverlap($compartment) then
            par
                setOriginalTime ($compartment):= true
                newTime ($compartment):= at(time(name($compartment)),drugIndex(
                    $compartment)) endpar endif endif
```

Code 3. Enforcement rule for scenarios MP1 and MP2

---

[3] https://github.com/asmeta/MRM

(a) Time to take fosamax, led on

(b) Open compartment, led blinking

(c) Close compartment, pill taken

(d) Time to take moment, led on

(e) After ten minutes, led blinking

(f) The enforcer reschedules the pill

Fig. 6. Safety enforcement for scenario MP1

When it is time to take fosamax (the first pill prescribed), the pill box turns on the corresponding red led and displays a message to the patient (Fig. 6a). When the patient opens the fosamax compartment the led starts blinking (Fig. 6b) until the patient closes the compartment and takes the pill (Fig. 6c). When the patient takes the pill, the consumption time is reported in the scheduling table. When it is time to take moment, the pill box turns on the corresponding red led and displays a message to the patient (Fig. 6d). Since the patient did not opened the compartment within the next 10 min, the red led starts blinking and the pill box reminds the patient that the pill must be taken in 10 min (Fig. 6e). Until now, the enforcer does not apply any adaptation plan because all the safety assumptions are observed. After 20 min from moment prescription, the pill box reports through the probing event `isPillMissed` that the pill is missed. The enforcer detects that the safety assumption `isPillMissed` for MP1 is violated. The safety repair guard `rescheduleNotOverlap` holds true and the enforcer reschedules the missed pill through the effectors (`setNewTime`, `newTime` and `setOriginalTime`) (Fig. 6f). An output message is displayed to the user to notify the pill rescheduling, and the new consumption time is displayed.

7 Conclusion and Future Work

We proposed a runtime enforcement framework to monitor and keep a software system behaviour in line with safety requirements by anticipating incorrect behaviour and countering it before it actually happens. The enforcer acts as an autonomic manager that wraps around the managed system and analyses and controls the system's operational changes and interactions with the environment with the help of an ASM used as runtime enforcement model.

In the future, we want to evaluate the generality of the proposed enforcement framework by targeting other systems and real-world application domains. In particular, we want to adopt our enforcement framework as an *autonomic midlleware* to retrofit pre-existing systems/legacy systems (e.g., *Software as a Medical Device*) and secure them with external autonomic capabilities, thus avoiding costly device offline repairs/recalls. Furthermore, we will investigate on the problem of deciding whether a given safety goal is enforceable or not through a gray-box enforcement mechanism. For this refined setting, we will give necessary and sufficient conditions on when and how a safety assertion is enforceable during the execution of the system and of the MAPE-K loop. In addition, we want to explore the applicability of our safety enforcement approach to autonomous systems whose runtime behaviour is highly unpredictable, such as AI-based systems. In particular, we want to explore the runtime use of probabilistic ASMs or other state-based stochastic formalisms to model and incorporate uncertainty issues explicitly [12] within the enforcement process.

References

1. Andersson, B., Chaki, S., de Niz, D.: Combining symbolic runtime enforcers for cyber-physical systems. In: Lahiri, S., Reger, G. (eds.) RV 2017. LNCS, vol. 10548, pp. 68–84. Springer, Cham (2017). https://doi.org/10.1007/978-3-319-67531-2_5
2. Andersson, J., Grassi, V., Mirandola, R., Perez-Palacin, D.: A conceptual framework for resilience: fundamental definitions, strategies and metrics. Computing **103**(4), 559–588 (2020)
3. Arcaini, P., Bombarda, A., Bonfanti, S., Gargantini, A., Riccobene, E., Scandurra, P.: The ASMETA approach to safety assurance of software systems. In: Raschke, A., Riccobene, E., Schewe, K.-D. (eds.) Logic, Computation and Rigorous Methods. LNCS, vol. 12750, pp. 215–238. Springer, Cham (2021). https://doi.org/10.1007/978-3-030-76020-5_13
4. Arcaini, P., Mirandola, R., Riccobene, E., Scandurra, P.: MSL: a pattern language for engineering self-adaptive systems. J. Syst. Softw. **164**, 110558 (2020)
5. Arcaini, P., Riccobene, E., Scandurra, P.: Modeling and analyzing MAPE-K feedback loops for self-adaptation. In: Proceedings of the 10th International Symposium on Software Engineering for Adaptive and Self-Managing Systems. ACM (2015)

6. Arcaini, P., Riccobene, E., Scandurra, P.: Formal design and verification of self-adaptive systems with decentralized control. ACM Trans. Auton. Adapt. Syst. **11**(4), 1–35 (2017)
7. Bombarda, A., Bonfanti, S., Gargantini, A.: Developing medical devices from abstract state machines to embedded systems: a smart pill box case study. In: Mazzara, M., Bruel, J.-M., Meyer, B., Petrenko, A. (eds.) TOOLS 2019. LNCS, vol. 11771, pp. 89–103. Springer, Cham (2019). https://doi.org/10.1007/978-3-030-29852-4_7
8. Bonfanti, S., Gargantini, A., Mashkoor, A.: Design and validation of a C++ code generator from abstract state machines specifications. J. Softw. Evol. Process **32**(2), e2205 (2020)
9. Börger, E., Raschke, A.: Modeling Companion for Software Practitioners. Springer, Heidelberg (2018). https://doi.org/10.1007/978-3-662-56641-1
10. Calinescu, R., Weyns, D., Gerasimou, S., Iftikhar, M.U., Habli, I., Kelly, T.: Engineering trustworthy self-adaptive software with dynamic assurance cases. IEEE Trans. Software Eng. **44**(11), 1039–1069 (2018)
11. Calinescu, R., Kikuchi, S.: Formal methods @ runtime. In: Calinescu, R., Jackson, E. (eds.) Monterey Workshop 2010. LNCS, vol. 6662, pp. 122–135. Springer, Heidelberg (2011). https://doi.org/10.1007/978-3-642-21292-5_7
12. Camilli, M., Gargantini, A., Scandurra, P.: Model-based hypothesis testing of uncertain software systems. Softw. Test. Verification Reliab. **30**(2), e1730 (2020)
13. Desai, A., Ghosh, S., Seshia, S.A., Shankar, N., Tiwari, A.: SOTER: a runtime assurance framework for programming safe robotics systems. In: 49th Annual IEEE/IFIP International Conference on Dependable Systems and Networks (2019)
14. Erlingsson, U., Schneider, F.B.: SASI enforcement of security policies: a retrospective. In: Proceedings of the 1999 Workshop on New Security Paradigms. NSPW 1999. Association for Computing Machinery (1999)
15. Falcone, Y., Mariani, L., Rollet, A., Saha, S.: Runtime failure prevention and reaction. In: Bartocci, E., Falcone, Y. (eds.) Lectures on Runtime Verification. LNCS, vol. 10457, pp. 103–134. Springer, Cham (2018). https://doi.org/10.1007/978-3-319-75632-5_4
16. Falcone, Y., Mounier, L., Fernandez, J., Richier, J.: Runtime enforcement monitors: composition, synthesis, and enforcement abilities. Formal Methods Syst. Des. **38**(3), 223–262 (2011)
17. Fernandez, E.B., Hamid, B.: Two safety patterns: safety assertion and safety assertion enforcer. In: Proceedings of the 22nd European Conference on Pattern Languages of Programs. EuroPLoP 2017. Association for Computing Machinery (2017)
18. Garlan, D., Schmerl, B.R., Cheng, S.: Software architecture-based self-adaptation. In: Zhang, Y., Yang, L., Denko, M. (eds.) Autonomic Computing and Networking, pp. 31–55. Springer, Boston (2009). https://doi.org/10.1007/978-0-387-89828-5_2
19. He, Y., Schumann, J.: A framework for the analysis of adaptive systems using Bayesian statistics. In: Proceedings of the IEEE/ACM 15th International Symposium on Software Engineering for Adaptive and Self-Managing Systems (2020)
20. Kephart, J.O., Chess, D.M.: The vision of autonomic computing. Computer **36**(1), 41–50 (2003)
21. Lutz, R.R.: Software engineering for safety: a roadmap. In: Proceedings of the Conference on the Future of Software Engineering. ICSE 2000. Association for Computing Machinery (2000)

22. de Niz, D., Andersson, B., Moreno, G.: Safety enforcement for the verification of autonomous systems. In: Dudzik, M.C., Ricklin, J.C. (eds.) Autonomous Systems: Sensors, Vehicles, Security, and the Internet of Everything, vol. 10643. International Society for Optics and Photonics, SPIE (2018)

23. Riccobene, E., Scandurra, P.: A formal framework for service modeling and prototyping. Formal Aspects Comput. **26**(6), 1077–1113 (2014)

24. Riccobene, E., Scandurra, P.: Exploring the concept of abstract state machines for system runtime enforcement. In: Raschke, A., Méry, D., Houdek, F. (eds.) ABZ 2020. LNCS, vol. 12071, pp. 244–247. Springer, Cham (2020). https://doi.org/10.1007/978-3-030-48077-6_18

25. Riccobene, E., Scandurra, P.: Model-based simulation at runtime with abstract state machines. In: Muccini, H., et al. (eds.) ECSA 2020. CCIS, vol. 1269, pp. 395–410. Springer, Cham (2020). https://doi.org/10.1007/978-3-030-59155-7_29

26. Riganelli, O., Micucci, D., Mariani, L.: Policy enforcement with proactive libraries. In: 12th IEEE/ACM International Symposium on Software Engineering for Adaptive and Self-Managing Systems. IEEE Computer Society (2017)

27. Riganelli, O., Micucci, D., Mariani, L.: Controlling interactions with libraries in android apps through runtime enforcement. ACM Trans. Auton. Adapt. Syst. **14**(2), 1–29 (2019)

28. Trapp, M., Schneider, D.: Safety assurance of open adaptive systems – a survey. In: Bencomo, N., France, R., Cheng, B.H.C., Aßmann, U. (eds.) Models@run.time. LNCS, vol. 8378, pp. 279–318. Springer, Cham (2014). https://doi.org/10.1007/978-3-319-08915-7_11

29. Weyns, D., Iftikhar, M.U.: Model-based simulation at runtime for self-adaptive systems. In: Kounev, S., Giese, H., Liu, J. (eds.) 2016 IEEE International Conference on Autonomic Computing, ICAC 2016. IEEE Computer Society (2016)

30. Wu, M., Zeng, H., Wang, C., Yu, H.: Safety guard: runtime enforcement for safety-critical cyber-physical systems: invited. In: Proceedings of the 54th Annual Design Automation Conference. ACM (2017)

Towards a Taxonomy of Autonomous Systems

Stefan Kugele[1](✉)[iD], Ana Petrovska[2][iD], and Ilias Gerostathopoulos[3][iD]

[1] Research Institute AImotion Bavaria, Technische Hochschule Ingolstadt,
Ingolstadt, Germany
`Stefan.Kugele@thi.de`
[2] Department of Informatics, Technical University of Munich,
Garching bei München, Germany
`ana.petrovska@tum.de`
[3] Faculty of Science, Vrije University in Amsterdam, Amsterdam, The Netherlands
`i.g.gerostathopoulos@vu.nl`

Abstract. In this paper, we present a precise and yet concise characterisation of autonomous systems. To the best of our knowledge, there is no similar work, which through a mathematical definition of terms provides a foundation for describing the systems of the future: autonomous software-intensive systems and their architectures. Such systems include robotic taxi as an example of 2D mobility, or even drone/UAV taxi, as an example in the field of 3D urban air mobility. The presented terms lead to a four-level taxonomy. We describe informally and formally the taxonomy levels and exemplarily compare them to the degrees of automation as previously proposed by the SAE J3016 automotive standard.

Keywords: Autonomous systems · Taxonomy · Architecture

1 Introduction

The world is changing, and so are systems. Woods [9] describes in his much-noticed article "Software Architecture in a Changing World" the evolution from monolithic systems back in the 1980s to intelligent connected systems in the 2020s. We share Woods's vision for future systems. Today's connected cyber-physical systems (CPSs) are not too far away from this vision. The missing link between the current systems and the autonomous systems that we outline for the future is twofold: First, systems will be capable of adapting their structure and behaviour in reaction to changes and uncertainties emerging from their environment and the systems themselves [4, 6, 8] – they will be adaptive systems. Second, they will be able to derive knowledge themselves during their operational time to infer actions to perform.

The modern CPSs, such as cooperative robotic systems or intelligent transportation systems, are per se distributed. The not too distant future probably brings hitherto unrivalled levels of human-robot interaction. In such scenarios,

S. Biffl et al. (Eds.): ECSA 2021, LNCS 12857, pp. 37–45, 2021.
https://doi.org/10.1007/978-3-030-86044-8_3

machines and humans share the same environment, i.e., operational context [1,4]. Examples for those shared environments are (i) production systems (cf. Industry 4.0) or (ii) intelligent transportation systems with both autonomous and human-operated mobility. As a result, autonomous behaviour becomes an indispensable characteristic of such systems.

The lack of shared understanding of the notion of autonomy makes it difficult for the works across various domains to be compared or even discussed since the same term is used with different semantics. For example, very often in the literature, Unmanned Aerial Vehicles (UAVs) are misleadingly referred to as autonomous, although an end user completely controls their flying operation. As another example, we take robots operating in a room, which use Adaptive Monte Carlo Localisation (AMCL) to localise themselves and navigate in the space. Even though the robots localising and navigating independently in the room is some form of autonomy, they simply cannot be called *fully autonomous systems* if they operate in a room in which they often collide or get in deadlocks. In these situations, human administrators need to intervene in order for the robots to be able to continue with their operation. The intervention from a user (i.e., human administrator) directly affects the system's autonomy.

In response, we present in this paper our first steps towards a unified, comprehensive, and precise description of autonomous systems. Based on the level of user interaction and system's learning capabilities, we distinguish four autonomy levels ($\mathbf{A_0}$–$\mathbf{A_3}$): non-autonomous, intermittent autonomous, eventually autonomous, and fully autonomous. Our goal is to offer a precise and concise terminology that can be used to refer to the different types/levels of autonomous systems and to present a high-level architecture for each level.

The remainder of this paper is structured as follows. In Sect. 2 we briefly sketch existing efforts to formalise autonomy and explain the formal notation we are using later on. In Sect. 3, we present our taxonomy. Finally, in Sect. 4, we discuss and conclude the paper and outline our further research agenda.

2   Background

2.1   Existing Efforts to Formalise Autonomy

An initial effort in the literature to formally define autonomy was made by Luck and d'Inverno [5]. In this paper, the authors argue that the terms agency and autonomy are often used interchangeably without considering their relevance and significance, and in response, they propose a three-tiered principled theory using the Z specification language. In their three-tiered hierarchy, the authors distinguish between objects, agents, and autonomous agents. Concretely, in their definition of autonomy, as a focal point, the authors introduce *motivations*— "higher-level non-derivative components related to goals." Namely, according to their definition, autonomous agents have certain motivations and some potential of evaluating their own behaviour in terms of their environment and the respective motivations. The authors further add that the behaviour of the autonomous agent is strongly determined by and dependent on different internal and environmental factors. Although the authors acknowledge the importance of considering different internal and environmental (i.e., contextual) factors while defining autonomy, in their formalisms, the importance of the user in defining autonomy is entirely omitted. On the contrary, in our paper, we put the strongest emphasis on the user. Concretely, how the involvement of the user in the operation of the system diminishes, proportionally to the increase of the system's autonomy. We define levels of system's autonomy by focusing on the system's function and how much from the user's logic is "shifted" to the system in the higher levels of autonomy. We further touch on the importance of *learning*, especially when 1) the systems operate in highly dynamic, uncertain and unknown environments, and 2) the user's control on the system reduces. To the best of our knowledge, there is no prior work that defines different levels of autonomy *formally*.

2.2   Formal Modelling Approach

Within this paper, we use the formal modelling notation FOCUS introduced by Broy and Stølen [2]. We restrict ourselves to only those concepts necessary for the understanding of this work. In FOCUS, systems are described by their (i) *syntactic* and their (ii) *semantic* interface. The semantic interface of a system is denoted by $(I \triangleright O)$ indicating the set of *input* and *output* channels, $I, O \subseteq C$, where C denotes the set of all channels. Systems are (hierarchically) (de-)composed by connecting them via channels. A *timed stream* s of messages $m \in M$, e.g. $s = \langle \langle m_1 \rangle \langle \rangle \langle m_3\ m_4 \rangle \dots \rangle$, is assigned to each channel $c \in C$. The set of timed streams $\mathcal{T}(M)$ over messages M associates to each positive point in time $t \in \mathbb{N}^+$ a sequence of messages M^*, formally $\mathcal{T}(M) = \mathbb{N}^+ \to M^*$. In case of finite timed streams, $\mathcal{T}_{\mathsf{fin}}(M)$ is defined as: $\mathcal{T}_{\mathsf{fin}}(M) = \bigcup_{n \in \mathbb{N}} ([1:n] \to M^*)$. In the example given, in the first time slot, $\langle m_1 \rangle$ is transmitted; in the second time slot, nothing is transmitted (denoted by $\langle \rangle$), and in the third depicted time slot, two messages $\langle m_3\ m_4 \rangle$ are transmitted. *Untimed streams* over messages M are captured in the set $\mathcal{U}(M)$ which is defined as $\mathcal{U}(M) = (\mathbb{N}^+ \to M) \cup \bigcup_{n \in \mathbb{N}} ([1:n] \to M)$, i.e., each time slot is associated with at most one message and there can be streams of finite length. By $\overrightarrow{C}$, we denote *channel histories* given by families of timed streams: $\overrightarrow{C} = (C \to \mathcal{T}(M))$. Thus, every timed history $x \in \overrightarrow{X}$ denotes an evaluation for the channels in C by streams. With $\#s$, we denote the number of arbitrary messages in stream s, with $m\#s$ that of messages m. For timed streams $s \in \mathcal{T}(M)$, we denote with $s\!\downarrow\!(t) \in \mathcal{T}_{\mathsf{fin}}(M)$ the finite timed stream until time t. The system's *behavioural function* (semantic interface) f is given by a mapping of *input* to *output histories*: $f \colon \overrightarrow{I} \to \wp(\overrightarrow{O})$.

3   A Taxonomy for Defining Autonomy

In this section, we first describe how autonomy of a system is related to autonomy of its functions, then present the main ideas behind our proposed taxonomy, and finally describe both informally and formally the different levels of autonomy.

3.1   Autonomy as a Property of Individual Functions

CPSs such as modern cars are engineered in a way to deliver thousands of customer or user functions. These are functions that are directly controlled by the
user, or at least the user can perceive their effect. Switching on the radio, for
example, results in music being played. This is a customer function. On the other
hand, there are functions, for example, for diagnosis or for offering encryption
services, which the customer cannot control directly, of whose existence often
nothing at all is known and whose effects are not visible to the user. Considering the above-mentioned, it is not trivial to classify a complete system as
autonomous or non-autonomous. Instead, autonomy is a property of individual
functions. Let us take a vehicle that drives autonomously. We assume that this
system still offers the functionality to the passengers to choose the radio station
or the playlist themselves. Thus, the CPS operates autonomously in terms of
driving but is still heteronomous in terms of music playback. A similar argu-
mentation applies, for example, to vehicles that are equipped with automation
functions of varying degrees of automation, as considered in the SAE J3016
standard. For this system, as well as for other multi-functional systems, it is not
meaningful to conclude from the autonomy of a single function, the autonomy
or heteronomy of the whole system. Therefore, the commonly used term of an
autonomous vehicle is too imprecise since the term autonomy refers exclusively
to its driving capabilities. Hence, also the SAE proposes not to speak about
"autonomous vehicles" but instead about "level [3, 4, or 5] Automated Driving
System-equipped vehicles" (cf. [7], §7.2).

The only two statements that can be made with certainty are the following:
(1) if all functions of a system are autonomous, then the system can also be called
autonomous, and (2) if no function is autonomous, then certainly the system
is not autonomous. Anything in between cannot be captured with precision.
Single-functional systems are a special case. In such systems, the autonomy or
heteronomy of the single function is propagated to the system. For the sake of
illustrating our taxonomy on a simpler case, we will focus on single-functional
systems in the rest of the paper.

3.2   Main Ideas Behind the Taxonomy for Autonomy

Our first main idea is to define autonomy levels of a system by focusing on the
system's function and specifically by looking at the level of interaction that a user
has with the system. Intuitively, the more user interaction is in place, the less
autonomous the system is. "More user interaction" can mean both more *frequent*
interaction and more *fine-grained* interaction. Actually, these two characteristics
very often go hand in hand: consider, for instance, the case of a drone: it can be
controlled with a joystick with frequent and fine-grained user interaction (lower
autonomy); it can also be controlled via a high-level target-setting routine with
less frequent and more coarse-grained user interaction (higher autonomy).

The second main idea behind our taxonomy is to distinguish between systems
that learn and ones that do not learn. By learning, we mean that systems can

observe both their context and user actions and identify behavioural patterns (e.g. rules or policies) in the observed data (e.g. by training and using a classifier). Such patterns can be used at run-time to reduce the amount of user interaction with the system gradually. Hence, the more capable a system is of learning behavioural patterns, the more autonomous it can become.

Finally, the third main idea is to define a system as autonomous within an assumed operational context. The assumed context can be narrow (e.g. a drone operating in a wind range of 0–4 Beaufort) or very broad (e.g. a drone operating under any weather conditions). The specification of the context can also be uncertain or incomplete, i.e., the designers of the system might not be able to anticipate and list all possible situations that may arise under a specific context assumption. In any case, the more broad context is assumed, the harder it becomes for a system to reach high autonomy.

3.3 Taxonomy Levels

The four levels of autonomous systems in our taxonomy are shown in Fig. 1. Figure 2 shows the interaction between the user u, the context c, and the system s, as well as the (very high level) architecture of the system at each level in the taxonomy.

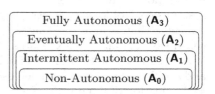

Fig. 1. Taxonomy levels.

The lowest level, A_0, refers to systems that are *not autonomous*. For these systems, user input is needed at all times for controlling their operation. Examples are using the radio in a car or controlling the movement of a robot via a remote controller. As can be seen in Fig. 2(a), on this level, the system s (i.e., the system function sf) is completely controlled by the user and does not assume any input from the context (although this input might be already taken indirectly into account by the user). Note that the function sf might internally do something in the background that does not depend on the user input. A user can control the movement and trajectory of a drone; however, each drone internally provides attitude stabilisation that is not dependent on user input but is part of this system function.

The next level, A_1, refers to systems that are *intermittent autonomous*: they can operate autonomously in-between two consecutive user inputs. In this case, the system can receive user input periodically or sporadically. As shown in Fig. 2(b), part of the logic of the user is shifted to the system as a control logic cl′, which interacts with the system function sf. Input to the control logic can also be provided by the context. For instance, consider the movement of a robotic vacuum cleaner: the system perceives its environment through its sensors (obtains context input) and operates autonomously until it gets stuck (e.g. because of an obstacle or a rough surface); at this point, a user is required to intervene to restart the robot or point it to the right direction.

Level A_2, shown in Fig. 2(c), refers to *eventually autonomous* systems: here, the user interaction reduces over time until the system reaches a point where

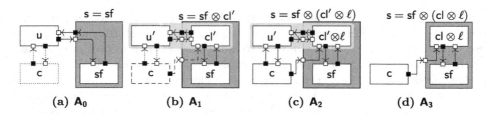

Fig. 2. From user-operation to autonomy: (a) A human user u controls the system s (i.e., the system's function sf). (b) The control logic is divided between the user u′ and the system cl′, i.e., $u = u' \otimes cl'$. (c) The control logic of the system cl′ could be enhanced with a learning component ℓ to better address e.g. changes in the context c. (d) The control logic cl with the usually necessary learning component ℓ is entirely performed by the system itself.

it does not require any user interaction (user control). For this to happen, the system's control logic cl′ is usually enhanced and equipped with a learning component ℓ that is able to identify the user interaction patterns associated with certain system and context states. An example is a robotic vacuum cleaner that is able to learn how to move under different floor types (e.g. faster or slower) and avoid crashes that would necessitate user interaction. Clearly, the degree and sophistication of monitoring and reasoning on context changes and user actions is much higher than in intermittent autonomous systems.

Finally, level **A₃** refers to *fully autonomous* systems, where no user input is needed (except the provision of initial strategic or goal-setting information), as it can be seen in Fig. 2(d). Systems on this level of autonomy can observe and adjust their behaviour to *any* context by potentially integrating learning in their control logic cl. Please note that the necessity and the sophistication of the learning is proportionate to 1) the complexity and the broadness of the context, and 2) the specifications of the context in the systems, as previously explained in Sect. 3.2. For instance, a robotic vacuum cleaner can move in a fully autonomous way when its context is more simplistic and could be fully anticipated (e.g. prescribed environment that contains only certain floor and obstacle types). To achieve this, the system needs to be equipped with sensing and run-time reasoning capabilities to adjust its movement behaviour and remain operational without human interaction. However, the difficulty for the same system to remain fully autonomous increases proportionally to the complexity of its context. For example, the context can be dynamic in ways that could not be anticipated, resulting in uncertain and incomplete context specifications. Since the user on this level is entirely out of the loop, this would require new, innovative, and more sophisticated learning methods in the *fully autonomous* systems.

We note that one can also imagine relatively simple systems without context impact that are configured *once or not at all* by a user and then work *without any user interaction or learning* (e.g. an alarm clock); while these systems also technically fall under **A₂** or **A₃**, they are less complex and sophisticated.

3.4   Formalisation of Taxonomy Levels

The intuitively described taxonomy levels are specified mathematically in the following. We denote with u the input stream from the user to the system.

Definition 1 (Non-autonomous, A_0). *A system is called* non-autonomous, *iff it solely depends on user inputs:* $\forall t \in \mathbb{N}^+ : u(t) \neq \langle \rangle$.

If there is less and less intervention or input by users, this becomes necessary repeatedly; we speak of intermittent autonomy.

Definition 2 (Intermittent Autonomous, A_1). *A system is called* intermittent autonomous, *iff user interaction is necessary from time to time (periodic or sporadic), i.e.:* $\forall t \in \mathbb{N}^+ \ \exists t', t'' > t, t', t'' \in \mathbb{N}^+, t' \neq t'' : u(t') \neq \langle \rangle \land u(t'') = \langle \rangle$.

We emphasised that *learning* is essential in order to reach even higher levels of autonomy. By learning, the system converges to a point t after which no user interaction is needed anymore. Such systems are called *eventually autonomous*.

Definition 3 (Eventually Autonomous, A_2). *A system is called* eventually autonomous, *iff after time* $t \in \mathbb{N}^+$ *no user input or intervention is needed anymore to fulfil the mission goals:* $\exists t \in \mathbb{N}^+ : \forall t' > t : u(t') = \langle \rangle$.

In other words, only a finite number n of messages were transmitted up to t and no further messages will be transmitted beyond that time: $\#u\!\downarrow\!(t) = n$, with $n \in \mathbb{N}$. The smaller t is, the earlier the point of autonomy is reached. If this is already the case from the beginning, we speak of *fully autonomous* systems.

Definition 4 (Fully Autonomous, A_3). *A system is called* fully autonomous *if no user interaction or intervention is necessary at all, i.e.,* $\forall t \in \mathbb{N}^+ : u(t) = \langle \rangle$.

Eventual and full autonomy make strict demands on the ability to precisely perceive and analyse the context, and draw conclusions and learn from it. However, in many respects, it will probably not be possible to achieve them in the foreseeable future for a not highly restricted operational context. Reasons for this are manifold and include the limited ability to fully perceive and understand the context and be prepared for all conceivable operational situations. Therefore, let us now consider intermittent autonomy. Assume the case that every other time step (e.g. every second minute), there is user interaction on an infinite timed stream, see u_1 below. This results in an infinite number of interactions. In another case, there could be one interaction every millionth minute, as shown in u_2. These two cases are equivalent or indistinguishable by definition.

$$u_1 = \langle \langle m \rangle \langle \rangle \langle m \rangle \langle \rangle \ldots \langle m \rangle \langle \rangle \ldots \rangle, \ u_2 = \langle \langle m \rangle \langle \rangle^{10^6-1} \langle m \rangle \langle \rangle^{10^6-1} \ldots \langle m \rangle \langle \rangle^{10^6-1} \ldots \rangle$$

This is due to Cantor's concept of infinity. Intuitively, however, a system that depends on user input every two minutes acts less autonomously than a system that can operate for almost two years (1.9 years in u_2) independently. Therefore, intermittent autonomy extends from "almost" no autonomy towards "almost" eventually autonomy. The classification in this spectrum can be made more precise if we take a closer look at the frequency of user input. Because of the above discussion on infinity, we only consider prefixes of finite length of (in)finite streams, i.e., $u\downarrow(t)$. Let $\alpha \in (0,1)$ be the ratio between times without user input and the interval $[1;t]$, i.e., $\alpha = \langle\rangle\#u/t$. The closer α gets to one, the more autonomous the system is.

4   Discussion and Conclusion

Comparison to SAE Levels (L0–L5) [7]. No driving automation (L0) refers to A_0–*no autonomy*, L1/2 (driver assistance, partial driving automation) can be defined with the notion of intermittent autonomy–A_1, conditional driving automation (L3), applies for $\alpha \approx 1$ in a limited operational context such as highway autopilots. Finally, high driving automation (L4) and full driving automation (L5) are captured by our level A_3, *full autonomy*. For both, different assumptions, w.r.t. the context or the operational design domain, need to be made.

Future Extensions. It would be relevant to investigate the relation between the higher levels of autonomy and *self-** properties (cf. [3]) of the systems, e.g. self-adaptation. In our current understanding, adaptivity is a precondition for a higher autonomy since it enables the system to deal with various unanticipated changes and uncertainties; however, a clear distinction and definition of these two notions is still open. Another open issue refers to the notion of messages exchanged in intermittent autonomous systems. We have tried to distinguish between two intermittent autonomous systems based on their frequency of message exchange, but the expressiveness of messages is also important. Not every message has to have the same "information content". It is a matter for future research and discussion whether this point can be captured using, e.g. Shannon's definition of information content (a limitation of this approach is the assumption of statistical independence and idempotence of messages). To what extent or when is this a permissible limitation is an open question.

Conclusion. In this paper, we proposed a taxonomy that supports the formal specification of different levels of autonomous systems. We have also proposed a high-level architecture for each level to exemplify the user, context, and system interaction. Our goal is to propose a terminology that, if broadly accepted, can be used for more effective communication and comparison of autonomy levels in software-intensive systems that goes beyond the well-known SAE J3016 for automated driving.

References

1. Broy, M., Leuxner, C., Sitou, W., Spanfelner, B., Winter, S.: Formalizing the notion of adaptive system behavior. In: ACM Symposium on Applied Computing (SAC), pp. 1029–1033. ACM (2009)

2. Broy, M., Stølen, K.: Specification and Development of Interactive Systems-Focus on Streams, Interfaces, and Refinement. Monographs in Computer Science, Springer, New York (2001). https://doi.org/10.1007/978-1-4613-0091-5
3. Kephart, J.O., Chess, D.M.: The vision of autonomic computing. Computer **36**(1), 41–50 (2003)
4. de Lemos, R., et al.: Software engineering for self-adaptive systems: a second research roadmap. In: de Lemos, R., Giese, H., Müller, H.A., Shaw, M. (eds.) Software Engineering for Self-Adaptive Systems II. LNCS, vol. 7475, pp. 1–32. Springer, Heidelberg (2013). https://doi.org/10.1007/978-3-642-35813-5_1
5. Luck, M., d'Inverno, M.: A formal framework for agency and autonomy. In: First International Conference on Multiagent Systems, pp. 254–260. The MIT Press (1995)
6. Salehie, M., Tahvildari, L.: Self-adaptive software: landscape and research challenges. ACM Trans. Auton. Adapt. Syst. (TAAS) **4**(2), 1–42 (2009)
7. Society of Automotive Engineers: Taxonomy and definitions for terms related to driving automation systems for on-road motor vehicles, SAE j3016 (2018)
8. Weyns, D.: Software engineering of self-adaptive systems. In: Cha, S., Taylor, R., Kang, K. (eds.) Handbook of Software Engineering, pp. 399–443. Springer, Cham (2019). https://doi.org/10.1007/978-3-030-00262-6_11
9. Woods, E.: Software architecture in a changing world. IEEE Softw. **33**(6), 94–97 (2016)

Machine Learning For Software Architecture

Explaining Architectural Design Tradeoff Spaces: A Machine Learning Approach

Javier Cámara[1]([⊠])[iD], Mariana Silva[1], David Garlan[2][iD],
and Bradley Schmerl[2][iD]

[1] University of York, York, UK
{javier.camaramoreno,mariana.silva}@york.ac.uk
[2] Carnegie Mellon University, Pittsburgh, USA
{garlan,schmerl}@cs.cmu.edu

Abstract. In software design, guaranteeing the correctness of run-time system behavior while achieving an acceptable balance among multiple quality attributes remains a challenging problem. Moreover, providing guarantees about the satisfaction of those requirements when systems are subject to uncertain environments is even more challenging. While recent developments in architectural analysis techniques can assist architects in exploring the satisfaction of quantitative guarantees across the design space, existing approaches are still limited because they do not explicitly link design decisions to satisfaction of quality requirements. Furthermore, the amount of information they yield can be overwhelming to a human designer, making it difficult to distinguish the forest through the trees. In this paper, we present an approach to analyzing architectural design spaces that addresses these limitations and provides a basis to enable the explainability of design tradeoffs. Our approach combines dimensionality reduction techniques employed in machine learning pipelines with quantitative verification to enable architects to understand how design decisions contribute to the satisfaction of strict quantitative guarantees under uncertainty across the design space. Our results show feasibility of the approach in two case studies and evidence that dimensionality reduction is a viable approach to facilitate comprehension of tradeoffs in poorly-understood design spaces.

Keywords: Tradeoff analysis · Uncertainty · Dimensionality reduction

1 Introduction

Architecting modern software-intensive systems requires exploring design spaces that are often poorly understood due to the increasing complexity and range of design choices that have to be made (and their potential interactions), as well as to the high levels of uncertainty under which these systems are expected to operate, being subject to faults, changes in resource availability and network conditions, as well as to attacks [13]. In this setting, achieving a good design that is able to guarantee the correctness of run-time system behavior while striking an

© Springer Nature Switzerland AG 2021
S. Biffl et al. (Eds.): ECSA 2021, LNCS 12857, pp. 49–65, 2021.
https://doi.org/10.1007/978-3-030-86044-8_4

acceptable balance among multiple nonfunctional properties is challenging – in particular when: (i) the context in which the system has to run contains unknown attributes that are difficult to anticipate, and (ii) design decisions involve selecting and composing loosely coupled, pre-existing components or services that have different attributes (e.g., performance, reliability, cost).

There are many existing approaches that help to automate the search for a good architecture and that rely on a variety of techniques such as stochastic search and Pareto analysis [1,3,21], as well as quantitative verification [6,9] that enable architects to explore how the satisfaction of quality of service requirements varies as the value of design parameters and environment variables change. Despite being informative, these approaches do not always make clear why and how architectures were selected because: (i) they do not explicitly link design decisions and environmental factors to the satisfaction of requirements, (ii) they yield vast amounts of data that are not easy to interpret by a human designer, and (iii) results include both useful information and noise that obscures understanding of the relation among variables.

Architects need tools and techniques to help them understand the tradeoffs of complex design spaces and guide them to good designs, enabling them to answer questions such as: Why are these tradeoffs being made, and not others? What are the most important parameters and qualities that are driving the key design decisions? How sensitive to a particular set of decisions is the satisfaction of constraints or the achievement of optimality? Which choices are correlated with others, either positively or negatively?

Providing such tool support demands investigating questions such as:

(RQ1) How can we link architectural design decisions and requirements satisfaction in a way that highlights the most important dependencies among them?

(RQ2) How much can we reduce the complexity of the information presented to the architect while preserving most of the relevant design tradeoff information?

This paper explores these questions by introducing an approach to enable the explainability of architectural design spaces that addresses the limitations described above. Our approach employs a dimensionality reduction technique called principal component analysis (PCA) [16], which is typically employed to compress information in machine learning (ML) pipelines e.g., by reducing the number of features provided as input to a neural network classifier [17], as well as in natural sciences like biology to interpret high-dimensional data [20]. In our case, we combine dimensionality reduction with quantitative verification to facilitate understanding how design decisions contribute to the satisfaction of quantitative requirements across the architectural design space. Concretely, our approach consists of: (i) extracting design features and quality metrics of a population of architectural configuration samples generated via synthesis and quantitative verification [9], (ii) applying PCA to tease out the main variables that influence the qualities of configurations, as well as to establish a link between design variables (e.g., component selection, topological arrangement, configuration parameter values) and the qualities of the resulting configurations.

Our results show feasibility of the approach in two case studies and evidence that dimensionality reduction is a viable technique to facilitate understanding of tradeoffs in poorly-understood design spaces.

2 Motivating Scenario: Tele-Assistance System (TAS)

TAS [26] is a service-based system whose goal is tracking a patient's vital parameters to adapt drug type or dose when needed, and taking actions in case of emergency. TAS combines three service types in a workflow (Fig. 1, left). When TAS receives a request that includes the vital parameters of a patient, its *Medical Service* analyzes the data and replies with instructions to: (i) change the patient's drug type, (ii) change the drug dose, or (iii) trigger an alarm for first responders in case of emergency. When changing the drug type or dose, TAS notifies a local pharmacy using a *Drug Service*, whereas first responders are notified via an *Alarm Service*.

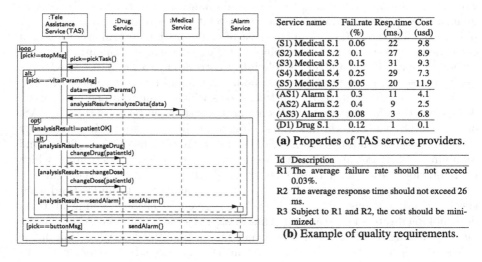

Service name	Fail.rate (%)	Resp.time (ms.)	Cost (usd)
(S1) Medical S.1	0.06	22	9.8
(S2) Medical S.2	0.1	27	8.9
(S3) Medical S.3	0.15	31	9.3
(S4) Medical S.4	0.25	29	7.3
(S5) Medical S.5	0.05	20	11.9
(AS1) Alarm S.1	0.3	11	4.1
(AS2) Alarm S.2	0.4	9	2.5
(AS3) Alarm S.3	0.08	3	6.8
(D1) Drug S.1	0.12	1	0.1

(a) Properties of TAS service providers.

Id	Description
R1	The average failure rate should not exceed 0.03%.
R2	The average response time should not exceed 26 ms.
R3	Subject to R1 and R2, the cost should be minimized.

(b) Example of quality requirements.

Fig. 1. TAS workflow, service provider properties, and quality requirements.

The functionality of each service type in TAS is provided by multiple third parties with different levels of performance (response time), reliability (failure rate), and cost (Fig. 1a). Finding an adequate design for the system entails understanding the tradeoff space by selecting the set of system configurations that satisfy: (i) structural constraints, e.g., the *Drug Service* must not be connected to an *Alarm Service*, (ii) behavioral correctness properties (e.g., the system will eventually provide a response – either by dispatching an ambulance or notifying the pharmacy), and (iii) quality requirements, which can be formulated as a combination of quantitative constraints and optimizations (Fig. 1b).

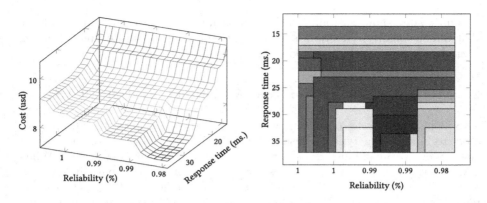

Fig. 2. TAS analysis results.

Figure 2 shows the analysis results of TAS obtained by applying our prior work that combines structural synthesis and quantitative verification to analyze quantitative formal guarantees across the architectural design space [8,9]. The plot on the left shows the minimized cost of configurations for different levels of constraints on response time and reliability. This plot conveys the intuition that higher response times and lower reliability correspond to lower costs, whereas peaks in cost are reached with lowest failure rates and response times.

The plot on the right is a map that shows which configurations best satisfy design criteria. Out of the set of 90 configurations that can be generated for TAS, only 24 satisfy the criteria in some subregion of the state space. If we consider that designers are interested e.g., in systems with response times ≤26 ms and reliability ≥99%, we can employ the same analysis technique to determine which configurations best satisfy these constraints (highlighted in red in the figure).

Although these plots are informative and help architects to understand what specific configurations might work well in a given situation, looking at them does not facilitate understanding what design decisions influence these trade-offs. Answering to what extent improvements on qualities are a function of the choice of a specific service implementation, the topological arrangement of the composition, or the value of configuration parameters (e.g., maximum number of retries, or timeout duration when services fail) is not possible with existing approaches.

One of the main challenges in facilitating the understanding of the tradeoff space relates to the high dimensionality of the data and how to make it digestible to a human designer: there are too many characteristics of configurations (and relations among them) to track, and some of them contribute more than others to the variation of quality attributes. For instance, even in the relatively simple system illustrated earlier, it is unclear if selecting specific services contributes more to system quality variation than workflow configuration parameters like timeout length. In the next section, we describe how to address this challenge.

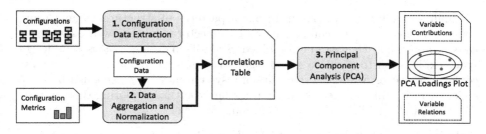

Fig. 3. Overview of the approach.

3 Approach

The inputs to our approach for explaining design tradeoffs (Fig. 3) are a set of legal configurations (i.e., those that satisfy the constraints of a given architectural style), captured as attribute-annotated graphs, and a set of quantitative metrics that can capture aspects related to e.g., the energy consumption, timeliness, or safety of configurations. The output of the process is a plot that captures a description of the relations between design and QoS variables (e.g., response time is negatively correlated with reliability, selection of component X contributes to lower response times and higher cost), as well as their contributions to differences among architectural configurations. The approach consists of three stages:

1. *Configuration Data Extraction* collects relevant information about the charac- teristics of architecture configurations. Data extracted includes both topologi- cal information (e.g., centrality and cardinality measures of nodes correspond- ing to different architectural types and bindings) and information related to properties of components, connectors, and other parameters.
2. *Data Aggregation and Normalization.* In this step, the configuration data produced in (1) and the configuration metrics provided as input to the process are aggregated into a single correlations table. Table data is normalized so that all variables will have the same weight in subsequent analysis steps.
3. *Principal Component Analysis (PCA)* is employed to discover how architec- tural configurations differ, and which variables contribute the most to that difference. Moreover, PCA enables us to discriminate whether variables con- tribute in the same way or a different way (i.e., are positively or negatively correlated, respectively), or if instead, are independent from each other. This enables architects to relate response variation (QoS, quantitative guarantees) to design variables.

In the remainder of this section, we first introduce some preliminaries, and follow with a detailed description of the three stages of our approach.

3.1 Preliminaries

Design spaces are often constrained by the need to design systems within certain patterns or constraints. Architectural styles [22] characterize the design space of families of software systems in terms of patterns of structural organization, defining a *vocabulary* of component and connector types, as well as a set of *constraints* on how they can be combined. Styles help designers constrain design space exploration to within a set of legal structures to which the system must conform. However, while the structure of a system may be constrained by some style, there is still considerable design flexibility left for exploring the tradeoffs on many of the qualities that a system must achieve.

Definition 1 (Architectural Style). *Formally, we characterize an architectural style as a tuple* $(\Sigma, \mathcal{C}_S)$, *where:*

– $\Sigma = (CompT, ConnT, \Pi, \Lambda)$ *is an architectural signature, such that:*
  • *CompT and ConnT are disjoint sets of component and connector types. For conciseness, we define* $ArchT \equiv CompT \cup ConnT$.
  • $\Pi : ArchT \rightarrow 2^{\mathcal{D}}$ *is a function that assigns sets of symbols typed by datatypes in a fixed set* $\mathcal{D}$ *to architectural types* $\kappa \in ArchT$. $\Pi(\kappa)$ *captures properties associated with type* κ. *To refer to a property* $p \in \Pi(\kappa)$, *we simply write* $\kappa.p$.
  • $\Lambda : ArchT \rightarrow 2^{\mathcal{P}} \cup 2^{\mathcal{R}}$ *is a function that assigns a set of symbols typed by a fixed set* $\mathcal{P}$ *to components* $\kappa \in CompT$. *This function also assigns a set of symbols in a fixed set* $\mathcal{R}$ *to connectors* $\kappa \in ConnT$. $\Lambda(\kappa)$ *represents the ports of a component (conversely, the roles if* κ *is a connector), which define logical points of interaction with* κ*'s environment. To denote a port/role* $q \in \Lambda(\kappa)$, *we write* $\kappa :: q$.
– $\mathcal{C}_S$ *is a set of structural constraints expressed in a constraint language based on first-order predicate logic in the style of Acme [14] or OCL [25] constraints (e.g.,* ∀ w:TASWorkflowT •∃ a:AlarmServiceT • connected(w,a) – *"every TAS workflow must be connected to at least one alarm service").*

In the remainder of this section, we assume a fixed universe $\mathcal{A}_\Sigma$ of architectural elements, i.e., a finite set of components and connectors for Σ typed by $ArchT$. The type of an architectural element $c \in \mathcal{A}_\Sigma$ is denoted by $type(c)$. We assume that elements of $\mathcal{A}_\Sigma$ are indexed and designate the ith element by $\mathcal{A}_\Sigma^i$.

A *configuration* is a graph that captures the topology of a legal structure of the system in a style $\mathcal{A}$ (we designate $\mathcal{A}$'s set of legal configurations by $\mathcal{G}_\mathcal{A}^*$).

Definition 2 (Configuration). *A configuration in a style* $(\Sigma, \mathcal{C}_S)$, *given a fixed universe of architectural elements* $\mathcal{A}_\Sigma$, *is a graph* $\mathcal{G} = (\mathcal{N}, \mathcal{E})$ *satisfying the constraints* $\mathcal{C}_S$, *where:* $\mathcal{N}$ *is a set of nodes, such that* $\mathcal{N} \subseteq \mathcal{A}_\Sigma$, *and* $\mathcal{E}$ *is a set of pairs typed by* $\mathcal{P} \times \mathcal{R}$ *that represent* attachments *between ports and roles.*

To determine if two architectural elements are attached on any of their port/roles, we define the function $att : \mathcal{A}_\Sigma \times \mathcal{A}_\Sigma \rightarrow \mathbb{B}$ as $att(n, n') = \top$ if $\exists p \in \mathcal{P}, r \in \mathcal{R} \bullet n :: p \wedge n' :: r \wedge (p, r) \in \mathcal{E}$, and $att(n, n') = \bot$ otherwise. We say that two components are *bound* if there is a connector attached to any of their ports on both ends. This is captured by function $bnd : CompT \times CompT \rightarrow \mathbb{B}$, $bnd(n, n') = \top$ if $\exists n'' \in \mathcal{N}$, s.t. $att(n, n'') \wedge att(n'', n')$, and $bnd(n, n') = \bot$ otherwise.

3.2 Configuration Data Extraction

The first stage of our approach extracts the set of relevant attributes that correspond to different design decisions made to form any legal configuration (i.e., that conforms to the architectural style), which are provided as input to the process. Our approach is agnostic to the mechanisms employed to generate the set of configurations that conform to an architectural style: this process is out of scope of this paper, but existing prior work has addressed this problem in a variety of ways (see [9] for one example).

The attributes extracted from a configuration $\mathcal{G} = (\mathcal{N}, \mathcal{E})$ form a tuple of *design variable* values $\mathcal{D}_\mathcal{G}(C, T, P) \in \mathcal{DG}$, where:

- $C \in \mathbb{R}_{>0}^n$ is a vector that contains data items corresponding to constituent architectural elements of the configuration (e.g., the presence and number of specific components and connectors). Concretely, this vector is formed by concatenating the result of the following functions:
    1. *Architectural element presence extraction* $f_{ep} : \mathcal{G}_\mathcal{A}^* \to \{0,1\}^{|\mathcal{A}_\Sigma|}$, returns a vector $\langle p_1, \ldots, p_{|\mathcal{A}_\Sigma|} \rangle$ that encodes the presence of specific architectural elements (i.e., component and connector instances) in a configuration, where $p_i = 1$, $i \in \{1..|\mathcal{A}_\Sigma|\}$ if $\mathcal{A}_\Sigma^i \in \mathcal{N}$, and $p_i = 0$, otherwise.
    2. *Architectural type cardinality extraction* $f_{tc} : \mathcal{G}_\mathcal{A}^* \to \mathbb{N}^{|ArchT|}$, returns a vector $\langle x_{tc}(\kappa_1), \ldots, x_{tc}(\kappa_{|ArchT|}) \rangle$ encoding the number of component and connectors of each type present in a configuration. For $\kappa \in ArchT$, we define function $x_{tc} : ArchT \to \mathbb{N}$ as $x_{tc}(\kappa) = |\{n \in \mathcal{N} \mid type(n) = \kappa\}|$.
- $T \in \mathbb{R}_{>0}^n$ is a vector of data items that correspond to the topology of the configuration like the presence of certain attachments among architectural elements, and other topological measures like centrality indices, which characterize important nodes in the configuration topology [2,4]. Concretely, this vector is formed by concatenating the results of the following functions:
    1. *Binding presence extraction* $f_{bp} : \mathcal{G}_\mathcal{A}^* \to \{0,1\}^{|\mathcal{A}_\Sigma| \cdot |\mathcal{A}_\Sigma|}$ returns a vector $\langle p_{1,1}, \ldots, p_{|\mathcal{A}_\Sigma|,1}, \ldots, p_{|\mathcal{A}_\Sigma|,|\mathcal{A}_\Sigma|} \rangle$ that encodes the presence of bindings between specific components, with $p_{i,j} = 1$, $i,j \in \{1..|\mathcal{A}_\Sigma|\}$ if $bnd(\mathcal{A}_\Sigma^i, \mathcal{A}_\Sigma^j)$, and $p_{i,j} = 0$ otherwise.
    2. *Binding type cardinality extraction* $f_{btc} : \mathcal{G}_\mathcal{A}^* \to \mathbb{N}^{|CompT| \cdot |CompT|}$, returns a vector $\langle x_{btc}(\kappa_1, \kappa_1), \ldots, x_{btc}(\kappa_{|CompT|}, 1), \ldots, x_{btc}(\kappa_{|CompT|}, |CompT|) \rangle$ encoding the number of bindings between specific pairs of component types. For the pair of component types (κ, κ'), we define function $x_{btc} : CompT \times CompT \to \mathbb{N}$ as $x_{btc}(\kappa, \kappa') = |\{(n, n') \in \mathcal{N} \times \mathcal{N} \mid type(n) = \kappa \wedge type(n') = \kappa' \wedge bnd(n, n')\}|$.
    3. *Betweenness centrality extraction* Function $f_{C_B} : \mathcal{G}_\mathcal{A}^* \to \mathbb{R}^{|\mathcal{A}_\Sigma|}$, returns a vector $\langle C_B(\mathcal{A}_\Sigma^1), \ldots, C_B(\mathcal{A}_\Sigma^{|\mathcal{A}_\Sigma|}) \rangle$ that encodes the betweenness centrality of each node in the configuration graph, which quantifies the number of times that a node acts as a bridge along the shortest path between two other nodes [12]. Concretely, $C_B : \mathcal{A}_\Sigma \to \mathbb{R}_{\geq 0}$ is defined as: $C_B(n) = \sum_{s \neq n \neq t \in \mathcal{N}} (\sigma_{st}(n) / \sigma_{st})$, where σ_{st} is the total number of shortest paths from node s to t in the configuration graph, and $\sigma_{st}(n)$ is the number of those paths that pass through n.

- $P \in \mathbb{R}^n$ is a vector containing data items corresponding to the values of relevant configuration parameters. We assume that these can be directly obtained from the values of properties associated with the different architectural elements of the configuration (e.g., configuration parameter for number of maximum service retries in TAS is stored in property TASWorkflow0.max_timeouts, where TASWorkflow0 is an instance of TASWorkflowT).

3.3   Data Aggregation and Normalization

The second input to our approach is a set of vectors $\mathcal{RG}$ of the form $\mathcal{R}_\mathcal{G} = \langle r_1, \ldots, r_n \rangle$, $r_i \in \mathbb{R}, i \in \{1..n\}$ containing *response variables* that correspond to the values of the quantified metrics for the different quality dimensions in a configuration $\mathcal{G}$. Our technique is agnostic to the mechanisms employed to quantify the quality metrics of a configuration. However, in the particular instantiation of the approach used in this paper, we obtain these values by checking a variety of probabilistic temporal logic properties encoded in an extension of PCTL using HaiQ [8], a tool that performs probabilistic model checking on collections of structural design variants that uses Alloy [15] and PRISM [19] in its backend.

The purpose of data aggregation and normalization is to generate a *correlations table* that can be provided as input to PCA:

- *Data aggregation.* Given a design variable value tuple $\mathcal{D}_\mathcal{G}(C, T, P) \in \mathcal{DG}$, and a response variable vector $\mathcal{R}_\mathcal{G} = \langle r_1, \ldots, r_n \rangle \in \mathcal{RG}$ for the same configuration $\mathcal{G}$, we define the *configuration sample* for $\mathcal{G}$ as $\mathcal{R}_\mathcal{G} \frown \mathcal{D}_\mathcal{G}$, where $\frown$ denotes concatenation. The (non-normalized) correlations table is formed by the samples that correspond to all input configurations.
- *Data normalization.* The correlations table contains variables that span varying degrees of magnitude and range. To avoid bias in PCA towards variables that may have a higher magnitude, we scale the data employing unity-based normalization, meaning that for any data item in the correlations table $x_{i,j}$ for sample i and variable j, the new value of the data item is defined as $x'_{i,j} = (x_{i,j} - x_j^{min})/(x_j^{max} - x_j^{min})$, where x_j^{min}, x_j^{max} are the minimum/maximum values of j across all samples.

Example 1. Figure 4 shows a TAS configuration and an excerpt of its encoding in the correlations table. The first and second top-most tables show the presence of architectural elements and type cardinalities (f_{ep} and f_{tc}, respectively). In this case, we can observe that the cardinality of all architectural types is 1, except for HttpConnT The two tables at the bottom describe the presence of bindings between components (f_{bp}), and their betweenness centrality (f_{C_B}). TAS is built as a service orchestration with a centralized workflow, meaning that all components but the workflow itself will have a betweenness centrality of zero.

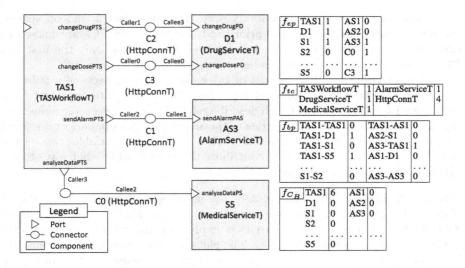

Fig. 4. Sample TAS configuration (left), along with an excerpt of its encoding (right).

3.4   Principal Component Analysis

Data resulting from analyzing architectural spaces usually contain a large amount of information, which is often too complex to be easily interpreted. Principal Component Analysis (PCA) [16] is a statistical projection method commonly used in ML and natural science that can facilitate understanding that information. To begin with, PCA can help to find out in what respect some architectural configurations differ from others, and which variables contribute to this difference. In some cases, variables contribute in the same way (i.e., are correlated) or do so independently. Moreover, PCA also enables quantifying the amount of useful information in a data set, as opposed to noise or meaningless variations.

If we consider the data in the correlations table geometrically, we can say that two samples (i.e., architectural configurations) are *similar* if they have close values for most variables (i.e., they are in the same region of the multidimensional space) and *different*, otherwise. Considering this, the purpose of PCA is finding the directions in space in which the distance between points is the largest. That is equivalent to finding the linear combinations of the variables that contribute most to making the samples (i.e., configurations) different from each other. These directions or linear combinations are called *principal components*.

Principal components (PC) are computed in an iterative manner, in such a way that the first PC is the one that carries most information (most explained variance), whereas the second PC will carry the maximum share of the information not taken into account by the previous PC, and so on. All PCs are orthogonal to each other and each one carries more information than the next one. In fact, this is one of the characteristics of PCA that makes it appealing as an underlying mechanism to enable the explainability of architectural design tradeoff spaces: the interpretation of PCs can be prioritized, since the first PCs are known to carry the most information. Indeed, it is often the case that only the first two PC contain genuine information, whereas the rest describe noise [16].

The main results of PCA consist of three complementary sets of attributes: (i) *variances*, which tell us how much information is taken into account by the successive PCs, (ii) *loadings*, which describe relationships between variables, and (iii) *scores*, which describe properties of the samples. In this paper, we focus on variances and loadings, which will tell us what are the main variables (i.e., either design or response variables) that contribute the most (and in what way) to the differences among configurations.

Example 2. The PCA loadings plot of the samples analyzed for TAS (Fig. 5) displays the first two PCs, which carry a large amount of information, explaining 83% of the variance of data, with PC1 explaining the most (68%) and PC2 explaining much less variance (13%). The plot contains two ellipses that indicate how much variance is taken into account. The outer ellipse is the unit-circle and indicates 100% explained variance, whereas the inner ellipse indicates 50% of explained variance. Variables that are found between the edges of the two ellipses, and particularly those positioned near the edge of the outer ellipse, are those that are more important to differentiate the configurations.

QoS metrics like reliability, cost, and response time are all important to differentiate configurations with response time being the most relevant (close to -1 in PC1, which accounts for almost 70% of the overall variability). Reliability and cost are important for PC2, but comparatively have less influence.

In addition to teasing out the most important variables, the plot displays the relationships between variables. In the plot, the angle between the vectors that go from the origin of coordinates to a variable point is an approximation of the correlation between the variables. A small angle indicates the variables are positively correlated, an angle of 90 degrees indicates the variables are not correlated, and an angle close to 180 degrees indicates the variables are negatively correlated. In our example, we can observe that reliability and cost are positively correlated, whereas response time is negatively correlated with both of them. These observations are consistent with the results in Fig. 2, which show that low response times and high reliability correspond to higher costs.

So far, we have been discussing QoS variables, but the loading plot also enables architects to observe the influence of design variables on variability. Here, we can see in the lower-right quadrant of the ellipse that some of the most influential variables for PC1 correspond to the presence of alarm service instance AS3 in a configuration, as well as to its binding to the workflow (TASWorkflow0). We observe that all these design variables related to AS3 are positively corre- lated with reliability and cost, and negatively correlated with response time. This indicates that the selection of AS3 has a remarkable influence on the qualities of the resulting configurations and is consistent with the fact that the alterna- tive alarm service implementations have considerably higher failure rates and response times than AS3, as well as lower cost per invocation (see Fig. 1a). Also,

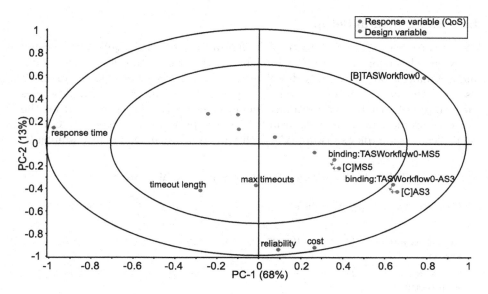

Fig. 5. Correlation loading PCA plot for TAS.

the alarm service is invoked more times in the workflow than any other service. Consequently other services like MS5, which are also influential and have the same QoS correlations as AS3, have a comparatively moderate impact (its associated design variables are within the inner edge of the ellipse) because they are invoked only once in the workflow. Regarding configuration parameters, we can see that, as expected, both timeout length and maximum number of timeouts for service invocations are positively correlated with response time with respect to PC1, but also to a lesser extent with reliability and cost with respect to PC2. This observation is consistent with the fact that more service invocation retries lead to increased reliability and cost, at the expense of higher response times. Finally, the betweenness centrality of the workflow ([B]TASWorkflow0) on the right-upper corner of the diagram is a relevant variable, although it is not particularly significant in this case, given that TAS is a centralized service orchestration in which the workflow is always at the center of the composition.

4   Evaluation

The objective of our evaluation is to: (i) assess the *feasibility* of linking design decisions to requirement satisfaction (RQ1) and (ii) assess the tradeoff between the information reduction and the amount of variance explained (RQ2).

In this section, we first describe our experimental setup. We then briefly introduce a scenario that we have incorporated into our evaluation in addition to TAS. Finally, we discuss results, relating them to our research questions.

4.1   Experimental Setup

We generated the set of architectural configurations and their QoS metrics using an extended version of HaiQ that implements the data extraction, aggregation, and normalization procedures described in Sects. 3.2–3.3 and the set of models for TAS and the network virus example described in [8]. Table 1 describes the number of variables and samples included in the datasets generated for the two case studies. Data analysis using PCA was performed employing "CAMO Analytics Unscrambler software (v11)" (https://www.camo.com/unscrambler/).

Table 1. Dataset dimensions for experimental evaluation.

Case study	# Variables								#samples
	QoS	f_{ep}	f_{tc}	f_{bp}	f_{btc}	f_{C_B}	Parameters	Total	
Tele-assistance system	3	10	10	27	27	10	2	89	1080
Network architecture	2	9	4	46	11	9	3	84	2400

4.2   Scenario: Network Architecture

Architecting network-based systems that are resilient to uncontrollable environment conditions, such as network delays, or undesirable events such at virus infections, entails structuring the system in a way that maximizes the chances of continued service provision in spite of the adverse conditions that it is subject to. The scenario introduced by Kwiatkowska et al. [18] models the progression of a virus infecting a network formed by a grid of N×N nodes. The virus remains at a node that is infected and repeatedly tries to infect any uninfected neighbors by first attacking the neighbor's firewall and, if successful, trying to infect the node. In the network there are 'low' and 'high' nodes divided by 'barrier' nodes that scan the traffic between them. Ideally, the architecture of the network should: (i) minimize the probability of successful infection of high nodes in the network within 50 time units, and (ii) maximize the number of node infection or attack attempts that the virus carries out to spread itself through the high nodes.

Results. The PCA loadings plot (Fig. 6) displays the first two PCs, which explain 75% of the data variation (43% for PC1 and 32% for PC2). Both QoS metrics for the virus infection success and maximum number of virus attacks are very important to differentiate configurations. Being at the two opposite ends of the horizontal axis, they are negatively correlated, indicating that configurations that are less resilient require more virus infection attempts. Although this may be counter-intuitive, it may be explained by the fact that the values for the virus attack success probability variable are obtained from a time-bound probabilistic analysis of the network model, meaning that scenarios in which the virus successfully infects high nodes after 50 time units are not captured in the samples. In contrast, the values for the maximum number of attacks are not time-bound.

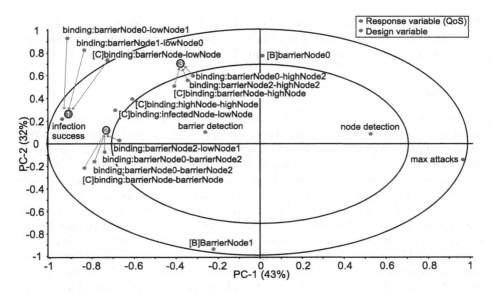

Fig. 6. Correlation loading PCA plot for the network architecture.

Concerning design variables, we can observe that the most influential cluster of variables for PC1 (identified by ①) corresponds to the bindings between low nodes and barrier nodes. Concretely, the number of bindings between barrier nodes and low nodes ([C]binding:barrierNode-lowNode) is positively correlated with the virus infection success and negatively correlated with the number of attacks. This is consistent with the fact that more bindings between low nodes and barrier nodes gives the virus more chances to spread faster to barrier nodes, compared to having to infect other low nodes first. The second most influential cluster of variables corresponds mostly to bindings between barrier nodes ②. These variables are also positively correlated with virus infection success and negatively correlated with the number of attacks. This is expected because having more bindings between barrier nodes gives more opportunities for the virus to spread, although the effect is more moderate because barrier nodes always have a higher probability of detecting virus attacks than high and low nodes. As expected, the number of bindings to the node that is initially infected in the network, and the number of bindings between high nodes also influence infection success probability and number of attacks in the same way, although with a more moderate impact. The cluster of variables that relates to bindings between barrier nodes and high nodes ③ is also influential in the same way, with a clear contribution both to PC1 and PC2. In PC2, we can also observe that the betweenness centrality of barrier nodes is also influential to explain variability, although there is no clear correlation with QoS variables, which are very close to PC1 and form angles close to 90 degrees with [B]barrierNode0/1. Finally, node and barrier virus detection probabilities are somewhat significant in terms of

PC1, but interestingly, not much compared to other variables that are related to the topology of the configurations. This emphasizes the importance of topology for the resilience of the network, compared to attributes of individual nodes.

4.3   Discussion

(RQ1) Feasibility. PCA analysis results performed on the TAS and network architecture scenarios has shown that our approach is able to extract information that explains the relation among QoS variables and design variables. When studying the relation among QoS variables, results are consistent with observations obtained from existing analysis techniques [8,9]. For the relation between design variables and QoS variables, results are also consistent with observations obtained from careful examination of models and simulations of the studied systems. Moreover, our results have been obtained from two different types of architecture (a centralized service-based system and a decentralized network architecture). In the centralized system, component variability has a more prominent role in explaining QoS variation, whereas in the decentralized system, it is configuration topology that explains most QoS variation. The ability of the approach to yield compelling results in both cases indicates its potential applicability to a broad range of scenarios.

(RQ2) Information Reduction-Explained Variance Tradeoff. Table 2 summarizes the information reduction and explained variance for the two scenarios described in the paper. In the table, information reduction is calculated as the percentage of the original variables in the dataset that remain as relevant in the PC1-PC2 correlation loadings plot (i.e., positioned within the 50%–100% explained variance ellipses), whereas the total explained variance for PC1-PC2 is one of the outputs provided by PCA. Total residual variance corresponds to the remainder of PCs, i.e., variance that is left unexplained by PC1 and PC2.

We can observe that in both scenarios, there is a remarkable reduction in the information that has to be examined by an architect to analyze the tradeoff space, which is in the range 80–93%. At the same time, the total residual variance ranges between 19 and 25%. Although non-negligible, these are moderate levels of residual variance, especially if we consider them in the context of the drastic dimensionality reduction in the set of explanatory variables.

Table 2. Information reduction and explained variance summary.

Case study	#dataset vars.	#relevant PCA vars.	Information reduction	Explained variance	Residual variance
Tele-assistance system	89	6	93.25 %	81 %	19 %
Network architecture	84	16	80.95 %	75 %	25 %

5   Related Work

Evaluation of software architectures under uncertainty is a subject that has been broadly explored [23]. Due to space constraints, we focus on the subset of works akin to our proposal, which can be categorized into:

Architecture-based quantitative analysis and optimization approaches, which focus on analyzing and optimizing quantitative aspects of architectures using mechanisms that include e.g., stochastic search and Pareto analysis [1,3,21]. Other recent approaches to architectural design synthesis and quantitative verification [5,8,9] generate and analyze alternative system designs, enabling exploration of quantitative guarantees across the design space. These techniques ([8,9] being our prior work) do not address explainability, but produce (large) datasets that can be used as input to the approach described in this paper.

Learning-based architecture evaluation adopts ML techniques to enhance the evaluation with observations of system properties over time [7,10,11,24]. These works employ Bayesian learning [7] to update model parameters, Model Tree Learning (MTL) to tune system adaptation logic [11], and reinforcement learning [10,24] to analyze architectural decisions made at run-time.

While all the approaches described above provide some form of architectural tradeoff analysis (sometimes employing ML techniques), none of them make any claims about explicitly linking design variables with requirement satisfaction or facilitating the explainability of the design tradeoff space. Indeed, a recent comprehensive literature review on architectural evaluation under uncertainty [23] reveals no approaches covering the research gap addressed by our technique.

6   Conclusions and Future Work

In this paper, we have presented what is, to the best of our knowledge, the first approach that explicitly relates QoS and architectural design variables using dimensionality reduction techniques employed in ML, enabling architects to interpret the main tradeoffs of an architectural design space based on a graphical summary of the relations among the main variables that explain differences between configurations. Our results show feasibility of the approach (RQ1) and indicate that a remarkable reduction of the amount of information required to explain the main tradeoffs of an architectural design space is attainable while the reduction in explained variance remains moderate (RQ2).

Although our approach works well in the case studies presented, PCA works optimally only in the situation where variable correlations are linear, or an approximation thereof. Future work will involve exploring alternatives to PCA that enable the analysis of systems with strong non-linear correlations. Moreover, our approach is currently limited to component-and-connector static architectures with binary connectors. Our future work will also explore extensions to the catalogue of metrics and extraction functions required to enable richer analysis of various styles of architectural representation, including dynamic architectures.

Acknowledgements. This work is partly supported by award N00014172899 from the Office of Naval Research (ONR) and award H9823018D0008 from the NSA. Any views, opinions, findings and conclusions or recommendations expressed in this material are those of the authors and do not necessarily reflect the views of the ONR or NSA.

References

1. Aleti, A., Bjornander, S., Grunske, L., Meedeniya, I.: Archeopterix: an extendable tool for architecture optimization of AADL models. In: ICSE Workshop on Model-Based Methodologies for Pervasive and Embedded Software, pp. 61–71 (2009)
2. Bonacich, P.: Power and centrality: a family of measures. Am. J. Sociol. **92**(5), 1170–1182 (1987)
3. Bondarev, E., Chaudron, M.R.V., de Kock, E.A.: Exploring performance trade-offs of a JPEG decoder using the deepcompass framework. In: 6th WS on Software and Performance, WOSP, pp. 153–163. ACM (2007)
4. Borgatti, S.P.: Centrality and network flow. Soc. Netw. **27**(1), 55–71 (2005)
5. Calinescu, R., Ceska, M., Gerasimou, S., Kwiatkowska, M., Paoletti, N.: Designing robust software systems through parametric Markov chain synthesis. In: International Conference on Software Architecture, ICSA, pp. 131–140. IEEE (2017)
6. Calinescu, R., Ceska, M., Gerasimou, S., Kwiatkowska, M., Paoletti, N.: Efficient synthesis of robust models for stochastic systems. J. Syst. Softw. **143**, 140–158 (2018)
7. Calinescu, R., Johnson, K., Rafiq, Y.: Using observation ageing to improve Markovian model learning in QOS engineering. In: 2nd ACM/SPEC International Conference on Performance Engineering, ICPE 2011, pp. 505–510. ACM (2011)
8. Cámara, J.: HaiQ: synthesis of software design spaces with structural and probabilistic guarantees. In: FormaliSE@ICSE 2020: 8th International Conference on Formal Methods in Software Engineering, pp. 22–33. ACM (2020)
9. Cámara, J., Garlan, D., Schmerl, B.: Synthesizing tradeoff spaces with quantitative guarantees for families of software systems. J. Syst. Softw. **152**, 33–49 (2019)
10. Cámara, J., Muccini, H., Vaidhyanathan, K.: Quantitative verification-aided machine learning: a tandem approach for architecting self-adaptive IoT systems. In: International Conference on Software Architecture, ICSA, pp. 11–22. IEEE (2020)
11. Esfahani, N., Elkhodary, A., Malek, S.: A learning-based framework for engineering feature-oriented self-adaptive software systems. IEEE Trans. Soft. Eng. **39**(11), 1467–1493 (2013)
12. Freeman, L.C.: A set of measures of centrality based on betweenness. Sociometry 35–41 (1977)
13. Garlan, D.: Software engineering in an uncertain world. In: Proceedings of the Workshop on Future of Software Engineering Research, FoSER, pp. 125–128 (2010)
14. Garlan, D., Monroe, R.T., Wile, D.: Acme: architectural description of component-based systems. Found. Component-Based Syst. **68**, 47–68 (2000)
15. Jackson, D.: Alloy: a lightweight object modelling notation. ACM Trans. Softw. Eng. Methodol. **11**(2), 256–290 (2002)
16. Jolliffe, I.T.: Principal component analysis and factor analysis. In: Jolliffe, I.T. (ed.) Principal Component Analysis, pp. 115–128. Springer, New York (1986). https://doi.org/10.1007/978-1-4757-1904-8_7

17. Khalid, S., Khalil, T., Nasreen, S.: A survey of feature selection and feature extraction techniques in machine learning. In: Science and Information Conference, pp. 372–378 (2014)
18. Kwiatkowska, M., Norman, G., Parker, D., Vigliotti, M.: Probabilistic mobile ambients. Theoret. Comput. Sci. **410**(12–13), 1272–1303 (2009)
19. Kwiatkowska, M., Norman, G., Parker, D.: PRISM 4.0: verification of probabilistic real-time systems. In: Gopalakrishnan, G., Qadeer, S. (eds.) CAV 2011. LNCS, vol. 6806, pp. 585–591. Springer, Heidelberg (2011). https://doi.org/10.1007/978-3-642-22110-1_47
20. Lever, J., Krzywinski, M., Altman, N.: Principal component analysis. Nat. Methods **14**(7), 641–642 (2017)
21. Martens, A., Koziolek, H., Becker, S., Reussner, R.: Automatically improve software architecture models for performance, reliability, and cost using evolutionary algorithms. In: International Conference on Performance Engineering, WOSP/SIPEW, pp. 105–116. ACM (2010)
22. Shaw, M., Garlan, D.: Software Architecture - Perspectives on an Emerging Discipline. Prentice Hall, Hoboken (1996)
23. Sobhy, D., Bahsoon, R., Minku, L., Kazman, R.: Evaluation of software architectures under uncertainty: a systematic literature review. ACM Trans. Softw. Eng. Methodol. (2021)
24. Sobhy, D., Minku, L., Bahsoon, R., Chen, T., Kazman, R.: Run-time evaluation of architectures: a case study of diversification in IoT. J. Syst. Soft. **159**, 110428 (2020)
25. Warmer, J., Kleppe, A.: The Object Constraint Language: Getting Your Models Ready for MDA. Addison-Wesley, Boston (2003)
26. Weyns, D., Calinescu, R.: Tele assistance: a self-adaptive service-based system exemplar. In: 10th IEEE/ACM International Symposium on Software Engineering for Adaptive and Self-Managing Systems, SEAMS 2015, pp. 88–92. IEEE CS (2015)

A Machine Learning Approach to Service Discovery for Microservice Architectures

Mauro Caporuscio[1]([✉])[iD], Marco De Toma[2], Henry Muccini[2][iD],
and Karthik Vaidhyanathan[2][iD]

[1] Linnaeus University, Växjö, Sweden
mauro.caporuscio@lnu.se
[2] University of L'Aquila, L'Aquila, Italy
{marco.detoma,henry.muccini,karthik.vaidhyanathan}@univaq.it

Abstract. Service discovery mechanisms have continuously evolved during the last years to support the effective and efficient service composition in large-scale microservice applications. Still, the dynamic nature of services (and of their contexts) are being rarely taken into account for maximizing the desired quality of service. This paper proposes using machine learning techniques, as part of the service discovery process, to select microservice instances in a given context, maximize QoS, and take into account the continuous changes in the execution environment. Both deep neural networks and reinforcement learning techniques are used. Experimental results show how the proposed approach outperforms traditional service discovery mechanisms.

Keywords: Service discovery · Machine learning · Microservices architecture

1 Introduction

Microservices have become enormously popular since traditional monolithic architectures no longer meet the needs of scalability and rapid development cycle. The success of large companies (Netflix among them) in building and deploying services is also a strong motivation for other companies to consider making the change. The loosely coupled property of microservices allow the independence between each service thus enabling the rapid, frequent and reliable delivery of large, complex applications [7].

Like most transformational trends, implementing microservices poses its own *challenges:* Hundreds of microservices may be composed to form a complex architecture; tens of instances of the same microservice can run on different servers; the number or locations of running instances could change very frequently. Moreover, the set of service instances changes dynamically because of autoscaling, failures, and upgrades. Therefore, one of the challenges in a microservice architecture concerns how services *discover, connect,* and *interact* with each other. Consequently, elaborated *service discovery mechanisms* are required [19].

© Springer Nature Switzerland AG 2021
S. Biffl et al. (Eds.): ECSA 2021, LNCS 12857, pp. 66–82, 2021.
https://doi.org/10.1007/978-3-030-86044-8_5

Service discovery mechanisms has continuously evolved during the last years (e.g., Consul, Etcd, Synapse, Zookeeper, etc.). A huge effort has been reported to make the service discovery effective and efficient by improving the functional matching capability, i.e., – discovering all the available instances of a specific microservice very quickly –, while delegating QoS concerns to external load-balancing components (e.g., AWS Elastic Load Balancing).

These solutions do not take explicitly into account the *context* and *quality of services*, that are transient and continuously change over time because of several different reasons – e.g., a service consumer/provider can change its context because of mobility/elasticity, a service provider can change its QoS profile according to day time, etc. In this settings, our approach envisages a new service discovery mechanism able to deal with uncertainty and potential adverse effects attributed to frequent variability of the context and QoS profile of services.

This paper proposes the use of Machine Learning (ML) techniques as part of the service discovery process, so to perform context-driven, QoS-aware service discovery. During the process of service discovery, our approach *i*) uses deep neural networks to predict the QoS of microservice instances; *ii*) extracts context information from service consumer such as location, time of request, etc.; *iii*) keeps track of the execution context of each microservice instances; *iv*) leverages the context and QoS data obtained using Reinforcement Learning (RL) technique to select the instance that is expected to guarantee the optimal QoS.

The *contribution* of this work is as follows: i) it proposes a machine learning approach to be used for service discovery; ii) it defines a microservices architecture framework that integrates ML in service discovery and service selection; iii) it provides experimental results comparing QoS offered by traditional service discovery mechanism with that of our ML approach.

In the *rest of the paper*, Sect. 2 presents related work on (ML for) service discovery in (micro)service applications. Section 3 introduces the terminology and notation used in the paper. Section 4 presents our ML-based service discovery proposal. Section 5 evaluates the benefits of our approach through an exemplar application. Conclusions are provided in Sect. 6.

2   Related Work

Work related to the general concept of *discovery* is manifold and ranges from architecture (e.g., centralized, decentralized) to matching mechanisms (e.g., QoS-aware, context-aware, and semantic-aware) and selection criterion (e.g., single objective, multi-objectives).

While a large body of work exists in the context of SOA for each of these categories, we summarize hereafter only those approaches which consider QoS in conjunction with context.

Contextualization refers to the ability to discover, understanding and selecting services of interest deployed within the environment. To this end, a key role is played by ontologies, which have been employed to make service discovery context-aware [23]. The SAPERE framework implements a service discovery that accounts for contextual and QoS factors [21] in pervasive networking environments. The EASY framework focuses on pervasive services and specifically targets extra-functional properties by rating services according to user preferences on extra-functional properties [16]. Finally, in [3] service discovery considers contextual factors while discovering and assembling services of interest satisfying QoS constraints.

ML have been already employed for developing recommendation systems for Web Services, and demonstrated to be effective and efficient. In [18], the authors propose a number of data mining methods to improve service discovery and facilitate the use of Web services. In [2], authors introduce a framework for optimizing service selection based on consumer experience (i.e., context), and preferences (i.e., utility). The framework maintains a set of predefined selection rules that are evolved at run time by means of a reinforcement learning strategy.

More recently, various ML techniques have been exploited for addressing important aspects related to microservice architectures. In [1], unsupervised learning is used to automatically decompose a monolithic application into a set of microservices. In [6] reinforcement learning has been used for considering QoS factors while assembly services. In [4], bayesian learning and LSTM are used to fingerprint and classify microservices. In [13], reinforcement learning is used to autoscale microservices applications, whereas in [15] random forest regression is used to implement intelligent container scheduling strategy. Finally, in [12] authors describe a data-driven service discovery for context-aware microservices.

In this work, we make use of ML techniques for selecting services of interest that fulfill the QoS requirements in a given context. In particular, we rely on ML to mitigate the uncertainty and variability emerging from frequent changes in services context and QoS profiles. To this end, next sections will present the approach formalization, and evaluation.

3   System Model

In this section we introduce the terminology and notation used in the rest of the paper, define the model of the system we are considering, and formally define the performance indexes we will use to measure the effectiveness of our approach.

Figure 1 shows the structure of the *server-side discovery* pattern [19], where the clients – i.e., the API Gateway or another services – make requests via the *Router*, which is deployed at a known location. The *Router* queries a *Service Registry*, selects the proper service instance, and forwards the request to it. *Service Registry* usually is a database of services, their instances and their locations. Service instances are registered with the *Service Registry* on startup and unregistered on shutdown.

The model of the system under consideration builds on such a general definition of the Server-side Service Discovery Pattern. In particular, let $\mathcal{S}$ be a set of services, hosted by different nodes in a networked system (e.g., edge, fog, or cloud architecture). A Service $s \in \mathcal{S}$ is defined as a tuple (i, c, p, e), where: $s.i \in \mathcal{I}$ denotes the *interface* provided by the service (i.e., the functionality provided by

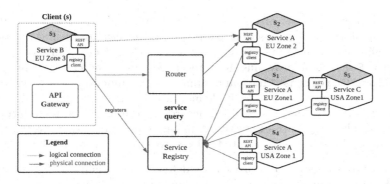

Fig. 1. Server-side service discovery pattern

s^1), $s.c \in C$ denotes the *context* of the service s, $s.p \in \mathcal{P}$ denotes the *quality profile* of the service s, and $s.e \in \mathcal{E}$ denotes the *endpoint* of the service s.

Further, a selection criteria $q \in \mathcal{Q}$ is a couple (c, p), where $q.c \in C$ denotes the context of interest, and $q.p \in \mathcal{P}$ denotes the quality profile of interest.

Given a selection criteria $q \in \mathcal{Q}$, and a service set $S \in 2^S$, the *Service Discovery* mechanism is defined according to two different functions, namely *match* and *select*. On the one and *match* $: \mathcal{I} \times 2^S \to 2^S$ is a function that given a interface $i \in \mathcal{I}$ and a set of services $S \subseteq \mathcal{S}$, returns a set of services $\overline{S} \subseteq S$ such that $\overline{S} = \{s | s.i = i\}$. On the other hand, *select* $: \mathcal{Q} \times 2^S \to \mathcal{S}$ is a function that given a selection criteria $q \in \mathcal{Q}$ and a set of services $S \subseteq \mathcal{S}$ returns a service $\hat{s} \in S$ such that $(\hat{s}.c \cong q.c) \wedge (\forall s \neq \hat{s} : \hat{s}.p \succeq s.p)$, where $\cong$ and $\succeq$ are defined according to some suitable methods [3,6].

Therefore, the Service Discovery mechanism can be defined as a function that, given an interface of interest i, a selection criteria q and a set of registered services $RS \subseteq \mathcal{S}$, returns a service instance $\hat{s}$, such that:

$$\hat{s} \leftarrow ServiceDiscovery(i) \equiv select(q, match(i, RS))$$

Example 1. Let $RS \subseteq \mathcal{S}$ be the set of services stored within the Service Registry depicted in Fig. 1:

$s_1 = (\text{``Service A''}, (\texttt{loc}, \texttt{EU}), ((\texttt{responseTime}, 0.5\texttt{s}), (\texttt{throughput}, 100\texttt{r/s})), \texttt{IP}_1)$
$s_2 = (\text{``Service A''}, (\texttt{loc}, \texttt{EU}), ((\texttt{responseTime}, 0.3\texttt{s}), (\texttt{throughput}, 300\texttt{r/s})), \texttt{IP}_2)$
$s_3 = (\text{``Service B''}, (\texttt{loc}, \texttt{EU}), ((\texttt{responseTime}, 0.2\texttt{s}), (\texttt{throughput}, 500\texttt{r/s})), \texttt{IP}_3)$
$s_4 = (\text{``Service A''}, (\texttt{loc}, \texttt{USA}), ((\texttt{responseTime}, 0.1\texttt{s}), (\texttt{throughput}, 100\texttt{r/s})), \texttt{IP}_4)$
$s_5 = (\text{``Service C''}, (\texttt{loc}, \texttt{USA}), ((\texttt{responseTime}, 0.6\texttt{s}), (\texttt{throughput}, 200\texttt{r/s})), \texttt{IP}_5)$

Let suppose s_3 (of type `Service B`) is interested in sending a request to a service of type $i = $ "`Service A`". The *Router* invokes the Service Discovery mechanism implemented by the *Service Registry* by providing i as input parameter. Applying the *match* function we obtain $\overline{S} = \{s_1, s_2, s_4\} \leftarrow match(i, RS)$.

---

[1] We use interchangeably the terms *interface* and *type* to denote the functionality of a service s.

Once retrieved the set of instances $\overline{S}$ implementing Service A, the *Router* makes use of the *select* function by providing a selection criteria q opportunely defined. For example, let suppose s_3 (which is located in EU) is interested in a Service A providing best response time. Therefore, defining $q \in \mathcal{Q} = ((\texttt{loc}, \texttt{EU}), \texttt{responseTime})$ and applying the function *select*, we obtain $\hat{s} = s_2 \leftarrow select(q, \overline{S})$ where, $\cong$ is defined according to geographical proximity (i.e., "close to"), and $\succeq$ is defined according to a less-is-better relationship (i.e., "$\leq$"). Then, s_2 is the Service A instance providing the "best response time" among those instances located "close" to s_3 (i.e., s_1, and s_2).

In order to evaluate our approach, we define a performance index measuring the *QoS* delivered by all services. To this end, let $SB_t \subseteq S$ be the set of services bound at a given time t. To measure the overall system performance, we define the *Average QoS* delivered by all services in SB_t:

$$\overline{QoS}(SB_t) = \frac{1}{|SB_t|} \sum_{s \in SB_t} s.p$$

4   ML Based Service Discovery

In this section, we describe how our approach uses a combination of ML techniques to perform context-aware service discovery.

For each query, $q \in \mathcal{Q}$ received by the *Service Registry* from a service consumer s, the overall goal of the approach is to select the matching service provider $\hat{s} \in RS$ so as to maximize the QoS perceived by s with respect to the context of the service consumer, s as well as with that of $\hat{s}$.

Figure 2 shows the overall flow of the approach. On receiving a service query, the *Service Registry* component first identifies a matching set, $\overline{S}$ of instances based on the strategy defined in Sect. 3. It then uses a combination of ML techniques to select the best instance $\hat{s}$ from $\overline{S}$.

The first part of the *select* function is to estimate the expected QoS of every instance in $\overline{S}$. This is due to the fact that, based on the change in contexts such as time of request, execution memory of instance, etc., there can be variations in the QoS offered by instances in $\overline{S}$ and neglecting this can lead to sub-optimal selections. Towards this, our approach uses deep neural networks which considers the historical QoS data offered by the instance along with their context data to *predict* the expected QoS for every instance in $\overline{S}$. The QoS forecasts alone are not sufficient for selection as the perceived QoS of $\hat{s}$ changes based on the context of s. In order to accommodate this, our approach further uses RL technique to select the best instance $\hat{s}$ from $\overline{S}$.

The overall ML process of the approach primarily consists of two phases (as represented in the Fig. 2) namely the *Batch Phase* and the *Real-Time Phase*. Training and building ML models for performing forecasts is a time consuming process. For this reason our approach involves periodic execution of *Batch Phase* where the historical *Quality Profile* information of each service $s_i \in RS$ as well as their context information are used for training and building models for forecasting the QoS. The *Real-Time Phase* on the other hand, consist of the instance selection process that happens in real-time. In order, to achieve this, it uses the latest ML models available from the batch phase to continuously forecast the expected *Quality Profile* of each service $s_i \in \overline{S}$. It further processes this forecast along with context of s using RL technique to *select*, $\hat{s}$ from $\overline{S}$.

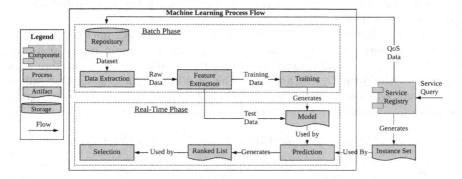

Fig. 2. Machine learning process flow

4.1   Data Extraction

The Quality Profiles (i.e., $s.p$) of all the service instances (e.g., response time, throughput, etc.) as well as the context information (i.e., $s.c$) which includes details such as instance memory, geographical location, etc. are continuously monitored and stored in a *Repository* component in the *Service Registry*. This forms the raw QoS/Context data. During the batch phase, the *Data Extraction process* retrieves the QoS/Context data from the *Repository*. This raw monitoring data contains the information of different QoS/Context attributes of every instance for different intervals of time. This data is sent to *Feature Extraction* process for further processing.

4.2   Feature Extraction

This process converts the raw monitoring data extracted during the data extraction process into structured set of features as required by the ML technique.

This data has a temporal nature and we use this to convert the problem of predicting QoS into a *time-series forecasting* problem. The QoS data with respect to time forms a *continuous time-series* [5]. For the ease of analysis, we first convert this into a *discrete time-series* by aggregating the data into uniform time intervals.

Let us assume to have m different service instances $s_1, \ldots, s_m$ providing a given interface $i \in \mathcal{I}$, which have been running for n units of time. Each of these m instances has an associated d dimensional *Context Feature-set* $C_f \subseteq \mathcal{C}$ describing the context of each running instance s_j.

Definition 1 (Context Feature-set). *We define context feature as a set* $C_f \subseteq \mathcal{C} = \{c_1, c_2, .., c_n\}$ *where* c_j *represents a pair* (l, v) *such that* l *is a unique label identifier for a context attribute, and* v *denotes the value of the context attribute.*

For example, $C_f = \{(\texttt{loc}, \texttt{IT}), (\texttt{day}, \texttt{Mon}), (\texttt{hour}, 10), (\texttt{min}, 30)\}$ denotes that a given service instance $s \in S$ is located in $\texttt{Italy}$, day is $\texttt{Monday}$ and the current time of invocation is $\texttt{10:30}$.

Then for each instance, the observation at any instant of time t can be represented by a matrix $O \in V^{d \times n}$ where V denotes the domain of the observed features. The process of generating time-series results in the formation of a sequence of the form $O_1, O_2, O_3 .... O_t$. The problem of forecasting QoS values is then reduced to predicting the most likely k-length sequence in future given the previous j observations that include the current one:

$$O_{t+1}, ..., O_{t+k} = \underset{O_{t+1}, ... O_{t+k}}{argmax} \ P(O_{t+1}, ..., O_{t+k} | O_{t-j+1}, O_{t-j+2}, ..., O_t)$$

where P denotes the conditional probability of observing $O_{t+1}, ..., O_{t+k}$ given $O_{t-j+1}, O_{t-j+2}, ..., O_t$. Since we also consider the context data for forecasting the QoS level of each instance, the observation matrix, O can be considered as a multivariate time-series dataset and as the forecasting needs to be done for the next k steps, the problem of time series forecasting becomes a multivariate multi-step forecasting problem [5].

Each column in O represents a feature vector, v. The process of feature scaling is applied to each column v such that $v_i \mapsto [0, 1] \ \forall v \in O$. O is then divided into two data sets, training set, O_{train} and testing set, O_{test} in the ratio 7:3 respectively. The training set obtained is further sent to the *Training* Process.

4.3   Training

The training process uses the training set, O_{train} to create ML models for forecasting the expected QoS of every service instance, $s_j \in RS$ for a given time period known as forecast horizon, H.

Definition 2 (Forecast Horizon). *We define a forecast horizon, H as a couple (h, u) where $h \in \mathbb{R}$ represents the time horizon value, and u is the unit identifier for the time horizon value specified.*

The approach makes use of Long Short Term Memory (LSTM) network [11], a class of Recurrent Neural Network (RNN) [8] for building the forecast models. LSTM's have shown to be very effective in time-series forecasting [20] as they have the ability to handle the problem of long-term dependency better known in the literature as the *Vanishing Gradient Problem* [10], as compared to traditional RNN's. In our previous work [17], we have shown how LSTM networks can be used for forecasting QoS of the sensor components and why they are more effective when compared to traditional models like ARIMA. In this work, we use the same approach to train the LSTM network for forecasting the QoS of service instances. The training process results in the creation of a *Model* which is further tested for accuracy using the test set, O_{test}. In the event of a low accuracy, the approach performs a retraining by tuning the neural network parameters. The tested models are further used by the *Prediction* process.

Training is executed as batch process in regular intervals to update the models so as to avoid the problems of concept drift [22].

4.4   Prediction

Prediction is a real-time process responsible for forecasting QoS of the matching instances. For every service discovery request received by the service registry, the prediction process uses the trained LSTM models to generate the QoS forecasts for each $s_j \in \overline{S} \leftarrow match(i, SR)$.

Definition 3 (QoS Forecasts). *We define the QoS forecasts as a set, $F = \{p_1, p_2, .., p_n\}$ where p_j represents the forecasted quality profile. Note that, $p_j = (a, v)$ where a identifies the quality attribute and $v \in \mathbb{R}$ denotes the forecasted quality value over the duration of the time horizon h.*

For example, $H = (10, \mathsf{sec})$ and $F = \{(\mathsf{responseTime}, 0.2), (\mathsf{throughput}, 200)\}$ for a given instance s denotes that s is expected to have an average response time of 0.2 s and a throughput of 200 requests/second in the next 10 s.

These QoS forecasts for each of the service instances $s_j \in \overline{S}$ are then sent to the *Selection* process for further processing.

4.5   Selection

The role of selection process is to select the best instance $\hat{s}$, such that, $\hat{s} \leftarrow select(q, \overline{S})$, based on the context of the service consumer as well as the forecasts of the expected QoS of each instance $s_j \in \overline{S}$. In order to achieve this our approach uses a RL technique in particular Q-learning [24]. Q-learning is a widely used method for decision-making scenarios due to their ability to come up with optimal decisions through a model-free learning approach. The key part of using Q-learning is to divide the problem into set of states, W, actions, A and rewards, R. The state space of our Q-learning approach is determined by two important attributes: (*i*) *QoS Categories*, and (*ii*) *Context Feature-set*.

Definition 4. *(QoS Categories) We define QoS category, QC as a discrete set $\{qc_1, qc_2, ...qc_n\}$ where qc_j represents the expected category for the QoS metrics j, obtained by mapping the values of the QoS forecasts f_j to a unique label, $l \in \mathcal{L}$.*

For instance, let $F = \{(\mathsf{responseTime}, 0.3), (\mathsf{throughput}, 100)\}$ represent the forecast vector and $L = \{\mathsf{lowRt}, \mathsf{highRt}, \mathsf{lowTh}, \mathsf{highTh}\}$ denote a set of labels. Then we can define a simple mapping function for the QoS attribute, *responsetime* such that $[0, 0.2] \mapsto \mathsf{lowRt}, [0.2, \infty] \mapsto \mathsf{highRt}$. Similarly, we can define another mapping function for the QoS attribute, *throughput* such that

---

Algorithm 1. Instance Selection Algorithm

Require: :
1: States $W = \{w_1, w_2, w_3, ..., w_n\}$
2: Actions $A = \{0, 1, 2....m\}$ ▷ represents the selection of each m instance
3: Labels $L = \{l_1, l_2, l_3, ...l_p\}$ ▷ Threshold categories
4: Forecasts $F = \{f_1, f_2, ..f_n\}$ ▷ Forecasts of QoS attributes
5: Rewards $R = \{r_1, r_2, ..., r_n\}$ ▷ Reward for each of the state
6: **procedure** DECISION-MAKER($W,A,L,F,R,\mathcal{C},\alpha,\gamma$)   ▷ Find the state of the system from the
   forecasts and context
7:    $QC \leftarrow identify\_category(F, L)$ ▷ Get Category from Forecasts
8:    $w \leftarrow (QC, c)$ ▷ combine category and context to form the state
9:    $r \leftarrow R[w]$ ▷ Reward for attaining the state, w
10:    $(w', a') \leftarrow argmax_a Q(w, a)$
11:    $Q'(w, a) = (1 - \alpha) * Q(w, a) + \alpha * (r + \gamma * max(Q(w', a)))$
12:    $a \leftarrow a'$ ▷ The action to reach that state
13:    **return** a

$[0, 40] \mapsto$ `lowTh`, $[40, \infty] \mapsto$ `highTh`. We can then combine this to generate a QoS category set, QC for the given F as $QC = \{highRt, highTh\}$.

Based on this, the state space, $W \subseteq QC \times \mathcal{C}$ is defined over the set of possible QoS categories and the set of all context features in $\mathcal{C}$.

Action space, A, consists of a set of actions $\{a_1, a_2, a_3, .., a_m\}$ such that $a_j \in A$ denotes the selection of instance s_j in $\overline{S}$. Rewards, R on the other hand is a set $\{r_1, r_2, ..r_n\}$ where $r_j \in \mathbb{Z}$ denotes the reward value for attaining a state, $w_j \in W$.

W and A together form a $n \times m$ matrix where n denotes the number of states and m denotes the number of actions. Q-Table forms the heart of the Q-learning approach where each value corresponds to a (w, a) pair and it's value denotes the relevance of selecting an action, a from a state w. In other words, it denotes the benefit for selecting an instance s_j given the context of the service consumer and the expected QoS category of the instance. This property is leveraged by the selection process to select the best instance during the process of service discovery. The complete instance selection algorithm based on Q-learning is presented in Algorithm 1. It uses two key parameters, α and γ where $0 < \alpha \leq 1$ denotes the learning rate which represents the importance given to the learned observation at each step, and $0 < \gamma \leq 1$ denotes the discount factor, which can be considered as the weight given to the next action (instance selection).

The algorithm first maps the forecasts received from the prediction process, F into a set of QoS Categories, QC based on the labels, L. The QC identified along with the context of the service consumer, $\mathcal{C}$ is combined to identify the current state, w inside the Q-Table (lines 7–8). The algorithm then assigns a reward for attaining the state, w. Following this, the maximum value of state-action pair, (w', a') that can be reached from the current state is identified (lines 9–10). The q-table is then updated using the q-function (line 11) and the action (instance, $\hat{s}$) is returned (lines 12–13).

In this manner for every query, q, our algorithm selects the best instance $\hat{s}$ by selecting the action that maximizes the reward. By assigning negative rewards (penalties) to selection of instances that offers sub-optimal QoS, the approach ensures that any incorrect selection is penalized in the form of a high negative reward and this means as the time progresses, given a q, the algorithm continuously improves the selection process to guarantee optimal QoS by ignoring instances that can lead to high penalties.

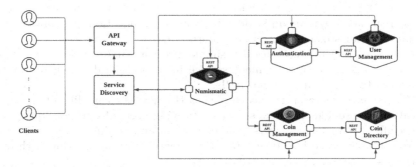

Fig. 3. High-level architecture of the prototype application

5 Evaluation

In this section, we elaborate on the evaluation of the proposed approach through a prototype microservice-based application developed for managing coin collections of the users. Due to space limitations, we omit here the implementation details. The interested reader can find the complete implementation, along with source code and dataset, at the project repository[2]. Rather, we describe the microservice architecture, the experimental setup, and the data and metrics used for the evaluation of our approach. We used *response time* as the key QoS parameter for the evaluation of our approach. Hence, for each $i \in \mathcal{I}$ requested by the service consumer, s, the objective will be to select the instance, $\hat{s}$ that is expected to provide the best response time.

5.1 Proof-of-Concept: The Coin Collection Application

The *Coin Collection* application provides different functionalities to users who want to collect coins. In particular, users can: i) register to the application by providing details such as name, location, etc.; ii) add information on the coins in hand (this information includes details such as name of the coin, country of use, etc.; iii) query information about the different types of coins available in the system; iv) retrieve information on the different coins of a specific user or of the nearby users of a given location. *Coin Collection* consists of five key microservices (see Fig. 3):

1. *User Management* microservice is responsible for handling user management related operations such as adding new users, deleting users and managing user profiles. It uses a database to store the user profile related information.

---

[2] https://github.com/karthikv1392/ML-SD.

2. *Authentication* microservice provides functionalities to ensure that only authenticated users have permission to view/manage user-profiles and other user-related information. It has a simple database to store user credentials.
3. *Coin Management* microservice provides functionalities to manage coins such as adding/removing coins to/from the collection. It consists of a database for storing coin related information.
4. *Coin Directory* microservice is a simple directory management service that supports the coin management service in fetching additional information related to coin from external APIs.
5. *Numismatic* microservice accomplishes the key functionality of the application. It provides features such as retrieving user information, querying a specific user or nearby users' coin collection, and adding or removing coins from a user collection. It achieves these features by interacting with other microservices, as shown in Fig. 3.

External clients interact with the system through the API Gateway, which further checks with the *Service Discovery* to fetch an instance of the desired microservice. Additionally, every microservice queries the service discovery before interacting with other microservices. For example, Numismatic service interacts with coin management microservice. This implies that every time Numismatic service has to interact with coin management microservice, it first needs to identify the instance that needs to be invoked using Service Discovery. The same holds true for other microservices.

5.2   Controlled Experiments

Experiment Specification. For experimentation and evaluation, we used the prototype application described in Sect. 5.1 consisting of 25 microservices. The microservices were implemented using Java Spring Boot. The service discovery module was primarily implemented in Java. The module also supports integration with technologies like Zookeeper, Netflix Eureka, etc. The LSTM part was implemented using Python (Keras framework with Tensorflow backend). Mean Squared Error (MSE) loss function and the efficient Adam version of stochastic gradient descent was used for optimization of the LSTM models [14]. Algorithm 1 was implemented using Java with parameters $\alpha = 0.1$ and $\gamma = 0.1$.

Experimental Setup. Our system was deployed on two VM instances in Google Cloud. The first one was run on a N1-Standard-4 CPU Intel Haswell Processor comprising 4 vCPU and 17 GB RAM with US-Central-a as the geographical zone. The second one ran on a N2-Standard-4 Intel Skylake processor comprising 2 vCPU and 28 GB RAM with Europe-West-a as the geographical zone. The microservice instances were distributed between the two VM instances. This was done to capture the different context dimensions that may arise from the type of CPU, number of cores, geographical zones, etc.

Evaluation Metrics. The objective of our evaluation is to assess the effectiveness and efficiency of the approach. The effectiveness of the approach is evaluated by i) measuring the *accuracy* of the response time forecasts produced; ii) calculating the *average response time* delivered by all service in SR, $\overline{QoS}(SB_t)$ as defined in Sect. 3; iii) computing the response time offered by the instance, $\hat{s}$ for every request made. Efficiency on the other hand is measured based on the average time taken for executing the process of matching and selection.

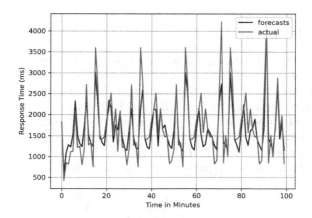

Fig. 4. LSTM response time forecasts

Data Setup. We deployed the system (using standard service discovery mechanism) for a period of one week and we developed 10 different clients to send requests to various microservices based on a Poisson distribution with different mean values based on the given day of the week. To simulate a different workload between instances of the same microservice, a delay has been added at each request that depends on the type of instance and current time. This was done to emulate the real scenario where the incoming request rate can vary depending on the day and time. The response time of all the instances were continuously monitored and recorded. This was then used to create the LSTM based forecast model with a forecast horizon, $H = <5, minutes>$.

Evaluation Candidates. We evaluated the approach by deploying the system integrated with each of the five different strategies for a period of 72 h. These strategies form the evaluation candidates:

1. *static-greedy (sta_gre)*: Instances are ranked based on the static response time registered by the instances during service registration. Selection is performed using a greedy strategy (select instance with the least response time). This strategy is the one used by standard service discovery mechanisms like Netflix Eureka, Apache Zookeeper, etc.

2. *linereg-greedy (lin_gre)*: Prediction of instance response time is performed using linear regression and selection is performed using a greedy strategy. We use linear regression as it is a standard regression baseline. It is implemented using Python scikit-learn package.

3. *timeseries-greedy (tim_gre)*: Prediction of instance response time is performed using time-series and selection using greedy.

4. *linereg-Q-Learn (lin_Qle)*: Prediction of instance response time is performed using linear regression and selection using Q-learning.

5. *timeseries-Q-Learn (tim_Qle)*: Our approach, which performs prediction of response time using time-series and selection using Q-learning.

5.3   Approach Effectiveness

Forecast Accuracy. The first part of evaluating the approach effectiveness was to measure the accuracy of the response-time forecasts produced by the LSTM models. The dataset was divided into training and testing set consisting of 8903 and 2206 samples respectively. We build the LSTM model with single hidden layer consisting of 60 neurons. This number was selected through experimentation. The model was fit in 250 epochs. We used Root Mean Square Error (RMSE) for evaluating the accuracy of LSTM models on the testing set, where RMSE for a dataset, O_{test} with n samples is given by the formula:

$$RMSE = \sqrt{\frac{1}{n} \sum_{i=1}^{n} \left(p_i - y_i \right)^2} \tag{1}$$

where p_i represents the predicted value and y_i represents the actual value.

The calculation resulted in a value of 406.73 ms which means on average there is an error of 406.73 ms in prediction. Figure 4 shows the plot of actual versus forecasted values. We can see that the prediction made by the LSTM model is almost able to follow the curve of actual response time. This is due to the fact that LSTM, being a deep neural network possesses ability to identify any non-linear dependency that might exist between the different features such as the context attributes to generate accurate forecasts.

Average QoS Per Minute. The second part of measuring the effectiveness was to calculate the metric, $\overline{QoS}(SB_t)$ as defined in Sect. 3. In order to accomplish this, we deployed our experiment by integrating the service discovery mechanism using each of the evaluation candidates for a period of 72 h. The batch training phase was executed every 12 h. The value of $\overline{QoS}(SB_t)$ was calculated for every minute and Fig. 5a shows the plot of the cumulative $\overline{QoS}(SB_t)$ while using each of the approaches. We can clearly that, the cumulative $\overline{QoS}(SB_t)$ offered by the different approaches starts diverging marginally during the initial stages but as time progresses, the gap between *tim_Qle* and other approaches slowly starts increasing. In particular we can see that, the gap between *tim_Qle* and the traditional *sta_gre* keeps increasing steadily after 1900 min thereby resulting in the improvement of *tim_Qle* (10449 s) over *sta_gre* (11762 s) by 12% at the end of 72 h. *lin_gre, tim_gre* on the other hand does perform better than *sta_gre* with *tim_gre* performing better than *lin_gre*. However, we can observe that the learning rate of these approaches is still less than *tim_Qle* and they are often inconsistent.

This is more visible especially after 1900 min. This is due to the ability of Q-Learning to continuously improve with the help of feedbacks obtained for every selection performed. For Q-learning, the feedback for decision at time, t obtained via forecast at time, $t + 1$. Hence poor forecast accuracy implies that Q-Learning favors selection of wrong instances and due to this reason, *lin_Qle* performs the worst.

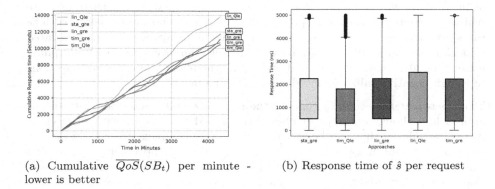

(a) Cumulative $\overline{QoS}(SB_t)$ per minute - lower is better

(b) Response time of $\hat{s}$ per request

Fig. 5. Effectiveness

Average QoS Per Request. In order to further evaluate the approach effectiveness in terms of the QoS offered by the instance, $\hat{s}$, we measured the response-time of $\hat{s}$ for every request made to $\hat{s}$. Figure 5b shows the box plot of the *response time* offered by $\hat{s}$ per request. The *tim_Qle* approach offers the least average response time of about 1236.23 ms which is $20\%, 19\%, 21\%$ and 16% better than the one offered by *sta_gre*, *lin_gre*, *lin_Qle* and *tim_gre* respectively. Also we can observe that most of the values fall between the range of 500 ms and 1800 ms which is much less compared to other approaches. Although, there are more outliers in the case of *tim_Qle* due to the initial phase of Q-learning where wrong selections are made, on average the response time perceived by s when using by *tim_Qle* is significantly lower compared to the others.

5.4   Approach Efficiency

The efficiency of the approach was evaluated by measuring the time taken by the whole service discovery process when integrated with our approach. The results show that on average the approach takes 0.10 s for performing the whole process. The speed can be mainly attributed to the fact that Q-Learning being a model-free technique performs only a lookup operation in the Q-Table. The majority of the time is taken by the prediction process as although it's a constant time process, the prediction needs to be done for service instances in each of the

5 services. LSTM training which happens every 12 h takes around 125 min to complete but this does not impact the real-time process as only the trained models are used for service discovery.

5.5 Threats to Validity

Threats to *construct validity* is related to the use of a controlled experimental setup and incorrect selections. Even though we performed *real-time execution* of the system, we simulated the context and quality change in order to emulate real-world scenarios as close as possible. In particular, the context setup such as the server locations, request simulations, dynamic delays were all incorporated to achieve this goal. In order to improve the selection accuracy, the build phase is executed at regular intervals and by keeping the reward for incorrect selections to a high negative value, wrong decisions can be penalized.

Threats to *external validity* concern the generalizability and scalability of our approach. Although our approach has been applied on a system with 25 services, it uses techniques that can be generalized to more complex systems. Moreover, our approach can be gathered to large scale systems by optimizing Q-Learning (for instance by using Deep Q-Learning [9]) to solve the effectiveness and efficiency issue that might arise from the increased state, action space.

6   Conclusion

This paper has proposed a novel service discovery mechanism that takes into account the frequent variability of the consumers and providers contexts and QoS profile of services. Therefore, the overall goal of the approach is to select the matching service provider $\hat{s}$ so as to maximize the QoS perceived by the service consumer s with respect to its context, as well as with that of $\hat{s}$.

In this work, we have demonstrated how we can incorporate a combination of supervised and reinforcement learning into microservice architectures, especially for service discovery, without creating additional overheads as opposed to traditional ML integration (thanks to the use of build and real time phases). Moreover, our approach implementation also supports integration with existing server-side discovery patterns. Further, we believe that with the increasing usage of microservice-based architectural styles, this kind of approach, which effectively combines different ML techniques, can aid architects in guaranteeing the satisfaction of different non-functional requirements. We believe that this is just the beginning, and a lot more problems can be solved with the effective use of ML techniques.

To this extent, future work includes, but is not limited to: (*i*) extending the approach to large scale systems by considering multiple QoS parameters and the trade-offs among them; (*ii*) exploring the possibility of using transfer learning to make the approach more robust across different classes of systems.

References

1. Abdullah, M., Iqbal, W., Erradi, A.: Unsupervised learning approach for web application auto-decomposition into microservices. J. Syst. Softw. **151**, 243–257 (2019)
2. Andersson, J., Heberle, A., Kirchner, J., Lowe, W.: Service level achievements - distributed knowledge for optimal service selection. In: 2011 IEEE Ninth European Conference on Web Services, pp. 125–132 (2011)
3. Caporuscio, M., Grassi, V., Marzolla, M., Mirandola, R.: GoPrime: a fully decentralized middleware for utility-aware service assembly. IEEE Trans. Softw. Eng. **42**(2), 136–152 (2016)
4. Chang, H., Kodialam, M., Lakshman, T., Mukherjee, S.: Microservice fingerprinting and classification using machine learning. In: 2019 IEEE 27th International Conference on Network Protocols (ICNP), pp. 1–11 (2019)
5. Chatfield, C.: Time-Series Forecasting. Chapman and Hall/CRC, London (2000)
6. D'Angelo, M., Caporuscio, M., Grassi, V., Mirandola, R.: Decentralized learning for self-adaptive QoS-aware service assembly. Future Gener. Comput. Syst. **108**, 210–227 (2020)
7. Di Francesco, P., Malavolta, I., Lago, P.: Research on architecting microservices: trends, focus, and potential for industrial adoption. In: 2017 IEEE International Conference on Software Architecture (ICSA), pp. 21–30 (2017)
8. Graves, A.: Supervised sequence labelling. In: Supervised Sequence Labelling with Recurrent Neural Networks. Studies in Computational Intelligence, vol. 385. Springer, Heidelberg (2012). https://doi.org/10.1007/978-3-642-24797-2_2
9. Hester, T., et al.: Deep q-learning from demonstrations. In: AAAI (2018)
10. Hochreiter, S., Bengio, Y., Frasconi, P., Schmidhuber, J., et al.: Gradient flow in recurrent nets: the difficulty of learning long-term dependencies (2001)
11. Hochreiter, S., Schmidhuber, J.: Long short-term memory. Neural Comput. **9**(8), 1735–1780 (1997)
12. Houmani, Z., Balouek-Thomert, D., Caron, E., Parashar, M.: Enhancing microservices architectures using data-driven service discovery and QoS guarantees. In: 20th International Symposium on Cluster, Cloud and Internet Computing (2020)
13. Khaleq, A.A., Ra, I.: Intelligent autoscaling of microservices in the cloud for real-time applications. IEEE Access **9**, 35464–35476 (2021)
14. Kingma, D.P., Ba, J.: Adam: a method for stochastic optimization. arXiv preprint arXiv:1412.6980 (2014)
15. Lv, J., Wei, M., Yu, Y.: A container scheduling strategy based on machine learning in microservice architecture. In: 2019 IEEE International Conference on Services Computing (SCC), pp. 65–71 (2019)
16. Mokhtar, S.B., Preuveneers, D., Georgantas, N., Issarny, V., Berbers, Y.: EASY: efficient semantic service discovery in pervasive computing environments with QoS and context support. J. Syst. Softw. **81**, 785–808 (2008)
17. Muccini, H., Vaidhyanathan, K.: PIE-ML: a machine learning-driven proactive approach for architecting self-adaptive energy efficient IoT systems. Tech. rep., University of L'Aquila, Italy (2020). https://tinyurl.com/y98weaat
18. Nayak, R., Tong, C.: Applications of data mining in web services. In: Zhou, X., Su, S., Papazoglou, M.P., Orlowska, M.E., Jeffery, K. (eds.) WISE 2004. LNCS, vol. 3306, pp. 199–205. Springer, Heidelberg (2004). https://doi.org/10.1007/978-3-540-30480-7_22
19. Richardson, C.: Microservices Patterns. Manning, New York (2018)

20. Siami-Namini, S., Tavakoli, N., Namin, A.S.: A comparison of ARIMA and LSTM in forecasting time series. In: 2018 17th IEEE International Conference on Machine Learning and Applications (ICMLA), pp. 1394–1401. IEEE (2018)
21. Stevenson, G., Ye, J., Dobson, S., Pianini, D., Montagna, S., Viroli, M.: Combining self-organisation, context-awareness and semantic reasoning: the case of resource discovery in opportunistic networks. In: Proceedings of the 28th Annual ACM Symposium on Applied Computing, SAC 2013, pp. 1369–1376 (2013)
22. Tsymbal, A.: The problem of concept drift: definitions and related work. Comput. Sci. Dep. Trinity Coll. Dublin **106**(2), 58 (2004)
23. W3C: OWL-S: Semantic Markup for Web Services (2004)
24. Watkins, C.J., Dayan, P.: Q-learning. Mach. Learn. **8**(3–4), 279–292 (1992)

FLRA: A Reference Architecture for Federated Learning Systems

Sin Kit Lo[1,2](✉) , Qinghua Lu[1,2] , Hye-Young Paik[2] , and Liming Zhu[1,2]

[1] Data61, CSIRO, Sydney, Australia
kit.lo@data61.csiro.au
[2] University of New South Wales, Sydney, Australia

Abstract. Federated learning is an emerging machine learning paradigm that enables multiple devices to train models locally and formulate a global model, without sharing the clients' local data. A federated learning system can be viewed as a large-scale distributed system, involving different components and stakeholders with diverse requirements and constraints. Hence, developing a federated learning system requires both software system design thinking and machine learning knowledge. Although much effort has been put into federated learning from the machine learning perspectives, our previous systematic literature review on the area shows that there is a distinct lack of considerations for software architecture design for federated learning. In this paper, we propose FLRA, a reference architecture for federated learning systems, which provides a template design for federated learning-based solutions. The proposed FLRA reference architecture is based on an extensive review of existing patterns of federated learning systems found in the literature and existing industrial implementation. The FLRA reference architecture consists of a pool of architectural patterns that could address the frequently recurring design problems in federated learning architectures. The FLRA reference architecture can serve as a design guideline to assist architects and developers with practical solutions for their problems, which can be further customised.

Keywords: Software architecture · Reference architecture · Federated learning · Pattern · Software engineering · Machine learning · Artificial intelligence

1 Introduction

The ever-growing use of industrial-scale IoT platforms and smart devices contribute to the exponential growth in data dimensions [23], which, in turn, empowers the research and applications in AI and machine learning. However, the development of AI and machine learning also significantly elevates data privacy concerns, and General Data Protection Regulation (GDPR)[1] stipulates a range of data protection measures with which many of these systems must comply.

---

[1] https://gdpr-info.eu/.

© Springer Nature Switzerland AG 2021
S. Biffl et al. (Eds.): ECSA 2021, LNCS 12857, pp. 83–98, 2021.
https://doi.org/10.1007/978-3-030-86044-8_6

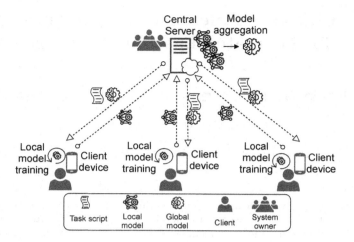

Fig. 1. Federated learning overview [25].

This is a particular challenge in machine learning systems as the data that is ready for model training is often insufficient and they frequently suffer from "data hungriness issues". As data privacy is now one of the most important ethical principles of machine learning systems [17], there needs to be a solution that can deliver sufficient amount of data for training while the privacy of the data owners is respected.

To tackle this challenge, Google proposed federated learning [28] in 2016. Federated learning is a variation of distributed machine learning techniques that enables model training on a highly distributed client devices network. The key feature of federated learning is the training of models using the data collected locally, without transferring the data out of the client devices. A global model is initialised on a central server and broadcast to the participating client devices for local training. The locally trained model parameters are then collected by the central server and aggregated to update global model parameters. The global model parameters are broadcast again for the next training round. Each local training round usually takes a step in the gradient descent process. Figure 1 presents an overview of the federated learning process.

A federated learning system can be viewed as a large-scale distributed system, involving different components and stakeholders with diverse requirements and constraints. Hence, developing a federated learning system requires both software system design thinking and machine learning knowledge [25]. Further, despite having various reference architectures for machine learning, big data, industrial IoT, and edge computing systems, to the best of our knowledge, there is still no reference architecture for an end-to-end federated learning system. Based on findings in several federated learning reviews [18,24], the application of federated learning is still limited and immature, with only certain stages of an end-to-end federated learning architecture are extensively studied, leaving many unfilled gaps for architecture and pipeline development. In contrast, many reusable solutions and components were proposed to solve the different challenges of federated learning systems and this motivates the design of a general federated learning system reference architecture. Therefore, this paper presents a pattern-oriented reference architecture that serves as an architecture design guideline and to facilitate the end-to-end development and operations of federated learning systems, while taking different quality attributes and constraints into considerations. This work provides the following contributions:

- A pattern-oriented federated learning reference architecture named FLRA, generated from the findings of a systematic literature review (SLR) and mining of industrial best practices on machine learning system implementations.
- A pool of patterns associated with the different components of the FLRA reference architecture that target to address the recurring design problems in federated learning architectures.

The structure of the paper is as follows. Section 2 introduces the methodology for the reference architecture design, followed by the presentation of the reference architecture in Sect. 3. Section 4 presents the related work. Section 5 presents the discussions of this work and finally concludes this paper.

2   Methodology

We have employed parts of an empirically-grounded design methodology [11] to design the federated learning reference architecture. Firstly, the design and development of this reference architecture are based on empirical evidence collected through our systematic literature review on 231 federated learning academic literature from a software engineering perspective [24]. The review is conducted based on Kitchenham's guideline [19] with which we designed a comprehensive protocol for the review's initial paper search, paper screening, quality assessments, data extractions, analyses, and synthesis. We have also adopted the software development practices of machine learning systems in [35] to describe the software development lifecycle (SDLC) for federated learning. Using the stages of this lifeycycle as a guide, we formulated our research questions as: (1) Background understanding; (2) Requirement analysis; (3) Architecture design; and (4) Implementation & evaluation. One major finding of the SLR is that federated learning research and applications are still highly immature, and certain stages of an end-to-end federated learning architecture still lack extensive studies [24]. However, we have also identified many solutions and components proposed to solve the different challenges of federated learning systems, which can be reused and adapted. This motivates the design of a federated learning system reference architecture.

Based on the findings, we specifically adopted the qualitative methods in empirical studies of software architecture [34] to develop and confirm the theory for the reference architecture design. The proposition is generated based on syntheses and validations of the different recurring customers and business needs of

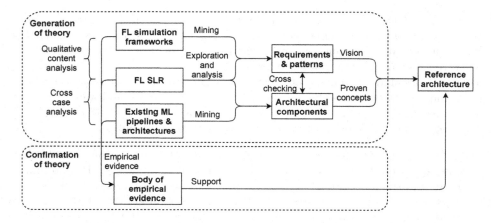

Fig. 2. Methodology for federated learning reference architecture design.

the federated learning systems, in addition to the collections and analyses of the reusable patterns to address these architectural needs. We then conducted studies on some of the best practices in centralised and distributed machine learning systems to cover some of the components that are not covered in the federated learning studies. The main processes are the: (1) *generation of theory* and (2) *confirmation of theory*. The architecture design methodology is illustrated in Fig. 2.

2.1   Generation of Theory

The generation of the initial design of the reference architecture theory is performed in this stage. Since there is no standard reference architecture for federated learning yet, we generated the theory by referring to the architecture of a machine learning system. Here, we adopted *cross-case analysis* [34] as the theory generation method, which is an analysis method that compares two different cases based on some attributes and examines their similarities and differences. We performed a *cross-case analysis* on the pipeline design of conventional machine learning and federated learning systems. Here, we reviewed several machine learning architectures proposed by well-known companies, such as Google[2], Microsoft[3], and Amazon[4], specifically on their machine learning pipeline designs. Furthermore, based on our previous project implementation experience, we defined a general federated learning pipeline based on the standards proposed by these industry players that covers *job creation, data collection, data preprocessing (cleaning, labeling, augmentation, etc.), model training, model evaluation, model deployment,* and

---

[2] https://cloud.google.com/architecture/mlops-continuous-delivery-and-automation-pipelines-in-machine-learning.

[3] https://docs.microsoft.com/en-us/azure/machine-learning/concept-model-management-and-deployment.

[4] https://docs.aws.amazon.com/sagemaker/latest/dg/multi-model-endpoints.html.

model monitoring stage. Since federated learning was first introduced by Google, the pipeline components analysis and mining are performed heavily on the federated learning standards proposed by Google researchers in [5,18,28], and the frameworks for federated learning system benchmark and simulation, such as Tensorflow Federated (TFF)[5], LEAF[6], and FedML[7]. From the findings, we were able to conclude that the *data collection* is fairly similar whereas *data preprocessing, model training, model evaluation, model deployment,* and *model monitoring* stages for federated learning systems are different from machine learning pipelines. Especially for the *model training* stage, the federated learning pipelines encapsulate *model broadcast, local model training, model upload and collection,* and *model aggregation* operation under this single stage. Furthermore, the iterative interaction between multiple client devices with one central server is the key design consideration of the federated learning architecture, and therefore, most academic work extensively studied the *model training* stage and proposed many solutions which can be adapted as reusable components or patterns to address different requirements.

Besides observing the pipeline design and the components, we performed *qualitative content analyses* on existing machine learning and federated learning systems proposed by industrial practitioners and academics to extract requirements, reusable patterns, and components for the design of the reference architecture. In the SLR, a series of system quality attributes are defined based on ISO/IEC 25010 System and Software Quality model[8] and ISO/IEC 25012[9] Data Quality model to record the different challenges of a federated learning system addressed by researchers. The empirical evidence associated with each quality attribute and business need is analysed and validated as the support for the design proposition of the reference architecture. After the generation of theory for the hypothesis of the reference architecture, we designed the reference architecture according to the theory.

2.2 Confirmation of Theory

In this stage, we confirmed and verified the viability and applicability of the reference architecture proposed. Since this reference architecture is built from scratch based on the patterns and requirements collected through qualitative analyses, we evaluated the architecture by building a convincing body of evidence to support the reference architecture, which is different from conventional evaluation approaches. We employed the qualitative validation method known as *triangulation* [34]. The basic idea is to gather different types of evidence to support a proposition. The evidence might come from different sources, be collected using different methods, and in our case, the evidence is from the SLR

---

[5] https://www.tensorflow.org/federated.
[6] https://github.com/TalwalkarLab/leaf.
[7] https://fedml.ai/.
[8] https://iso25000.com/index.php/en/iso-25000-standards/iso-25010.
[9] https://iso25000.com/index.php/en/iso-25000-standards/iso-25012.

and the industrial implementations of machine learning systems from renowned institutions and companies, and our previous implementation experience.

We have reviewed these evidence based on the SLDC lifecycle of machine learning systems we developed for the SLR to identify the adoptions of the different reusable patterns or components, in addition to the basic machine learning pipeline components that are mentioned in these evidence. These mentions and adoptions are collected to prove applicability of the instantiated components in the federated learning reference architecture. In short, the *triangulation* process justified that the reference architecture is applicable as it is supported by various empirical evidence we collected and analysed.

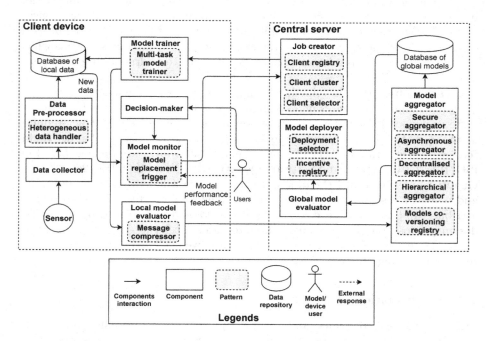

Fig. 3. FLRA: a reference architecture of federated learning systems.

3   FLRA Reference Architecture

In this section, we present FLRA, a pattern-oriented reference architecture for federated learning systems. Figure 3 illustrates the overall reference architecture. A base version of a federated learning system consists of two main participants: (1) central server and (2) client devices. A central server initialises a machine learning job and coordinates the federated training process, whereas client devices perform model training using local data and computation resources.

Underneath the two participants, there are two types of components: (1) Mandatory components and (2) optional components. The mandatory components provide the basic functions required by a federated machine learning pipeline. To fulfill the different software quality requirements and design constraints in federated learning systems, we collected and defined a set of patterns based on our SLR results and the mining of some existing federated learning simulation frameworks. Each pattern is embedded as optional components to facilitate the architecture design.

We summarised all the mandatory and optional components of the reference architecture and briefly highlighted the functionalities and responsibility of each component in Table 1. The table presents the details of each component associated with the federated learning pipeline stages.

3.1   Job Creation

The federated learning process starts with the creation of a model training job (including initial model and training configurations) via *job creator* on the central server. Within the *job creator* component, three optional components could be considered are: *client registry*, *client cluster*, *client selector*. In a federated learning system, client devices may be owned by different parties, constantly connect and drop out from the system. Hence, it is challenging to keep track of all the participating client devices including dropout devices and dishonest devices. This is different from distributed or centralised machine learning systems in which both clients and the server are typically owned and managed by a single party [27]. A *client registry* is required to maintain all the information of the client devices that are registered, (e.g., ID, resource information, number of participating rounds, local model performance, etc.) Both IBM Federated Learning Framework[10] and doc.ai[11] adopted client registry in their design to improve maintainability and reliability of the system since the system can manage the devices effectively and quickly identify the problematic ones via the *client registry* component. FedML which is a federated learning benchmarking and simulation framework has also explicitly covered the client manager module in their framework that serves the same purpose as the *client registry*. However, the system may sacrifice client data privacy due to the recording of the device information on the central server.

The non-IID[12] data characteristics of local raw data and the data-sharing restriction translates to model performance challenge [18,21,28,42]. When the data from client devices are non-IID, the global models aggregated is less generalised to the entire data. To improve the generalisation of the global model and speed up model convergence, a *client cluster* component can be added to

---

[10] https://github.com/IBM/federated-learning-lib.

[11] https://doc.ai/.

[12] Non-Identically and Independently Distribution: Highly-skewed and personalised data distribution that vary heavily between different clients and affects the model performance and generalisation [33].

Table 1. Components of the federated learning reference architecture

Stages	Types	Components	Responsibility
Job creation	Mandatory	Job creator	Initialises training job and global model
	Optional	Client registry	Improves system's **maintainability** and **reliability** by maintaining client's information
		Client cluster	Tackles **statistical heterogeneity** & **system heterogeneity** by grouping clients with similar data distribution or resources before aggregation
		Client selector	Improves **model & system's performance** by selecting high performance client devices
Data collection & preprocessing	Mandatory	Data collector	Collects raw data through sensors or smart devices deployed
		Data preprocessor	Preprocesses raw data
	Optional	Heterogeneous Data Handler	Tackles **statistical heterogeneity** through data augmentation methods
Model training	Mandatory	Model trainer	Trains local model
		Local model evaluator	Evaluates local model performance after each local training round
		Model aggregator	Aggregates local models to produce new global model
	Optional	Multi-task model trainer	Improves **model performance** (personalisation) by adopting multi-task training methods
		Message compressor	Improves **communication efficiency** through message size reduction to reduce bandwidth consumption
		Secure aggregator	Improves **data privacy** & **system security** through different secure multiparty computation protocols
		Asynchronous aggregator	Improves **system performance** by reducing aggregation pending time of late client updates
		Decentralised aggregator	Improves system **reliability** through the removal of single-point-of-failure
		Hierarchical aggregator	Improves **system performance** & tackle **statistical heterogeneity** & **system heterogeneity** by aggregating models from similar clients before global aggregation
		Model co-versioning registry	Improves system's **accountability** by recording the local models associated to each global models to track clients' performances
Model deployment	Mandatory	Model deployer	Deploys completely-trained-models
		Decision maker	Decides model deployment
	Optional	Deployment selector	Improves **model performance** (personalisation) through suitable model users selection according to data or applications
		Incentive registry	Increases clients' **motivatability**
Model monitoring	Mandatory	Model monitor	Monitors model's data inference performance
	Optional	Model replacement trigger	Maintains **system & model performance** by replacing outdated models due to performance degrades

cluster the client devices into groups according to their data distribution, gradient loss, and feature similarities. This design has been used in Google's IFCA algorithm[13], TiFL system[8], and Massachusetts General Hospital's patient system[13]. The side effect of *client cluster* is the extra computation cost caused by client relationship quantification.

The central servers interacts with a massive number of client devices that are both system heterogeneous and statistically heterogeneous. The magnitude of client devices number is also several times larger than that of the distributed machine learning systems [18,24]. To increase the model and system performance, client devices can be selected every round with predefined criteria (e.g., resource, data, or performance) via *client selector* component. This has been integrated into Google's FedAvg [28] algorithm and IBM's Helios [39].

3.2 Data Collection and Preprocessing

Each client device gathers data using different *sensors* through the *data collector* component and process the data (i.e., feature extraction, data cleaning, labeling, augmentation, etc.) locally through the *data preprocessor* component, due to the data-sharing constraint. This is different from centralised or distributed machine learning systems in which the non-IID data characteristic is negligible since the data collected on client devices are usually shuffled and processed on the central server. Thus, within the *data preprocessor*, an optional component *heterogeneous data handler* is adopted to deal with the non-IID and skewed data distribution issue through data augmentation techniques. The known uses of the component include Astraea[14], FAug scheme [14] and Federated Distillation (FD) method [2].

3.3 Model Training

Local Model Training. Once the client receives the job from the central server, the *model trainer* component performs model training based on configured hyperparameters (number of epochs, learning rate, etc.). In the standard federated learning training process proposed by McMahan in [28], only model parameters (i.e., weight/gradient) are mentioned to be sent from the central server, whereas in this reference architecture, the models include not only the model parameters but also the hyperparameters. For multi-task machine learning scenarios, a *multi-task model trainer* component can be chosen to train task-related models to improve model performance and learning efficiency. Multitask Learning is a machine learning approach to transfer and share knowledge through training of individual models. It improves model generalisation by using the domain information contained in the parameters of related tasks as an inductive bias. It does this by learning tasks in parallel while using a shared representation; what is learned for each task can help other tasks be learned

---

[13] https://github.com/felisat/clustered-federated-learning.
[14] https://github.com/mtang724/Self-Balancing-Federated-Learning.

better [7]. In federated learning scenarios, this technique is particularly relevant when faced with non-IID data which can produce personalised model that may outperform the best possible shared global model [18]. This best practice solution is identified based on Google's MultiModel[15] architecture, and Microsoft's MT-DNN[16].

Model Evaluation. The *local model evaluator* component measures the performance of the local model and uploads the model to the *model aggregator* on the central server if the performance requirement is met. In distributed machine learning systems, the performance evaluation on client devices is not conducted locally, and only the aggregated server model is evaluated. However, for federated learning systems, local model performance evaluation is required for system operations such as client selection, model co-versioning, contributions calculation, incentive provision, client clustering, etc.

Model Uploading. The trained local model parameters or gradients are uploaded to the central server for model aggregation. Unlike centralised machine learning systems that performs model training in a central server or distributed machine learning systems that deals with fairly small amount of client nodes, the cost for transmitting model parameters or gradients between the bandwidth-limited client devices and central server is high when the system scales up [18,24]. A *message compressor* component can be added to improve communication efficiency. The embedded pattern are extracted from Google Sketched Update [20], and IBM PruneFL [16].

Model Aggregation. The *model aggregator* formulates the new global model based on the received local models. There are four types of aggregator-related optional components within the *model aggregator* component: *secure aggregator*, *asynchronous aggregator*, *decentralised aggregator*, and *hierarchical aggregator*. A *secure aggregator* component prevents adversarial parties from accessing the models during model exchanges through multiparty computation protocols, such as differential privacy or cryptographic techniques. These techniques provide security proof to guarantee that each party knows only its input and output. For centralised and distributed machine learning settings that practice centralised system orchestration, communication security between clients and server is not the main concern. In contrast, for federated learning settings, this best practices are used in SecAgg [6], HybridAlpha [38], and TensorFlow Privacy Library[17]. *Asynchronous aggregator* is identified from ASO-fed [9], AFSGD-VP [12], and FedAsync [37]. The *asynchronous aggregator* component enables the global model aggregation to be conducted asynchronously whenever a local model update arrives. Similar technique have been

---

[15] https://ai.googleblog.com/2017/06/multimodel-multi-task-machine-learning.html.
[16] https://github.com/microsoft/MT-DNN.
[17] https://github.com/tensorflow/privacy/.

adopted in distributed machine learning approaches such as iHadoop [10] and it is proven that this can effectively reduce the overall training time. The conventional design of a federated learning system that relies on a central server to orchestrate the learning process might lead to a single point of failure. A *decentralise aggregator* performs model exchanges and aggregation in decentralised manner to improve system reliability. The known uses of *decentralised aggregator* include BrainTorrent [31] and FedPGA [15]. Blockchain can be employed as a decentralised solution for federated learning systems. In distributed machine learning systems, p2p network topology is employed to in MapReduce [27] to resolve the single-point-of-failure threat on parameter servers. A *hierarchical aggregator* component can be selected to improve system efficiency by adding an intermediate edge layer to aggregate the model updates from related client devices partially before performing the final global aggregation. This pattern has been adopted by HierFAVG [22], Astraea, and HFL [1].

In addition to aggregator-related optional components, a *model co-versioning registry* component can be embedded within the *model aggregator* component to map all the local models and their corresponding global models. This enables the model provernance and improves system accountability. The *model co-versioning registry* pattern is summarised and adopted from the version control methods in DVC[18], Replicate.ai[19], and Pachyderm[20].

3.4   Model Deployment

After the aggregation, the *global model evaluator* assesses the performance of the global model. One example is TensorFlow Extended (TFX)[21] that provides a model validator function to assess the federated learning model performance. If the global model performs well, the *model deployer* component deploys the global model to the client device for decision-making through the *decision-maker* component. For instance, TensorFlow lite[22] prepares the final validated model for deployment to the client devices for data inference. Within the *model deployer* component, there are two optional components for selection: *deployment selector* and *incentive registry*. The *deployment selector* component examines the client devices and selects clients to receive the global model based on their data characteristics or applications. The *deployment selector* pattern has been applied in Azure Machine Learning[23], Amazon SageMaker[24], and Google Cloud[25] to improve model performance. The incentive registry component maintains all the client devices' incentives based on their contributions

---

[18] https://dvc.org.

[19] https://replicate.ai.

[20] https://www.pachyderm.com.

[21] https://www.tensorflow.org/tfx.

[22] https://www.tensorflow.org/lite.

[23] https://docs.microsoft.com/en-us/azure/machine-learning/concept-model-management-and-deployment.

[24] https://docs.aws.amazon.com/sagemaker/latest/dg/multi-model-endpoints.html.

[25] https://cloud.google.com/ai-platform/prediction/docs/deploying-models.

and agreed rates to motivate clients to contribute to the training. Blockchain has been leveraged in FLChain [3] and DeepChain [36] to build a *incentive registry*.

3.5 Model Monitoring

After the deployment of models for the actual data inference, a *model monitor* keeps track of the model performance continuously. If the performance degrades below a predefined threshold value, the *model replacement trigger* component notifies the *model trainer* for local fine-tuning or sends an alert to the *job creator* for a new model generation. The *model replacement trigger* pattern is identified based on the known uses including Microsoft Azure Machine Learning Designer[26], Amazon SageMaker[27], Alibaba Machine Learning Platform[28].

4 Related Work

The most widely mentioned definition of a reference architecture is defined by Bass et al. [4] as "a reference model mapped onto software elements (that cooperatively implement the functionality defined in the reference model) and the data flow between them. Whereas a reference model divides the functionality, a reference architecture is the mapping of that functionality onto a system decomposition." Nakagawa et al. collected a series of definitions of reference architectures by various researchers and summarised them as follows: "the reference architecture encompasses the knowledge about how to design system architectures of a given application domain. It must address the business rules, architectural styles (sometimes also defined as architectural patterns that address quality attributes in the reference architecture), best practices of software development (architectural decisions, domain constraints, legislation, and standards), and the software elements that support the development of systems for that domain [29]."

Reference architectures for machine learning applications and big data analysis were researched comprehensively. For instance, Pääkkönen and Pakkala proposed a reference architecture of big data systems for machine learning in an edge computing environment [30]. IBM AI Infrastructure Reference Architecture is proposed to be used as a reference by data scientists and IT professionals who are defining, deploying, and integrating AI solutions into an organization [26].

Reference architectures for edge computing systems are also widely studied. For example, H2020 FAR-Edge-project, Edge Computing Reference Architecture 2.0, Intel-SAP Reference Architecture, IBM Edge computing reference architecture, and Industrial Internet Reference Architecture (IIRA) are proposed by practitioners to support the development of multi-tenant edge systems.

---

[26] https://azure.microsoft.com/en-au/services/machine-learning/designer.
[27] https://aws.amazon.com/sagemaker.
[28] https://www.alibabacloud.com/product/machine-learning.

There are existing works proposed to support federated learning system and architecture design. For instance, Google was the earliest to introduce a system design approach for federated learning [5]. A scalable production system for federated learning in the domain of mobile devices, based on TensorFlow described from a high-level perspective. A collection of architectural patterns for the design of federated learning systems are summarised and presented by [25]. There are also many architectures and adoptions of federated learning systems proposed by researchers for diverse applications. For instance, Zhang et al. [40] proposed a blockchain-based federated learning architecture for industrial IoT to improve client motivatability through an incentive mechanism. Samarakoon et al. [32] have adopted federated learning to improve reliability and communication latency for vehicle-to-vehicle networks. Another real-world federated learning adoption by Zhang et al. [41] is a dynamic fusion-based federated learning approach for medical diagnostic image analysis to detect COVID-19 infections. We observed that there have been multiple studies on federated learning from different aspects and their design methods are highly diverse and isolated which makes their proposals challenging to be reproduced.

Motivated by the previous works mentioned above, we intend to fill the research gap by putting forward an end-to-end reference architecture for federated learning systems development and deployment which has been distinctly lacking in the current state-of-the-art.

5   Discussion and Conclusion

A reference architecture can be served as a standard guideline for system designers and developers for quick selection of best practice solutions for their problems, which can be further customised as required. To the best of our knowledge, there is still no reference architecture proposed for an end-to-end federated learning system while many reusable components and patterns have been proposed. Thus, in this paper, we proposed FLRA, a pattern-oriented reference architecture for federated learning system design to increase the real-world adoption of federated learning.

To design the reference architecture, we developed an empirically-grounded qualitative analysis method as the basis of design theory generation. The empirical evidence to support the reference architecture design is a collection of findings (requirements, patterns, and components) gathered and defined by our previous systematic literature review on federated learning and well-known industry practices of machine learning systems.

After developing the reference architecture, we compared it with existing machine learning architectures of Google, Amazon, Microsoft, and IBM to examine its applicability. The key differences between centralised or distributed machine learning with federated learning are the non-IIDness of training data, variation in the data partitioning (e.g., vertical, horizontal, and transfer federated learning) and device partitioning (e.g., cross-device, cross-silo), the ownership and security requirements of different client devices, the system heterogeneity, and the participation of client nodes. The proposed FLRA architecture adopted many reusable machine learning and federated learning patterns while maintaining most of the mandatory machine learning pipeline components. This ensures that the reference architecture is generalised to support the basic model training tasks in the real world.

While there are different constraints when developing a federated learning system for different applications and settings, the possible trade-offs and the pattern solutions to these challenges are discussed comprehensively. The confirmation of theory justified the applicability of FLRA and the patterns associated with the support of empirical evidence collected. Hence, the FLRA proposed is applicable in the real world for a general, end-to-end development of federated learning systems. Our future work will focus on developing an architecture decision model for federated learning system design. We will also work on the architecture design for trust in federated learning systems.

References

1. Abad, M.S.H., Ozfatura, E., GUndUz, D., Ercetin, O.: Hierarchical federated learning across heterogeneous cellular networks. In: ICASSP 2020–2020 IEEE International Conference on Acoustics, Speech and Signal Processing (ICASSP), pp. 8866–8870 (2020)
2. Ahn, J., Simeone, O., Kang, J.: Wireless federated distillation for distributed edge learning with heterogeneous data. In: 2019 IEEE 30th Annual International Symposium on Personal, Indoor and Mobile Radio Communications (PIMRC), pp. 1–6 (2019)
3. Bao, X., Su, C., Xiong, Y., Huang, W., Hu, Y.: Flchain: a blockchain for auditable federated learning with trust and incentive. In: 2019 5th International Conference on Big Data Computing and Communications (BIGCOM), pp. 151–159 (2019)
4. Bass, L., Clements, P., Kazman, R.: Software Architecture in Practice. Addison-Wesley Professional, Boston (2003)
5. Bonawitz, K., et al.: Towards federated learning at scale: System design. arXiv preprint arXiv:1902.01046 (2019)
6. Bonawitz, K., et al.: Practical secure aggregation for privacy-preserving machine learning. Association for Computing Machinery, New York (2017)
7. Caruana, R.: Multitask learning. In: Thrun, S., Pratt, L. (eds.) Learning to Learn, pp. 95–133. Springer, Boston (1998). https://doi.org/10.1007/978-1-4615-5529-2_5
8. Chai, Z., et al.: TiFL: a tier-based federated learning system. In: Proceedings of the 29th International Symposium on High-Performance Parallel and Distributed Computing, HPDC 2020, pp. 125–136. Association for Computing Machinery, New York (2020)
9. Chen, Y., Ning, Y., Slawski, M., Rangwala, H.: Asynchronous online federated learning for edge devices with non-IID data. In: 2020 IEEE International Conference on Big Data (Big Data), pp. 15–24. IEEE (2020)
10. Elnikety, E., Elsayed, T., Ramadan, H.E.: iHadoop: asynchronous iterations for mapreduce. In: 2011 IEEE Third International Conference on Cloud Computing Technology and Science, pp. 81–90 (2011)

11. Galster, M., Avgeriou, P.: Empirically-grounded reference architectures: a proposal. In: Proceedings of the Joint ACM SIGSOFT Conference - QoSA and ACM SIGSOFT Symposium - ISARCS on Quality of Software Architectures - QoSA and Architecting Critical Systems - ISARCS, QoSA-ISARCS 2011, pp. 153–158. Association for Computing Machinery, New York (2011)

12. Gu, B., Xu, A., Huo, Z., Deng, C., Huang, H.: Privacy-preserving asynchronous federated learning algorithms for multi-party vertically collaborative learning. arXiv preprint arXiv:2008.06233 (2020)

13. Huang, L., Shea, A.L., Qian, H., Masurkar, A., Deng, H., Liu, D.: Patient clustering improves efficiency of federated machine learning to predict mortality and hospital stay time using distributed electronic medical records. J. Biomed. Inform. **99**, 103291 (2019)

14. Jeong, E., Oh, S., Kim, H., Park, J., Bennis, M., Kim, S.L.: Communication-efficient on-device machine learning: federated distillation and augmentation under non-IID private data. arXiv preprint arXiv:1811.11479 (2018)

15. Jiang, J., Hu, L.: Decentralised federated learning with adaptive partial gradient aggregation. CAAI Trans. Intell. Technol. **5**(3), 230–236 (2020)

16. Jiang, Y., et al.: Model pruning enables efficient federated learning on edge devices. arXiv preprint arXiv:1909.12326 (2019)

17. Jobin, A., Ienca, M., Vayena, E.: The global landscape of AI ethics guidelines. Nat. Mach. Intell. **1**(9), 389–399 (2019)

18. Kairouz, P., et al.: Advances and open problems in federated learning. arXiv preprint arXiv:1912.04977 (2019)

19. Kitchenham, B., Brereton, O.P., Budgen, D., Turner, M., Bailey, J., Linkman, S.: Systematic literature reviews in software engineering-a systematic literature review. Inf. Softw. Technol. **51**(1), 7–15 (2009)

20. Konečnỳ, J., McMahan, H.B., Yu, F.X., Richtárik, P., Suresh, A.T., Bacon, D.: Federated learning: strategies for improving communication efficiency. arXiv preprint arXiv:1610.05492 (2016)

21. Li, X., Huang, K., Yang, W., Wang, S., Zhang, Z.: On the convergence of FedAvg on non-IID data. arXiv preprint arXiv:1907.02189 (2019)

22. Liu, L., Zhang, J., Song, S.H., Letaief, K.B.: Client-edge-cloud hierarchical federated learning. In: ICC 2020–2020 IEEE International Conference on Communications (ICC), pp. 1–6 (2020)

23. Lo, S.K., Liew, C.S., Tey, K.S., Mekhilef, S.: An interoperable component-based architecture for data-driven IoT system. Sensors **19**(20), 4354 (2019)

24. Lo, S.K., Lu, Q., Wang, C., Paik, H.Y., Zhu, L.: A systematic literature review on federated machine learning: from a software engineering perspective. ACM Comput. Surv. **54**(5), 1–39 (2021)

25. Lo, S.K., Lu, Q., Zhu, L., Paik, H.Y., Xu, X., Wang, C.: Architectural patterns for the design of federated learning systems. arXiv preprint arXiv:2101.02373 (2021)

26. Lui, K., Karmiol, J.: AI Infrastructure Reference Architecture. IBM Systems (2018). https://www.ibm.com/downloads/cas/W1JQBNJV

27. Marozzo, F., Talia, D., Trunfio, P.: P2P-MapReduce: parallel data processing in dynamic cloud environments. J. Comput. Syst. Sci. **78**(5), 1382–1402 (2012). jCSS Special Issue: Cloud Computing 2011

28. McMahan, B., Moore, E., Ramage, D., Hampson, S., Arcas, B.A.: Communication-efficient learning of deep networks from decentralized data. In: Artificial Intelligence and Statistics, pp. 1273–1282. PMLR (2017)

29. Nakagawa, E.Y., Oliveira Antonino, P., Becker, M.: Reference architecture and product line architecture: a subtle but critical difference. In: Crnkovic, I., Gruhn, V., Book, M. (eds.) ECSA 2011. LNCS, vol. 6903, pp. 207–211. Springer, Heidelberg (2011). https://doi.org/10.1007/978-3-642-23798-0_22

30. Pääkkönen, P., Pakkala, D.: Extending reference architecture of big data systems towards machine learning in edge computing environments. J. Big Data **7**(1), 1–29 (2020). https://doi.org/10.1186/s40537-020-00303-y

31. Roy, A.G., Siddiqui, S., Pölsterl, S., Navab, N., Wachinger, C.: Braintorrent: a peer-to-peer environment for decentralized federated learning. arXiv preprint arXiv:1905.06731 (2019)

32. Samarakoon, S., Bennis, M., Saad, W., Debbah, M.: Federated learning for ultra-reliable low-latency V2V communications. In: 2018 IEEE Global Communications Conference (GLOBECOM), pp. 1–7 (2018)

33. Sattler, F., Wiedemann, S., Müller, K.R., Samek, W.: Robust and communication-efficient federated learning from non-I.I.D. data. IEEE Trans. Neural Netw. Learn. Syst. **31**(9), 3400–3413 (2020)

34. Seaman, C.: Qualitative methods in empirical studies of software engineering. IEEE Trans. Software Eng. **25**(4), 557–572 (1999)

35. Wan, Z., Xia, X., Lo, D., Murphy, G.C.: How does machine learning change software development practices? IEEE Trans. Software Eng. 1 (2019)

36. Weng, J., Weng, J., Zhang, J., Li, M., Zhang, Y., Luo, W.: Deepchain: auditable and privacy-preserving deep learning with blockchain-based incentive. IEEE Trans. Dependable Secure Comput. 1 (2019)

37. Xie, C., Koyejo, S., Gupta, I.: Asynchronous federated optimization. arXiv preprint arXiv:1903.03934 (2019)

38. Xu, R., Baracaldo, N., Zhou, Y., Anwar, A., Ludwig, H.: Hybridalpha: an efficient approach for privacy-preserving federated learning. In: Proceedings of the 12th ACM Workshop on Artificial Intelligence and Security, AISec 2019, pp. 13–23. Association for Computing Machinery, New York (2019)

39. Xu, Z., Yu, F., Xiong, J., Chen, X.: Helios: heterogeneity-aware federated learning with dynamically balanced collaboration. arXiv preprint arXiv:1912.01684 (2019)

40. Zhang, W., et al.: Blockchain-based federated learning for device failure detection in industrial IoT. IEEE Internet Things J. **8**(7), 5926–5937 (2021)

41. Zhang, W., et al.: Dynamic fusion-based federated learning for COVID-19 detection. IEEE Internet Things J. 1 (2021)

42. Zhao, Y., Li, M., Lai, L., Suda, N., Civin, D., Chandra, V.: Federated learning with non-IID data. arXiv preprint arXiv:1806.00582 (2018)

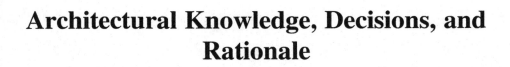

Architectural Knowledge, Decisions, and Rationale

Trace Link Recovery for Software Architecture Documentation

Jan Keim[1]([✉])(iD), Sophie Schulz[1,2](iD), Dominik Fuchß[1](iD), Claudius Kocher[1],
Janek Speit[1], and Anne Koziolek[1](iD)

[1] Karlsruhe Institute of Technology (KIT), Karlsruhe, Germany
{jan.keim,sophie.schulz,dominik.fuchss,koziolek}@kit.edu,
{claudius.kocher,janek.speit}@student.kit.edu
[2] Competence Center for Applied Security Technology (KASTEL),
Karlsruhe, Germany

Abstract. Software Architecture Documentation often consists of different artifacts. On the one hand, there is informal textual documentation. On the other hand, there are formal models of the system. Finding related information in multiple artifacts with different level of formality is often not easy. Therefore, trace links between these can help to understand the system. In this paper, we propose an extendable, agent-based framework for creating trace links between textual software architecture documentation and models. Our framework SWATTR offers different pipeline stages to extract text and model information, identify elements in text, and connect these elements to model elements. In each stage, multiple agents can be used to capture necessary information to automatically create trace links. We evaluate the performance of our approach with three case studies and compare our results to baseline approaches. The results for our approach are good to excellent with a weighted average F_1-Score of 0.72 over all case studies. Moreover, our approach outperforms the baseline approaches on non-weighted average by at least 0.24 (weighted 0.31).

Keywords: Software Architecture Documentation · Trace link recovery · Modeling · Natural language processing · Information retrieval

1 Introduction

The success of a software system is highly dependent on its architecture and the architecture inhibits or enables many of the system's quality attributes [1]. Software architecture defines early design decisions about a system's remaining development, its deployment, and its maintenance. Documenting the architecture is important to capture necessary information for these tasks.

Software Architecture Documentation (SAD) is currently created in two fashions. On the one hand, there are formal models of the system. Modeling systems

© Springer Nature Switzerland AG 2021
S. Biffl et al. (Eds.): ECSA 2021, LNCS 12857, pp. 101–116, 2021.
https://doi.org/10.1007/978-3-030-86044-8_7

helps the architect to track changes in a software architecture and brings additional benefits like early evaluation and simulation to predict performance and other quality attributes [15]. On the other hand, there is informal SAD. In textual informal SAD, knowledge about the system including underlying design decisions are captured. Both are key factors to understand a system and provide essential insight.

However, combining information from both artifact types is challenging. Finding information to a certain part of a system within informal documentation is not always easy, especially in large-scale systems. Vice versa, finding the model realizations from a part of the informal documentation can be time consuming. Therefore, connecting different artifacts using trace links is useful. For example, a part of the formal architecture model like a component changed. As a consequence, you need to find and update information in the informal documentation. However, a common occurrence is different naming in different artifacts [21], therefore, simple search strategies (like string comparisons) do not work. If no explicit trace links exist, identifying all locations that need to be updated can be challenging and time consuming. Additionally, trace links can help finding (in-) consistencies between artifacts, one of our long-term goals (cf. [6]).

In our work, we want to automate trace link recovery between informal textual documentation and formal models. Usually, automated trace link recovery is done for requirements to code and, to the best of our knowledge, has not been done for this case, yet. There are major differences in available information. Compared to architectural models, source code contains more explicit information, e.g., code comments and method bodies that can be used in retrieval (IR) and natural language understanding (NLU) approaches. As a result, many approaches cannot be applied easily and due to lack of information will yield worse results. Therefore, we want to close this gap.

We propose the framework SoftWare Architecture Text Trace link Recovery (SWATTR) for creating trace links between textual informal SAD and formal models. Trace links are created between elements from different artifacts; for example, in Fig. 1, where the *logic component* is realized in the model and mentioned within the text. Trace links are also created between elements where naming is only similar but not exact like between *database* and *SQL Datastore*. Within our approach, we use NLU and IR techniques to identify elements, match these elements and create these trace links.

The SWATTR framework consists of different stages: Text and Model Extraction, Element Identification, and Element Connection. Each stage uses agents to enable extensibility. This way, the framework supports adding further approaches to improve NLU and the recovery of trace links. Furthermore, the framework can be easily extended for further tasks (via additional stages) such as the previously mentioned inconsistency identification.

As a result, our research question is: How accurately can we identify trace links between textual informal SAD and models with our approach? With this work, we make the following contributions: We present an approach for creating trace links between textual informal SAD and formal models. The approach is

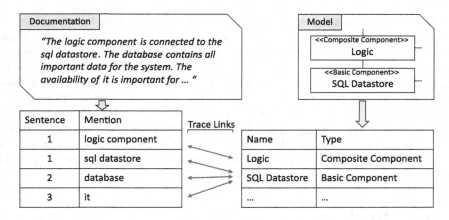

Fig. 1. Textual mentions of architectural elements are collected. Then, they are linked to their corresponding model elements.

embedded in an extendable agent-based framework. We also provide our framework, the results of our experiments, as well as a reproduction package online [7].

2   Related Work

We closely relate to the automated trace link recovery community and the problem of connecting requirement documents to code.

For the task of recovering requirements-to-code trace links, there are many approaches that are based on IR. These IR techniques dominated the trace link recovery scene for more than a decade [2]. Recent approaches like the approach by Rodriguez and Carver [16] report good results by employing machine learning techniques like evolutionary approaches. Rodriguez and Carver, for example, combine two IR metrics and use the *Non-dominated Sorting Genetic Algorithm (NSGA-II)* [3] to explore and find trace links. However, there are different problems regarding these IR approaches, including polysemy of words [20]. Moreover, underlying semantics are often disregarded.

Many more recent approaches try to understand and interpret the semantics more thoroughly, using natural language processing (NLP) and NLU techniques as well as deep learning. For example, Zhang et al. [22] use synonyms and verb-object phrases. They combine these information with structural information to create a similarity score. This score is then used to recover trace links. Guo et al. [4] use word embeddings and recurrent neural networks (RNNs), Wang et al. tackle polysemy to resolve coreferences and find terms with identical meanings [20]. These approaches often use only single measures, a shortcoming that is approached by Moran et al. [12] with a Bayesian hierarchical network. However, such approaches need lots of (training) data. Mills et al. try to face this downside with an active learning approach [10].

Tang et al. present an approach that supports traceability between requirements and architecture design [19]. They define an ontology in which specifications and architectural artifacts can be defined manually. The latter are documented in a semantic wiki. Rempel and Mäder propose traceability metrics in the context of agile development to use graph-based metrics to link requirements and test cases [14]. Building on that, Molenaar et al. propose their RE4SA approach that aims to align requirements and architecture [11]. More specifically, RE4SA creates links between Epic Stories, User Stories, modules, and features.

All these approaches investigate some form of requirements-to-code trace link recovery. However, our goal is to automatically create trace links between SAD and models, which is a slightly different problem.

3   Our Approach

The main goal of our framework SWATTR is the creation of trace links between entities of formal software architecture models and their textual informal architecture documentations. For this, we have different requirements: We want to recover trace links between mentions of a model element in text to the corresponding counterpart in the model(s) (see also Fig. 1). The trace link recovery should be resilient enough to cover slightly different naming, as this is a common occurrence [21]. The framework should base on a very generic metamodel to be independent of specific ones. With this, it can be applied on different kinds of models. Additionally, the framework should have a modular design to enable easy extension. All used mechanisms should be exchangeable or configurable to adapt the framework dynamically based on given contexts. Lastly, we focus, for this paper, on the creation of trace links between text elements and, on the model side, entities like components. This means, we disregard trace links that may link to relations between components, but plan to include such in the future.

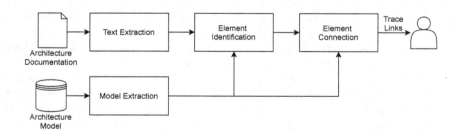

Fig. 2. The core framework consists of multiple sequential steps.

As a result, our framework SWATTR has multiple execution steps (see Fig. 2) that execute different agents. The different steps are the following: *NLP Pre-Processing, Text Extraction, Model Extraction, Element Identification, Element Connection*. At first, the text is analyzed with NLP techniques. This includes, among others, part-of-speech (POS) tagging, sentence splitting, lemmatizing, and dependency parsing. Based on this, the *Text Extraction* runs to extract relevant information from the architecture documentation. Simultaneously, the *Model Extraction* extracts model elements from the architecture model. After both extraction steps, the *Element Identification* uses the extracted information from text and metamodel to identify potential elements in the text. Here, we focus on metamodel information to maintain the possibility to also identify architectural elements in the text that do not occur in the model. Lastly, the *Element Connection* connects identified elements in the text with their counterpart in the model and, thus, creates trace links.

Each step is a module that runs selected analyses. The analyses, as well as their order, are determined by configurations and can be adapted flexibly. Each analysis writes its result in a state that is held by the module, following the blackboard design pattern (cf. [9]). Additionally, every (incoming) information is associated with a confidence, so following steps can use this information.

Consequently, this design only expands promising results (dependent on the analyses) in each subsequent step. Therefore, it is important to explore many possibilities and to not discard viable solutions too early to maintain a high recall, especially in early steps such as the text extraction step. If mentions are wrongly discarded, they will not be considered for trace links. Therefore, we keep less likely options early and each step analyses and filters out very unlikely ones.

With all these measures, we try to ensure good precision and good recall.

Overall, this design leads to a modular, extendable, and exchangeable framework. In the following, we detail each of the steps within our framework.

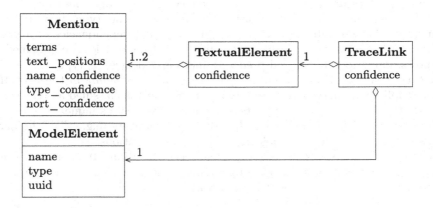

Fig. 3. Model of trace links in our approach

Extracting Text Information. After initial pre-processing with NLP techniques, the text is analyzed for potential mentions. The goal of this processing step is to find out which words or compound terms denote named elements or types of elements (e.g., *component*). The mentions (cf. Fig. 3) are collected in the text extraction's state. Each mention has a confidence for each classification.

Strictly looking at names and types might diminish the performance of succeeding steps, restricting the chance to identify trace links. To approach this problem, our classification approach is more lenient and also classifies mentions that could be either, a name or type (short: *nort*). Since the category *nort* is more generic, not distinct from the others, and ambiguous, *name* and *type* classifications are preferred in later steps.

For example, if an analysis classified with a 70% confidence that *database* is a *nort* and another analysis classifies that the term is with 20% confidence a *name*, the module still prefers the latter as *names* are more specific than *norts*. To ease the handling of different results, mentions also point to their most likely classification. The confidences are saved within the mention and can be used in succeeding steps, for instance, to overrule the classification.

Apart from the classification of mentions, the text extraction step clusters terms based on their word similarity. The underlying assumption here is consistent naming, thus same or similar names within the documentation are used for the same model elements. Thereby, *database* and *datastore* might occur as one entity. A similarity threshold is used to allow case-based fine-tuning for this clustering and can optionally be turned off to disable this behavior altogether.

The following enumeration describes the various analyses and heuristics that we use in this step:

Nouns – Extracts all nouns of the text and classifies them as name-or-type. If a noun occurs in plural, the noun is classified as type.

Incoming Dependencies – Examines the incoming dependencies (obtained by the dependency parser) of a word to classify it as name, type, or nort.

Outgoing Dependencies – Examines the outgoing dependencies of a word. Sources of agent and relative clause modifier dependencies are classified as norts, numeric modifier and predeterminer dependencies as type.

Pattern search – Searches for the pattern *article-type-name* in the text. If a nort follows an *article-name* combination, the nort is classified as type. If an *article-nort-type* pattern appears, the nort is classified as name.

Separators – Searches for terms that contain separators (e.g. "-"). The parts as well as the term as a whole are added to the mentions.

Compound Terms – Searches for name and type mentions. If a nort that is not yet classified as type is followed by a name, a new mention of the compound terms is created. The type detection works analogously.

Extracting Model Information. The model extraction step retrieves instances from the model and saves their name, their type, and a uniquely traceable identifier (see Fig. 3). These attributes can be seen as a generic definition of a model element that our approach builds upon. Exchangeable adapters can extract needed information from different metamodels and transform them into our model element definition. Right now, these attributes are sufficient for the cases we encountered. If necessary, this definition can also be extended.

The applications in our evaluation (cf. Sect. 4) use Palladio Component Models (PCM) [15] as architecture models. To read in models, we first transform them into an ontology using our Ecore2OWL tool[1]. We choose the ontology approach here because we plan to unify the extraction for different metamodels and we plan to extend (pre-) processing with the help of ontologies in future work. An adapter reads in the provided ontology of a PCM and extracts information to create internal representations of model elements. Additional adapters for other metamodels can be implemented similarly.

As an illustration, a PCM contains the basic component *sql datastore*. The model extractor retrieves its name, its type, and its ID using the PCM adapter. Thereby, the internal model element has the name *sql datastore* and the type *basic component* along with its id.

Identifying Elements. This step uses types derived by the model extraction step and mentions from the text extraction step to identify possible elements out of mentions (from text) that should occur in the architecture model. The analyses of this step are independent from the actual model but can use metamodel information. This step also combines different identified mentions (see Fig. 3) to combine names and types.

Take following sentence as example: "The logic entity gets its data from the database component". Here, the text extractor classifies *database* as name and *component* as type and both mentions are combined. The model extractor provides the information that there is the type *basic component*. In this case, the similarity between *component* and *basic component* is close enough to identify the *database component* as potential element. Additionally, the *datastore component* is in the same cluster and, thus, is treated the same.

We use two analyses here: One builds an element whenever a *nort-type* or *type-nort* pattern occurs. The other one creates elements out of compound terms. We additionally add a copy of each element in a *name-type* combination containing only its name to avoid errors due to wrongly combined names and types. This is in line with our paradigm to keep less likely but still valid options.

Because of its independence from the actual model, the results of this step can also be used in future work within an inconsistency analysis to identify elements that are mentioned in text but are missing in the model.

Connecting Elements and Creating Trace Links. In this last step, trace links are created. Here, information from textual processing as well as model processing are combined. We compare elements built out of textual mentions on one side and elements that have been extracted from a model on the other side. There are various agents that contribute to this comparison and an overall confidence for similarity is calculated. Hereby, textual elements and model instances are linked using the terms of the underlying mentions (cf. Fig. 3).

---

[1] https://github.com/kit-sdq/Ecore2OWL.

A trace link is created when the comparison results in a high enough confidence (cf. Fig. 3). Trace links that do not have enough confidence are discarded. Again, the minimum confidence level can be configured. Similar to previous steps, we annotate the confidence of the analysis.

For example, previous steps of the approach have identified *database component* as an potential element and the *database* mention is clustered together with the *datastore*. Moreover, the model extractor retrieved a model element with the name *sql datastore* and the type *basic component*. Depending on the similarity settings, this step links the potential element to the actual model element. Thereby, all clustered occurrences of *database* and *datastore* in the text are linked to the *basic component sql datastore* in the model.

4 Evaluation

In this evaluation, we quantify the performance of our framework and answer our research question: How accurately can we identify trace links between textual SAD and models with our approach? To answer this question, we created gold standards as described in Sect. 4.1 for multiple case studies. We use different metrics to measure the performance; we describe these metrics in Sect. 4.2. Finally, we examine the results and compare them to the results of baseline approaches (see Sect. 4.3).

4.1 Gold Standards

To achieve our evaluation goal, the gold standard declares trace links, each consisting of the ID of a sentence in the documentation and the ID of the corresponding model element. The focus here is to have trace links when model elements are mentioned.

We use several case studies to compare the quality of our approach to others and we created a gold standard for each case study. The first case study is *Mediastore* [18], a Java EE based case study representing a (fictional) digital store to buy and download music. The second case study is *TeaStore* [8], a micro-service reference application representing a web store for tea. The third case study is *Teammates* [13], a platform for managing peer evaluations and other feedback for students.

For each of these case studies, we use existing software architecture documentation. We first remove all figures and images. We also remove semicolons to have clear separations between sentences. We use consecutive sentence numbers as ID for the textual documentation.

For all but Teammates, there was an existing Palladio model[2]. For Teammates, we reverse engineered a repository model from the code and from figures of the architecture overview from the documentation. Although the figures are

---

[2] See   https://sdqweb.ipd.kit.edu/wiki/Media_Store   and   https://github.com/ArDoCo/CaseStudies/tree/master/TeaStore.

close to the documentation text, there are still differences, e.g., in naming. This makes the trace link recovery problem harder and is also more realistic.

We created a trace link between a sentence and a model element if the element was mentioned in the sentence. This also includes coreferences such as "it". Each gold standard was created by multiple authors, disagreements were discussed and resolved. One sentence can contain multiple mentions of model elements, therefore, multiple trace links per sentence can exist.

Table 1 gives an overview of the different case studies regarding their text size, number of model elements that are considered for trace links and number of trace links that are expected. Mediastore and TeaStore are both dense descriptions of the architecture with a comparably high number of trace links per sentence. Teammates is more extensive with many explanations and sentences that do not classify as a trace link.

Table 1. Used case studies with their number of sentences (#Sen.), trace links (#TraceLinks), model elements (#ModelElem.), the max. number of trace links per sentence (MaxTLperSen.) & the number of sentences w/o trace links (#Sen.w/oTL)

	#Sen.	#TraceLinks	#ModelElem.	MaxTLperSen.	#Sen.w/oTL
Mediastore	37	25	14	2	13
TeaStore	43	25	13	2	22
Teammates	198	80	8	7	131

4.2   Metrics

To quantify the results of the approaches, we use the metrics precision, recall, and F_1-Score. For this, we look at the created trace links of the approach and compare them to our gold standards. For a certain trace link, the referenced sentence id and model id must match to form a true positive case. If there is no trace link created by the approach but the gold standard expects one, we count it as false negative. If a trace link is created that is not in the gold standard, we count it as false positive. This also means, for example, if only a trace link is created between sentence 3 and the *logic component* (see Fig. 1) but the gold standard expected the *sql datastore component*, then we have both, a false positive as the link does not exist in the gold standard and a false negative because an expected link is not present.

For trace link recovery in general, recall is seen as more important than precision. According to Hayes et al. [5], analysts are better at detecting false trace links than finding omitted ones. So, a result with higher recall and lower precision is preferable to one with higher precision and lower recall. However, precision has still to be regarded as the additional work for discarding false positives diminishes some of the benefits of automated trace link recovery.

4.3   Results of SWATTR

Different configurations can have a big influence on the results of our approach. We identified the threshold that determines when mentions are clustered (see Sect. 3) as the biggest influence factor. Therefore, we examine the performance of our approach using different thresholds. To examine the influence, we varied the threshold from 0.5 to 1.0 in steps of 0.05. The results are shown in Fig. 4.

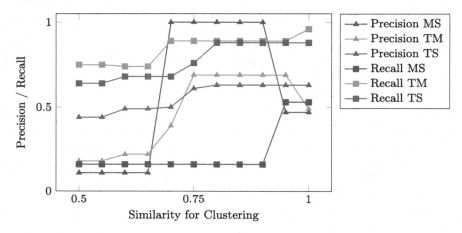

Fig. 4. Evolution of precision and recall in dependence of the similarity configuration for the clustering algorithm for Mediastore (MS), Teammates (TM), and TeaStore (TS)

Our experiments show that recall increases with higher clustering thresholds. If the threshold is set too low, many less similar terms are clustered in few mentions. The reference terms of these mentions might not be similar enough to the names of the model elements. Thereby, trace links are not found and the recall is low. A high threshold above 0.95 results in the best recall.

Looking into the precision, best results can be achieved with threshold values between 0.8 and 0.9. With a low threshold value, many dissimilar terms are collected in a mention. This results in many incorrectly created tracelinks. If the threshold is set too high, slight differences of mentions (e.g. *database* and *datastore*) are not treated as similar anymore.

The influence of the threshold on the F_1-Score can be seen in Fig. 5. Best results are achieved with thresholds between 0.8 and 0.95. The maximum F_1-Scores are 0.73 for TeaStore and 0.78 for Teammates. The performance for Mediastore is slightly worse with a F_1-Score of 0.53 at the best configuration.

According to Hayes et al. [5], the recall for TeaStore and Teammates are excellent and for Mediastore still acceptable. Precision values are good for Mediastore and excellent for TeaStore and Teammates. On average, recall values can be classified as good on the edge to excellent, precision values as excellent. For weighted average, the results can be classified as excellent.

We also looked at the source of errors in case of the best configuration. In the TeaStore case study, model elements, such as *image component*, have similar naming to general terms that were used in the text (e.g., *images*). This kind of mistake causes 46% of the false negatives. Regarding MediaStore, multiple mentions contain names of other model elements because of their similarity (e.g. *MediaManagement* and *UserManagement*). Thus, every found trace link of these mentions adds at least one false positive to the result. This problem causes 69% of the false positives for this case study. Two more issues can be found in the Teammates case study. Since Teammates has a *GAE Database* but often refers to the component as well as other parts of the service as *GAE* the term is hard to distinguish. Additionally, short terms like *GAE* or *Client* can easily be too similar to other terms. The first failure causes 47% of the false positives, the latter 25%. Over all case studies, 57% of false negatives are caused by trace links that are not created due to incorrectly low similarity values. These results indicate that we should refine clustering in the future. We also need to refine our similarity calculation, especially for shorter terms.

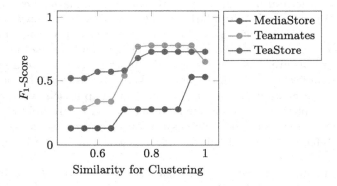

Fig. 5. Evolution of F_1-Score in dependence of the similarity configuration for the clustering algorithm for Mediastore, Teammates, and TeaStore

4.4 Comparison to Other Approaches

To compare our results with other approaches, we re-implemented the approaches by Rodriguez and Carver [16] and Zhang et al. [22]. We choose these approaches because they promise good (state-of-the-art) results. The second major benefit is that these approaches can be adapted to our trace link recovery problem without major problems; most needed information is still present when using models instead of code. In the following, we outline the approaches and our adaptations.

The approach as described by Rodriguez and Carver [16] uses Jaccard similarity and weighted cosine similarity and considers the trace link recovery problem as an optimization problem between these two metrics. They use the *Non-dominated Sorting Genetic Algorithm (NSGA-II)* [3] and create a population consisting of potential trace links, starting with random pairings. In each iteration, a new population is generated out of the best candidates from the previous population. Best candidates are kept and the rest of the population is created using mutation and crossover operators. As a result, the approach is highly reliant on specific configuration settings and randomness for its evolutionary aspect. We see this as a general problem of the approach, as the best configuration and best run cannot be predicted. We can mostly re-use the approach. The sole difference here is the reduced amount of text for the model side compared to code. Therefore, we expect the approach to perform worse compared to the original requirements trace link recovery problem. To cover the random factor of the approach and to identify the maximum performance of the approach, we run experiments 10 times and only select best results. Thus, results will be worse when applying this approach in a non-experimental setting.

For the second baseline approach by Zhang et al. [22], we have to adapt the described approach a little more. The approach uses synonyms, verb-object phrases, and structural information to calculate the similarity between requirements and source code. The similarity is calculated using a vector space model where the vector consists of weights for distinct words and phrases. The weights themselves are calculated based on term frequency and inverse document frequency. The terms are extracted using verb-object phrases in requirements and code and are unified by resolving synonyms. When terms on both sides are similar, a trace link is created. In contrast to the original approach, we have to adapt the verb-object phrase extraction for models and add a threshold for similarity to improve the precision. This worsens the recall slightly, so we run the approach with different threshold values and only select the best run according to the F_1-Score.

The results of our experiments for each case study are listed in Table 2. Additionally, we report two different average values. The first is the average that is calculated on the precision and recall values of the three case studies. The second one, weighted average, is the average that weights the results with the number of trace links that a case study contains. We report both values because there are slightly different semantics within these metrics. The non-weighted average mainly portrays the expected outcome for a project. The weighted average reflects the expected outcome for trace links. For example, a project with lower scores but only a small number of trace links does not affect the weighted average as much. However, both metrics have some bias. As the F_1-Score is the harmonic mean of precision and recall, we calculate the score out of the values for precision and recall, also for the average cases.

Overall, SWATTR outperforms the other approaches in the case studies TeaStore and Teammates. Moreover, our framework has better results on average, both weighted and non-weighted. Only in the Mediastore case study, the

Table 2. Results of trace link recovery for the three case studies and on average (including weighted average) with comparison to baseline approaches using Precision (P), Recall (R), and F_1-Score (F_1).

Approach	Mediastore			TeaStore			Teammates			Average			w. Avg.		
	P	R	F_1	P	R	F_1	P	R	F_1	P	P	F_1	P	R	F_1
SWATTR	.47	**.60**	**.53**	**.63**	**.88**	**.73**	**.69**	**.89**	**.78**	**.60**	**.79**	**.68**	**.64**	**.83**	**.72**
Rodriguez & C.	.07	.32	.12	.10	.20	.13	.10	.15	.12	.09	.22	.13	.10	.19	.13
Zhang et al.	**.76**	.52	**.62**	.35	.28	.31	.49	.30	.37	.53	.37	.44	.52	.34	.41

approach by Zhang et al. slightly outperforms our approach, mostly due to the comparably high precision of their approach for this case study. As mentioned earlier, some model elements are very similar and more direct string comparison metrics without clustering as used by Zhang et al. can perform better here.

5   Discussion and Threats to Validity

Our approach brings a few limitations that are based on current design decisions and assumptions that we made. Currently, our approach is dependent on word-based similarity. Although there are different metrics to calculate word similarity that could be exchanged, there are still few problems: First, if one word is not recognized as similar enough to its modeled counterpart, all of its mentions in the text are ignored. This obviously has a big impact on the performance, especially recall, of our approach. Second, our approach does not differentiate different contexts of mentions yet, which might affect its precision. This limitation is also based on our aforementioned assumption that naming is consistent.

Our framework achieves promising results. Still, there are currently rather simple agents and heuristics in this prototype and further improvements need to be made. However, it is highly questionable, how much impact better and more complex agents will have, given the good results. We want to analyze the structure and properties of documentation more in depth, especially in relation to other models. This way, we want to directly tackle found properties that our approach does not address yet. We also disregard information about relations to trace relations and to find further trace links.

For most parts, the case studies in investigation use similar naming in models and documentation. Therefore, approaches that consider naming and accept slight differences can yield quite good results already. The baseline approach by Rodriguez and Carver (cf. [16]) uses such metrics, but is affected by randomness and, thus, luck. The baseline approach by Zhang et al. (cf. [22]) also performs better when same or very similar terms are used.

In the following, we discuss the threats to validity based on the guidelines for case study research in software engineering by Runeson and Höst [17].

Construct Validity. We applied commonly in the trace link recovery community used experimental designs and metrics to mitigate potential risks regarding the construct validity. However, there might be a certain bias in the selection of the use cases. We used three case studies that have different project size as well as documentation and model size. We selected different kinds of case studies with different architecture styles and patterns. This way, we believe to have reduced the bias and have a representative selection to ensure construct validity. However, these were publicly available open source systems; documentation and models of other or non-open-source projects might differ. Moreover, we only looked at component-based architecture models, which might induce bias in our experimental design. In future work, we will extend our approach and our experiments to further architecture description languages to avoid this.

Internal Validity. In our case studies, we analyzed the provided documentation texts and compared it to models to create trace links. This assumes that both artifacts contain the same consistent information. Consequentially, this disregards inconsistencies between the different artifacts and further inabilities to properly map the documentation to the models. This also disregards that the abstraction level of the artifacts might be vastly different, thus a linking is less useful or applicable. We countered this factor by selecting case studies where the models and the documentation have similar abstraction and are well mappable for humans. This reduces the probability that other factors affect the investigation.

External Validity. In our evaluation, we examined three different case studies. Two of which originate from research. Teammates is used in practice, but also originates from a university context. With these three case studies, we risk that not all aspects and facets of the trace link recovery problem for SAD are covered. We carefully chose the cases studies, but documentation might differ for other projects or organizations and therefore our results might differ as well. One property of these case studies is that the naming within the textual documentation is close to the naming in the models. This should be the ideal case, but inconsistent language and naming is one of the main types of inconsistencies that practitioners encounter in practice [21]. In our datasets, there is slightly inconsistent naming present, but it is unclear how representative this is overall.

Reliability. For our experiments, we had to derive a gold standard for trace links in these projects ourselves. Multiple researchers each created independently a gold standard for our case studies. These gold standards where combined and the few occurring differences were discussed. This way, we tried to minimize a bias from a single researcher. However, there still can be a certain bias.

6 Conclusion and Future Work

Trace links between textual software architecture documentation and architectural models are important for tracing (in-) consistency or tracking changes. However, recovering these trace links to connect the different artifacts is not trivial and has, to the best of our knowledge, not been done, yet. In this paper, we presented the framework SWATTR for recovering trace links between these artifacts. The framework consists of multiple execution steps: Finding mentions in text, loading and analyzing provided models, identifying textual elements for potential trace links, and finally creating the actual trace links. In each step, there are different agents to provide different required analyses. This approach also allows us to flexibly add further analysis methods.

We evaluated our approach using three case studies for which we created gold standards. We calculated precision, recall, and F_1-Score for each approach. Here, our approach achieves an average F_1-Score of 0.68 (weighted 0.72) outperforming the other approaches. The average F_1-Score is 0.24 (weighted 0.31) higher than the next best baseline approach. The results of our approach are overall good to excellent according to the classification schema of Hayes et al. [5].

To overcome the identified limitations and to improve the performance of our approach, we plan to add more analyses in every step. With more specific analyses, precision as well as the recall could be increased. Especially in case of mentions, a context based disambiguation could be helpful.

We also want to look more deeply into considering and tracing relations. This can be useful, for example, to find where and how exactly the relation between two components is realized. Moreover, relations could ease the identification of trace links or help with verifying found ones.

Moreover, we want to extend our framework and combine it with other approaches. This way, we hope to improve the overall results. The most difficult research question in this regard is how to combine or select results. One basic strategy for this is to use results with most support, for example because two out of three approaches created a certain trace link. However, we also want to explore whether there are other combination strategies that can improve the overall performance of our framework.

Lastly, we want to use our framework to recognize inconsistencies between text and model. A low hanging fruit here is to classify elements in the text that could not be connected to the model as potential inconsistency.

Acknowledgment. This work was supported by the Competence Center for Applied Security Technology (KASTEL Project 46.23.01).

References

1. Bass, L., Clements, P., Kazman, R.: Software Architecture in Practice. Addison-Wesley Professional, Upper Saddle River (2003)
2. Borg, M., Runeson, P., Ardö, A.: Recovering from a decade: a systematic mapping of information retrieval approaches to software traceability. Empir. Softw. Eng. **19**(6), 1565–1616 (2013). https://doi.org/10.1007/s10664-013-9255-y
3. Deb, K., Pratap, A., Agarwal, S., Meyarivan, T.: A fast and elitist multiobjective genetic algorithm: NSGA-II. IEEE Trans. Evol. Comput. **6**(2), 182–197 (2002). https://doi.org/10.1109/4235.996017
4. Guo, J., Cheng, J., Cleland-Huang, J.: Semantically enhanced software traceability using deep learning techniques. In: 2017 IEEE/ACM 39th ICSE, pp. 3–14 (2017)

5. Hayes, J.H., Dekhtyar, A., Sundaram, S.K.: Advancing candidate link generation for requirements tracing: the study of methods. IEEE Trans. Software Eng. **32**(1), 4 (2006)

6. Keim, J., Koziolek, A.: Towards consistency checking between software architecture and informal documentation. In: 2019 IEEE ICSA, pp. 250–253 (2019)

7. Keim, J., Schulz, S., Fuchß, D., Speit, J., Kocher, C., Koziolek, A.: SWATTR Reproduction Package (2021). https://doi.org/10.5281/zenodo.4730621

8. von Kistowski, J., Eismann, S., Schmitt, N., Bauer, A., Grohmann, J., Kounev, S.: TeaStore: a micro-service reference application for benchmarking, modeling and resource management research. In: IEEE 26th MASCOTS, pp. 223–236 (2018)

9. Lalanda, P.: Two complementary patterns to build multi-expert systems. In: Pattern Languages of Programs. vol. 25 (1997)

10. Mills, C., Escobar-Avila, J., Bhattacharya, A., Kondyukov, G., Chakraborty, S., Haiduc, S.: Tracing with less data: active learning for classification-based traceability link recovery. In: 2019 IEEE ICSME, pp. 103–113 (2019)

11. Molenaar, S., Spijkman, T., Dalpiaz, F., Brinkkemper, S.: Explicit alignment of requirements and architecture in agile development. In: Madhavji, N., Pasquale, L., Ferrari, A., Gnesi, S. (eds.) REFSQ 2020. LNCS, vol. 12045, pp. 169–185. Springer, Cham (2020). https://doi.org/10.1007/978-3-030-44429-7_13

12. Moran, K., et al.: Improving the effectiveness of traceability link recovery using hierarchical Bayesian networks. In: ICSE 2020, pp. 873–885. ACM (2020)

13. Rajapakse, D.C., et al.: Teammates (2021). https://teammatesv4.appspot.com

14. Rempel, P., Mäder, P.: Estimating the implementation risk of requirements in agile software development projects with traceability metrics. In: Fricker, S.A., Schneider, K. (eds.) REFSQ 2015. LNCS, vol. 9013, pp. 81–97. Springer, Cham (2015). https://doi.org/10.1007/978-3-319-16101-3_6

15. Reussner, R.H., et al.: Modeling and Simulating Software Architectures: The Palladio Approach. MIT Press, Cambridge (2016)

16. Rodriguez, D.V., Carver, D.L.: Multi-objective information retrieval-based NSGA-II optimization for requirements traceability recovery. In: 2020 IEEE EIT, pp. 271–280. https://doi.org/10.1109/EIT48999.2020.9208233. ISSN 2154-0373

17. Runeson, P., Höst, M.: Guidelines for conducting and reporting case study research in software engineering **14**(2), 131. https://doi.org/10.1007/s10664-008-9102-8

18. Strittmatter, M., Kechaou, A.: The media store 3 case study system (2016). https://doi.org/10.5445/IR/1000052197

19. Tang, A., Liang, P., Clerc, V., van Vliet, H.: Traceability in the co-evolution of architectural requirements and design. In: Avgeriou, P., Grundy, J., Hall, J.G., Lago, P., Mistrík, I. (eds.) Relating Software Requirements and Architectures, pp. 35–60. Springer, Heidelberg (2011). https://doi.org/10.1007/978-3-642-21001-3_4

20. Wang, W., Niu, N., Liu, H., Niu, Z.: Enhancing automated requirements traceability by resolving polysemy. In: IEEE 26th RE, pp. 40–51 (2018)

21. Wohlrab, R., Eliasson, U., Pelliccione, P., Heldal, R.: Improving the consistency and usefulness of architecture descriptions: guidelines for architects. In: 2019 IEEE ICSA, pp. 151–160 (2019). https://doi.org/10.1109/ICSA.2019.00024

22. Zhang, Y., Wan, C., Jin, B.: An empirical study on recovering requirement-to-code links. In: 17th IEEE/ACIS SNPD, pp. 121–126 (2016)

An Exploratory Study on Architectural Knowledge in Issue Tracking Systems

Mohamed Soliman[1]([✉]) [ID], Matthias Galster[2] [ID], and Paris Avgeriou[1] [ID]

[1] University of Groningen, Groningen, Netherlands
{m.a.m.soliman,p.avgeriou}@rug.nl
[2] University of Canterbury, Christchurch, New Zealand
mgalster@ieee.org

Abstract. Software developers use issue trackers (e.g. Jira) to manage defects, bugs, tasks, change requests, etc. In this paper we explore (a) how architectural knowledge concepts (e.g. architectural component behavior, contextual constraints) are textually represented in issues (e.g. as adjectives), (b) which architectural knowledge concepts commonly occur in issues, and (c) which architectural knowledge concepts appear together. We analyzed issues in the Jira issue trackers of three large Apache projects. To identify "architecturally relevant" issues, we linked issues to architecturally relevant source code changes in the studied systems. We then developed a code book by manually labeling a subset of issues. After reaching conceptual saturation, we coded remaining issues. Our findings support empirically-grounded search tools to identify architectural knowledge concepts in issues for future reuse.

Keywords: Software architecture · Architecture design decisions · Architecture knowledge · Issue tracking systems · Software engineering

1 Introduction

Architectural design decisions (ADDs) about software components, their dependencies and behavior are one of the most significant types of ADDs [1] made by practitioners [14]. For example, an enterprise application could have multiple ADDs regarding the components in each layer and dependencies between them. In the Architectural Knowledge (AK) ontology of Kruchten et al. [11], ADDs related to component design are identified as *structural ADDs* (SADDs).

Making SADDs, requires AK [11] about important quality attributes and their trade-offs, and about instantiating architectural solutions (e.g. patterns or tactics). Without the required AK, software engineers might make uncertain and risky assumptions about the ADDs. However, this AK is mostly acquired through experience with multiple different projects within the same domain [26].

M. Soliman—We would like to thank ITEA3 and RVO for their support under grant agreement No. 17038 VISDOM (https://visdom-project.github.io/website).

S. Biffl et al. (Eds.): ECSA 2021, LNCS 12857, pp. 117–133, 2021.
https://doi.org/10.1007/978-3-030-86044-8_8

If one does not have such experience, one needs to be able to search and locate the pertinent AK.

One potential source of AK is issue tracking systems (e.g. Jira): previous research has shown that software engineers share some AK (e.g. previously made ADDs) in issues [3,18]. Developers create issues to discuss and manage defects, tasks, change requests, etc. However, similar to other sources of AK (e.g. developer communities [19,20] or simply Google searching [23]), it is challenging to manually recognize and re-use AK within issue tracking systems. First, the majority of issues do not discuss architectural problems [3]; instead, they focus on detailed development problems (e.g. bug fixing or testing). Second, text in issues is not explicitly structured and classified; rather, AK is represented as unstructured text within an issue's description, comments and attachments.

Recently, there has been research work on automatic mining of AK from issues: there are studies that identify types of ADDs [3] and types of architectural issues [18]. However, they do not explore **AK concepts** (i.e. conceptual elements that describe and characterize AK), such as *types of architectural solutions* (e.g. components behavior and tactics) [10,28], *decision factors* like constraints, and *decision rationale* [25] like assumptions, benefits and drawbacks of solutions [21]. Moreover, current studies [3] limit their analysis to issue descriptions which are only a small part of the whole issue (often the shortest) without exploring comments in issues or attachments. Finally, current studies do not explore how AK concepts are textually represented (e.g. using adjectives or explicit keywords) in issues. These three limitations make it nearly impossible to determine AK concepts in architectural issues, and prevent approaches to find, capture and re-use AK from issue tracking systems.

We contribute in addressing these shortcomings by *exploring the different AK concepts for making SADDs and their representation in architectural issues* (see research questions in Sect. 3). We look at the entire issue, instead of only its description. Achieving this goal supports automating AK capturing approaches with concrete representations for AK concepts. Moreover, it supports determining the most suitable scenarios for re-using AK from issue tracking systems (e.g. when searching for alternative solutions or comparing solutions).

To achieve this goal, we conduct a case study on three large Apache projects. We analyze *architecturally relevant* issues from the projects' issue tracker. The issues are first identified by static analysis of the source code of the projects, and then the textual contents of issues are verified as architecturally relevant and analyzed to explore their contained AK concepts (see Sect. 3). In summary, our study leads to the following contributions:

- A corpus of 98 architectural issues, and 3,937 annotations for AK concepts. This helps future research, e.g. using machine learning to capture AK.
- Common textual variants for each AK concept in architectural issues. This is useful to identify and search for AK concepts in issue tracking systems.
- A list of the most discussed AK concepts in issue tracking systems. This supports identifying scenarios in which AK from issues can be re-used.

– Common co-occurrences of different AK concepts in architectural issues. This supports capturing relationships between AK concepts from these issues.

The paper is structured as follows: In Sect. 2, we provide a background on relevant AK concepts. In Sect. 3, we explain our research questions and steps. We then present our results in Sects. 4, 5 and 6, which are subsequently discussed in Sect. 7. The threats to validity and related work are discussed in Sects. 8 and 9, while the paper is concluded in Sect. 10.

2   Background - Architectural Knowledge Concepts

In this section, we give an overview of AK concepts in the literature, which are relevant to this study. We consider AK concepts from different studies, because there is no comprehensive ontology with all AK concepts. Each concept is represented by an abbreviation, that is used in the rest of the paper.

Software engineers consider different *decision factors* [1, 21]:

– *Requirements and constraints* (REQ) could be *quality attribute requirements*, such as performance, maintainability, security [1], *user functional requirements*, such as use cases and user stories, or *contextual constraints* such as external systems or constraints from managers [1].
– *Architecture of existing system* (EXA) may constrain new ADDs [8].
– *Quality issues of existing system* (EXQ) can involve *run-time quality issues* (e.g. performance issues) or *technical debt items* (e.g. architectural smells). While REQ may represent the target value for a quality requirement, EXQ is the current value that needs improvement (e.g. security vulnerabilities).

Furthermore, ADDs require deciding on one or more *architectural solutions* [28]. These could have several types, such as:

– *Architectural component behavior* (CB) describes the behavior of an architecture component, including the implemented logic and complexity [19].
– *Architectural configuration* (CONF) describes the dependencies of components [13, 19].
– *Architectural tactics* (TAC) address specific quality attributes, for example, caching data (tactic) improves performance [1].

Finally, ADDs should be based on a certain *rationale* [25] (i.e. the reason for selecting architectural solutions). This involves several AK concepts:

– *Architectural solution benefits and drawbacks* (ABD) describe strengths and weaknesses for certain architectural solutions [21].
– *Assumptions* (ASSUM) capture facts which are assumed without proof when deciding on an architectural solution [27].
– *Trade-offs* (TRO) describe balanced analysis of what is an appropriate option after prioritizing and weighing different design options [25].
– *Risks* (RIS) capture considerations about uncertainties of design options [25].

3 Study Design

3.1 Research Questions

To achieve our goal, we ask the following research questions:

- (**RQ1**) *How are AK concepts textually represented within architectural issues that discuss SADDs?* Since AK concepts (Sect. 2) are high-level conceptual entities, their textual representation could come in multiple different forms. Determining how AK concepts are actually represented (e.g. using certain keywords or adjectives) in architectural issues can support improving the accuracy of automatically identifying AK concepts.
- (**RQ2**) *Which AK concepts are commonly used by practitioners within architectural issues to discuss SADDs?* While researchers have empirically explored several AK concepts (Sect. 2) and how they are used by practitioners (e.g. on Stack Overflow [19]), it is unknown which AK concepts are shared in issue tracking systems to make SADDs. Identifying AK concepts, which are commonly discussed in issues, is useful in determining scenarios to re-use the AK in architectural issues.
- (**RQ3**) *Which AK concepts co-occur with each other when discussing SADDs in architectural issues?* The discussion of SADDs in an issue, often does not pertain to a single AK concept, but may involve multiple related AK concepts. Conceptual relationships between AK concepts in ADDs have been discussed in literature (e.g. [10,28]). However, it is unknown how practitioners use different AK concepts together to discuss SADDs in architectural issues. Determining common co-occurrences between AK concepts provides contextual relationships between the different AK concepts. These are important to support capturing related AK concepts from architectural issues.

3.2 Research Process

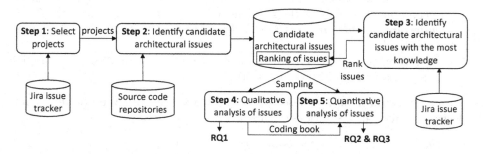

Fig. 1. Research steps

We followed five steps (see Fig. 1) as explained in the following sub-sections.

Step 1 - Select Projects: We selected Apache Java projects, similarly to previous research on AK in issues [3,18], and based on the following criteria:

1. *Larger than 200 KLOC*: This is to ensure sufficiently large projects with a sufficient number of architectural issues.
2. *Use of Jira*: Jira is a commonly used issue tracking system. It also provides useful features for managing issues (e.g. an API to download issues).
3. *Traceability between code commits and issues*: To identify candidate architectural issues (Step 2) based on links between code commits and issues, we require that issue IDs are used in commit messages of the code repository.
4. *Sufficient knowledge within issues*: Not all Apache projects discuss decisions within issues. Some projects use other communication methods (e.g. mailing lists). Thus, we have to ensure that Jira not only lists tasks, but also communications. We calculated the average number of comments within issues for each project, and the percentage of issues with no comments (i.e. no discussions in issues). We then ranked projects (available online[1]) to identify projects with the most issues and the most comments within issues.

We selected the top three Apache projects from the resulted ranking in the fourth criterion (with the most issues and comments in issues): Apache Hadoop, Cassandra, and Tajo.

Step 2: Identify Candidate Architectural Issues: Some issues involve architectural changes [18]. However, most issues in tracking systems do not trigger architectural changes [18], because they involve small changes within components (e.g. small bug fixes). Thus, we need to identify the issues which trigger architectural changes. This has been addressed previously in different ways:

1. *Top-down*: Bhat et al. [3] manually analyze issues to determine if they involve discussions on architectural decisions. This requires significant effort, because of the sheer volume of issues (e.g. Hadoop has more than 50,000 issues). Thus, the selected architectural issues based on this approach might not be representative for the most significant architectural issues.
2. *Bottom-up*: Shahbazian et al. [18] analyze source code, and construct dependency graphs for consecutive versions of a project. Differences between dependency graphs are compared to assess if changes within each version are architectural. The source code versions are then traced back to issues to identify architectural issues. The approach can effectively identify candidates for architectural issues. However, inaccuracy in the assessment of architectural changes might miss architectural issues or identify false positives.

Similar to Shahbazian et al. [18], we follow a bottom-up approach to identify candidate architectural issues with the most architectural changes. However, we further filtered issues with the most AK and to reduce false positives. In detail, we followed three steps to identify candidate architectural issues:

1. *Construct dependency graphs from source code*: We used Arcan's system reconstructor [6] to create dependency graphs (one graph for each version) between classes and packages of the three projects.

---

[1] github.com/m-a-m-s/ECSA-2021.

2. *Estimate architectural changes*: We compared the dependency graph of each version with the dependency graph of its preceding version and determined added or removed Java packages, added or removed dependencies between packages and changes in the allocations of classes to packages. We chose Java packages as architectural components, because they have been explicitly designed by the developers. Moreover, packages are at a higher abstraction level than classes. Thus, changes at package level are likely more architectural than changes at class level. To compare the architecture of two consecutive versions we calculated the Architecture-to-Architecture (a2a) metric [2]:

   (a) Calculate *Minimum Transform Operation (MTO)* for two consecutive versions in a repository. The MTO between two versions is the sum of added packages, removed packages, added dependencies, removed dependencies and the number of re-allocated classes between packages.

   (b) Calculate the a2a metric [2] for each version in a repository as the percentage of MTO for a certain version compared to the size of the architecture (i.e. total number of packages, dependencies and classes).

   The a2a metric has been previously used by Shahbazian et al. [18], and can provide a reliable estimation for the size of architectural changes.

3. *Filter and rank architectural issues*: We identified versions in source code repositories with a2a > 0 and identified related issues. Issues have been discovered by following the traceability links (Jira issue ID's, e.g. TAJO-88, used in commit messages on GitHub) between versions in GitHub and issues in Jira. We have identified 2,575 candidate architectural issues (from over 28,000 issues in the three projects), which are responsible for possible architectural changes. The candidate architectural issues are shared online[2].

Step 3: Identify Candidate Architectural Issues with Most AK: From the 2575 candidate architectural issues, we need to select those that contain actual AK and of sufficient quantity. Thus, we identified the issues with the most AK based on three steps:

1. *Identify parent issues and sub-task issues*: For all candidate architectural issues (Step 2), we identified their parent issue (if the issue is a sub-task), and their sub-task issues (if the issue is a parent issue).

2. *Estimate amount of AK per issue*: For all candidate architectural issues (Step 2), their parents and sub-tasks, we counted the number of words, considering issue description, comments and attachments (e.g. pdf documents).

3. *Rank candidate architectural issues*: We ranked issues per project according to their architectural significance (based on the a2a metric from Step 2) and the amount of knowledge per issue (based on the number of words per issue). The ranked issues present the population from which a sample of issues are selected for analysis in Step 4 and another sample in Step 5.

Step 4: Qualitative Analysis of AK Concepts in Issues: To answer RQ1, we analyzed a sample of issues with the most AK from the ranked list of candidate architectural issues (from Step 3) qualitatively. We followed deductive category assignment content analysis as defined by Mayring [12]:

---

[2] github.com/m-a-m-s/ECSA-2021.

1. *Identify AK concepts from literature*: To identify AK concepts, we needed a category system based on existing literature. Thus, we reviewed literature in the field of AK and identified AK concepts (Sect. 2). The AK concepts and their definition were the starting point for the coding book.

2. *Preliminary coding to create initial coding book*: The first two authors annotated independently a sample of architectural issues with the AK concepts identified from literature. Before annotating an issue, we manually validated that an issue is actually an architectural issue, and that it contains AK. During annotation, we followed two *annotation rules*:
   - We annotated AK concepts (Sect. 2) as clauses or sentences or paragraphs, because AK concepts do not appear as single words.
   - We ignored all textual segments with no relationship to AK concepts, such as code examples and test executions.

   For each issue, the first two authors compared annotations and discussed differences in meetings. After each meeting, we refined the coding book with concrete definitions and examples for each AK concept. Our aim was to operationalize abstract AK concepts (from literature) into concrete definitions (in the issues). After several iterations and annotating 20 randomly selected issues from the sample with more than 300 annotations, we reached theoretical saturation (i.e. no new AK concepts appeared in issues).

3. *Identify textual variants of AK concepts in issues*: Based on the preliminary coding, we identified textual variants for each AK concept to answer RQ1. For example, benefits and drawbacks of solutions are expressed explicitly using certain keywords (e.g. advantages) or adjectives. Moreover, we added the textual variants for each AK concept to the coding book. This supports other researchers to annotate the same AK concepts reliably. The most common textual variants for each AK concept are presented in Sect. 4.

Step 5: Quantitative Analysis of AK Concepts in Issues: To answer RQ2 and RQ3, we performed the following steps:

1. *Expand annotations to ensure statistical significance*: We provided the coding book (from the previous two steps) to two independent researchers to annotate AK concepts in selected architectural issues from the population of candidate architectural issues. We randomly selected issues proportional to their ranking in the list of candidate issues (from Step 3). This method of sampling supports selecting issues with the most AK to ensure exploring AK concepts. The first author explained the coding book to the two researchers who followed the same annotation rules as in the preliminary coding. In several iterations, a sample of issues were independently annotated by the first author to ensure agreement. Disagreements were discussed to ensure understanding of the coding book. Before annotating an issue, the first author checked its architectural relevance.

   To answer RQ2 and RQ3, we need to ensure that the number of annotations is sufficient for higher confidence level and lower error margin. However, some issues involve lots of discussions and thus can involve hundreds of annotations,

Table 1. Variants of most common **decision factors** AK concepts

AK concepts and variants	Description and examples
Quality attribute as one type of requirements (REQ)	
├─Explicitly	Uses common quality attribute-related terms like "extensibility" or "performance". For example: *"This improves the code **readability** and **maintainability**"* [TAJO-121]
├─Implicitly using adjectives	Describes the quality of certain system or component using adjectives. For example *"For the sake of **efficient** join order enumeration,..."* [TAJO-229] could point to performance.
Existing system quality (EXQ)	
├─Negation of quality	Refers to a component of a system with negation keywords and adjectives. For example, *"It is rather **complicated** and **does not** guarantee data recoverability"* [HADOOP-702]
├─Explicit quality issues	Describes well-known quality issues using their terms explicitly For example, *"The dependencies between them should be enforced to avoid **cyclic dependencies**. At present they all have **dependencies on each other**"* [HADOOP-3750]

while others are nearly empty. Thus, we had to first estimate the possible number of annotations in our population of candidate architectural issues. We did this by dividing the total number of words ($\approx$20 millions words) in all candidate architectural issues (from Step 3) by the average size of each annotation ($\approx$25 words, see Sect. 5). Thus, the estimated number of annotations in the whole population is $\approx$800,000 annotations. Accordingly, we created a statistically significant sample size [15] of 3,937 annotations with 95% confidence level and 1.6% error margin. The annotations are created from 98 architectural issues with the most architectural significance and most AK inside them.

2. *Analyze annotations to answer research questions*: For RQ2 we counted the number of annotations for each AK concept. To determine their sizes, we counted words after removing stop-words. For RQ3 we counted the number of co-occurrences of annotations (for each AK concept) which occur together in either an issue description or comment. We then tested the significance of each co-occurrence of AK concepts using a $\tilde{\chi}^2$ test [16]. For example, for the AK concepts *Benefits and drawbacks (ABD)* and *Component behavior (CB)*, we considered frequencies for the following four situations: 1) Text annotated as ABD co-occur with annotations for CB. 2) Text annotated as ABD co-occur with annotations other than CB. 3) Text annotated with AK concepts other than ABD co-occur with annotations for CB. 4) Text annotated with AK concept other than ABD co-occur with annotations other than CB. We excluded co-occurrences with $\tilde{\chi}^2 < 10$ to ensure that all co-occurrences were statistically significant at p-value < 0.05. The significant co-occurrences between AK concepts are presented in Sect. 6.

Table 2. Variants of most common **rationale** AK concepts

AK concepts and variants	Description and examples
Benefits and drawbacks (ABD)	
Explicitly	Using terms like "advantages", "limitations', etc. For example "*Keeping things config-file based has two **drawbacks**:...*" [CASSANDRA-44].
Using adjectives	Adjectives could be generic like "good", "ugly", etc. For example, "*it would be a **fragile** solution to the identified problem*" [HADOOP-1053]. It could also be more related to special quality attribute. For example "*The serialization mechanism proposed so far is...so **general***" [HADOOP-1986].
Using quality measurement	Expressing special quality measurements. For example, "*We can do group by aggregations on **billions of rows with only a few milliseconds***" [TAJO-283].
Problems in a solution	Problems which are a consequence from using a particular solution. For example "*multiget-within-a-single-row still **has all the problems*** of multiget-across-rows...it doesn't parallelize across machines" [CASSANDRA-2710].
Assumptions (ASSUM)	
Explicitly	Explicit references to assumptions, e.g., the word "assumption" or synonyms. For example, "***Assume** that Jobs and interfering cache updates won't occur concurrently*" [HADOOP-288]
Using uncertainty terms	Uncertain and vague terms, such as "I think", "it might'". For example, "***I think**, saving values would limit fexibility of the cache interface...*" [CASSANDRA-3143]

4   RQ1: Representation of AK Concepts in Issues

Based on the analysis of architectural issues (see Sect. 3), we identified the representation of AK concepts in terms of common textual variants for each AK concept. The most frequent textual variants for the most common AK concepts (see Sect. 5) are explained in Tables 1, 2, and 3. Further variants are provided online[3]. Some of the decision factors (Table 1) and rationale AK concepts (Table 2) occur explicitly or implicitly. The explicit variants can be easily identified, because they depend on the occurrence of certain keywords (e.g. "performance" for quality attributes or "advantage" for benefits and drawbacks). Implicit variants are more difficult to distinguish, since they rely on a combinations of words, which must appear together in a certain context to deliver the meaning of the AK concept. For example, both quality attributes and benefits and drawbacks could be expressed using adjectives. However, benefits and drawbacks are expressed in combination with a certain architectural solution, while quality attributes are expressed in relation to certain requirements. This presents a challenge to accurately identify AK concepts.

We also observed domain-specific terms in some of the variants to describe the architecture solutions (Table 3). For example, optimization of queries is a core

---

[3] github.com/m-a-m-s/ECSA-2021.

functionality in Apache Tajo, and the term "optimizer" refers to an architectural component. This might not be the case in other systems, where an optimizer might be a tool to improve source code. Thus, AK in architectural issues depends strongly on the domain and context. This poses a challenge in finding AK in issue trackers, which describes the architecture components of a system.

Table 3. Variants of most common **architectural solutions** AK concepts

AK concepts and variants	Description and examples
Architectural component behavior (CB)	
─Approach	Describes the main approach (e.g. algorithm) on which behavior of component is based. For example "*So the* **approach** *I propose is...to iterate through the key space on a per-CF basis, compute a hash...*" [CASSANDRA-193].
─Sub-components	Describes sub-components (e.g. interfaces or data structures) which implement the component's behavior, e.g. "*This optimizer will* **provide the interfaces** *for join enumeration algorithms and rewrite rules*" [TAJO-24 attachment].
Architectural design configuration (CONF)	
─Static dependencies	Dependencies between components independent of their sequence. The dependencies can use connector verbs such as "access" and "obtain" [19]. For example "*a management tool to* **contact** *every node via JMX*" [CASSANDRA-44].
─Dynamic dependencies	Sequence of interactions between components, for example "*YARN mode 1. TajoClient request query to TajoMaster. 2. YarnRMClient request QueryMaster(YARN Application Master)...*" [TAJO-88 attachment]

5   RQ2: Prominent AK Concepts in Issues

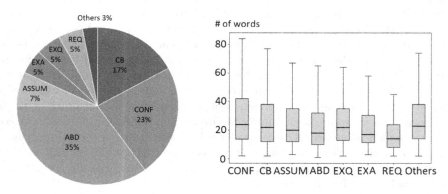

(a) % of annotations for each AK concept   (b) Size of annotations for each AK concept

Fig. 2. The amount and size of annotations for each AK concept

Figure 2 shows the percentages of annotations related to each AK concept, as well as their size (number of words). There are no significant differences in the percentages or sizes of annotations among issue descriptions and issue comments. Issues tend to include AK regarding proposed architectural solutions ($\approx40\%$) and their rationale ($>40\%$) more frequently than decision factors ($\approx15\%$). AK regarding architectural solutions focuses mainly on components behavior (CB) and architectural configurations (CONF), which align with the scope of this paper to explore SADDs. The benefits and drawbacks (ABD) of architectural solutions dominate the rationale of ADDs in architectural issues, followed by Assumptions (ASSUM). However, trade-offs and risks are rarely shared in architectural issues. Also, descriptions of architectural solutions (i.e. CONF and CB) tend to be larger than their rationale (i.e. ABD and ASSUM). This means that developers describe their architectural solutions extensively, but provide brief justifications for decisions.

Most decision factors are about the architecture (EXA) and quality issues (EXQ) of an existing system (both $\approx10\%$). Discussions on requirements and constraints (REQ) are rare ($\approx5\%$). Also, REQ annotations are the shortest, which indicates limited discussions about architectural significant requirements.

6   RQ3: Significant Co-occurrences Between AK Concepts

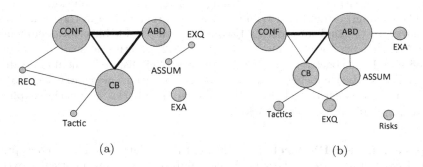

(a)   (b)

Fig. 3. Significant co-occurrences (based $\tilde{\chi}^2$) between AK concepts in the description of issues (a) and issue comments (b). Node size indicates the significance of co-occurrences between annotations of the same AK concept with each other, while edge width is the significance of co-occurrence between annotations from different AK concepts.

Figure 3 shows the co-occurrence networks for the significant co-occurrences between AK concepts in issue descriptions and comments, respectively. Significance has been computed using the $\tilde{\chi}^2$ test as explained in Sect. 3. From Fig. 3, we can observe that annotations of benefits and drawbacks (ABD) have the most significant co-occurrences with architectural configurations (CONF) and component behavior (CB), both in the issue description and comments. This means that practitioners usually share their AK on components design solutions, and associate it with their benefits and drawbacks as a rationale.

When comparing Fig. 3a and 3b, we observe some differences: First, require-ments (REQ) (functional and non-functional) only significantly co-occur with other AK concepts in issue descriptions, but not in issue comments. This shows that discussions on architecturally significant requirements happen in issue descriptions rather than in issue comments. Second, assumptions (ASSUM) co-occur significantly only with Existing system quality (EXQ) (e.g. technical debt items) in issue descriptions, while they co-occur significantly with EXQ and Ben-efits and drawbacks (ABD) in issue comments. This shows that assumptions is a multifaceted AK concept, which appears in issue descriptions to express uncer-tainties about system quality, while in issue comments they additionally express uncertainty regarding the benefits and drawbacks of a proposed solution.

7   Discussion

7.1   RQ1: Representation of AK Concepts in Issues

Implications for Practitioners. The textual variants for AK concepts in Sect. 4 can support practitioners to search for AK in issue trackers. For instance, to search for benefits and drawbacks, practitioners can use regular expressions, which require either adjectives and names of architectural solutions (e.g. tac-tics like caching) or quality attribute terms (e.g. scalability) in the same search. Moreover, the textual variants of AK concepts can provide ideas for documenting each AK concept. For example, following Table 2, practitioners could document benefits and drawbacks as follows: 1) create explicit lists of benefits and draw-backs, 2) describe the benefits and drawbacks of solutions using adjectives, 3) use quality measurement to justify the benefits and drawbacks, 4) mention explicitly problems of solutions as drawbacks.

Implications for Researchers. The textual variations for AK concepts in Sect. 4 can support researchers to develop approaches to automatically extract AK concepts from issue trackers. Concretely, when using machine learning to identify and classify AK concepts from architectural issues, a corpus of annota-tions of AK concepts in issues is needed. A high quality corpus for improving the quality of classification would consider the different textual variants for AK con-cepts as presented in Sect. 4. Moreover, our corpus (3,937 annotations from 98 architectural issues) provides a starting point to train machine learning models on identifying and classifying AK concepts from issue trackers.

The variants of AK concepts in architectural issues show the benefits and challenges in capturing AK from issue trackers compared to developer commu-nities (e.g. Stack Overflow). On the one hand, developers in issue trackers use domain-specific terms (e.g. "optimizer" or "reduce") to describe the architecture of a system, while developers in communities use generic terms (e.g. "server" or "code"). This makes capturing generic AK from issue trackers more challenging.

On the other hand, developers share AK in issues with extensive details; in contrast, developers in developer communities omit many of the details of a system when sharing their AK. This makes the AK in issue trackers more comprehensive than the AK in developer communities.

7.2   RQ2: AK Concepts in Issues

Implications for Practitioners. Knowing which AK concepts are mostly shared in architectural issues supports practitioners to effectively direct their search for AK. For instance, practitioners could search for AK in issue tracking system, if they are looking for alternatives of component design. This is because architectural solutions on component design present the majority of AK concepts in architectural issues. In contrast, it may not be effective to search in issue tracking systems for architecturally significant requirements (e.g. quality attributes), because these are rarely discussed in issue tracking systems.

Implications for Researchers. The results from RQ2 support researchers determining architectural scenarios, in which the re-use of AK from issue tracking system could be most useful. Specifically, the AK in architectural issues could be useful in these two scenarios:

- *Architectural recovery*: Current architectural recovery techniques capture components and their dependencies from source code or byte code. However, such approaches cannot easily capture the behavior of components solely based on the source code. Thus, AK in issue tracking systems could complement architectural recovery techniques with additional natural language descriptions for component behaviors and configurations.
- *Selecting architectural solutions*: Results of RQ2 in Sect. 5 shows that 40% of AK concepts contain the rationale of ADDs (mostly benefits and drawbacks of solutions). Re-using this AK could facilitate comparing architectural solutions and selecting among alternatives based on their pros and cons.

7.3   RQ3: Significant Co-Occurrences Between AK Concepts

Implications for Practitioners. Because architectural issues involve lots of discussions, the significant co-occurrences between AK concepts in issues (as presented in Fig. 3) can guide practitioners when browsing for AK in architectural issues. For instance, if a practitioner found an architectural solution (e.g. an architectural configuration) in a comment, she may keep looking for the rationale of this solution: it is likely written in the same comment. The same applies when finding quality attributes or functional requirements in issue descriptions; these are likely to be accompanied with a certain architectural solution (i.e. an architectural configuration or component behavior).

Implications for Researchers. The significant co-occurrences between AK concepts can guide AK extraction approaches to effectively identify the relationships between AK concepts. For example, we can design a heuristic-based AK extraction approach, which links annotations on architectural configurations with annotations on benefits and drawbacks from the same issue section (i.e. issue description or comment); based on our results in Fig. 3, architectural configurations and benefits and drawbacks significantly co-occur in the same issue section. Associate architectural solutions with their rationale is very useful for the re-use of AK.

Moreover, some significant co-occurrences between AK concepts are worth further detailed analysis. For example, Assumptions seem to co-occur with different AK concepts, especially decision factors like technical debt items, as well as rationale of decisions like benefits and drawbacks. However, it is unknown why and how such significant co-occurrences happen. Thus, further research could determine how and why assumptions co-occur with each of the AK concepts.

8 Threats to Validity

8.1 External Validity

Similar to other studies ([3,18]), our study depends on selecting issues from open source Apache projects and analyzing issues from Jira. This might be a threat, when generalizing the results to industrial projects or other ecosystems. Moreover, our analysis is based on a limited number of architectural issues and annotations, which might be a threat to the generalizability of our results. However, we have carefully selected these issues since they contain the most AK in the projects. Moreover, we created a significant sample of annotations, which are sufficient to report our quantitative results in Sects. 5 and 6 with the smallest error margin as possible.

8.2 Construct Validity

The considered AK concepts in Sect. 2 might not be exhaustive. However, during our qualitative analysis (see Sect. 3), we reached theoretical saturation, and thus covered most AK concepts in architectural issues.

8.3 Reliability

The agreement on the AK concept for each annotation presents a threat to reliability. However, we considered the agreement between researchers in each phase of the study. Moreover, we created a coding book (provided online[4]) with concrete textual variants to facilitate reaching agreement on the AK concepts. We measured the agreement between researchers using Kappa as 0.73. This shows good agreement beyond chance. In addition, we provide the list of identified architectural issues and annotations to support further replication steps.

---

[4] github.com/m-a-m-s/ECSA-2021.

9   Related Work

AK concepts (as presented in Sect. 2) are established based on several studies, such as [11,24,28]. Recent research efforts explore AK for specific domains (e.g. microservices [5]), as well as human and social aspects when making ADDs [17]. However, these studies do not explore concrete representation of AK concepts in any AK source like issue trackers to support finding or capturing AK.

Recently, researchers explored and captured AK concepts in multiple different sources, such as developer communities (e.g. Stack Overflow [4,19,20,22]), Google search results [23], technology documentation [9] and mailing lists [7]. However, these studies do not explore or capture AK in issue tracking systems.

Bhat et al. [3] propose a machine learning approach to classify issues in issue trackers, which contain certain types of ADDs. The approach depends on classifying issue descriptions without considering issue comments or attachments. Moreover, the approach does not explore different AK concepts (see Sect. 2) in details. Our study on the other hand explores different AK concepts, their textual representation and relationships, considering the different sections of issues in more details.

Shahbazian et al. [18] proposed an approach to identify architectural issues by analyzing source code and applying clustering algorithms. The approach can additionally differentiate between simple, compound and crosscutting decisions, and identify relationships between source code and issues. However, Shahbazian et al. did not analyze the textual content of architectural issues to explore the different AK concepts. The approach from Shahbazian et al. has inspired our study design to identify candidates architectural issues. However, our study goes beyond identifying architectural issues, and analyzes the textual content of architectural issues to explore the representation of AK concepts and their relationships within issues.

10   Conclusions

Our goal in this study is to explore the AK concepts within architectural issues to support re-using this AK. Our results cover existing AK concepts within architectural issues, as well as their textual representation and relationships. These support determining how the AK in issues could be re-used. Our future work aims to expand our study to explore different types of decisions in issue trackers, and to identify and extract the AK concepts automatically from issues.

References

1. Bass, L., Clements, P., Kazman, R.: Software Architecture in Practice, 3rd edn. Addison-Wesley Professional, Boston (2012)
2. Behnamghader, P., Le, D.M., Garcia, J., Link, D., Shahbazian, A., Medvidovic, N.: A large-scale study of architectural evolution in open-source software systems. Empir. Softwa. Eng. **22**(3), 1146–1193 (2016). https://doi.org/10.1007/s10664-016-9466-0

3. Bhat, M., Shumaiev, K., Biesdorf, A., Hohenstein, U., Matthes, F.: Automatic extraction of design decisions from issue management systems: a machine learning based approach. In: Lopes, A., de Lemos, R. (eds.) ECSA 2017. LNCS, vol. 10475, pp. 138–154. Springer, Cham (2017). https://doi.org/10.1007/978-3-319-65831-5_10

4. Bi, T., Liang, P., Tang, A., Xia, X.: Mining architecture tactics and quality attributes knowledge in Stack Overflow. J. Syst. Softw., 111005 (2021)

5. El Malki, A., Zdun, U.: Guiding architectural decision making on service mesh based microservice architectures. In: Bures, T., Duchien, L., Inverardi, P. (eds.) ECSA 2019. LNCS, vol. 11681, pp. 3–19. Springer, Cham (2019). https://doi.org/10.1007/978-3-030-29983-5_1

6. Fontana, F.A., Pigazzini, I., Roveda, R., Tamburri, D., Zanoni, M., Nitto, E.D.: Arcan: a tool for architectural smells detection. In: Proceedings - 2017 IEEE International Conference on Software Architecture Workshops, ICSAW 2017: Side Track Proceedings, pp. 282–285. IEEE Inc., June 2017

7. Fu, L., Liang, P., Li, X., Yang, C.: Will data influence the experiment results?: a replication study of automatic identification of decisions. In: SANER 2021, pp. 614–617. IEEE, March 2021. https://doi.org/10.1109/SANER50967.2021.00076

8. Gerdes, S., Lehnert, S., Riebisch, M.: Combining architectural design decisions and legacy system evolution. In: Avgeriou, P., Zdun, U. (eds.) ECSA 2014. LNCS, vol. 8627, pp. 50–57. Springer, Cham (2014). https://doi.org/10.1007/978-3-319-09970-5_5

9. Gorton, I., Xu, R., Yang, Y., Liu, H., Zheng, G.: Experiments in curation: towards machine-assisted construction of software architecture knowledge bases. In: IEEE/IFIP ICSA 2017, pp. 79–88, April 2017

10. Jansen, A., Bosch, J.: Software architecture as a set of architectural design decisions. In: WICSA, pp. 109–120 (2005)

11. Kruchten, P., Lago, P., van Vliet, H.: Building up and reasoning about architectural knowledge. In: Hofmeister, C., Crnkovic, I., Reussner, R. (eds.) QoSA 2006. LNCS, vol. 4214, pp. 43–58. Springer, Heidelberg (2006). https://doi.org/10.1007/11921998_8

12. Mayring, P.: Qualitative content analysis. In: Forum Qualitative Sozialforschung/Forum: Qualitative Social Research, vol. 1 (2000)

13. Medvidovic, N., Taylor, R.N.: A classification and comparison framework for software architecture description languages. IEEE Trans. Softw. Eng. **26**(1), 70–93 (2000). https://doi.org/10.1109/32.825767

14. Miesbauer, C., Weinreich, R.: Classification of design decisions – an expert survey in practice. In: Drira, K. (ed.) ECSA 2013. LNCS, vol. 7957, pp. 130–145. Springer, Heidelberg (2013). https://doi.org/10.1007/978-3-642-39031-9_12

15. Neuendorf, K.A.: The Content Analysis Guidebook, 2nd edn. SAGE Publications

16. Pearson, K.: On a criterion that a given system of deviations from the probable in the case of correlated system of variables is such that it can be reasonably supposed to have arisen from random sampling, pp. 157–175 (1900)

17. Razavian, M., Paech, B., Tang, A.: Empirical research for software architecture decision making: an analysis. J. Syst. Softw. **149**, 360–381 (2019). https://doi.org/10.1016/j.jss.2018.12.003

18. Shahbazian, A., Kyu Lee, Y., Le, D., Brun, Y., Medvidovic, N.: Recovering architectural design decisions. In: Proceedings - 2018 IEEE 15th International Conference on Software Architecture. ICSA 2018, pp. 95–104. IEEE Inc., July 2018

19. Soliman, M., Galster, M., Riebisch, M.: Developing an ontology for architecture knowledge from developer communities. In: IEEE/IFIP ICSA 2017, pp. 89–92, April 2017. https://doi.org/10.1109/ICSA.2017.31
20. Soliman, M., Galster, M., Salama, A.R., Riebisch, M.: Architectural knowledge for technology decisions in developer communities: an exploratory study with Stack-Overflow. In: IEEE/IFIP WICSA 2016, pp. 128–133, April 2016
21. Soliman, M., Riebisch, M., Zdun, U.: Enriching architecture knowledge with technology design decisions. In: WICSA, pp. 135–144, May 2015. https://doi.org/10.1109/WICSA.2015.14
22. Soliman, M., Rekaby Salama, A., Galster, M., Zimmermann, O., Riebisch, M.: Improving the search for architecture knowledge in online developer communities. In: Proceedings - ICSA 2018, pp. 186–195. IEEE Inc., July 2018
23. Soliman, M., Wiese, M., Li, Y., Riebisch, M., Avgeriou, P.: Exploring web search engines to find architectural knowledge. In: 2021 IEEE 18th International Conference on Software Architecture (ICSA), pp. 162–172. IEEE, March 2021
24. Tang, A., Jin, Y., Han, J.: A rationale-based architecture model for design traceability and reasoning. J. Syst. Softw. 80(6), 918–934 (2007). https://doi.org/10.1016/j.jss.2006.08.040
25. Tang, A., Van Vliet, H.: Software architecture design reasoning. In: Ali Babar, M., Dingsøyr, T., Lago, P., van Vliet, H. (eds.) Software Architecture Knowledge Management: Theory and Practice, pp. 155–174. Springer, Heidelberg (2009). https://doi.org/10.1007/978-3-642-02374-3_9
26. van Vliet, H., Tang, A.: Decision making in software architecture. J. Syst. Softw. 117, 638–644 (2016)
27. Yang, C., et al.: An industrial case study on an architectural assumption documentation framework. J. Syst. Softw. 134, 190–210 (2017). https://doi.org/10.1016/j.jss.2017.09.007
28. Zimmermann, O., Koehler, J., Leymann, F., Polley, R., Schuster, N.: Managing architectural decision models with dependency relations, integrity constraints, and production rules. J. Syst. Softw. 82(8), 1249–1267 (2009). https://doi.org/10.1016/j.jss.2009.01.039

Human Behavior-Oriented Architectural Design

Moamin B. Abughazala[1] , Mahyar T. Moghaddam[1,2](✉) , Henry Muccini[1] ,
and Karthik Vaidhyanathan[1]

[1] University of L'Aquila, L'Aquila, Italy
moamin.abughazala@graduate.univaq.it,
{henry.muccini,karthik.vaidhyanathan}@univaq.it
[2] University of Southern Denmark, Odense, Denmark
mtmo@mmmi.sdu.dk

Abstract. This paper highlights humans' social and mobility behaviors'
role in the continuous engineering of sustainable socio-technical Internet
of Things (IoT) systems. Our approach relates the humans' characteristics and intentions with the system's goals, and models such interaction.
Such a modeling approach aligns the architectural design and associated
quality of service (QoS) with humans' quality of experience (QoE). We
design a simulation environment that combines agent-based social simulation (ABSS) with architectural models generated through a model-
driven engineering approach. Our modeling approach facilitates choosing
the best architectural model and system configuration to enhance both the
humans' and system's sustainability. We apply our approach to the Uffizi
Galleries crowd management system. Taking advantage of real data, we
model scenarios related to humans' speed, vision variations, grouping, and
social attachment, which impact QoE. We then assess various architectural models with different SW/HW configurations to propose the optimal
model based on different scenarios concerning QoS-QoE requirements.

Keywords: IoT · Software architecture · Agent-based modeling ·
Human behavior · Sustainability · Quality of experience · Quality of
service

1 Introduction

Architectural design decisions are historically driven by technical reasoning and
concerns [1]. More recently, other aspects such as business value [2] and sustainability [3]. The growing importance of sustainable development is highlighting
additional concerns regarding social, individual, economics, and environmental interlinked with technical dimensions [4]. Literature on sustainable software
development generally focuses on environmental aspects; still, little attention
is dedicated to *social and individual* human sustainability. These dimensions
become especially relevant in the context of socio-technical Internet of Things
(IoT) applications, where humans are *immersed* in the system, and *their behavior
impacts system's quality and functionality* [5].

© Springer Nature Switzerland AG 2021
S. Biffl et al. (Eds.): ECSA 2021, LNCS 12857, pp. 134–143, 2021.
https://doi.org/10.1007/978-3-030-86044-8_9

In this paper, we propose a *human-oriented architecture design approach* for IoT applications. Our approach interconnects and improves humans sustainability and system sustainability in the context of architecting IoT applications. More specifically, we analyze how the understanding of human behavior may drive the selection of different and alternative architectural models [6] and configurations, with the objective of minimizing energy consumption. In order to do so, we present a comprehensive approach comprising the following activities:

- proposing an agent-based modeling (ABM) approach to model IoT ecosystems, in which humans and IoT resources interact;
- integrating ABM and model-driven engineering approach to associate software architecture models to human behavior. Such models support design decisions and create a knowledge baseline for quality-driven architectural reconfiguration;
- developing a simulation environment (fed by real data) that simulates human behavior with respect to IoT resources, and chooses the best architectural model and system configuration to enhance both the humans' and system's sustainability;
- applying the approach to a real case, a museum crowd management system, by tracking and analyzing human social and mobility behavior in the museum.

Our proposed approach puts humans and their context, goals, and quality of experience (QoE) at the heart of IoT socio-technical systems design while considering the software quality of services (QoS) improvement. This desirable adjustment (or sometimes trade-off) between humans' QoE and the system's QoS could be achieved by modeling humans' expected behavior and assessing its impacts on IoT architectures and configuration. We apply our approach to a real socio-technical system: the Uffizi Galleries crowd management. During our 5 years of experience (from 2016), we found humans behavior as the source of many challenges: in huge queues, in the ticketing system, in congestion on famous artworks, in bottlenecks on entrances, and more interestingly, in system's functionality and QoS issues. Evaluation results of our approach on the Uffizi case show how a human-oriented approach can allow software architects to assess various design alternatives and select an architecture that optimizes the overall QoS/QoE offered by the system.

The paper is organized as follows. Background and case study are presented in Sect. 2. Our agent-based and architectural modeling methodologies are presented in Sect. 3. The method is applied to a real case study in Sect. 4, and the conclusions are finally drawn in Sect. 5.

2   Background and Case Study

2.1   Agent-Based Modeling and Simulation

In agent-based modeling (ABM), the environment and what is included in it are modeled as agents. Each agent (such as humans, robots, cars, etc.) has a set of characteristics and behaviors. For simulation of human behavior, agent-based social simulations (ABSS) are generally used. In ABSS, an agent is defined as an autonomous software entity that can act upon and perceive its environment [7]. When agents are put together, they form an artificial society, each perceiving, moving, performing actions, communicating, and transforming the local environment, much like human beings in real society. An effective method used to model pedestrian dynamics in agent-based systems is the social force model [8]. In this paper, we use PedSim [9] to simulate IoT environment and moving agents. The main setting in our simulation is that, *IoT sensors* are modeled as static points in the environment with different coverage. When human agents fall within the sensors' coverage area, the information will be sent to the IoT simulator.

2.2   Architectural Modeling and Simulation

Modeling the IoT system's architecture implies considering the IoT components, their interactions, the underlying hardware configurations of the different IoT components, as well as constraints from the environment in which these IoT components will be deployed. To this end, we use our CAPS modeling framework[1] [10] to provide a multi-view (software, hardware, physical space) approach based on the IEEE/ISO/IEC 42010 standard [11]. Different simulators (e.g., NS-3, IoTSim, OMNET++, etc.) are used in research and practice for simulating IoT systems to gather various types of QoS information. In this work, we use CupCarbon, a state-of-the-art smart city IoT simulator[2] [12], widely used in research, especially for energy and data simulation of IoT systems.

2.3   Case Study: The Uffizi Galleries

The Uffizi Gallery in Florence is one of the most visited museums in Italy. In 2018, it had more than 2 million visitors. The museums' congestion is a socio-physical phenomenon where visitors, decision-makers, and IoT system dynamically interact [13]. Within our crowd management project with the Uffizi Gallery, we gathered real data that supports simulating realistic scenarios. This could provide situational awareness and optimal IoT architectures associated with humans' mobility behavior.

3   Methodology

This section presents the methodology that links ABM and ABSS with IoT architectural modeling and simulation, thereby allowing architects to analyze the models and design an optimal architecture with respect to QoS and QoE requirements. Our methodology (refer Fig. 1) consists of four stages:

1. *Agent Modeling and Simulation.* Stage that deals with the modeling and simulation of different agents using the ABM and ABSS approaches. The agent-based model for IoT socio-technical systems consists of four classes of

---

[1] http://caps.disim.univaq.it/.
[2] http://cupcarbon.com/.

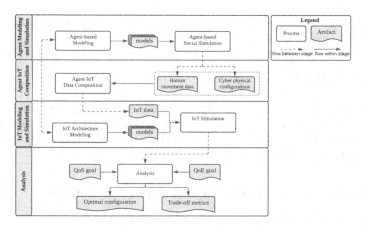

Fig. 1. Methodology overview

agents: *humans, cyber elements, physical space, and IoT resources* which all are part of the *environment* class. A class is, by definition, a template for an agent. When the model is implemented, and the simulator is run, various agents within the same class but with potentially different attributes satisfy the social behavior and contextual heterogeneity. For instance, many human agents with the same attributes are created but with possibly different values for the attributes, thus creating a heterogeneous artificial society.

2. **Agent-IoT composition.** This stage receives the results of the agent-based simulations to generate the data required for the IoT simulation. This step consists of a single process, namely, Agent IoT Data Composition (AIDC). It transforms the human movement data generated by the agent-based social simulation process to sensor data as required by the IoT Simulation process. Towards this, the AIDC takes two different inputs, i.e., Human movement data (containing the information on the flow of humans in a given space) and physical configurations (containing the list of the sensors along with their corresponding location and coverage information). The AIDC uses those data to generate the sensor data required for IoT simulation.

3. **IoT modeling and simulation.** This stage involves modeling and simulation of different architectural models and configurations based on the data received from the agent-IoT composition step. It consists of two processes: *i)* *IoT Architecture Modeling* using CAPS framework and *ii)* *IoT Architecture Simulation* using CupCarbon.

4. **Analysis.** This stage processes the IoT simulation results by taking into account the QoS/QoE goals (which can be specified by stakeholders). It then identifies the optimal architectural model and configuration for a given agent behavior. It achieves this with the help of a utility metric, namely trade-off score, $t_s = w_s * Q_s + w_e * Q_e$; where w_s and w_e represents the weights given to QoS and QoE goals respectively and Q_s and Q_e are piece-wise functions that captures the satisfaction of QoS and QoE goals respectively. This stage

also provides a detailed evaluation of the different architectural models with respect to QoS/QoE metrics trade-offs.

4   Application

We apply our approach to the Uffizi case. We first design the ABSS environment of the Uffizi and assign characteristics to various agents. While simulating, the humans' mobility data captured by IoT resources will drive quality-driven SW/HW optimal configurations.

4.1   Agent-Based Modeling Scenarios and Simulations

In our agent-based model of the Uffizi galleries, we set the simulation parameters either by real data gathered or according to the literature. For instance, we gathered information about the daily museum population and the population over each day. The museum has a limited capacity, and no more than 900 persons could be in the museum at a time. The entry rate of people to the museum varies from 80 to 200 persons in 15 min time slots. We set potential points of interest and their associated visiting time accordingly that are different for agents. However, the agents could change their target based on some contextual situations such as visible congestion and the intention of their friends or relatives. We ran all the experiments on a *Corei7 2.7GHz* computer with *16Gb* of RAM memory under Windows 10 pro *64-bits*.

We considered two scenarios. In the *first scenario* we used the Uffizi historical data to assign different characteristics to human agents regarding age, gender, origin, and physical condition. In fact, each human agent has a profile including vision, maximum speed, and target force that are impacted by their characteristics. We observed various challenges regarding congestion, physical bottlenecks, grouping, social distancing, and panic in disasters. These challenges impact the visitors' QoE. In the *second scenario* we modeled social attachment and grouping in Uffizi to assess its impact on QoE and QoS. A group of agents is a single immutable entity that move together. We consider groups consisting of 3 to 7 agents. People also may have social attachment to each other and they may reach together before doing a specific activity. We observed that walking velocity highly depends on the company and the speed of the slowest person in the group. We also observed that groups move together and block other visitors way, which impact the QoE. The performed agent-based social simulations' main objective was to model humans' movement behavior in realistic scenarios captured by IoT resources. The results of this ABSS will input the agent-IoT composition engine to assess their impact on architectures.

4.2   IoT Architectures Modeling and Simulations

We modeled the IoT architecture of the Uffizi case study using the CAPS modeling framework (refer Sect. 2.2). In the Uffizi museum, IoT devices need to be deployed in the entrance, exits, and corridors to monitor the movement of humans into, outside of, and within the museum. The IoT device's choice can impact the overall QoS and QoE offered by the system. To this end, after discussion with different stakeholders, including the museum's director and IoT experts, we came up with a list of six different architectural alternatives. These were modeled using CAPS to create six different software architectural models. The details on the different types and number of IoT devices used to create the models are reported in Table 1. These numbers were decided based on our experience at the Uffizi. Further, in each of the models, the IoT device components were connected to 4 controller components that managed the data flow and further sent it to the Uffizi server component. This resulted in a total of 18 components per architectural model. Further, to define the configuration of the IoT components in the models, we use the concept of modes provided by CAPS. Every IoT component operates in two modes, *i)* normal mode when the sensor reads/sends data at a lower frequency; *ii)* critical mode where the sensor reads/sensor at a higher frequency due to some critical condition (high queuing). However, the choice of the frequency in either mode can impact the QoS and QoE. Towards this, we defined three different configurations for each IoT component. This is reported in Table 2. These models along with their configurations were converted to CupCarbon Simulation projects using the CAPSim tool [14].

The CupCarbon simulation of the six different architectural models along with three configurations was performed based on the two different scenarios listed in Sect. 4.1. This resulted in a total of 36 simulations (6 models × 3 configurations × 2 scenarios). Each simulation was performed for a total time of 2 h in a Windows-based desktop machine running on an Intel i7, 2.6–3.2 GHz processor with 16 Gb RAM.

Table 1. Details of the components used to create the different architectural models.

Model	Entrance sensor)	Exit sensor	Corridor sensors
M1	1 QR Reader	3 Counters	5 Cameras, 4 RFID
M2	1 QR Reader	3 QR Readers	5 Cameras, 4 RFID
M3	1 Counter	3 Counters	5 Cameras, 4 RFID
M4	1 Counter	3 QR Readers	5 Cameras, 4 RFID
M5	1 QR Reader	3 Counters	9 Cameras
M6	1 QR Reader	3 Counters	9 RFID

Table 2. Configuration of sensors (N and C represents Normal and Critical mode frequencies in seconds).

Configuration	QR Reader		Camera		RFID		People Counter	
	N (s))	C (s)	N (s)	C (s)	N (s)	C (s)	N (s)	C (s)
C1	10	1	30	10	30	10	10	1
C2	20	5	120	60	40	20	20	5
C3	30	15	60	30	150	75	30	15

4.3 Results

This section describes the results obtained after simulating the different architectural models. We analyze the results to identify the optimal architectural model and configuration for the two scenarios (refer Sect. 4.1). To this end, we defined scenario-specific QoS and QoE goals. The simulation results were analyzed using a set of Python scripts. We used total energy consumed by the system for every 15 min as the parameter for measuring QoS and the total count of humans gathered by the server every 15 min as the parameter for measuring QoE (slow updates in a high crowd situation can lead to queuing affecting the overall experience of humans). The goal of the analysis was to understand if and how different types of human behavior can impact the overall architectural design of an IoT system with respect to the QoS and QoE goals. We identified 2 research questions.[3]

Table 3. Simulation results of applying the models on different human behaviour scenarios. E_{avg} is the average energy consumed, H_{avg} is the average number of humans captured by the system, and t_s is the trade-off score.

Model	Scenario 1			Scenario 2		
	E_{avg} (**J**)	H_{avg}	t_s	E_{avg} (**J**)	H_{avg}	t_s
M1_C1	162.18	85	7.0	348.04	1177	7.0
M1_C2	197.78	784	62.65	192.27	631	82.22
M1_C3	137.12	534	56.12	133.32	432	98.61
M2_C1	402.02	1503	25.04	290.10	1247	47.43
M2_C2	217.11	788	56.55	212.49	649	70.37
M2_C3	149.44	533	54.79	145.99	445	98.13
M3_C1	**182.10**	**1486**	**97.16**	171.40	1176	120.92
M3_C2	105.60	778	81.01	102.13	628	112.37
M3_C3	74.51	529	59.79	71.77	433	102.43
M4_C1	239.62	1584	82.26	232.72	1333	92.56
M4_C2	130.88	830	83.82	127.90	696	116.67
M4_C3	84.25	494	55.72	78.11	377	98.11
M5_C1	171.78	883	80.63	168.85	810	107.28
M5_C2	86.17	444	50.68	83.89	389	98.09
M5_C3	42.25	66	16.33	40.56	76	74.37
M6_C1	243.09	1898	86.49	241.06	1760	98.89
M6_C2	147.51	1005	94.64	**147.47**	**954**	**129.02**
M6_C3	98.52	664	71.57	97.87	616	115.19

---

[3] The results replication package can be found at: https://github.com/karthikv1392/PedCupSim.

RQ1. Which architectural model and configuration ensures optimal QoE by guaranteeing an overall QoS in scenario 1 (Congestion)?

In scenario 1, people may move bidirectionally resulting in congestion (refer Sect. 4.1). To identify the architectural model that provides optimal QoE in Scenario 1, we calculate the trade-off score (t_s) by giving more weight to QoE. We set the goals such that we want the system to consume not more than 100 J and the server to capture the movement of at least 1200 people every 15 min. The results are reported in Scenario 1 section of Table 3. It shows that $M3\_C1$ provides the highest ts by giving more preference to QoE without compromising too much on the QoS. This is because having a combination of RFID readers (in rooms) and cameras (in corridors) allows $M3\_C1$ to gather data at higher accuracy compared to model(s) that uses only RFID (good for covering small areas) or only cameras (lower accuracy). In addition, the use of people counters in exits and entrances allows data to be captured faster compared to using QR Readers, which requires manual intervention (this is costly, especially in Scenario 1 where congestion takes place). Further, the use of $C1$ configuration (refer Table 2) allows the system to collect and send data in near real-time to the server, thereby ensuring higher QoE. There are some architectural model configuration pair that offers less E_{avg} (eg: $M1\_C1$, $M6\_C2$, etc.) but they offer less H_{avg}. On the other hand, there are other model configuration pair that offers higher H_{avg} (eg: $M6\_C1$, $M2\_C1$, $M4\_C1$, etc.). However, they end up consuming higher energy on average compared to the goals specified.

RQ2. Which architectural model and configuration balances QoS and QoE in scenario 2 (social attachment)?

In scenario 2, due to social attachment, people move in groups, and sometimes this leads to congestion and other times not, as the speeds of people also vary (refer Sect. 4.1). To understand which architectural model and configurations balances QoS and QoE in scenario 2, we calculated the trade-off score, t_s for each of the model configuration pair, with the goal of consuming not more than 150 J and the server to capture the movement of at least 800 people every 15 min. The results are reported in Scenario 2 part of Table 3. We can observe that as opposed to Scenario 1 discussed in RQ1, $M6\_C2$ offers the highest t_s value as it is able to balance between E_{avg} and H_{avg}. Differently from Scenario 1, even though $M3\_C1$ (higher H_{avg}) offers second highest t_s, $M6\_C2$ is able to offer higher t_s as in Scenario 2, as $M3\_C1$ uses cameras which consumes more power than RFID readers and thereby impacts the overall QoS. In Scenario 2, due to social attachment, people tend to move in groups. This allows RFID readers in the corridors and rooms to capture data with a comparable accuracy without consuming too much energy with respect to using a combination of cameras and RFID readers. Similarly, $M4\_C2$ consumes lesser energy than $M6\_C2$ and offers comparable t_s value. However, it has a lower H_{avg} value primarily due to the use of QR Readers in the exits, as explained in the analysis of RQ1. The same holds for other model configuration pairs as well. There are models that satisfy the QoS goal ($M1\_C3$, $M2\_C3$, etc.) but not the QoE goals, and there are models that satisfy the QoE goal ($M1\_C1$, $M2\_C1$, etc.) but not QoS. However, the model configuration pair, $M6\_C2$ is able to balance both.

> The results of our evaluations in RQ1 and RQ2 indicate how our approach could allow architects to model the expected human behavior and further select the appropriate architectural models and configurations that can optimize the overall QoS/QoE (or a combination) offered by the system. Moreover, our approach provides architects with a set of models and configurations to handle different types of human behavioral scenarios.

5   Conclusion

In this work, we demonstrated that using a human-oriented approach can allow software architects to better design socio-technical IoT systems. It achieves this with the help of a model-driven approach which enables architects to model the expected behaviors of humans, the architecture of the IoT system and further provides mechanisms to simulate and perform trade-off analysis of different design alternatives with respect to QoE and QoS requirements. Our evaluation on a real case study shows that our approach can allow architects to select optimal architectural models and configurations by considering the expected human behavior. With respect to future work, the first research avenue that we plan to explore is scalability. This will entail enabling the approach to synthesize multiple models and configurations based on different behavioral scenarios as well as considering various QoS/QoE parameters (thereby also extending the trade-off analysis mechanism). The second extension of our approach is to explore the possibility of using machine learning for run-time proactive, dynamic architectural reconfiguration based on the expected human behavior. Finally, we plan to evolve this approach into a tool that can be used by software architects to better design socio-technical IoT systems.

Acknowledgment. We would like to acknowledge the support given by the Uffizi Galleries and its director Dr. Eike Schmidt. This research is also supported by the VASARI PON R&I 2014–2020 and FSC project.

References

1. van Vliet, H., Tang, A.: Decision making in software architecture. J. Syst. Softw. **117**, 638–644 (2016)
2. Harris, M.D.S.: The Business Value of Software. CRC Press, Boca Raton (2017)
3. Lago, P.: Architecture design decision maps for software sustainability. In: Proceedings of the 41st International Conference on Software Engineering: Software Engineering in Society. ICSE-SEIS 2019, pp. 61–64. IEEE Press (2019)
4. Becker, C., et al.: Sustainability design and software: the karlskrona manifesto. In: 2015 IEEE/ACM 37th IEEE International Conference on Software Engineering, vol. 2, pp. 467–476. IEEE (2015)

5. Dugdale, J., Moghaddam, M.T., Muccini, H.: Human behaviour centered design: developing a software system for cultural heritage. In: Proceedings of the ACM/IEEE 42nd International Conference on Software Engineering: Software Engineering in Society, pp. 85–94 (2020)
6. Muccini, H., Moghaddam, M.T.: IoT architectural styles. In: Cuesta, C.E., Garlan, D., Pérez, J. (eds.) ECSA 2018. LNCS, vol. 11048, pp. 68–85. Springer, Cham (2018). https://doi.org/10.1007/978-3-030-00761-4_5
7. Ferber, J., Weiss, G.: Multi-agent Systems: An Introduction to Distributed Artificial Intelligence, vol. 1. Addison-Wesley, Reading (1999)
8. Helbing, D., Molnar, P.: Social force model for pedestrian dynamics. Phys. Rev. E **51**(5), 4282 (1995)
9. PedSim pedestrian simulator. https://www.pedsim.net/. Acessed 17 May 2021
10. Muccini, H., Sharaf, M.: Caps: architecture description of situational aware cyber physical systems. In: 2017 IEEE International Conference on Software Architecture (ICSA), pp. 211–220, April 2017
11. ISO/IEC/IEEE Systems and software engineering - Architecture description. ISO/IEC/IEEE 42010:2011(E) (Revision of ISO/IEC 42010:2007 and IEEE Std 1471–2000), pp. 1–46 (2011)
12. Bounceur, A.: CupCarbon: a new platform for designing and simulating smart-city and IoT wireless sensor networks (SCI-WSN). In: Proceedings of the International Conference on Internet of Things and Cloud Computing. ICC 2016, p. 1:1. ACM, New York (2016)
13. Dugdale, J., Moghaddam, M.T., Muccini, H.: Agent-based simulation for IoT facilitated building evacuation. In: 2019 International Conference on Information and Communication Technologies for Disaster Management (ICT-DM), pp. 1–8. IEEE (2019)
14. Sharaf, M., Abughazala, M., Muccini, H., Abusair, M.: CAPSim: simulation and code generation based on the CAPS. In: Proceedings of the 11th European Conference on Software Architecture: Companion Proceedings, pp. 56–60 (2017)

Architecting for Quality Attributes

Updating Service-Based Software Systems in Air-Gapped Environments

Oleksandr Shabelnyk[1,2]($\boxtimes$), Pantelis A. Frangoudis[2], Schahram Dustdar[2], and Christos Tsigkanos[2]

[1] Preparatory Commission for the Comprehensive Nuclear-Test-Ban Treaty Organization, Vienna, Austria
[2] Distributed Systems Group, TU Wien, Vienna, Austria

Abstract. Contemporary component-based systems often manifest themselves as service-based architectures, where a central activity is management of their software updates. However, stringent security constraints in mission-critical settings often impose compulsory network isolation among systems, also known as air-gap; a prevalent choice in different sectors including private, public or governmental organizations. This raises several issues involving updates, stemming from the fact that controlling the update procedure of a distributed service-based system centrally and remotely is precluded by network isolation policies. A dedicated software architecture is thus required, where key themes are dependability of the update process, interoperability with respect to the software supported and auditability regarding update actions previously performed. We adopt an architectural viewpoint and present a technical framework for updating service-based systems in air-gapped environments. We describe the particularities of the domain characterized by network isolation and provide suitable notations for service versions, whereupon satisfiability is leveraged for dependency resolution; those are situated within an overall architectural design. Finally, we evaluate the proposed framework over a realistic case study of an international organization, and assess the performance of the dependency resolution procedures for practical problem sizes.

Keywords: Software updates · Air-gapped environments · Service-based architectures

1 Introduction

Contemporary software architectures reflect decades-long software engineering research and practice, where separation of concerns with respect to the wide-ranging functionality available throughout a software system is strongly emphasized. This leads to systems formed via composition of loosely coupled independent software components, which are also often distributed. The trend towards

Research partially supported by Austrian Science Foundation (FWF) project M 2778-N "EDENSPACE".

S. Biffl et al. (Eds.): ECSA 2021, LNCS 12857, pp. 147–163, 2021.
https://doi.org/10.1007/978-3-030-86044-8_10

breaking down software into increasingly smaller pieces introduces numerous advantages, however, it increases overall system complexity, including over its maintenance and managed evolution. This component-based view has culminated in service-orientation, where service-oriented architectures (SOA) have seen wide applicability.

Software systems however are not static, but rather *evolve*, undergoing continual change, with software maintenance thus constituting a major activity [1]. This is evident also in service-oriented component-based architectures, where software is designed, developed and maintained by different teams in often agile processes. As such, software updates are a central theme, something exacerbated in mission-critical settings in highly regulated, mission critical environments where stringent security constraints impose compulsory network isolation among distributed systems, also known as *air-gap*. Even though network isolation does not counter all security concerns [2–4], such a design is a prevalent choice in different sectors involving critical systems, be it within private, public or governmental organizations. Air-gap isolation generally imposes challenges in the lifecycle management of service-based software systems, the lack of constant availability of resources being a major issue, and is in contrast with the spirit of modern DevOps practices [5]. In working environments where an air-gap is in place, the lack of Internet connectivity also has a negative impact on productivity [6]. Challenges arise especially when there is a need to initially provision and later update distributed component-based software systems – an update of a software component may introduce breaking changes to other dependents. Naturally, software updates, their modelling and dependency resolution are problems that have been treated by the community extensively and in several forms [7–10].

However, updating air-gapped systems raises several issues from a software architecture perspective, especially given the overall mission-critical setting; those include: (i) the configuration of components produced to update the system should be verifiably correct, since there is significant cost-to-repair for incorrect updates, (ii) service-based architectures entail containerized services, with support of different runtime environments, and (iii) update actions should be recorded in a traceable manner, in order to support auditability and regulatory compliance. As such, we adopt an architectural viewpoint and present a technical framework for updating distributed software systems in air-gapped environments. Our main contributions are as follows:

- We detail the domain characterized by network isolation and identify requirements, update workflow and modelling notations for service versions;
- We leverage satisfiability for dependency resolution, providing alternative strategies with correctness guarantees and address the trade-off between their execution time and resolution quality;
- We describe an architectural design to instrument updates for air-gapped service-based systems, which we implement end-to-end, and finally
- We evaluate the proposed framework over a realistic case of an air-gapped update elicited from the Comprehensive Nuclear-Test-Ban Treaty Organiza-

tion (CTBTO[1]). We further assess the performance of the dependency resolution procedures for practical problem sizes.

The rest of this paper is structured as follows. Sect. 2 gives an overview of the proposed approach along with the challenges brought by the air-gapped setting. Sect. 3 describes an architecture and workflow instrumenting air-gapped updates, while Sect. 4 elaborates on characteristic dependency resolution strategies. Sect. 5 provides an assessment over a case study along with a performance evaluation. Related work is considered in Sect. 6, and Sect. 7 concludes the paper.

2   Updating Service-Based Air-Gapped Systems

An *air-gap* is a security measure employed to ensure that a computer system is physically network-isolated from others, such as the Internet or other local area networks. The air-gap design may manifest in computers having no network interfaces to others, while residing in a physically isolated location. This is because a network – often used to update software – represents a security vulnerability or regulatory violation. To transfer data (or programs) between the network-connected world and air-gapped systems, one typically uses a removable physical medium such as a hard drive, while access is regulated and controlled [11]. The key concept is that an air-gapped system can generally be regarded as closed in terms of data and software, and unable to be accessed from the outside world. However, this has implications regarding contemporary systems, which may need to be upgraded as part of software maintenance activities. Although existing package management solutions can be theoretically used (e.g., by storing an entire repository on a physical medium), this may be inefficient and not readily applicable in a service-based setting; repositories can be sizable and snapshotting to removable media may be impractical or even infeasible.

Figure 1 illustrates a birds-eye view of the domain and proposed approach. On the problem domain (left part of Fig. 1) a series of air-gapped systems host software services, each having some version. Those comprise the service version configuration state of each air-gapped system, which is assumed to be known or adequately communicated. Software development takes place off-site, and services may need to be updated. Services – as software components – have dependencies, specified at development time. To perform an update on an air-gapped system (right part of Fig. 1), the process entails resolution of service dependencies per air-gapped system, building a valid service configuration taking into account its current configuration state, and pulling of appropriate artifacts (such as containers) from development repositories, storing them in a removable physical medium. Subsequently, the air-gapped system is visited, the service configuration is verified against the local state and the update is performed; services are then provisioned accordingly based on execution environments.

---

[1] CTBTO Preparatory Commission, http://www.ctbto.org/.

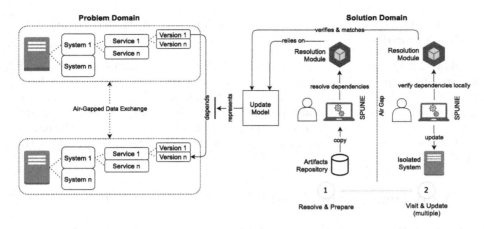

Fig. 1. Updating service-based air-gapped systems – Overview.

3   Architecture for Instrumenting Air-Gapped Updates

As evident from Fig. 1, updating service-based air-gapped systems requires a dedicated software architecture, capable of coping with the particularities of the domain, workflow, and execution environments. To this end, this section first outlines design requirements a software architecture for instrumenting air-gapped updates should fulfil, before presenting its materialization and accompanying update workflow.

3.1   Design Requirements

As air-gapped systems are typically employed in mission-critical settings, key themes regarding the design of a software architecture concern dependability of the update process performed, interoperability with respect to the software supported and auditability regarding update actions performed. Specifically:

DR1 Dependability & Verifiability: The configuration of components produced in order to update a system should be verifiably correct. Given the criticality of the domain and the network isolation, there is significant cost-to-repair incorrect updates, something exacerbated by the fact that a physical visit to the air-gapped site is required to apply the update. Moreover, the air-gapped system should be able to verify locally that the update configuration to be applied is correct before installing (recall Fig. 1), as rollbacks induce further cost.

DR2 Interoperability & Extensibility: Since in service-based systems, software is designed, developed and maintained by different teams in often agile processes, loose coupling is desired, in practice realized by pluggable (and interchangeable) components. Functional blocks should manifest themselves as containerized services, different runtime environments of which may be supported (e.g., Docker). Components should expose interfaces, in order to be agnostic of underlying programming languages and other internals.

DR3 Traceability & Auditability: User and system access and update actions should be recorded in a traceable manner, in order to both aid the development and deployment lifecycle and to ensure regulatory compliance. This is key to support required forensic processes for external regulators or inspectors of the update workflow, that are typically in place in mission-critical administrative domains, and is a fundamental requirement in our particular case study which we present in Sect. 5.1.

3.2 Functional Components

Figure 2 illustrates functional components of the architecture we advocate for updating air-gapped systems. The architecture is itself service-based, in order to support interoperability as per DR2; components address separation of concerns such that their development can be supported by different teams or processes, something which is the typical case in large organizations involved with mission-critical systems. The Gateway provides a Web UI and is responsible for routing (authenticated) users' requests to the right service, making use of a Service Registry which records and discovers available services available to consist an update. Additionally, a collection of air-gapped systems is maintained along with their current service version configuration – this amounts to book-keeping of their remote state, and may be instrumented in case-specific ways which are out of the scope of the present paper. Thereupon, the Dependency Resolver service is responsible for resolving version dependencies according to DR1, yielding update configurations that are verifiably correct, to be shipped to target air-gapped systems. Upon the physical visit, the update configuration is validated against the service configuration already present in the system.

The rightmost part of Fig. 2 illustrates functional components outside the core architecture, namely interaction with different execution environments the system may employ – Docker is assumed to be the main service containerization technology, but mobile application containers or images may be also be included. In practice, Docker Swarm implements an interface to ensure loose coupling and avoid vendor lock-in (DR2). The depicted artifact repositories provide, for example, container images. Finally, logging and monitoring facilities address traceability and auditability according to DR3; to this end, all user actions, update operations and system interactions are recorded. Concrete technological choices for implementation of the functional components are illustrated in grey in Fig. 2; those represent contemporary technologies that can be adopted for implementation.

3.3 Update Workflow

Given the architecture of Fig. 2 and upon a user's request, the update workflow for an air-gapped system is comprised of the following steps, which are sufficiently recorded per session, in order to ensure traceability and auditability:

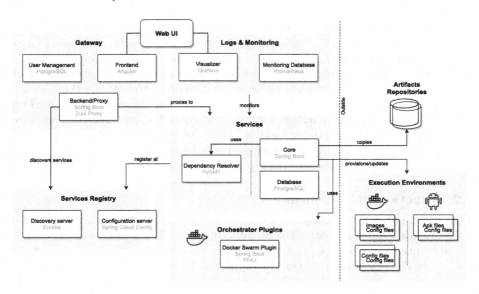

Fig. 2. Service-based architecture supporting updates of air-gapped systems.

1. The user responsible for the preparation and deployment of an update (e.g., the designated release engineer) selects an available system and defines which of its services should be updated and to which versions (DR3).
2. The Dependency Resolver yields a satisfiable combination of service versions (ref. DR1).
3. The Core service, accordingly invoking the Dependency Resolver prepares the corresponding artifacts by copying them to a physical medium from external repositories, and creates a Deployment Plan.
4. Given the Deployment Plan produced, the target air-gapped system is physically visited, the update configuration is verified against the local service configuration (as per DR1), and the update is applied; the services can be provisioned in the target host.

4   Service Dependency Resolution

At the heart of the update workflow lies a dependency resolution step. In this section we first discuss how to model service versions, including how the problem of resolving their dependencies can be formulated in order to enable its automatic resolution. This regards an implementation of the critical *Dependency Resolver* component of Fig. 2. As this component amounts to a black box, we outline a characteristic manner in which it can be implemented; recent literature on the topic can further extend it to cover more specialized cases.

4.1 Problem Formulation

Dependency resolution entails finding the right combination of software components while preserving certain constraints such as version compatibility; the underlying problem is NP-Complete [12]. Dependency resolution is particularly pertinent in component-based software architectures, where it is manifested in various forms; in free and open source software for instance, the components are often called packages and are handled by package managers. Although package managers differ in how they handle dependency resolution, dependencies/packages usually have certain common traits [8,9]: i) name and version which are uniquely identifiable, ii) dependencies to other components (also called *positive* requirements), iii) conflicts expressing absence of certain other components (also called *negative* requirements), and iv) features, identifiers of "virtual" components that may be used to satisfy dependencies of other components.

For our service-based setting, we adopt semantic versioning [13], where three numbers separated by a dot are used, e.g. "2.4.1." The first number indicates a *major* release typically introducing breaking changes. The middle number reflects a *minor* version change, signalling that new functionality has been added but with full backwards compatibility preserved. The last number stands for *patch or micro* changes which indicates bug fixes; patch changes are also fully backwards compatible. Dietrich et al. [14] propose a comprehensive classification of version constraints, including describing fixed, soft, variable dependencies, or typical version semantics such as at least, at most, or latest; the approach we advocate can be further extended to support them.

Resolving which versions are needed to perform a valid update of a system has been approached in several ways including boolean satisfiability (SAT), Mixed Integer Linear Programming (MILP), Answer Set Programming (ASP), or Quantified Boolean Formulae (QBF) [8,9,15,16]. A typical way is working within Satisfiability Modulo Theories (SMT), where solving consists in deciding the satisfiability of a first-order formula with unknowns and relations lying in certain theories; formulas are constructed over usual boolean operators, quantifiers over finite sets, as well as integer linear arithmetic operators. In the following, we informally describe the construction of such a formula which integrates known facts about a system, along with certain constraints; the interested reader can consult technical literature on the topic [17]. The intuition is as follows. Facts capture the current state of the system as well as its desired state; for example, consider that services A and B with versions "1.3" and "18.2.1" respectively are installed, and A is sought to be upgraded to version "1.4." Constraints encode dependencies between services; for example, service B of version "18.2.*" requires service C of fixed version "1.2.5". In essence, given (i) a configuration of already installed services of certain versions, (ii) a service of a newer version which is sought to be updated, (iii) dependency relations between services, and (iv) a set of available versions per each service, we seek to identify which versions of services are required to perform a valid update. A valid update is one that satisfies all service dependencies, and transitions the system to an upgraded (resp. for some service) state. Specifically, the components of the problem regard the desired state, dependencies and the current service configuration:

- **upgrade-versions**: One or more versions of different services that should be upgraded. For example, the user may desire to upgrade service A to version n and service B to version m due to newly introduced features in the first one and a recently fixed bug in the second.
- **available-versions**: Versions of services that are available to be installed, sourced for instance from development repositories.
- **dependencies**: A dependency of a service to versions of another, for example service A with patch constraint "7.5.*" depends on service B with minor constraint "10.*.*."
- **installed-versions**: Versions of services which are already installed in the system; this is the current state of the system.

We abstain from providing a formal representation; existence of versions amounts to assignment to variables (e.g., within linear arithmetic in SMT), while dependencies consist of implications (e.g., selection of service A version 2.1 requires B version 3.4). As such, informally, the dependency resolution problem amounts to: "Given service versions the user wants to update to, versions available and services already installed, derive a set of service versions that adhere to version dependencies, if such a set exists".

Algorithm 1. ALL-VER
Input upgrade version(s), dependency constraint(s), available version(s) per component, installed version(s)
Output set of all valid versions per component
1: /* Construct domain */
2: *domain* ← dependencies
3: /* Construct facts */
4: *hardFacts* ←upgrade-versions,exactly-one
5: *hardFacts* ←+ available-versions
6: *softFacts* ← installed-versions
7: /* Construct problem */
8: *problem* ← *domain, hardFacts, softFacts*
9: /* Iterate over service versions */
10: **for** i ← 1, *versions* **do**
11:     /* pr is partial result */
12:     **for** *pr* ← **solve**(problem,i) **do**
13:         /* add partial to results */
14:         result.add(pr)
15:         /* negate partial result */
16:         problem.not(pr)
17:     **end for**
18: **end for**
19: **Return** *result*

Algorithm 2. MAX-VER
Input upgrade version(s), dependency constraint(s), available version(s) per component, installed versions
Output set of maximum versions per component
1: /* Construct domain */
2: *domain* ← dependencies
3: /* Construct facts */
4: *hardFacts* ←upgrade-versions,exactly-one
5: *hardFacts* ←+ available-versions
6: *softFacts* ← installed-versions
7: /* Construct problem */
8: *problem* ← *domain, hardFacts, softFacts*
9: *components* ← available version(s)
10: /* Iterate over components */
11: **for** i ← 1, *components* **do**
12:     /* Apply ALL-VER to component i */
13:     *versions* ← **all_ver**(problem, i)
14:     *max_ver* ← **max**(versions)
15:     result.add(max_ver)
16:     /* Version holds for component i */
17:     problem.add(**max_ver**, i)
18: **end for**
19: **Return** *result*

4.2 Dependency Resolution Strategies

The generic setting previously presented amounts to a generic problem formulation; thereupon, one can build further strategies for dependency resolution, with different objectives, beyond merely being satisfiable. In particular, we advocate two reference strategies: the MAX-VER strategy determines the most recent versions that constitute a valid update, while ALL-VER discovers all feasible versions. The latter is intended to enable some other selection criterion – for example, selecting a version which has been more widely deployed (thus perhaps more bug-free) – but naturally, at a higher computational cost. We note that the strategies describe the general process – optimizations (taking into account solver particularities, for example), are further possible.

The strategies employed are illustrated in Algorithms 1 and 2 . Both take as input the desired service version(s), the dependency constraints, the available versions per component, and the current installed configuration. The ALL-VER strategy consists of three steps: (i) construct the domain using dependency constraint(s), (ii) construct facts using available and installed version(s), (iii) find solutions. The latter step entails considering each version variable, querying the solver for a partial model (a set of valid results), storing the results, negating the partial model, and querying the solver again until all partial models are delivered. Conversely, the MAX-VER strategy identifies first all versions for the current service, subsequently obtains the partial model and negates the intermediary results. Thereupon, all valid options for the component are found, and the maximum (most recent) is selected. The iteration continues – each time the problem is increasingly constrained.

5 Evaluation

To provide concrete support for our air-gapped update framework, we realized a prototypical end-to-end system; technological choices made for implementation of the functional components are the ones illustrated in grey in Fig. 2. Thereupon, we evaluate our approach over a characteristic scenario elicited from the Comprehensive Nuclear-Test-Ban Treaty (CTBT) Organization. Subsequently, we assess performance aspects. We conclude with a discussion. Our evaluation goals are two-fold; we seek to investigate (i) *applicability* of the proposed solution, in terms that the architecture and system used are able to be used in practice (Sect. 5.1), and (ii) *performance* in realistic settings (Sect. 5.2). The former entails considering a realistic scenario in a mission-critical setting, where the workflow and architecture advocated are employed end-to-end. The latter requires assessing dependency resolution over typical problem sizes.

5.1 Applicability

The Comprehensive Nuclear-Test-Ban Treaty Organization (CTBTO) is an international body tasked with verifying the ban on nuclear tests, operating a worldwide monitoring system and, after the treaty's entry into force, conducting On-Site Inspections (OSIs). Being the final verification measure under the treaty, the purpose of an On-Site Inspection is to collect evidence on whether or not a nuclear explosion has been carried out. The inspection team consists of scientific experts, while the strict regulatory compliance framework in place enforces stringent security requirements on data handling, which imposes strict

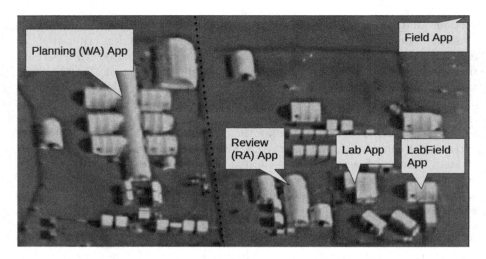

Fig. 3. Fragment of an On-Site-Inspection Exercise illustrating air-gapped sites hosting applications (Image credit: CTBTO OSI Division).

air-gapped isolation upon all software systems involved. The scenario we consider was elicited via interviews from key stakeholders, and concerns a characteristic case where air-gapped update is required.

When an On-Site Inspection is dispatched to a remote location, all software systems are carefully prepared, configured and shipped fully provisioned during the launch phase. Figure 3 illustrates an airborne photograph of this setup during an Integrated Field Exercise. The shown software systems help the inspection team to conduct an inspection by: planning field missions (Planning WA App), collecting data and metadata in the field depending on the used inspection technique (Field App), field data review and classification (Review RA App), conducting radionuclide measurements of environmental samples (LabApp), and receiving or handing over samples (Lab Field App). Observe that the site is network-isolated – there is no uplink, and furthermore sub-systems are not connected to each other; for instance, there is a strict air gap between the Working Area (WA) and Receiving Area (RA) applications, indicated with the red dotted line in Fig. 3. The software setup is comprised of particular versions as shown in Fig. 4. However, they may need to be updated; this may be a case where the Inspected State Party (ISP – the nation or state in which inspection is performed) provides a piece of equipment to conduct e.g., radionuclide measurements in the mobile laboratory, requiring new software to be deployed. As such, the Laboratory Application must be updated to a newer version. In such a case, an officer assesses the change requested and plans the update procedure. Figure 4 highlights in red the application which uses the equipment directly, and it highlights in orange four other components which must now incorporate changes as well. The diagram also shows how communication between components is implemented, and indicates the air-gap with dotted lines between applications.

Observe that in order to update the Laboratory Application to version 3.9.1, new versions of others are required: Field Application (A component), LabField Application (A component), Planning (WA) App PWA (W component), Lab App (W component). The procedure amounts to the following phases:

- **Bootstrapping.** Versions, dependency constraints and artifacts are obtained. Those are defined beforehand by the respective software teams managing them: for the case considered, those are Lab App W "3.9.*" requires LabField App A "3.1.0", Lab App W "3.9.*" requires Field App A "7.9.*," Lab App W "3.9.*" requires Planning (RA) App W "20.1.*," and Lab App W "3.9.*" requires Planning (WA) App PWA "20.1.*." Recall Sect. 4.1 and observe that the dependee version is restricted to only a fixed one of LabField App A, while in the rest only major and minor versions specified and the patch one is open.
- **Update Plan.** The plan to perform needed updates is calculated, and the relevant service artifacts are obtained – those include appropriate container images, data or other binaries. Specifically, the officer selects Lab App W (current installed version "3.8.2"), which is intended to be updated to version "3.9.1." The framework resolves dependencies and returns a list of mandatory updates for other components: LabField App A "3.1.0," Field App A "7.9.0," Planning (RA) App W "20.1.0," and Planning (WA) App PWA "20.1.0." Subsequently, the appropriate artifacts corresponding to the components are obtained from development repositories.
- **Update Execution.** Updates are performed by physically visiting each air-gapped host – details of this step involve protocols outside the scope of this paper.

Overall, we observe that design requirements DR1-DR3 regarding dependability of the update process performed, interoperability with respect to the software supported and auditability regarding update actions are featured in the case performed, pointing to increased applicability of the architecture and end-framework.

5.2 Dependency Resolution Performance

The strategies employed to resolve dependencies represent the most computationally intense activity of the update process; as such, our quantitative evaluation concerns performance assessment with typical problem sizes as elicited from stakeholders (see previous section). Recall that the dependency resolution strategies employ multiple calls to an SMT solver; moreover, they do so differently with MAX-VER deriving (conservative) maximum version resolution only, while ALL-VER targets resolution of all versions, at higher computational cost.

Experiments Setup. Our experiment setup entails (i) generating a suitable dataset and (ii) deploying the proposed framework on a commodity laptop computer typically used in the setting described in the previous section. To obtain a suitable dataset for our experiments, we automatically generate versions in

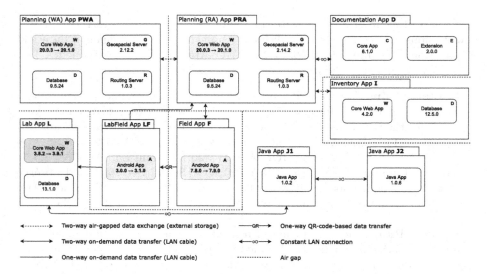

Fig. 4. Service-based software architecture of the OSI case study, illustrating applications comprised of services, with versions (before and after the update) in bold. Applications' air-gapped deployment is denoted with dotted lines.

predefined ranges, while constraints and components are set manually to ensure satisfiable solutions. Thereupon, problem instances are synthesized, varying the number of components and the number of versions per component. Experiments were performed on a laptop computer featuring an Intel® Core™ i7-6820HQ CPU clocked at 2.70GHz, using PySMT 0.9.0 for the programmatic formula construction and MathSAT 5.6.1 as the underlying solver.

Experiments Results. Quantitative results are illustrated in Fig. 5, for configurations of 50 and 125 versions and increasing the number of services considered. We are interested to investigate i) execution time, and ii) the memory footprint, due to the size of the formulas constructed. Results show that strategies MAX-VER and ALL-VER can handle a realistic number of versions per component within acceptable time budgets. For a system with 15 components and 50 versions for each, the execution time is in the order of seconds, depending on the applied strategy. Although the memory footprint does not grow linearly with the size of the problem, it is arguably insignificant for modern systems.

5.3   Discussion

Based on our evaluation results, we believe to have demonstrated that our framework facilitates the update process for air-gapped systems. A typical scenario was elicited and modelled in Sect. 5.1, demonstrating applicability; we successfully modelled a realistic scenario elicited from stakeholders without running into any conceptual issues with regard to our notions of service versions, dependency management and architecture materializing air-gapped updates. On a functional

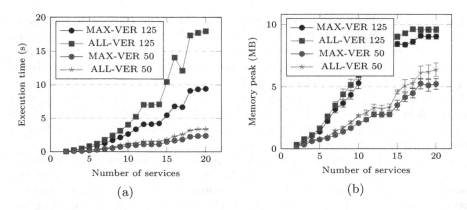

Fig. 5. Dependency resolution performance (a) and memory footprint (b) of MAX-VER and ALL-VER strategies, over number of services for 50 and 125 versions each.

level, a satisfiable combination of versions is computed and a deployment plan is formed, to be installed via the physical visit where the service artifacts are pushed to the target host. Furthermore, the architecture illustrated in Fig. 2 provides for an end-to-end solution, including configuration management, user authentication and container management. Since we followed versioning best practices (tailored for contemporary service-based systems) and employed satisfiability which is widely applied for version management, we believe internal threats to validity of our results to be minimal. However, we note that the case study, although realistic and catering to the needs of an international organization, implied certain type and number of service components, as well as certain design choices in the overall service-based architecture. This is additionally relevant to the quantitative analysis of the dependency resolution; vastly different systems or with different update procedures would imply changes to the workflow and dependency resolution strategies. This would point that results of the case study may not apply to highly diverse cases, which is a threat to external validity. We believe identifying variation points in the architecture presented as a promising avenue of future work.

6   Related Work

The architectural framework proposed is founded on the general area of updating software systems. Accordingly, we classify related work into software evolution management and related approaches dealing with air-gapped environments.

The process of updating service-oriented software systems has been extensively studied, especially concerning so-called dynamic updates [18–20], aiming for reducing downtime while an update is performed. Panzica et al. [19] present a model-driven approach to support software evolution of component-based distributed systems. It requires to build a model, interface automata, to automatically identify the specific class of update. The class is derived based on information locally available in the component and indicates in which state and under which environment condition the system can be correctly updated. In our case, due to the air-gapped nature of the environment, (i) distributed transactions do not take place, and (ii) updates need not happen at runtime. This makes our problem more akin to an offline one; the runtime context of distributed components is thus not relevant and need not be maintained. Importantly, works on dynamic updates focus on *when* to update, while our focus is on *what* to include in an update.

Software update usually relies on dependency resolution (also known as dependency solving) to identify suitable components and compatible versions. Dependency resolution has been approached by using various types of solvers such as boolean satisfiability (SAT), Mixed Integer Linear Programming (MILP), Answer Set Programming (ASP), or Quantified Boolean Formulae (QBF) [8,9,15,16]. Abate et al. [9] argue that dependency solving should be treated as a separate concern from other component management concerns, proposing a modular software construct to decouple the evolution of dependency solving from that of specific package managers and component models, with a Domain Specific Language (DSL) called CUDF as the interface – the DSL can be used to encode component metadata and user update requests. We identify integrating such advanced features as an interesting avenue of future work.

An alternative approach to updates over a network is to take advantage of mobile agents [21,22]. Software packages are updated on a central server, then mobile agents installed on a client receive the update. However, this approach does not target air-gapped networks, as it relies on at least occasional network connectivity for transfer of updates. Gravity [23] is a delivery system for provisioning cloud-native applications in regulated, restricted, or remote environments. It allows packaging complex Kubernetes clusters into portable images for later delivery to a cloud-hosted provider-agnostic environment. Among others, deployment in air-gapped environments is additionally targetted allowing to package a whole cluster, including dependencies, to a tarball, eliminating the need for utilizing a network connection during installation. Gravity aims at packaging and transferring of complex Kubernetes clusters, abstaining however from addressing versions – our approach further provides plugin-style support for different target runtime environments, addressing Docker support out-of-the-box while also similarly allowing Kubernetes for orchestration.

Azab et al. [24] target an isolated infrastructure for storing and processing sensitive research data, providing procedures to provision Docker containers in isolated environments. Additionally, security-related disadvantages of Docker containers are identified, and mitigations are proposed. We believe this reinforces the technological choices made in the architecture of Fig. 2 – furthermore [24] showed that Docker can be indeed successfully applied to provision software in network-isolated environments. The study of security limitations of containers and their secure deployment [25,26] are also important aspects to be taken into account in the overall air-gapped context.

7   Conclusion and Future Work

A central activity within the lifecycle of service-based systems is management of their software updates. Although it is a problem that has been widely tackled by the community in the past, settings where security constraints impose compulsory network isolation call for specialized treatment. To this end, we adopted an architectural viewpoint and presented a technical framework for updating service-based systems in air-gapped environments. After describing the particularities of the domain, we provided suitable modelling notations for service versions, whereupon satisfiability is used for dependency resolution; an overall architecture was presented in an end-to-end solution. We evaluated the applicability of the framework over a realistic case study of an international organization, and assessed the performance of the dependency resolution procedures for practical problem sizes. As for future work, we identify providing a complete reference architecture that engineers and organizations can use for air-gapped updates of service-based systems as per ISO/IEC/IEEE 42010. Moreover, within the update workflow, dependency constraints defined between components and their versions are left to be set by developers without any verification whether the specified constraint is valid; automatic discovery of dependencies could mitigate this problem, which we identify as future work. Similarly, architecture description languages may be used to ensure that the provided interfaces of services match the required ones of their dependents. Adequately keeping track of the remote state of air-gapped systems is an adjacent problem as well. Finally, explicitly considering the criticality of the domain, security is often a key concern that permeates processes, software architectures and software construction and maintenance and as such warrants further investigation.

Disclaimer. The views expressed herein are those of the authors and do not necessarily reflect the views of the CTBTO Preparatory Commission.

References

1. Lehman, M.M.: Programs, life cycles, and laws of software evolution. Proc. IEEE **68**(9), 1060–1076 (1980)
2. Byres, E.: The air gap: Scada's enduring security myth. Commun. ACM **56**(8), 29–31 (2013)
3. Guri, M., Kedma, G., Kachlon, A., Elovici, Y.: Airhopper: bridging the air-gap between isolated networks and mobile phones using radio frequencies. In: 2014 9th International Conference on Malicious and Unwanted Software: The Americas (MALWARE), pp. 58–67. IEEE (2014)
4. Guri, M., Zadov, B., Elovici, Y.: ODINI: escaping sensitive data from faraday-caged, air-gapped computers via magnetic fields. IEEE Trans. Inf. Forensics Secur. **15**, 1190–1203 (2019)
5. Morales, J.A., Yasar, H., Volkmann, A.: Implementing devops practices in highly regulated environments. In: Proceedings of 19th International Conference on Agile Software Development (XP 2018), Companion (2018)

6. Wong, S., Woepse, A.: Software development challenges with air-gap isolation. In: Proceedings of the 2018 26th ACM Joint Meeting on European Software Engineering Conference and Symposium on the Foundations of Software Engineering, ESEC/FSE 2018, pp. 815–820. Association for Computing Machinery, New York (2018)
7. Mancinelli, F., et al.: Managing the complexity of large free and open source package-based software distributions. In: Proceedings of 21st IEEE/ACM International Conference on Automated Software Engineering (ASE 2006) (2006)
8. Abate, P., Di Cosmo, R., Boender, J., Zacchiroli, S.: Strong dependencies between software components. In: 2009 3rd International Symposium on Empirical Software Engineering and Measurement, pp. 89–99. IEEE (2009)
9. Abate, P., Di Cosmo, R., Treinen, R., Zacchiroli, S.: Dependency solving: a separate concern in component evolution management. J. Syst. Softw. **85**(10), 2228–2240 (2012)
10. Abate, P., Cosmo, R.D., Gousios, G., Zacchiroli, S.: Dependency solving is still hard, but we are getting better at it. In: Proceedings of 27th IEEE International Conference on Software Analysis, Evolution and Reengineering (SANER 2020) (2020)
11. Tsigkanos, C., Pasquale, L., Ghezzi, C., Nuseibeh, B.: On the interplay between cyber and physical spaces for adaptive security. IEEE Trans. Dependable Sec. Comput. **15**(3), 466–480 (2018)
12. Russ, C.: Version sat (2016). http://research.swtch.com/version-sat. Accessed 22 Oct 2020
13. Preston-Werner, T.: Semantic versioning 2.0.0. 2013 (2019). http://semver.org
14. Dietrich, J., Pearce, D., Stringer, J., Tahir, A., Blincoe, K.: Dependency versioning in the wild. In: 2019 IEEE/ACM 16th International Conference on Mining Software Repositories (MSR), pp. 349–359. IEEE (2019)
15. Le Berre, D., Parrain, A.: On sat technologies for dependency management and beyond (2008)
16. Lonsing, F., Biere, A.: DepQBF: a dependency-aware QBF solver. J. Satisfiability Boolean Model. Comput. **7**(2–3), 71–76 (2010)
17. Barrett, C., Tinelli, C.: Satisfiability modulo theories. In: Handbook of Model Checking, pp. 305–343. Springer, Cham (2018). https://doi.org/10.1007/978-3-319-10575-8_11
18. Baresi, L., Ghezzi, C., Ma, X., La Manna, V.P.: Efficient dynamic updates of distributed components through version consistency. IEEE Trans. Software Eng. **43**(4), 340–358 (2016)
19. Panzica La Manna, V.: Local dynamic update for component-based distributed systems. In: Proceedings of the 15th ACM SIGSOFT Symposium on Component Based Software Engineering, pp. 167–176 (2012)
20. Ajmani, S., Liskov, B., Shrira, L.: Modular software upgrades for distributed systems. In: Thomas, D. (ed.) ECOOP 2006. LNCS, vol. 4067, pp. 452–476. Springer, Heidelberg (2006). https://doi.org/10.1007/11785477_26
21. Bettini, L., De Nicola, R., Loreti, M.: Software update via mobile agent based programming. In: Proceedings of the 2002 ACM Symposium on Applied Computing, pp. 32–36 (2002)
22. Lange, D.B.: Mobile objects and mobile agents: the future of distributed computing? In: Jul, E. (ed.) ECOOP 1998. LNCS, vol. 1445, pp. 1–12. Springer, Heidelberg (1998). https://doi.org/10.1007/BFb0054084
23. Marin, J.: Deploying applications into air gapped environments (2019). http://goteleport.com/blog/airgap-deployment. Accessed 24 Mar 2021

24. Azab, A., Domanska, D.: Software provisioning inside a secure environment as docker containers using stroll file-system. In: 2016 16th IEEE/ACM International Symposium on Cluster, Cloud and Grid Computing (CCGrid), pp. 674–683. IEEE (2016)
25. Martin, A., Raponi, S., Combe, T., Pietro, R.D.: Docker ecosystem - vulnerability analysis. Comput. Commun. **122**, 30–43 (2018)
26. Xu, Q., Jin, C., Rasid, M.F.B.M., Veeravalli, B., Aung, K.M.M.: Blockchain-based decentralized content trust for docker images. Multimedia Tools Appl. **77**(14), 18223–18248 (2017). https://doi.org/10.1007/s11042-017-5224-6

Architectural Tactics for Energy-Aware Robotics Software: A Preliminary Study

Katerina Chinnappan[1], Ivano Malavolta[1], Grace A. Lewis[2],
Michel Albonico[3(✉)], and Patricia Lago[1,4]

[1] Vrije Universiteit Amsterdam, Amsterdam, The Netherlands
{k.p.chinnappan,i.malavolta,p.lago}@vu.nl
[2] Software Engineering Institute, Carnegie Mellon University, Pittsburgh, USA
glewis@sei.cmu.edu
[3] Federal University of Technology, Paraná - UTFPR, Francisco Beltrão, Brazil
michelalbonico@utfpr.edu.br
[4] Chalmers University of Technology, Gothenburg, Sweden

Abstract. In software engineering, energy awareness refers to the conscious design and development of software that is able to monitor and react to energy state. Energy awareness is the key building block for energy efficiency and for other quality aspects of robotics software, such as mission completion time and safety. However, as of today, there is no guidance for practitioners and researchers on how to architect robotics software with energy awareness in mind. The goal of this paper is to identify architectural tactics for energy-aware robotics software. Specifically, using a dataset of 339,493 data points extracted from five complementary data sources (*e.g.,* source code repositories, Stack Overflow), we identified and analyzed 97 data points that considered both energy consumption and architectural concerns. We then synthesized a set of energy-aware architectural tactics via thematic analysis. In this preliminary investigation we focus on two representative architectural tactics.

1 Introduction

Energy is a critical resource for a company's competitiveness and environmental sustainability; its management can lead to controlled operational expenses and low carbon emissions. However, data shows that energy consumption has increased considerably over time. For instance, it is projected that the industrial sector will increase energy consumption by 44% between 2006 and 2030 [13]. Furthermore, Information and Communications Technology (ICT) also plays an important role in energy consumption, where it is expected that by 2040 it will alone consume the equivalent of today's global energy production [1]. Robotics software may impact both these scenarios.

© Springer Nature Switzerland AG 2021
S. Biffl et al. (Eds.): ECSA 2021, LNCS 12857, pp. 164–171, 2021.
https://doi.org/10.1007/978-3-030-86044-8_11

Software is becoming the prominent aspect in robotics [11]. Robotics software is becoming more and more complex in terms of control and communication, which inevitably leads to greater energy consumption [10]. Making robotics software energy-aware can lead to cost and sustainability benefits. Additionally, energy awareness is a key factor for battery-operated robots, such as autonomous cars, drones, and service robots. Being energy-aware can lead to better quality of service for the whole robotic system because the robot can operate for a longer time, more safely, and more reliably [3].

Rethinking software development is a good starting point to reason about how software systems consume energy [7]. This principle also applies to robotics software [9]. The first step towards designing energy-aware robotics software is to establish a set of concrete design options known as *architectural tactics* [4] that roboticists can use as the foundation to achieve energy awareness. In this study, we follow the definition of energy-aware software provided by Fonseca *et al.*: software that is consciously designed and developed to monitor and react to energy preferences and usage [8]. Accordingly, energy-aware tactics for robotics software can be defined as those tactics whose response is system-wide monitoring and communication of the energy levels of the robots; the monitored energy levels can be used by other components within the robotic system for different purposes, one of them (not the only one) being energy efficiency.

The goal of this paper is to *identify and document existing energy-aware tactics in state-of-the-practice robotics software*. We consider software running on the Robot Operating System (ROS) [2] as it is the de-facto standard for robotics software [10]. To achieve this goal, we build on a previously constructed dataset [9] containing online data sources specifically related to the ROS community and millions of lines of code from open-source ROS projects. The initial dataset contains 339,493 data points, which have been filtered to obtain only those data points where roboticists discuss/refer to energy consumption and discuss architecturally-relevant concerns. This filtering step produced 97 data points that were analyzed using the thematic analysis technique. As a result, we identified a set of architectural tactics for energy awareness in robotics software. In this preliminary investigation we focus on two architectural tactics, namely: (AT1) Energy Savings Mode and (AT2) Stop Current Task & Recharge. We select those tactics among the others since (i) they are among the most occurring tactics applied in the mined projects and (ii) they are complementary with respect to their objective (AT1 is about energy-level provisioning and AT2 is about mission recondiguration at runtime).

2   ROS-Based Robotics Software

ROS has become a de-facto standard that supports different robotics project domains [11]. It currently supports more than 140 types of robots [2]. Its popularity is a reflection of the vibrant ROS community, which has more than 59k questions posted on the ROS Answers forum[1], and another 2.6k discussions on

---

[1] https://answers.ros.org.

ROS Discourse[2]. ROS is also a framework that includes tools, libraries, and conventions for developing robotics software [2]. Its goal is to support a collaborative and open development environment, and function as middleware for robotics software, supporting the development of more complex solutions in which different high-skilled teams provide different components.

In ROS, each robotics ecosystem component (*e.g.,* robot, sensor, control application) is designed as a *node*. ROS nodes can be distributed across multiple tiers, and communicate with each other using three communication patterns: *topics, services,* and *actions. Topics* implement a publish-subscribe pattern, *i.e.,* one node publishes its data into a topic that other nodes can subscribe to and then retrieve the published data. *Services* are based on remote procedure calls (RPC), which are implemented following RPC conventions. *Actions* are used for long-running processes, where one node requests an action from another node, which starts the process, periodically publishes intermediate results, and notifies the requester node when the process is finished. These three patterns are simple and based on well-known distributed system techniques, which simplifies the development of robot communication interfaces. Furthermore, with the second version of ROS (ROS2), part of the communication relies on a Data Distribution Service (DDS) middleware, which further simplifies network programming.

3   Mining the Architectural Tactics

We extracted the architectural tactics in four distinct phases: 1) we build an initial dataset of 339,493 data points by crawling open data sources for ROS-specific data (*e.g.,* ROS Answers, Stack Overflow, GitHub); 2) we filter the dataset to extract the *562* data points that are specifically related to energy by means of a combination of keyword-based search and manual analysis; 3) we identify 97 data points where architecturally-relevant concerns are also discussed; and 4) we synthesize the architectural tactics for energy-aware robotics software via thematic analysis. Phases 1, 2, and 3 were already carried out in the context of previous work [9], where we targeted tactics for energy efficiency, *i.e.,* tactics whose response is the *reduction* of energy consumption when performing a given task. In this study, we carry out Phase 4 with a different goal, which is to identify architectural tactics for *energy awareness.*

Due to space constraints, in this paper we only provide a high-level overview of the main characteristics of two representative architectural tactics. The complete description of those tactics (including the raw data we analyzed) is available in the replication package for this study[3].

4   Results

In this section we describe in two of the tactics we extracted: (AT1) Energy Savings Mode and (AT2) Stop Current Task & Recharge. Those tactics are among the most occurrent ones in our dataset and their objectives are complementary.

---

[2] https://discourse.ros.org.
[3] https://github.com/S2-group/ecsa-2021-replication-package.

AT1 aims to provides energy-level values to other nodes in the system, a user, or a third party; differently, AT2 update the current mission according to currently available energy, specifically by interrupting a task when the energy level becomes critical. For each tactic we provide the following information: (i) the *intent* of the tactic, (ii) the *solution* in terms of a component-and-connector and sequence diagrams that shows the main components that play a key role in the tactic and their interaction, (iii) an *example* of a concrete implementation of the tactic from our dataset.

4.1   Energy Savings Mode (AT1)

Intent. This tactic provides a shared space for storing information about the robot's state (*i.e.*, blackboard architecture pattern), which ensures that all the robotics software components are energy-aware. Thus, it informs components when they need to start saving energy and adjust their behavior accordingly.

Solution. This tactic dictates to the components in a system whether or not to enter into a state in which energy must be saved (enable or disable the energy-savings mode).

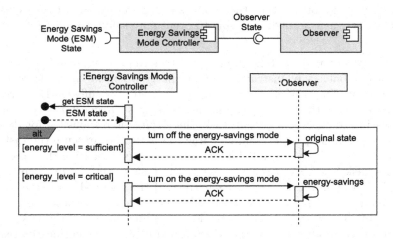

Fig. 1. Energy savings mode tactic (AT1)

Figure 1 shows a C&C and sequence diagram for this tactic. The *Energy Savings Mode Controller* acts as a decentralized *blackboard* component [12]. Specifically, it keeps track of the current energy-savings mode of the robotic system and then makes it available to the other components in the system. In the majority of cases, the *Energy Savings Mode Controller* is proactive: it requests the current energy-savings mode from one component in the system and, based on the response, it dictates to the rest of the components to either disable or enable the energy-savings mode and change their state accordingly. Every *Observer* component receives the current energy-savings mode, switches to it, and updates the *blackboard* by sending an acknowledgment message. With this approach, all of the *Observers* are aware of the current energy-savings mode of the system, and the blackboard is aware of whether or not each component switched to the instructed energy-savings mode.

Example. The `rov-control` project[4] implements this tactic in a Remotely Operated Vehicle (ROV) system with two components: the *stepper* node that maps to the *Observer* component, and the *manipulator* node that maps to the *Energy Savings Mode Controller* component. The *stepper* represents nodes in the system which must comply with a certain behavior depending on the current manipulator command (*e.g.*, energy-savings mode). The *manipulator* node publishes the current command to a *manipulator_command* topic, while the *stepper* node subscribes to it. After receiving the current *manipulator* command and complying with it, the *stepper* node publishes its new state to the *stepper_state* topic, which is in turn subscribed to by the manipulator node.

4.2   Stop Current Task & Recharge (AT2)

Intent. This tactic is used to ensure that robots are able to complete their tasks. Human intervention is not always available when the battery level is critical. Therefore, it is important that the robot is energy-aware, able to replenish its battery power when needed, and able to eventually safely complete its current mission.

Solution. This tactic gracefully interrupts a task to prevent the robot from fully discharging its battery by instructing it to recharge when the energy level reaches a critical point. The task is resumed when the battery is sufficiently charged.

Figure 2 shows the tactic components. The *Task Requestor* is responsible for requesting to execute a certain task, the *Arbiter* is responsible for deciding whether or not to stop a task and recharge the battery or execute the task, and the *Task Executor* is responsible for either stopping or executing the task. After creating a task, the *Task Requestor* sends the task to the *Arbiter*, which then checks the energy-level of the robot's battery. If the energy-level is critical, the *Arbiter* immediately removes the task and the task is not forwarded to the *Task Executor*. In the case when the energy-level is sufficient, the *Arbiter* sends the task to the *Task Executor* and the *Task Executor* starts executing the task. In parallel, the *Arbiter* starts checking the energy-level of the robot within a loop. If throughout the entire execution of the task the energy-level stays sufficient, the *Task Requestor* is notified about the completion of the task. If during the execution of the task the energy-level becomes critical, the *Arbiter* instructs the *Task Executor* to stop the task and request another component in the system to recharge the battery. Once the battery is recharged (*i.e.*, the energy level is sufficient), the *Arbiter* instructs the *Task Executor* to resume the task. Finally, when the task is completed, the *Task Executor* sends a completion message to the *Arbiter*, which in turn forwards the completion message to the *Task Requestor*.

---

[4] https://github.com/vortexntnu/rov-control.

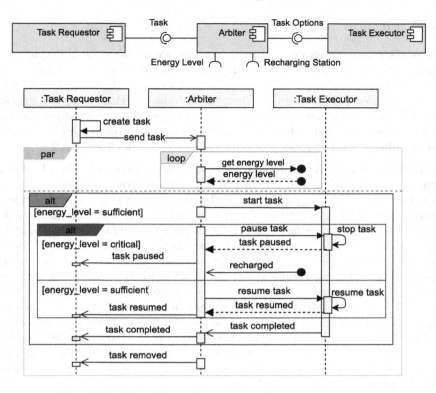

Fig. 2. Stop current task & recharge tactic (AT2)

Example. The aau_multi_robot project[5] implements this tactic in an autonomous multi-robot ROS-based system with two nodes: *explorer* and *exploration_planner*. In the system, the *explorer* implements the *Task Requestor* and the *Arbiter* components, while the *exploration_planner* implements the *Task Executor*. Because all the tactic decisions are made in the *explorer* (*Arbiter*), it subscribes to the *battery_state* ROS topic where the robot repeatedly publishes its battery level. Then, the *explorer* instructs the *exploration_planner* to execute an exploration task. If the battery level is not critical (set by a threshold) the *exploration_planner* node starts executing the task and reports to the *explorer* when it is finished. It is possible that during task execution the battery reaches the critical level, which is when the *explorer* saves the current progress of the task and instructs the *explorer_planner* (on the robot) to recharge the battery. The robot goes to the recharging station, and once its battery is charged, it notifies the *explorer* node, which then provides it the necessary information to continue the task.

---

[5] https://github.com/aau-ros/aau_multi_robot.

5   Discussion

Roboticists are concerned about energy awareness. In this study, we mined ROS data sources to identify and extract architectural tactics for energy-aware robotics software. We discovered that there were in fact multiple data points that used energy-aware tactics, which indicates that there are existing methods available for roboticists to design and implement energy-aware robotics software. The tactics range from only profiling energy consumption (like in AT1) to controlling the robot to stop or pause its current task (like in AT2).

Data points are mostly for battery-operated robots, but the identified architectural tactics can be applied to other robot types. It is also interesting to note that the majority of the tactics are associated with battery-operated robots even though we did not intend to only focus on such robots. This might highlight the fact that batteries such as *Lithium Ion* and *Lithium Polymer* have a limited energy budget, and therefore battery-operated robots require an intelligent energy-management scheme. Additionally, several robotic tasks are followed by idle times where the robot needs to recharge its batteries; those idle times generally correspond to a loss of productivity [5]. Reducing idle times can lead to a better quality of service because the robot can run for a longer time and therefore more tasks can be completed. Even though most of the tactics were extracted from data points related to battery-operated robots, we argue that most of the identified tactics are applicable to robots that are powered directly from a cable (and also apply to other domains, such as cloud computing and the Internet of Things).

Roboticists tend not to explicitly document the architecture of their software. There are several benefits in documenting software architectures [6], such as helping new developers to understand projects and being able to discuss possible trade-offs. However, the analyzed data points do not present any structured documentation or diagram that model the robotics software. In this study, we provide some architecture views and tactic descriptions which may inspire roboticists to do the same as they design their software.

6   Conclusions and Future Work

In this study, we mined architectural tactics for energy-aware robotics software from data sources related to ROS-based systems. To identify energy-aware tactics in existing systems, we carried out a multi-phase study that resulted in seven *energy-awareness* tactics. To foster the applicability of the identified tactics (even beyond the ROS community), we describe them in a generic, implementation-independent manner by means of diagrams inspired by the UML component and sequence diagram notation. The presented energy-aware tactics can serve as guidance for roboticists, as well as other developers interested in architecting and implementing energy-aware software. Furthermore, the extracted energy-aware tactics can help researchers by providing empirically-grounded insights about how practitioners are designing energy-aware robotics software.

As future work, we will build a complete catalog of architectural tactics for both energy-awareness and energy-efficiency in the context of robotics software. Moreover, we are planning to conduct an empirical assessment on how different implementations of the identified tactics might impact the overall quality of robotic systems by using real robots in real missions. For example, different implementations of tactics might lead to different trade-offs with other quality attributes, such as performance and reliability.

Acknowledgments. This research is partially supported by the Dutch Research Council (NWO) through the OCENW.XS2.038 grant; and the CNPQ/FA through the PPP-CP-20/2018 call.

References

1. International Technology Roadmap for Semiconductors. https://www.itrs2.net/itrs-reports.html. Accessed 04 June 2021
2. ROS.org — Powering the world's robots. https://www.ros.org/. Accessed 12 Mar 2021
3. Albonico, M., Malavolta, I., Pinto, G., Guzmán, E., Chinnappan, K., Lago, P.: Mining energy-related practices in robotics software. In: International Conference on Mining Software Repositories, MSR, New York, NY. IEEE/ACM, May 2021
4. Bass, L., Clements, P., Kazman, R.: Software Architecture in Practice, 3rd edn. Addison-Wesley Professional, Boston (2012)
5. Carabin, G., Wehrle, E., Vidoni, R.: A review on energy-saving optimization methods for robotic and automatic systems. MDPI (2017)
6. Clements, P., Garlan, D., Little, R., Nord, R., Stafford, J.: Documenting software architectures: views and beyond. In: Proceedings of 25th International Conference on Software Engineering, pp. 740–741. IEEE (2003)
7. De Matteis, T., Mencagli, G.: Proactive elasticity and energy awareness in data stream processing. J. Syst. Softw. **127**, 302–319 (2017)
8. Fonseca, A., Kazman, R., Lago, P.: A manifesto for energy-aware software. IEEE Softw. **36**(6), 79–82 (2019)
9. Malavolta, I., Chinnappan, K., Swanborn, S., Lewis, G., Lago, P.: Mining the ROS ecosystem for green architectural tactics in robotics and an empirical evaluation. In: Proceedings of the 18th International Conference on Mining Software Repositories, MSR, pp. 300–311. ACM, May 2021
10. Malavolta, I., Lewis, G., Schmerl, B., Lago, P., Garlan, D.: How do you architect your robots? State of the practice and guidelines for ROS-based systems. In: IEEE/ACM 42nd International Conference on Software Engineering: Software Engineering in Practice (ICSE-SEIP), pp. 31–40 (2020)
11. Malavolta, I., Lewis, G.A., Schmerl, B., Lago, P., Garlan, D.: Mining guidelines for architecting robotics software. J. Syst. Softw. **178**, 110969 (2021)
12. Shaw, M., Garlan, D.: Software Architecture: Perspectives on an Emerging Discipline. Prentice-Hall, Hoboken (1996)
13. Vikhorev, K., Greenough, R., Brown, N.: An advanced energy management framework to promote energy awareness. J. Clean. Prod. **43**, 103–112 (2013)

Taxonomy of Edge Blockchain Network Designs

Nguyen Khoi Tran$^{(\boxtimes)}$ ⓘ and Muhammad Ali Babar ⓘ

The University of Adelaide, Adelaide, South Australia, Australia
{nguyen.tran,ali.babar}@adelaide.edu.au

Abstract. Blockchains have been increasingly employed in use cases at the network's edge, such as autonomous vehicles and edge computing. These use cases usually establish new blockchain networks due to operation costs, performance constraints, and the lack of reliable connectivity to public blockchains. The design of these edge blockchain networks heavily influences the quality attributes of blockchain-oriented software deployed upon them. This paper presents a taxonomy of edge blockchain network designs successfully utilized by the existing literature and analyzes their availability when facing failures at nodes and networks. This taxonomy benefits practitioners and researchers by offering a design guide for establishing blockchain networks for edge use cases.

Keywords: Blockchain · Distributed ledger · Design pattern

1 Introduction

Blockchain is a type of distributed system that enables tamper-proof transaction recording and facilitates incorruptible judgement without relying on a third party [7]. To establish a new blockchain, practitioners must design and develop an underlying blockchain network – *a distributed software system comprising connected computers that jointly maintain a blockchain according to a blockchain protocol.* Even though the term "blockchain networks" suggests that these systems operate at the computer network level, blockchain networks actually denote the distributed software system running on top of a computer network. Thus, designing blockchain networks is a software architecture topic, similarly to designing and configuring a distributed system.

Designing a blockchain network involves deciding on its protocol and topology. Despite the critical impact of blockchain networks on the characteristics of blockchain-oriented software, the design aspect of blockchain networks has been relatively under-investigated in the software architecture literature comparing to blockchain-oriented software topics such as patterns [9], tactics [6], and decision models [1]. Even less research has focused on edge blockchain networks [2]. While practitioners can selectively apply these existing work to edge blockchain networks, they would benefit further from a comprehensive description, classification, and analysis of concrete designs utilized successfully by the existing edge blockchain network prototypes.

© Springer Nature Switzerland AG 2021
S. Biffl et al. (Eds.): ECSA 2021, LNCS 12857, pp. 172–180, 2021.
https://doi.org/10.1007/978-3-030-86044-8_12

This paper targets the stated gap with a taxonomy of edge blockchain network designs. We constructed this taxonomy by systematically identifying, classifying, and evaluating edge blockchain network designs utilized by prototypes in the literature. First, we identified the relevant papers from a paper dataset of an existing systematic literature review on integrating blockchain and the Internet of Things [5]. Second, we extracted blockchain network design decisions from the prototypes reported by these papers using the blockchain network design space [4]. Third, these decisions were grouped into network designs and organized into a taxonomy (Fig. 1). Finally, we evaluated the identified designs regarding their availability for edge devices to read, write, and propagate updates when losing nodes, networks, and cloud backend. We focused on availability because of its criticality to edge use cases and its independence from the implementation technology and hardware infrastructure. The taxonomy of edge blockchain network designs and the availability analysis forms the contributions of this paper.

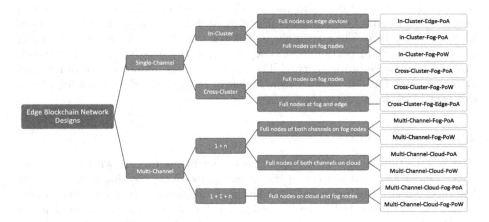

Fig. 1. Taxonomy of edge blockchain network designs

2 Background and Related Work

2.1 Blockchain Network Design

Blockchains can be considered a singleton, transaction-based state machine replicated across a group of networked computers – *a blockchain network* [7]. These computers operate according to *consensus protocol*, which dictates how a blockchain network agree on the validity and order of blockchain transactions to ensure that a blockchain's state is identical across the entire network. Public blockchains, which are open to anonymous participants on the Internet, generally employ *Proof-of-Work (PoW) consensus protocols*. These protocols are resistant against Sybil attacks, which involve a malicious party creating multiple fake identities to take over the consensus of an open and anonymous system. PoW protocols make Sybil attack prohibitively expensive by adding a cost to any consensus-related interaction, such as broadcasting a new set of transactions (i.e., a *block*). This cost assumes a cryptography puzzle that is challenging to solve but easy for anyone to validate. All participants that process transactions in a PoW-based blockchain network, also known as *miners*, race to solve puzzles and broadcast new blocks. Due to the independence of miners, PoW-based networks are resilient to network fragmentation because all fragments would continue operating instead of becoming hanged. An alternative to PoW consensus protocol is *Proof-of-Authority (PoA) consensus protocols*, which require participants to reveal their identity and coordinate closely to reach a consensus on the validity and order of transactions. Due to this tight coordination, PoA-based networks are less resource-intensive but more vulnerable to network disruptions.

Designing a blockchain network involves decisions covering both protocol and topology [4]. Protocol decisions include choosing and configuring the consensus protocol for a blockchain network. Topological decisions determine a blockchain network's structure. They cover the distribution of blockchain nodes and mining rights to blockchain participants. They describe the deployment of blockchain nodes on hardware infrastructure. They also cover the segmentation of a blockchain network into *channels*, which maintain separated ledgers and might use different blockchain protocols.

2.2 Related Work

The architecture design of software running on or interacting with blockchains have been studied extensively in the recent software engineering literature. For instance, Xu et al. [8] proposed considering blockchain as a new form of software connector and presented a pattern collection for blockchain-based applications [9]. Wessling et al. [6] proposed architectural blockchain tactics. Comuzzi [1] proposed a design space consisting of eight types of design decisions for consideration when transforming a centralised software system into a blockchain-based one. While these patterns, tactics, and design space are invaluable to blockchain-based software, they do not guide the design of blockchain networks beyond describing the typical characteristics of various blockchain types [10].

A few research have focused on the architectural aspect of the underlying blockchain network. For example, Tran et al. [4] proposed a design space for blockchain networks containing 19 dimensions with 51 choices. This design space applies to blockchain networks in most domains, including edge use cases. It provides a framework for systematically evaluating design decisions and describe blockchain network designs. More closely related to edge blockchain networks are four architectural styles proposed by Liao et al. [2], which specify where blockchain clients should be located in an IoT-based infrastructure. While practitioners can selectively apply these existing work to the design of edge blockchains, none has provided a comprehensive description, classification, and analysis of concrete designs for edge blockchain networks that support the design process of practitioners working on blockchain for edge use cases.

This paper addresses the stated gap by proposing a taxonomy of edge blockchain network designs. We apply the blockchain network design space [4] to identify and describe the common edge blockchain network designs employed by the existing prototypes. Comparing to the architectural styles proposed by Liao et al. [2], the taxonomy has a broader scope, covering both protocol and topology design decisions rather than limiting to blockchain client deployment. Moreover, we also evaluate the availability level of the identified edge blockchain network designs against five failure scenarios.

3   Taxonomy of Edge Blockchain Network Designs

3.1   Methodology

We developed the taxonomy following a three-step process. First, we identified the relevant papers about operating blockchains in an edge computing environment. These papers were selected from a dataset of an existing systematic literature review on Blockchain-integrated Internet of Things systems [5], combined with the top search results from Google Scholar on the keywords "blockchain" and "edge computing".

Second, we extracted design decisions from the selected papers using the blockchain network design space [4]. The extracted decisions fell into two classes. *Protocol decisions* cover the choice and configuration of blockchain protocols for operating the blockchain network. *Topological decisions* cover the following aspects:

- *Overall network's shape decisions* determine whether the network is segmented into interrelated channels and the coverage of those channels.
- *Full node decisions* dictate the distribution of full nodes to the network's participants and the deployment of full nodes on hardware infrastructure.
- *Mining nodes decisions* control the distribution of the mining rights and the placement of mining nodes on the hardware infrastructure.
- *Lightweight node decisions* determine whether a blockchain network employs lightweight blockchain nodes in its topology.
- *Network interface decisions* govern the type and deployment of blockchain networks' interfaces.
- *Remote node decisions* govern the distribution and deployment of remote nodes, which are programs that users use to query and send transactions to a blockchain.

In this step, we also synthesized a *Reference Edge Infrastructure* from the edge infrastructures utilized by the selected papers (Fig. 2). The reference edge infrastructure is arranged into clusters, representing devices deployed at different locations. Each cluster includes edge devices and a few fog nodes, which act as cluster heads and are responsible for communicating with other clusters and cloud servers. No direct communication is allowed between edge nodes and any device outside its cluster. The reference edge infrastructure normalizes deployment-related design decisions across different papers by defining a standard vocabulary for describing hardware nodes and networks on which edge blockchain networks are deployed. It also helped minimize the ambiguity of concepts such as edge, fog nodes, cloudlet, and edge computing.

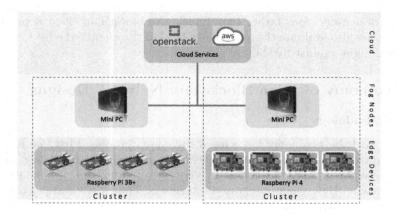

Fig. 2. Reference edge infrastructure for describing deployment decisions

The last step of our process was constructing the taxonomy of edge blockchain network designs. We identified common edge blockchain network designs, which are groups of design decisions that commonly appear together. We clustered these designs into a hierarchical structure, forming the taxonomy (Fig. 1).

3.2   Taxonomy of Edge Blockchain Network Designs

Despite the diversity of options, we found that the existing edge blockchain prototypes converged to a few designs, classified into two groups: single-channel designs and multi-channel designs.

Single-channel designs contain only one blockchain channel in the entire edge infrastructure or many independent channels that have no connection with each other, effectively forming smaller separate blockchain networks. Single-channel designs are divided into in-cluster and cross-cluster designs. *In-cluster designs* limit blockchain channels within the boundary of device clusters. Designers can choose between placing full and mining nodes on edge devices or offloading all blockchain-related responsibilities to fog nodes. Placing miners on edge devices limits the consensus protocol choice to PoA due to resource constraints. *Cross-cluster designs* deploy a blockchain channel across multiple device clusters. A popular design is placing all blockchain-related responsibilities on fog nodes that control clusters, reducing edge devices to simple blockchain clients. Alternatively, designers can place full and mining nodes on all fog nodes and edge devices. As we will see in the availability analysis, this design offers a superior availability level for reading from a blockchain. However, it limits protocol choice to PoA-based consensus protocols.

Multi-channel designs contain multiple blockchain channels covering different sets of hardware nodes in an edge computing infrastructure. We further classify these designs into $1 + n$ and $1 + 1 + n$ designs. The $1 + n$ designs combine n in-cluster channels with a cross-cluster channel. Both types of channels can be designed using the corresponding single-channel designs described above. The cross-cluster channel is generally hosted by cloud servers or fog nodes.

The $1 + 1 + n$ designs contain a cloud-level channel, a cross-cluster fog-level channel, and n in-cluster channels. For instance, Nyamtiga et al. [3] employed a three-level edge blockchain network to securely store and manage the data collected by edge devices. The bottom-level channels covered edge devices within clusters. The middle-level channel spanned fog nodes, connecting clusters. The top-level channel was deployed within cloud infrastructures to control and coordinate cloud resources. Even though $1 + 1 + n$ designs offer a high degree of flexibility, they were among the least popular edge blockchain network designs.

4 Availability Evaluation

We evaluated the availability level of edge blockchain network designs from the perspective of edge devices such as robots and autonomous vehicles because they are primary end-users of edge blockchain networks. We distinguished three types of availability as follows. *Read-availability* of a blockchain network design assesses whether edge devices can read the content stored on a blockchain. *Write-availability* assesses whether updates sent by edge devices can be committed to a blockchain, meaning that a device can reach a blockchain node and that node can process and append new transactions to a blockchain. *Update-availability* assesses whether the updates sent by an edge device can reach every device, only local devices, or no devices in an edge infrastructure. It should be noted that being write-available does not imply being update-available. For instance, a disconnected group of PoW-based blockchain clients is available for writing, but these updates would not reach all edge devices.

We analyzed the availability of edge blockchain network designs listed in the taxonomy in the context of the following failure scenarios: (1) losing (n/3) of edge devices in a local cluster, (2) losing a local fog node, (3) losing a cloud node, (4) losing a local edge network, and (5) losing a cross-cluster network.

As an example, let us consider the availability of the Cross-Cluster-Fog-Edge-PoA design when losing the cross-cluster network. All edge devices can still read from a blockchain when a failure happens because they host full blockchain nodes and thus have access to a complete ledger replica. However, the PoA consensus protocol used by a Cross-Cluster-For-Edge-PoA blockchain network would hang if its miners are disconnected. Therefore, none of the edge devices can write to a blockchain, which means none of the edge devices can receive any update from others. Thus, the Cross-Cluster-Fog-Edge-PoA design achieves the "all" level for read availability and "none" for both write availability and update availability. Following the a similar analysis, we evaluated all blockchain network designs identified in the taxonomy. Figure 3 and 4 presents the results.

a. Read Availability

Failure	In-cluster-Edge-PoA	In-Cluster-Fog-PoA	In-Cluster-Fog-PoW	Cross-Cluster-Fog-PoA	Cross-Cluster-Fog-PoW	Cross-Cluster-Fog-Edge-PoA	Multi-Channel-Fog-PoA	Multi-Channel-Fog-PoW	Multi-Channel-Cloud-PoA	Multi-Channel-Cloud-PoW	Multi-Channel-Cloud-Fog-PoA	Multi-Channel-Cloud-Fog-PoW	
Lose 1 edge device in the cluster	All	All	All	All	All	All	All	All	All	All	All	All	0.00%
Lose the controlling fog node	All	All	All	None	None	All	None	None	None	None	None	None	66.67%
Lose the cloud node	All	All	All	All	All	All	All	All	None	None	All	All	16.67%
Lose the in-cluster network	All	All	All	None	None	All	None	None	None	None	None	None	66.67%
Lose the cross-cluster network	All	All	All	All	All	All	All	All	None	None	All	All	16.67%
	100.00%	100.00%	100.00%	60.00%	60.00%	100.00%	60.00%	60.00%	20.00%	20.00%	60.00%	60.00%	

b. Write Availability

Failure	In-cluster-Edge-PoA	In-Cluster-Fog-PoA	In-Cluster-Fog-PoW	Cross-Cluster-Fog-PoA	Cross-Cluster-Fog-PoW	Cross-Cluster-Fog-Edge-PoA	Multi-Channel-Fog-PoA	Multi-Channel-Fog-PoW	Multi-Channel-Cloud-PoA	Multi-Channel-Cloud-PoW	Multi-Channel-Cloud-Fog-PoA	Multi-Channel-Cloud-Fog-PoW	
Lose 1 edge device in cluster	All	All	All	All	All	All	All	All	All	All	All	All	0.00%
Lose the controlling fog node	All	None	None	None	None	None	None	None	None	None	None	None	91.67%
Lose the cloud node	All	All	All	All	All	All	All	All	None	None	All	All	16.67%
Lose the in-cluster network	None	None	None	None	None	None	None	None	None	None	None	None	100.00%
Lose the cross-cluster network	All	All	All	None	All	None	All	All	None	None	None	All	41.67%
	80.00%	60.00%	60.00%	40.00%	60.00%	40.00%	60.00%	60.00%	20.00%	20.00%	40.00%	60.00%	

Fig. 3. Read and write availability levels of the evaluated blockchain network designs

5   Concluding Remarks

This paper presents and evaluates the availability levels of twelve edge blockchain network designs commonly used by the existing edge blockchain prototypes. We found that the further we push blockchain clients to the edge, the more available an edge blockchain network becomes, particularly in read availability. Designs that place blockchain clients directly on edge computing devices enjoy the best read availability and in-cluster update availability. Cloud-only designs consistently offer the worst availability levels. Protocol-wise, we find that PoW-based designs generally provide better levels of write availability and update availability. While designs that use PoW consensus protocol and push blockchain clients to the edge offer higher availability levels, they are also significantly more resource-intensive and, as a result, potentially slower. These drawbacks make these designs infeasible for some edge use cases. This observation shows the trade-off between resource consumption, performance, and the availability of

Failure	In-cluster-Edge-PoA	In-Cluster-Fog-PoA	In-Cluster-Fog-PoW	Cross-Cluster-Fog-PoA	Cross-Cluster-Fog-PoW	Cross-Cluster-Fog-Edge-PoA	Multi-Channel-Fog-PoA	Multi-Channel-Fog-PoW	Multi-Channel-Cloud-PoA	Multi-Channel-Cloud-PoW	Multi-Channel-Cloud-Fog-PoA	Multi-Channel-Cloud-Fog-PoW	
Lose 1 edge device in cluster	In-Cluster Only	In-Cluster Only	In-Cluster Only	All	All	All	All	All	All	All	All	All	0.00%
Lose the controlling fog node	In-Cluster Only	None	None	None	None	None	None	None	None	None	None	None	91.67%
Lose the cloud node	In-Cluster Only	In-Cluster Only	In-Cluster Only	All	All	All	All	All	None	None	All	All	16.67%
Lose the in-cluster network	None	None	None	None	None	None	None	None	None	None	None	None	100.00%
Lose the cross-cluster network	In-Cluster Only	In-Cluster Only	In-Cluster Only	None	In-Cluster Only	None	In-Cluster Only	In-Cluster Only	None	None	None	In-Cluster Only	41.67%
Global Write Availability	0%	0%	0%	40%	40%	40%	40%	40%	20%	20%	40%	40%	
Local Write Availability	80%	60%	60%	40%	60%	40%	60%	60%	20%	20%	40%	60%	

Fig. 4. Update availability levels of the evaluated blockchain network designs

blockchain network designs. Thus, future research should empirically analyze the performance and resource consumption offered by edge blockchain network designs to establish a multi-dimensional decision support system for designing blockchain networks that consider trade-offs on all three aspects.

References

1. Comuzzi, M., Unurjargal, E., Lim, C.: Towards a design space for blockchain-based system reengineering. In: Matulevičius, R., Dijkman, R. (eds.) CAiSE 2018. LNBIP, vol. 316, pp. 138–143. Springer, Cham (2018). https://doi.org/10.1007/978-3-319-92898-2_11
2. Liao, C.-F., Hung, C.-C., Chen, K.: Blockchain and the internet of things: a software architecture perspective. In: Treiblmaier, H., Beck, R. (eds.) Business Transformation through Blockchain, pp. 53–75. Springer, Cham (2019). https://doi.org/10.1007/978-3-319-99058-3_3
3. Nyamtiga, B.W., Sicato, J.C.S., Rathore, S., Sung, Y., Park, J.H.: Blockchain-based secure storage management with edge computing for IoT. Electronics (Switzerland) 8(8), 1–22 (2019). https://doi.org/10.3390/electronics8080828
4. Tran, N.K., Ali Babar, M.: Anatomy, concept, and design space of blockchain networks. In: Proceedings - IEEE 17th International Conference on Software Architecture, ICSA 2020 (2020). https://doi.org/10.1109/ICSA47634.2020.00020
5. Tran, N.K., Ali Babar, M., Boan, J.: Integrating blockchain and Internet of Things systems: a systematic review on objectives and designs. J. Netw. Comput. Appl. **173**, 102844 (2020). https://doi.org/10.1016/j.jnca.2020.102844
6. Wessling, F., Ehmke, C., Meyer, O., Gruhn, V.: Towards blockchain tactics: building hybrid decentralized software architectures. In: 2019 IEEE International Conference on Software Architecture Companion (ICSA-C), pp. 234–237. IEEE (2019)
7. Wood, G.: Ethereum: A Secure Decentralized Generalized Transaction Ledger. Ethereum Yellow Paper (2014)
8. Xu, X., et al.: The blockchain as a software connector. In: 2016 13th Working IEEE/IFIP Conference on Software Architecture (WICSA), pp. 182–191 (2016). https://doi.org/10.1109/WICSA.2016.21

9. Xu, X., Pautasso, C., Zhu, L., Lu, Q., Weber, I.: A Pattern Collection for Blockchain-based Applications (2018). https://doi.org/10.1145/3282308.3282312
10. Xu, X., et al.: A taxonomy of blockchain-based systems for architecture design. In: 2017 IEEE International Conference on Software Architecture (ICSA), pp. 243–252. IEEE (2017)

An Analysis of Software Parallelism in Big Data Technologies for Data-Intensive Architectures

Felipe Cerezo⬤, Carlos E. Cuesta⬤, and Belén Vela$^{(\boxtimes)}$⬤

VorTIC3 Research Group, Universidad Rey Juan Carlos, C/ Tulipán S/N, Móstoles,
28933 Madrid, Spain
jf.cerezo.2019@alumnos.urjc.es, {carlos.cuesta,
belen.vela}@urjc.es

Abstract. Data-intensive architectures handle an enormous amount of information, which require the use of big data technologies. These tools include the parallelization mechanisms employed to speed up data processing. However, the increasing volume of these data has an impact on this parallelism and on resource usage. The strategy traditionally employed to increase the processing power has usually been that of adding more resources in order to exploit the parallelism; this strategy is, however, not always feasible in real projects, principally owing to the cost implied. The intention of this paper is, therefore, to analyze how this parallelism can be exploited from a software perspective, focusing specifically on whether big data tools behave as ideally expected: a linear increase in performance with respect to the degree of parallelism and the data load rate. An analysis is consequently carried out of, on the one hand, the impact of the internal data partitioning mechanisms of big data tools and, on the other, the impact on the performance of an increasing data load, while keeping the hardware resources constant. We have, therefore, conducted an experiment with two consolidated big data tools, Kafka and Elasticsearch. Our goal is to analyze the performance obtained when varying the degree of parallelism and the data load rate without ever reaching the limit of hardware resources available. The results of these experiments lead us to conclude that the performance obtained is far from being the ideal speedup, but that software parallelism still has a significant impact.

Keywords: Data-intensive architecture · Software parallelism · Partitioning · Big data technologies · Linear scalability

1 Introduction

The last decade has witnessed an exponential rise in the magnitude of information to be processed, causing the current interest in Big Data technologies. Even the advances in modern hardware have been unable to cope with this growth, and in order to bridge this gap, it has been necessary to resort to the widespread adoption of parallelism. When more processing power is required, more cores are added to a server, or more nodes are added to a processing cluster. These strategies, known as vertical and horizontal scalability [1], distribute the work between these new elements, which are partially or

© Springer Nature Switzerland AG 2021
S. Biffl et al. (Eds.): ECSA 2021, LNCS 12857, pp. 181–188, 2021.
https://doi.org/10.1007/978-3-030-86044-8_13

completely used by the process. In general terms, this approach to parallelism leads to a *linear* performance speedup [2, 3], although some contention factors [2, 4] must also be taken into account.

But simply increasing the processing power will not make it possible to achieve the required results. This has triggered a new interest in *software parallelism* [5], defined here as the partitioning and distribution strategy of our software. This provides the basis for z-axis (diagonal) scalability [1], in which data elements are partitioned and scattered in the parallel structure, and which is obviously relevant in the context of data-intensive architectures.

However, an adequate use of parallelism in big data tools has often been neglected. Existing tools provide several alternatives that can be used to define this, but they typically lack any sort of guidelines with which to define an optimal setting. This configuration usually depends on the number of threads available, and/or the number of parallel storage elements (partitions, shards) in which to allocate data entities.

This paper intends to analyze how the data partitioning mechanisms that define internal software parallelism in big data tools influence their performance from a comparative perspective. Our goal is to achieve a better comprehension of how these mechanisms affect the system as a whole and how they may affect the design of data-intensive software architectures [6]. In particular, the claim often made is that their parallelism provides the same sort of linear scalability [7] usually expected from parallel computer architectures. It is our intent to verify the validity of these assumptions.

As our goal is to study *software* parallelism, we have designed an experiment in which the hardware is stable and the resources are constant, explicitly avoiding the saturation regime. Rather than employing the approach normally used in hardware performance benchmarks (i.e., maintaining a constant workload while resources are increased), our experiment utilizes the complementary approach, that is, maintaining the same (constant) set of resources while scalability is tested by:

1. Increasing the number of internal parallelism elements, as defined by the system parameters of our big data tools, and
2. Increasing the data load rate in order to verify how much this software scales.

Our working hypothesis is that when the data insertion rate increases, an adequate configuration of these tools should provide a linear speedup of their performance.

Different big data tools use different parallelism mechanisms, even when several of them are variants of the same theoretical concepts. In order to obtain independent results, it is necessary to use several different tools. We focus on different approaches to *data* parallelism, as provided by horizontal partitioning and data sharing.

We designed an experiment in which we studied the impact of internal data partitioning mechanisms with several different configurations, when both the degree of parallelism and the data load rate were increased. The comparable alternatives chosen as representative of internal parallelism were Apache Kafka and Elasticsearch, two well-known and highly performant data-centered big data tools, both of which are widely used and established in industry.

Our results suggest that these configurations provide good initial results, with almost linear scaling, even with quite different speedup factors. But our experiment also shows that there are unexpected limits, clearly imposed by the software itself. The performance results obtained for the two tools are significantly dissimilar, and these scaling limits manifest themselves at very different stages of the experiment.

The remainder of the paper is organized as follows. Section 2 includes a comparison of the parallelization mechanisms of the chosen tools. In Sect. 3, we provide detailed descriptions of the design of the experiment and of the different choices about the parameters that affect internal parallelism and the increasing data load rate. We then go on to discuss the results of these experiments in Sect. 4. Finally, our main conclusions and future work are summarized in Sect. 5.

2 Software Parallelism in Big Data Tools

In order to perform an analysis of the parallelization mechanisms and their impact in data-intensive architectures, it was necessary to define the criteria for selecting the adequate Big Data tools. The first one was that we wished to select **open source and independent** big data tools whose use does not require additional software. The second requirement was that the tool should have a **configurable** internal parallelism mechanism. The third one was that we wished to analyze **standalone tools**, we discarded **execution frameworks** as they require the development of additional code in order to test them. The fourth was that the tools should be considered as **mature tools**, that means that they have a history of use and versions and are used widely in the industry. Finally, we also wished to select tools with a large **support and development community**, for which extensive documentation was available. After evaluating several tools, we chose Elasticsearch and Kafka because they comply with all these requirements.

Apache Kafka [8] is an independent, open source, big data tool whose first version dates to January 2011. Apache Kafka aims to provide a unified, high-throughput, low-latency platform to handle real-time data feeds. Kafka is developed in Java and Scala and allows the manual configuration of its internal parallelism mechanism.

Elasticsearch is an independent, open source, big data tool whose first version appeared in February 2010. ElasticSearch provides a distributed, multitenant-capable full-text search engine with web interface and schema-free documents. Elasticsearch is developed in Java. Its internal parallelism mechanism can be configured manually.

The internal data partitioning mechanisms are implemented as follows:

- In Kafka, the data processing unit is the topic (queue), and each topic can be configured with a number of different *partitions*. Each partition is fed and accessed independently, and both the performance obtained and the resources used for each topic will, therefore, depend on how many partitions are configured.
- In ElasticSearch, the data storage unit is the index. Each index can be configured in a number of different storage partitions (called *shards*). When writing to or reading from an index, each different thread actually writes to or reads from each of the shards, thus the application is generating an additional parallelism of its own.

3 Experiment Design

In this paper we conduct an experiment with the two big data tools chosen, Kafka and Elasticsearch, in order to analyze their performance (while maintaining the resources constant), varying the degree of internal parallelism and the data load rate.

The objective of this experiment was to verify two different aspects:

- How the performance is affected by the internal data partitioning mechanism,
- How the performance is affected when then load is increased.

The internal parallelism should increase the performance of the system. We studied the impact of different configuration alternatives on the performance.

In our experiment we focused on data load insertion, which requires an intensive use of all the hardware resources: CPU, disk, memory and network.

The following independent variables were, therefore, considered for both tools: (1) number of elements for internal partitioning, (2) data insertion rate.

We began our experiment by using a **basic configuration**: one parallelism element for each instance within the cluster. Smaller configurations do not make sense, as each instance must store at least a part of the data in order to take proper advantage of parallelism. We increased the number of storage elements per instance in each iteration.

We built a **multithreaded process.** Each atomic thread in this process was programmed to insert data at a constant rate. The insertion rate was increased by increasing the number of threads. When we refer to a "x3 load", we are increasing the insertion rate by the factor of three.

We also considered the possibility of performing simultaneous loads on different data entities. Therefore, in another set of tests, we ran two instances of the multithreaded process. Each instance loaded data into a different entity. The different loads within each process were combined in order to obtain a total load from x2 to x8.

Resource usage **monitoring** was key in our experiment. It was necessary for the tools to work without reaching, in any case, the limit of the available hardware resources; that is, CPU, disk, RAM memory or network bandwidth. If this resource saturation had been reached, the results would have been distorted.

A **test time** of 30 min was determined for each configuration (internal parallelism and load). This was sufficient time for the tools to pass through the transient start-up period of the load processes and to work in the normal regime.

We chose a **representative dataset** from the big data domain: 2.142.000 records, 25 fields of information with different datatypes, an average length of 312 bytes per record and a standard deviation in the size of the records of 28 bytes. The distinct fields have different cardinalities: from 2 different values up to 2 million.

We carried out our experiment using Elasticsearch and Kafka.

- In the case of Elasticsearch, we ran the insertion experiment 36 times. This covered all the combinations of a degree of internal parallelism from 1 to 6 and a data insertion load from x1 to x6.
- Kafka can support higher loads, so internal parallelism degrees used were 1 to 6, 8, 10 and 12 partitions in each instance, and a data insertion load from x1 to x8.

The use of all system resources, CPU, network, disk and memory remained below the maximum limits of the servers in all cases for both tools. The resources used were fairly homogeneous between the servers throughout the test and remained almost constant throughout the test.

In the part of the experiment in which we insert into two independent data entities, we have executed them only for a selected set of values, in order to evaluate internal data partitioning. We chose those values that had performed best in the previous tests: 2 elements for Elasticsearch (a total of 60) and 12 elements for Kafka (a total of 360).

We also verified whether different proportions of insertions had an impact on the global insertion rate. The fact that more than one combination provides the same total load (for example, x4 can be obtained as x2 + x2 or as x3 + x1) made it possible to assess this aspect.

4   Results

In this section, we present the results of the experiment with regard to the following two aspects: a) internal parallelism b) load increasing.

The following Fig. 1 shows the number of insertions per second. The horizontal axis shows the **internal parallelism** (number of shards in Elasticsearch and number of partitions in Kafka) used for the experiment. It is important to keep in mind that we used 30 instances, signifying that the numbers that appear are always multiples of 30. Each line represents a different, and increased, data insertion rate (data load).

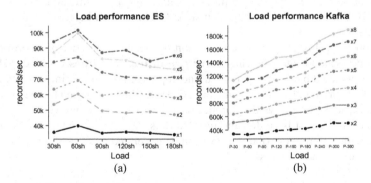

Fig. 1. Data load in Elasticsearch (a) vs. Kafka (b) (Color figure online)

The data partitioning mechanism implemented in these big data tools, when compared, show a very different behavior in each case.

In Elasticsearch there is a clear **optimal value of 2 elements per instance,** while in Kafka, a value of *12 elements per instance* was still attained, always increasing the performance of the data insertion process.

With regard to the **load increasing,** the Fig. 2 below shows the number of insertions into **a single entity** per second. The horizontal axis shows the data insertion rate (data load) used for the experiment. Each line represents the number of parallel elements (number of shards in Elasticsearch and number of partitions in Kafka).

When the degree of internal parallelism is kept constant for different data loads in each iteration of the experiment, the result can be approximated by a straight line. It is possible to consider that the growth with the insertion load is linear, the lowest correlation coefficient for the loads was r = 0.983 (Elasticsearch) and r = 0.996 (Kafka).

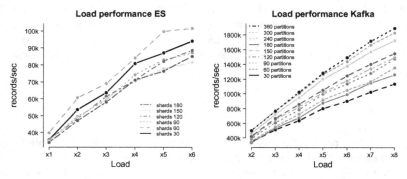

Fig. 2. Load performances of Elasticsearch vs. Kafka (Color figure online)

The growth rate should ideally be 100%: one thread obtains 100% output, two obtain 200%, three obtain 300%, etc. Actually, this ratio is 93% in Kafka. Its behavior is very close to that of the ideal theoretical models, with a linear growth and a ratio very close to 100%. In Elasticsearch, this ratio is just 30%. The growth behavior is linear, but its growth rate is very low.

The following Fig. 3 shows a comparison between the number of insertions (**load increase**) per second into **one** (in red) or **two different entities** (in blue). The ideal behavior is depicted by means of a green line, representing a linear increase with a ratio of 100%. The horizontal axis shows the insertion rate (data load) used for the experiment, while the vertical axis shows the number of insertions per second. Each experimental iteration is represented by a dot; the unfilled dots indicate the data loads that can be generated with different distributions (x4 can be generated as x2 + x2 or x3 + x1). The lines indicate the linear regression.

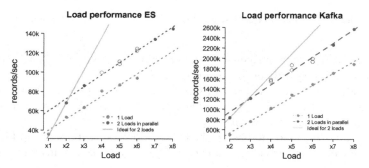

Fig. 3. Load performance when increasing the insert ratio: Elasticsearch vs. Kafka (Color figure online)

The results for both tools are very similar. The main difference between them is that Elasticsearch is much further away from the ideal behavior than Kafka is.

The performances of the executions represented by the unfilled dots (different distributions) are very close to each other in every case. It is, therefore, possible to conclude that the performance obtained in these scenarios depends only on the total insertion load, not on how the load is distributed between the two data entities.

The regression line of the two-process load is parallel to the single-process load line for both tools. A higher performance is attained when storing the data in two entities rather than one, and this increase is constant with the load.

In the case of ElasticSearch, there is a low increase in performance (30%) and also a performance bonus in the case of loading in two different data entities. These two insights lead to different architectural scenarios when scaling the data load: (i) a single cluster with a single data entity, (ii) a single cluster with two data entities, (iii) two different clusters, each with a single data entity. The performance will be very different in each of these scenarios. If the insertion ratio is doubled, the performance will increase by 50% (one cluster with one entity, i), 90% (one cluster with two entities) and 100% (two clusters). If the increase is quadruplicated, then we obtain 125% (one cluster with one entity), 180% (one cluster with two entities) and 200% (two clusters).

In the case of Kafka, since the growth with the load is close to 100%, all the scenarios are very similar, and the behavior is consistent.

5   Conclusions

In this paper we study the impact of software parallelism on data-intensive architectures by means of an experiment, in which two factors have been evaluated, namely internal partitioning mechanisms and increasing the load rate. When conducting our experiment, we chose two representative big data tools: Kafka and Elasticsearch. The results of these experiments lead us to conclude that these tools do not behave as expected, that is, the performance obtained is far from the assumed speedup. But our experiment also shows that the software parallelism mechanisms still have a significant impact on the performance. This improvement is entirely dependent on the implementation of the partitioning mechanism in each of the tools.

Throughout the experiment, our goal was always to analyse the performance without ever reaching the limit of available hardware resources. We considered constant hardware resources, signifying that any increment in the processing power had to be provided by internal parallelism mechanisms. Scalability was checked later by incrementing the data load rate.

In the case of internal parallelism mechanisms, it was reasonable to assume that performance would improve if we increased the number of parallelization elements: partitions in Kafka and shards in Elasticsearch. Our results show that this is not always true. In the case of Kafka, this actually occurred: increasing the internal parallelism also increased the performance obtained. But in the case of Elasticsearch, this occurred only until we attained a value that maximized the performance, after which the performance *decreased* as the number of internal parallelism elements *increased*.

In the case of the increasing data load, a linear growth of performance should be expected. The ratio between the data insertions and the processed data led to highly disparate values in both tools: 93% for Kafka and 30% for Elasticsearch. The tools should ideally have a load/processing ratio of 100%, that is, if we double the data load rate, the performance should scale in the same proportion. However, as stated in [2], there are non-parallelizable elements that can make the ratio obtained lower. In Kafka, the result is very close to the maximum expected value, but in Elasticsearch, the resulting value of 30% clearly indicates that it is far from the ideal expected behavior.

The fact that these tools do not perform according to expectations has important implications for data-intensive architectures in big data context. As mentioned previously, the performance of the tool would be different depending on the architectural scenario chosen (number of clusters, number of entities, number of internal storage elements…). Moreover, the difference between these scenarios as regards the performance rate becomes greater with an increasing data insertion rate.

Another implication of our study is that there is a great dependency on the specific big data tool. It is, therefore, necessary to perform detailed tests regarding the behavior of these tools in order to discover whether there is a performance limit and where this maximum value is located. In the case of Kafka, it will be noted that the speedup is maintained as the internal partitioning increases. It is not, however, possible to guarantee that there will be no upper limit with this tool in another scenario. In the case of Elasticsearch, we discovered that using two shards per instance allowed us to attain of an optimal performance as regards data loading. But it is again impossible to guarantee that this value will be optimal in all cases. It is possible that by modifying the number of physical instances within the cluster, this optimal parameter could also vary.

We therefore conclude that big data tools must be evaluated quantitatively for the particular scenario in which they will be used. When evaluating a data-intensive architecture, we cannot straightforwardly assume an increase in linear performance when applying software parallelism mechanisms.

References

1. Abbott, M.L., Fisher, M.T.: The Art of Scalability. Pearson, London (2009)
2. Amdahl, G.M.: Validity of single-processor approach to achieving large-scale computing capability. In: Proceedings of AFIPS Joint Computer Conference. AFIPS (1967)
3. Gustafson, J.L.: Reevaluating amdahl's law. Commun. ACM. **31**, 532–533 (1988). https://doi.org/10.1145/42411.42415
4. Gunther, N.J.: Guerrilla Capacity Planning: Tactical Approach to Planning for Highly Scalable Applications and Services. Springer, Heidelberg (2007). https://doi.org/10.1007/978-3-540-31010-5
5. Pacheco, P.: An Introduction to Parallel Programming. Morgan-Kaufmann, Burlington (2011)
6. Cerezo, F., Cuesta, C.E., Vela, B.: Phi: a software architecture for big & fast data (2021)
7. Gunther, N.J., Puglia, P., Tomasette, K.: Hadoop superlinear scalability. Commun. ACM. **58**, 46–55 (2015). https://doi.org/10.1145/2719919
8. Kafka Apache Kafka Project (2021). https://kafka.apache.org/. Accessed 21 Jan 2021

Architecture-Centric Source Code Analysis

State of the Practice in Application Programming Interfaces (APIs): A Case Study

Mikko Raatikainen[1]([✉])[ID], Elina Kettunen[1], Ari Salonen[2], Marko Komssi[3],
Tommi Mikkonen[1][ID], and Timo Lehtonen[4][ID]

[1] University of Helsinki, Helsinki, Finland
{mikko.raatikainen,elina.kettunen,tommi.mikkonen}@helsinki.fi
[2] Digia Plc, Turku, Finland
ari.salonen@digia.com
[3] F-Secure Plc, Helsinki, Finland
marko.komssi@f-secure.com
[4] Solita Ltd., Tampere, Finland
timo.lehtonen@solita.fi

Abstract. Application Programming Interfaces (APIs) have become prevalent in today's software systems and services. APIs are basically a technical means to realize the co-operation between software systems or services. While there are several guidelines for API development, the actually applied practices and challenges are less clear. To better understand the state of the practice of API development and management in the industry, we conducted a descriptive case study in four Finnish software companies: two consultancy companies developing software for their customers, and two companies developing their software products. As a result, we identified five different usage scenarios for APIs and emphasize that diversity of usage should be taken into account more explicitly especially in research. API development and technical management are well supported by the existing tools and technologies especially available from the cloud technology. This leaves as the main challenge the selection of the right technology from the existing technology stack. Documentation and usability are practical issues to be considered and often less rigorously addressed. However, understanding what kind of API management model to apply for the business context appears as the major challenge. We also suggest considering APIs more clearly a separate concern in the product management with specific practices, such as API roadmapping.

Keywords: Software engineering · Application programming interface · API · API management · API management · Case study

1 Introduction

Application Programming Interfaces (APIs) have become prevalent in today's software systems and services. APIs play an integral role in enabling software

© Springer Nature Switzerland AG 2021
S. Biffl et al. (Eds.): ECSA 2021, LNCS 12857, pp. 191–206, 2021.
https://doi.org/10.1007/978-3-030-86044-8_14

systems to interact with each other and in allowing applications to be built on the data or functionality of other systems. In fact, companies have been opening their products to third-party developers through various APIs for several years [4].

Despite being a central concept, the definitions for API are quite broad and diverse [11]. For instance, on one hand, the term API includes libraries, frameworks, and software development kits (SDKs). We refer these traditional APIs as *static APIs*. On the other hand, APIs are accessible over a network, such as SOAP or REST-based APIs from another component, system, or service. We refer to these as *web APIs*. Diversity exists also in the goals of using APIs. Rauf *et al.* [24] see three main tasks for APIs. The first task is to enable software reuse via defining the interfaces of software components. The second task is to provide interfaces to software services that are available over a network. The third task is to enable the publication of open data through APIs.

Various API development and management guidelines have been summarized in textbooks (e.g., in [8]). In addition, many specific concerns of APIs have been addressed in research, such as API learnability [25], evolution [13], and usability evaluation [24].

However, a holistic overview of the API development and management state of the practice has not been presented. Thus, our goal in this study was to capture an overview of the API development and management in an industrial context from the API owners' and developers' view rather than API users' or client developers' point of view. We limit the investigation broadly to technical concerns so that, e.g., API business or monetizing models are not our primary concerns. The research problem we are addressing is:

– *How are APIs technically developed and managed in the software industry and what are the main challenges?*

The study was carried out as a descriptive case study [27] in four Finnish software product and consultancy companies. We interviewed one API expert from each company. The case study method was selected as the research method because we desired to construct broad and holistic understanding about practices related to APIs in the industry.

The rest of the paper is organized as follows. Section 2 covers the background and related work. Section 3 presents the research method and in Sect. 4 are the results of the case study. Section 5 discusses the results and Sect. 6 considers the validity of the study. Conclusions are in Sect. 7.

2   Background and Previous Work

Murphy *et al.* [19] conducted a study in which they interviewed professional software engineers and managers from seven different companies. In the study, the focus is on how API developers learned or received training on API design and what processes are included in API design. In comparison to Murphy *et al.*, our study is more focused on technical concerns of API properties and API development and management practices.

In contrast to our focus on API developers viewpoint, empirical studies of API client developers have been carried out revealing that often APIs are difficult to learn due to insufficient documentation [11,25]. In addition to being difficult to learn, APIs also often have issues with usability [20]. APIs have been also discovered to form from the API user's perspective broader boundary resources [3]. APIs have been found to be prone to evolve over time, and often changes result in breaking the code of API clients [5,10,13,15]. Especially refactoring is one major cause for API breaking changes [10]. Thus, API evolution is considered one major challenge in API development. Moreover, there may be issues with APIs changing without a warning [11]. In research the literature, the recommendations for API developers often include providing useful examples of the interaction with the API, versioning system, API usage monitoring, and API usability testing [6,11].

In addition to empirical studies, different types of API design guidelines have been published by many companies that provide REST APIs to client developers. In fact, Murphy et al. [18] conducted a study comparing 32 industrial REST API style guideline sets and discovered how these guides handle some topics differently and emphasize different concepts in API design.

Several academic papers have been written about API design and management also give recommendations for API developers. In a paper on API design, Henning [12] gives several recommendations on designing good APIs and emphasizes considering the needs of API callers in the design process. Espinha et al. [11] base their recommendations on interviews of API client developers and the recommendations include avoiding changes in the API, having a versioning system, and including examples of the interaction with the API in the documentation.

Despite the popularity of APIs in the practice and research literature, there are only a few systematic literature reviews that focus and summarize concerns specifically on APIs. By adapting the search protocol of an earlier study ([23]), we found four systematic literature reviews or mapping studies that focus on APIs and their properties [6,7,22,24]. However, these reviews—as summarized below—can be characterized as mapping studies aiming at finding proposed practices or guidelines rather than summarizing empirical evidence.

Burns et al. [6] have reviewed papers that have empirical justification for their recommendations regarding API development divided into three categories: design, documentation, and methodology recommendations. Design recommendations include technical recommendations such as preferring simple architecture and forms of object creation, using constructors instead of factories, avoiding unnecessary inheritance and configuration files, and not forcing developers to set all parameters. Documentation recommendations mention having useful examples in the documentation, documentation integration with the IDE, and using unit tests as a form of documentation. Methodology recommendations suggest using actual developers to evaluate API usability and finding out the participants' assumptions about an API. The recommendations focus on static APIs.

Cummaudo *et al.* [7] have synthesized a five-dimensional taxonomy for constructs needed to create good API documentation:

1. Usage Description (how the developer should use the API).
2. Design Rationale (when the API is the right choice for a particular use case).
3. Domain Concepts (why choose this API for a particular domain).
4. Support Artefacts (what additional documentation is provided by the API).
5. Documentation Presentation (visualization of the above information).

Each class of the taxonomy is further divided into 12, 7, 3, 6, and 6 different, more concrete categories, respectively. Of these categories, the primary studies mention most often code snippets, step-by-step tutorials, and low-level reference documentation for the usage description; purpose or overview of the API as a low barrier to entry to the design rationale; and the consistency in the look and feel of the documentation for the documentation presentation. While the taxonomy provides a long list of options for the documentation, as a systematic mapping study, the level of empirical evidence is not covered.

Nybom *et al.* [22] have studied generative approaches available for creating and improving API documentation. Generation and its tool support make creating and maintaining API documentation easier, as without proper tools code updates may render the documentation at least in some parts obsolete or inadequate. The study lists tools in its primary studies and constructed taxonomies for different sources for the generation, generation outputs, and quality properties of generative approaches. They conclude that many approaches contribute to API documentation in the areas of natural language documentation and code examples. All primary studies focus on new tool proposals rather than study the existing, well-known tools, such as Javadoc or Swagger/OpenAPI. Therefore, the tools appear to be mostly research prototypes or at least detailed empirical evidence is not provided, but the taxonomies provide an overview of different possibilities in generation. The focus is at least implicitly mostly on static APIs.

Rauf *et al.* [24] have studied different methods for evaluating API usability outlining and categorizing the different methods. The majority of studies use empirical methods about *API use* to evaluate the usability of an API. A less used category is analytical methods about *API specification* that includes reviews and metrics (the least addressed). Many research articles using empirical evaluation methods aim to provide guidelines, recommendations, or general principles that could be useful to API designers and developers in evaluating API usability. Only a few studies aim to provide tools for usability evaluation and most of these tools are not available for the public. The study differentiates usability evaluation phases to be design, development, and post-development, where the last category is dominant. They conclude that usability is inherently subjective and there are several factors or concepts but a lack of synthesis or agreement between the studies about the usability concepts.

Finally, there are also systematic literature reviews or mapping studies where APIs are covered shortly as a part of a specific context or application domain, such as in microservices or software ecosystems [1,9,17,26]. Notably, API versioning or evolution are mentioned as recurring challenges in three of these reviews [9,17,26]. The problem of API portability can also be seen similarly as a challenge of different versions from the user perspective although the versions do not typically have drastic differences.

To summarize the previous research in terms of the objectives of this paper, we argue—in parallel with Rauf *et al.* [24]—that research needs also focus on the development concerns rather than the post-deployment phase and API users' or client developers' perspectives. Another notable shortcoming is that much of the research appears to be still done on static APIs rather than on web APIs. At least explicit differentiation between different types of APIs is not usually made. Finally, research often proposes guidelines or practices rather than characterizes industrial state-of-the-practice in terms of challenges and tested solutions.

3   Research Method: Case Study

This study was carried out as a descriptive case study [27] that studied APIs in four Finnish software companies. The primary selection of the companies for the study was two-fold: First, we selected consultancy companies that develop software for their customers both of them being large-sized and having several different customers. Second, we selected product companies that develop their own software being more focused on long-term development and maintenance of APIs. All products or projects were related to information systems, rather than, e.g., embedded systems, games, or mobile apps. We also practically knew that the selected companies considered APIs being important for their business. Otherwise, the case selection was based on convenience sampling, i.e. the companies that we had easy access to based on ongoing or earlier research collaboration.

The consultancy companies in the study are Digia Plc[1] and Solita Ltd[2]. Both of them are medium-sized having several projects and over 1000 employees. Both consultancy companies mainly operate on the Nordic or northern European markets. The third company, Vertex Systems Ltd[3], is a product-oriented company with around 100 employees. Vertex provides information management solutions for the industry, especially for industrial products and building construction design. The fourth company, F-Secure Plc[4], is a product- and service-oriented company with over 1700 employees providing cybersecurity solutions directly to their end-users and end-customers but also often through different partnership channels. Both these product companies operate on global markets.

The data was primarily collected by audio-recorded interviews that each took between one to two hours. Two university researchers acted as main interviewers with company representatives interested in the topic. One interview was carried out on the premises of the responding company while others were carried out by partly telecommuting due to the ongoing COVID-19 situation. Afterward, we asked a few clarification questions and let the respondents review and comment

---

[1] http://www.digia.com.
[2] http://www.solita.fi.
[3] https://www.vertex.fi.
[4] https://www.f-secure.com.

Table 1. The typical API technologies and practices in the case companies.

	Digia	Solita	Vertex	F-Secure
Use case	Integrations	Integrations, open APIs	Partner APIs	Partner APIs, internal APIs
Language	Java most common	Java most common	Java	Many
Framework	Spring Boot	Spring Boot	Spring Boot	Many
Cloud provider	Amazon, Azure, Google	Azure, Amazon, Google	None	Amazon
Container	Docker	Docker	No[a]	Docker
CI & CD	Yes	Yes	Partial	Yes
CI Tool	Jenkins	Jenkins	Bamboo	Jenkins
API Gateway	Yes	Yes	No	Yes
Monitoring	Yes	Yes	None	Yes
Logging	Elastic Stack, Splunk	Splunk, Elastic Stack	None	Splunk, proprietary
API Documentation	Annotation-driven (OpenAPI/ Swagger)	Annotation-driven (OpenAPI/ Swagger)	Postman	Endpoint reference, Open API, Github examples

[a]Container technology is currently being investigated.

on a draft of this paper. In addition, company representatives present in interviews co-author this paper but they are not the same representatives that were interviewed.

The interviews were semi-structured focusing on the projects or products that the respondent was familiar with. The questions in the interviews aimed to cover APIs holistically from the technological rather than business perspective. The interviews were structured by the following themes: technologies used for API development, deployment, and run-time; API testing; API monitoring and management; API documentation; API versioning practices; and API quality attributes. Thus, the themes covered roughly first the general life-cycle phases of API development and management, and then a few selected specific concerns. The SQuaRE product quality model of ISO25010:2011 [14] was used and shown to the respondent as a reference model for quality attributes during the study. The model covers eight main quality characteristics—functional suitability, performance efficiency, compatibility, usability, reliability, security, maintainability, and portability—that have further sub-characteristics.

4   Case Study Findings

We summarize a set of typical technologies and practices related to API development in the case companies in Table 1 that are elaborated in more depth in the following sections.

4.1   API Usage Scenarios

We identified four different usage scenarios for the concept of API. First, the consultancy companies developed most often APIs that exchange data between two or a few systems to integrate the systems for their customers—although there can be a few systems involved, we refer this to as *one-to-one integration APIs*. Second, all companies also developed *partner APIs* that their—or, in the case of consultancy companies, their customers'—partner organizations or customers can use. A partner API is similar to the one-to-one integration API but available to a broader audience of partners. Specifically, F-Secure has several partner APIs that their integration partners use for end-customer solutions. Third, especially Solita has projects to develop *open APIs* mainly to publish the data of public sector systems. The idea of such open APIs is that anyone can at least read data through the API. One example of open APIs are maritime traffic APIs (see [16]). Fourth, *internal APIs* are a means of reuse between products at F-Secure. F-Secure has many existing systems, some of which have been acquired by business mergers and acquisitions. These systems integrate through internally accessible APIs. However, some internal APIs are opened for trusted partner organizations, thus widening the scope of reuse to partner APIs.

All above APIs rely on web APIs except that F-Secure also applies static APIs for some of its internal APIs. Therefore, web APIs, especially in terms of REST-architecture and JSON-messages, have become prevalent industry-standard for all API usages. However, legacy systems still use SOAP or XML-based data and APIs, which must be considered especially in the consultancy companies when building APIs. Finally, other technologies for web APIs, such as GraphQL as an example of emerging technology, are not common although getting increasing interest in the industry.

4.2   Technologies and Adoption of New Technologies

While Table 1 highlights typical technologies and practices, there is a large selection of technologies that are used depending on the context of the project. Especially in the consultancy business, different technologies can be selected depending on the specific project. The product companies have a more focused selection of technologies but even F-Secure uses many different technologies, some of which pertain to the long history of the different systems, and some are inherited from business mergers and acquisitions. However, Java and Spring Framework are very common for all companies and projects.

The variety of technologies is well displayed by Digia's Tech Radar, which is used to understand and represent the ever-growing field of technological options

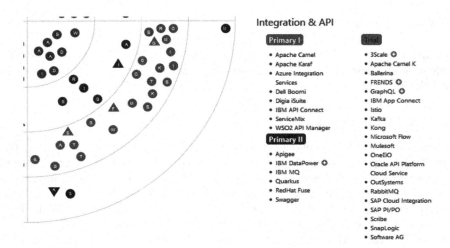

Fig. 1. A screenshot of the technology radar of Digia (https://techradar.digia.online).

both internally and to the customers. A screenshot of one quadrant in the Tech Radar is presented in the following[5]. The quadrant in Fig. 1, Integration & API, is the most relevant in the context of this paper. Tech Radar contains four prioritized classes of the most relevant technologies represented by four rings: Primary I (actively used and preferred), Primary II (widely used), Trial (emerging and fading away), and Hold (not yet used or avoided). Plus signs are used to indicate recent new entries and arrows the direction within the rings (not visible in the screenshot). The first two rings contain the most important technologies. For instance, in Integration & API quadrant, one of the primary technologies used is Apache Camel. In the trial ring, there is Camel K mentioned as an emerging technology. Technologies that are fading away in the Integration & API quadrant, are, for instance, Scribe/Tibco. The other quadrants also contain some relevant technologies for API development. For instance, in DevOps & Tools quadrant, commonly used technologies for infrastructure-as-code approach [2], e.g., Ansible and Docker, are mentioned.

The majority of preferred technologies are similar and alternative to each other although some variations exist between companies. For example, both consultancy companies, Digia and Solita, make extensive use of the open source Apache Camel framework as the main integration tool. Digia, as noted also above in Tech Radar, was also interested in newer Camel K, which can run integrations on Kubernetes. Solita, however, does not use Kubernetes as much and expressed no interest in adopting Camel K to their technology stack for the time being. There were also certain excluding selections, such as one company did not practically use IBM's tool stack at all. One key reason for not using a certain technology is license costs. A commercial stack may have remarkable license

---

[5] For readability and space reasons, we can only show one quadrant. Full Tech Radar is available at https://techradar.digia.online.

costs already at the beginning of the project, whereas a stack based on Open Source products is free from license costs. Consultancy companies make a profit by selling man-months, i.e., their business model is often based on providing consultancy services in long-term customer relationships without license costs.

Especially among the personnel of the consultancy companies, technologies are concentrated around interest groups with preferred technologies. For instance, the two consultancy companies have *tribes* or *competence communities* gathering around selected technologies that can complement each other, such as Amazon and Microsoft Azure cloud technologies. The groups of people share knowledge on the existing technologies and actively adopt new emerging technologies from the market or open source communities.

4.3   Deployment

Cloud deployment has become a de facto practice. A cloud readily offers some essential services, such as an API gateway, a developer portal, and federated user management. Of the cloud services, Amazon Web Servers (AWS) and Microsoft's Azure are the two most commonly used especially in the projects of the consulting companies. Google Cloud is used significantly less. Azure is very widely used in organizations in the public sector in Finland. A reason for the popularity was assumed to be the existing licenses to Microsoft products in the public sector customers in Finland, which makes Azure an easy add-on option to the existing technology stack of the organization. Containers, especially Docker, also are usually used. Serverless architecture is also becoming increasingly common but by no means prevalent. There are still server-based installations: Vertex had their software and APIs still running on their servers but transferring to a cloud environment and container technology is under investigation and planned in the near future.

Continuous integration and delivery (or deployment) (CI/CD) features have also become the status quo in all companies involved in the study. The differences are in the environments used. The consultancy companies have typically separate environments for development, test, and production with deployments by a modern CI tool, most often Jenkins. F-Secure has an additional partner-specific deployment and test environment where new versions are released. Vertex had currently only the development and production environments in addition to a playground server. The speed of CI/CD is the main challenge rather than CI/CD itself. Some software frameworks, such as Spring, require inconveniently long compiling time for today's CI/CD needs.

4.4   API Versioning

API versioning was considered a significant maintenance effort in the worst case, but not especially technically challenging per se. As probably the most rigorous example of versioning, F-Secure applies semantic versioning[6] in their APIs consisting of the major, minor, and patch version values (major.minor.batch). A new

---

[6] https://semver.org/.

major version can break backward compatibility but the end-of-life policy of F-Secure guarantees a transition period of at least 12 months. F-Secure aims to retain backward-compatibility so that the older API versions can be kept online together with the newer versions. The consultancy companies likewise apply API versioning although there are no such explicit guidelines or commitment as in F-Secure because versioning is also the responsibility of their customers. It was noted that especially integration APIs can be changed without versioning if backward compatibility is guaranteed, such as in the case of adding endpoints. Vertex, which in the early stages with APIs, had not yet adopted versioning practices. Although several versions of APIs can be available simultaneously, old versions are taken down when they are not used anymore. Monitoring the API usage is used as an indicator when the old version can be taken down.

4.5 API Documentation

As REST is the dominant architectural style for APIs, the endpoints in the consultancy companies are documented using OpenAPI Specification[7] (or Swagger as it was earlier known). The consultancy companies also sometimes set up a developer portal for their client companies. Solita mentioned using API catalogs that can contain also other written documentation, such as tutorials and guides, in addition to generated technological specifications. Vertex uses Postman to produce similar endpoint specifications as OpenAPI. F-Secure maintains a reference guide to its API endpoints that is constructed using a proprietary tool. Each endpoint has a description and types of its data, and one or a few simple examples of the calls and responses. In addition, there are a few more complex use cases. The APIs have also OpenAPI specifications. API usage code examples are given publicly in Github[8].

However, in all companies, the documentation consists mainly of technical endpoint specifications and code examples, and there are usually very few other kinds of documentation, such as tutorials or getting started guidelines. The companies cited the lack of resources as the main reason for not having more examples of the API usage in the documentation. For the consultancy companies, much of the documentation was considered more of the responsibility of their customers. The operations of one-to-one integration APIs were noted to be quite similar create, read, update and delete (CRUD) operations or other equivalent obvious functionality that a domain expert can learn from technical endpoint documentation without the need of more thorough documentation. Similarly, in the case of F-Secure, the users of APIs are often partner companies who build long collaboration relationships and have gained understanding about the domains and products of the APIs. Being partner companies, F-Secure can also give necessary guidance directly.

---

[7] https://swagger.io/specification/.
[8] E.g., https://github.com/F-Secure/atlant-api.

4.6   API Quality Attributes

The companies did not report major challenges related to quality attributes in APIs based on the SQuaRE [14] reference model. The existing standards, such as OpenID Connect for security, and technologies, such as cloud servers and API gateways for performance and scalability, provide typically sufficient solutions for the majority of quality characteristics.

At the moment, Vertex has no issues with quality attributes despite relying on server-based deployment. However, in the future, the company has plans for more cloud-based solutions as a means to ensure dependability and scalability with a more extensive user base. Challenges with quality attributes, especially run-time quality such as reliability and performance, pertain typically to the problems in the backend systems, such as databases, rather than APIs in all companies. In a similar manner in the case of large data, network bandwidth can also become a consideration.

The only issues concerning quality attributes were related to usability, portability, and maintainability. From the usability point of view, specific API testing was not conducted in any company. For example, F-Secure considers API testing as a part of product testing and usability is a part of general usability that the product management is responsible for. In terms of portability, the consultancy companies reported that portability—or adaptability as its sub-characteristic— may require additional effort although it is not problematic per se. A typical example is a deployment to a different cloud environment, or both to a cloud and a local server. Finally, reusability was seen as the main point of API development, but developing an API that is as reusable as possible and not difficult to use was noted to be an endless issue for the design.

4.7   API Management

The interest in API management among the customers of the consultancy companies was mentioned being increasing considerably during the past few years. Much like above, the existing technologies mostly provide sufficient tools: For instance, Azure was mentioned having a good tool for API management or dedicated tools can be used, such as WSO2, IBM API Connect, TreeScale, Kong, and ServiceMix. However, the respondents noted that despite the technologies exist, the concept of API management is still vague in terms of what API management should cover, and when and to what extend dedicated API management is needed. In addition, the business models based on APIs were perceived as immature. For instance, monetizing the APIs was not really considered by the consultancy companies, while Vertex and F-Secure apply a subscription model for their API for the paying customers.

As an example of technical API management, API monitoring appeared particularly mature. Both consultancy companies used designated tools for API monitoring and logs. For example, Solita strives to use a centralized log management system and a uniform log format. The Camel framework offers components for sending API log data. Digia mentioned using also Splunk, Elastic, and Kibana in real-time usage monitoring. As a cybersecurity company, F-Secure uses extensive API monitoring and multiple levels of logging: They have an internal monitoring system and logging with Splunk and they use the alert system of Amazon's cloud. The aim is to monitor the whole flow. Vertex is not yet using comprehensive API monitoring, but logs are used for basic access monitoring. However, they are very interested in developing their API management system and more detailed monitoring.

5   Discussion

Our findings show that the concept of API has become, and is getting broader and more diverse. We identified four usage scenarios for APIs: one-to-one integration APIs, internal reuse, partner APIs, and open APIs. All of these are widely based nowadays on the REST architectural style making web APIs prevalent in industrial software projects for information systems. However, more traditional static APIs of SDKs, libraries, or frameworks are still used within the code as the fifth usage scenario as evidenced by the use of various open source and cloud technologies. Similar static APIs are also still used as a means of intra-organizational reuse. While this presented classification is quite straightforwards, it is often implicit. Moreover, the classification can be refined and other classifications from other viewpoints can be proposed. However, rather than the classification alone, we emphasize that the diversity of API usage scenarios in practice should be more explicitly taken into account in research since much of the research appears to be implicit about the nature of API.

Existing tools and technologies make most of the technical tasks in API development, deployment, and management straightforward and ensure sufficient runtime quality of APIs. The main technological challenges are, in fact, related to the backend systems or computing infrastructure rather than to APIs themselves. The major decision for APIs is the selection of the desired technology from the existing technology stacks of multiple similar and comparable options for which many technologies are inherited from the backend technology selections. Mature techniques might be in some cases old-fashioned and inefficient, but on the other hand, newer fashionable technologies may suffer from immaturity. Similarly, personal preferences and familiarity can favor certain technologies. However, the technologies appear to be quite comparable, and advance and mature rapidly.

Despite being often presented as challenges in the literature (e.g., [11,13]), API evolution and versioning were not considered to be especially technically challenging by the practitioners. However, API evolution can be more problematic to the client developers, and the companies we studied mainly provide APIs, so the viewpoint is most likely different. API evolution is not either always visible to consultancy companies as they do not necessarily maintain the API for longer time. Nevertheless, API evolution, even if not being a challenge, requires considerable manual effort and rigor in order not to break the applications using the API. A research challenge is to reduce the manual work and help with ensuring continuity of APIs.

In contrast to evolution, documentation and usability appeared more as a practical issue. First, API documentation appeared often to be a somewhat under-addressed practice. Similar results were presented in [19]. Although API endpoint specifications are constructed using OpenAPI or a similar tool, more detailed API user guidelines are still often lacking. That is, a *developer journey* [21], which roughly means attracting and supporting new developers for an API, keeping them motivated as they learn to use the API, and provide specialized and detailed support and tools also for experts, is not actively considered. Second, API usability is not necessarily designed or it is treated as a part of the product quality cursorily. API usability might sometimes need reconsideration because the users of APIs are software developers that can be different from the end-users. Interestingly for example at F-Secure, the same product manager was responsible for a product and its APIs although the users of products and APIs are quite different. Who should be responsible for APIs is a topic that deserves further investigation.

However, it is important to take into account that even though API usability and documentation are not always extensively addressed in industrial practice, the rigor of addressing these disciplines depends on the API context and use cases. API usability and documentation become more important or even relevant when APIs are used in a broader context with external developers or even unknown developers rather than only internally or for integration.

API management appeared clearly as the vaguest and most challenging concept. API management was mentioned as being increasingly important for customers of the consultancy companies. As the discussion and information on APIs have become more widespread, some customers have become concerned about whether they too should have an API and API management system even though they might not have an exact idea of what an API actually is or if a full API management system is even completely necessary for their business. Likewise, for API development, there are several individual tools available for API monitoring and management, and the technical aspects of the process are not as challenging as deciding what to do and handling the received data. That is, besides using API monitoring for the availability, performance, and functional correctness of an API, monitoring could be used for understanding customers and API users. Thus, the greatest challenges pertain to better understanding the needs of API management such as what kinds of policies or models to use for API management in different situations from the business perspective.

Overall, APIs were always considered an integral part of products (or services) and managed as a part of the products. However, APIs have certain inherent characteristics that make them different from products. For example, the user and customer of an API can be different from that of a product. Furthermore, as several other systems and stakeholders can rely on APIs, the APIs cannot be developed quickly to prototype different features as in agile and DevOps practices for product development. Therefore, it could be beneficial to consider APIs at least more clearly a separate concern in the product management having certain dedicated practices. For instance, having a dedicated API roadmap planning could help in diminishing the technical effort required in API versioning. As APIs have become such a quintessential part of software systems and services, APIs could be considered at least a more separate concern in product management and business planning.

Finally related to APIs being a separate concern of a product, one interviewed API expert mentioned how API design and use are not taught at educational institutions similarly to software design in general. Therefore, all API developers have to be taught at work, at least to some extent. Similar notions of learning on the job were brought up by API developers interviewed in [19]. This raises questions on the need to emphasize API development and management in computer science curricula at educational institutions. Courses covering API development and design could help to prevent some of the API usability issues and help with technology transfer from research to practice. This is becoming more relevant as APIs are increasingly important in many software systems.

6   Study Validity

A threat to construct validity is that only limited sources of evidence were used relying on one or a few interviewees. However, to mitigate the threats to construct validity, we let the respondents read and comment on a version of this manuscript, and other representatives from companies co-author this paper. Another threat to construct validity relates to the respondents in the consultancy companies that described practices in several projects. Their selection of examples could have been unintentionally biased or they might have done generalizations across projects. To mitigate biases in cases, we purposefully selected different kinds of cases that represent product- or service-oriented business and consultancy business. We did not either initially limit our selection to four cases but considered during data collection that we had quite saturated understanding of the state of the practice and decided not to need additional cases.

A threat to external validity in qualitative studies pertains to the selection of cases. This study focused on companies and projects that develop information systems and are geographically limited. Therefore, the results may not be generalizable especially to other technological domains, such as mobile apps or embedded systems.

7   Conclusions

We presented a case study on four Finnish companies to characterize API development and management state-of-the-practice in the context of information systems. The study shows that APIs and API management are important and prevalent practices in the software industry. We identified internal reuse, partner APIs, one-to-one integration APIs, and open APIs as web-based complementing usage scenarios to more traditional static APIs in, e.g., SDKs, libraries, or frameworks. While these usage scenarios identify some diversity, we argue that the diversity in the nature of APIs—and especially web APIs—should be better and more explicitly taken into consideration in research and practice.

API development and management are technically well supported in the practice by existing tools and technologies especially related to cloud services and provided by cloud vendors. API usability and documentation as design problems are most challenging to be properly addressed. The main technical challenge remains to be the selection of the right technologies from the existing technology stacks. Although API management is supported technically, the challenges in practice include what kinds of policies or models to use for API management in different business contexts. We suggest considering APIs more clearly at least as a separate concern in the product management, which might require some novel API specific practices, such as API roadmapping. In terms of future research, solutions for API roadmapping could be proposed and a more extensive empirical investigation could be carried out even by quantitative methods.

Acknowledgements. We acknowledge the financial support of Business Finland as a part of 4APIs project.

References

1. Alshuqayran, N., Ali, N., Evans, R.: A systematic mapping study in microservice architecture. In: IEEE International Conference on Service-Oriented Computing and Applications, pp. 44–51 (2016)
2. Artac, M., Borovssak, T., Di Nitto, E., Guerriero, M., Tamburri, D.A.: DevOps: introducing infrastructure-as-code. In: IEEE/ACM International Conference on Software Engineering (Companion volume), pp. 497–498 (2017)
3. dal Bianco, V., Myllärniemi, V., Komssi, M., Raatikainen, M.: The role of platform boundary resources in software ecosystems: a case study. In: IEEE/IFIP Conference on Software Architecture, pp. 11–20 (2014)
4. Bosch, J.: From software product lines to software ecosystems. In: AMC International Conference Software Product Lines, pp. 111–119 (2009)
5. Brito, A., Valente, M.T., Xavier, L., Hora, A.: You broke my code: understanding the motivations for breaking changes in APIs. Empir. Softw. Eng. **25**(2), 1458–1492 (2019). https://doi.org/10.1007/s10664-019-09756-z
6. Burns, C., Ferreira, J., Hellmann, T.D., Maurer, F.: Usable results from the field of API usability: a systematic mapping and further analysis. In: IEEE Symposium on Visual Languages and Human-Centric Computing, pp. 179–182 (2012)
7. Cummaudo, A., Vasa, R., Grundy, J.: What should I document? A preliminary systematic mapping study into API documentation knowledge. In: ACM/IEEE International Symposium on Empirical Software Engineering and Measurement (2019)
8. De, B.: API Management. Apress, Berkeley (2017). https://doi.org/10.1007/978-1-4842-1305-6
9. De Lima Fontao, A., Dos Santos, R., Dias-Neto, A.: Mobile software ecosystem (MSECO): a systematic mapping study. Int. Comput. Softw. Appl. Conf. **2**, 653–658 (2015)
10. Dig, D., Johnson, R.: How do APIs evolve? A story of refactoring. J. Softw. Maint. Evol. Res. Pract. **18**(2), 83–107 (2006)

11. Espinha, T., Zaidman, A., Gross, H.: Web API growing pains: loosely coupled yet strongly tied. J. Syst. Softw. **100**, 27–43 (2015)
12. Henning, M.: API design matters. ACM Queue **5**(4), 24–36 (2007)
13. Hora, A., Robbes, R., Valente, M.T., Anquetil, N., Etien, A., Ducasse, S.: How do developers react to API evolution? A large-scale empirical study. Software Qual. J. **26**(1), 161–191 (2016). https://doi.org/10.1007/s11219-016-9344-4
14. ISO/IEC: 25010:2011, Systems and software engineering - Systems and software quality requirements and evaluation (SQuaRE) - system and software quality models (2011)
15. Jezek, K., Dietrich, J., Brada, P.: How Java APIs break - an empirical study. Inf. Softw. Technol. **65**, 129–146 (2015)
16. Joutsenlahti, J., Lehtonen, T., Raatikainen, M., Kettunen, E., Mikkonen, T.: Challenges and governance solutions for data science services based on open data and APIs. In: IEEE/ACM 1st Workshop on AI Engineering - Software Engineering for AI of International Conference on Software Engineering (2021)
17. Manikas, K.: Revisiting software ecosystems research: a longitudinal literature study. J. Syst. Softw. **117**, 84–103 (2016)
18. Murphy, L., Alliyu, T., Macvean, A., Kery, M.B., Myers, B.A.: Preliminary analysis of REST API style guidelines. Ann Arbor **1001**, 48109 (2017)
19. Murphy, L., Kery, M.B., Alliyu, O., Macvean, A., Myers, B.A.: API designers in the field: design practices and challenges for creating usable APIs. In: IEEE Symposium on Visual Languages and Human-Centric Computing, pp. 249–258 (2018)
20. Myers, B.A., Stylos, J.: Improving API usability. Commun. ACM **59**(6), 62–69 (2016)
21. Myllärniemi, V., Kujala, S., Raatikainen, M., Sevoń, P.: Development as a journey: factors supporting the adoption and use of software frameworks. Journal of Software Engineering Research and Development **6**(1), 1–22 (2018). https://doi.org/10.1186/s40411-018-0050-8
22. Nybom, K., Ashraf, A., Porres, I.: A systematic mapping study on API documentation generation approaches. In: Euromicro Conference on Software Engineering and Advanced Applications, pp. 462–469 (2018)
23. Raatikainen, M., Tiihonen, J., Männistö, T.: Software product lines and variability modeling: a tertiary study. J. Syst. Softw. **149**, 485–510 (2019)
24. Rauf, I., Troubitsyna, E., Porres, I.: Systematic mapping study of API usability evaluation methods. Comput. Sci. Rev. **33**, 49–68 (2019)
25. Robillard, M.P.: What makes APIs hard to learn? Answers from developers. IEEE Softw. **26**(6), 27–34 (2009)
26. Soldani, J., Tamburri, D., Van Den Heuvel, W.J.: The pains and gains of microservices: a systematic grey literature review. J. Syst. Softw. **146**, 215–232 (2018)
27. Yin, R.K.: Case Study Research: Design and Methods. Sage (2014)

Identifying Domain-Based Cyclic Dependencies in Microservice APIs Using Source Code Detectors

Patric Genfer(✉) and Uwe Zdun(✉)

Faculty of Computer Science, Research Group Software Architecture,
University of Vienna, Vienna, Austria
{patric.genfer,uwe.zdun}@univie.ac.at

Abstract. Isolation, autonomy, and loose coupling are critical success factors of microservice architectures. Unfortunately, systems tend to become strongly coupled over time, sometimes even exhibiting cyclic communication chains, making the individual deployment of services challenging. Such chains are highly problematic when strongly coupled communication e.g. based on synchronous invocations is used, but also create complexity and maintenance issues in more loosely coupled asynchronous or event-based communication. Here, cycles only manifest on a conceptual or domain level, making them hard to track for algorithms that rely solely on static analysis. Accordingly, previous attempts to detect cycles either focused on synchronous communication or had to collect additional runtime data, which can be costly and time-consuming. We suggest a novel approach for identifying and evaluating domain-based cyclic dependencies in microservice systems based on modular, reusable source code detectors. Based on the architecture model reconstructed by the detectors, we derived a set of architectural metrics for detecting and classifying domain-based cyclical dependencies. By conducting two case studies on open-source microservice architectures, we validated the feasibility and applicability of our approach.

Keywords: Microservice API · Domain-based cyclic dependencies · Metrics · Source code detectors

1 Introduction

One of the main goals of microservices is to reduce the complexity of large monolithic applications by splitting them up into smaller, autonomously acting services [30], each of them focused on a specific part of a (business) domain [4] and independently deployable [19]. In addition to being isolated from each other (and therefore also becoming more autonomous), lightweight inter-service communication is central in microservice architectures [20]. The goal is to support loose coupling of the services. Finding a balance between service isolation and interaction is often a challenging task.

© Springer Nature Switzerland AG 2021
S. Biffl et al. (Eds.): ECSA 2021, LNCS 12857, pp. 207–222, 2021.
https://doi.org/10.1007/978-3-030-86044-8_15

Communication dependencies are often problematic when they form cycles, where a chain of service calls ends in the same service where it began [27]. As cycles increase the coupling between individual services, their independent deployment is no longer possible [6,33]. Cyclic communication paths make the system more complex, which might also lead to higher maintenance and development efforts and costs in the long run [17].

Several solutions for this problem have been suggested, all with their specific advantages or disadvantages: Applying the *API Gateway* pattern [28], as recommended by Taibi and Lenarduzzi [27], is a possible way of decoupling the system, switching to an asynchronous communication model is another [7,19]. While the first approach reduces the coupling, it bears the risk of creating a single point of failure in the system [15]. Worse, in this solution there is still a cycle in the system, but just via the API gateway. Changing the communication flow to asynchronous messaging is also debated among researchers. While it certainly improves the testability of the overall system as parts of the communication can easily be replaced by using message stubs, asynchronous communication makes the system also more complex and difficult to reason about [20]. Wolff [33] even argues in this context that switching from synchronous to asynchronous communication alone does not resolve any cyclic dependencies, but instead only shifts them to a different level. Before the transformation, cycles manifested through direct synchronous communication links, such as HTTP REST calls or Remote Procedure Calls (*RPC*), and were easily recognizable in the infrastructure code. But using asynchronous communication flow, these dependencies are expressed implicitly through the semantic information stored in the content of asynchronously transferred messages. For this Wolff coined the term *Unintended Domain-Based Dependencies* [33]. These dependencies – and especially the cycles resulting from them – now manifest as part of the domain or business logic and can only be resolved by redesigning the architecture. Especially tracking these communication links is now even more complicated. On the one hand, conventional metrics such as *cohesion* or *coupling* cannot correctly capture them, and most static code analysis approaches also fall short in detecting them [33].

Some authors (see e.g. [15,33]) suggest that the only effective way to resolve these domain-based communication cycles is redesigning the architecture on the domain level. However, for this, the cyclic connections first have to be identified, which is not always a trivial task, considering the polyglot nature of microservice implementations [26]. Besides, the communication flow within a microservice system is often distributed over several endpoints, which makes tracking the communication paths difficult. Another caveat lies in the fact that those architectures have often evolved organically over time and their documentation is not up-to-date, thus making architectural reconstruction tedious. The focus on research so far has mainly been on recognizing cycles based on synchronous connections [17,32]. Tracking and analyzing asynchronous communication on API operation level, as it would be necessary to identify domain-based cycles, has only been occasionally the subject of research so far (see e.g. [5,12]). This work aims at filling this gap by presenting a novel approach for identifying both, technical and domain-based cyclic dependencies on microservice API operation level. To achieve this, our approach uses modular, reusable source code parsers, called *detectors* [21] for reverse engineering a communication model from an underlying microservice's source code. Based on this model, we define a set of architectural metrics for detecting and evaluating potential cyclic dependency structures within the architecture. In this context, we will study the following research questions:

RQ1 How is it possible to identify domain-based cyclic dependencies between microservices by only analyzing static source code artifacts?

RQ2 What is a minimal communication model need for tracking cyclic dependencies on API operation level?

RQ3 Can architectural metrics for supporting software architects in redesigning domain-based cycles be defined based on this model?

The structure of this paper is as follows: Section 2 compares to related works. Next, Sect. 3 explains how our model of the inter-service communication is generated with the help of our source code detectors. Based on this communication model, Sect. 4 defines various metrics for tracking and evaluating technical and domain-based communication cycles in a given microservice system. Section 5 subsequently applies these metrics on two open source example projects as part of two case studies. The remaining Sect. 6, 7 and 8 conclude with a discussion of the research results, threat to validity, and future work.

2 Related Work

Cyclic dependencies are not a new phenomenon and have to be taken into account not only in microservice systems but also in monolithic applications [14]. However, their relevance for microservice systems has also been recognized in recent years by various authors [6,17,27,33]. In particular, Wolff [33] distinguishes between *technical* and *domain-based* dependencies, with the latter describing dependencies that exist on a conceptual level and are difficult to track trough static analysis methods. Ma et al. [17] classify synchronous cyclic dependencies into strong and weak cycles: Strong cycles are communication paths with the exact same start and endpoint, while weak cycles end in the same microservice, but at least at a different endpoint. According to the authors, strong cycles are way more problematic as they bear the risk of potential deadlocks in case the cycle has no termination condition. Our work adopts this concept of strong and weak cycles, and extends the analyses also to asynchronous communication models.

To be able to analyze a microservice system in detail, many studies follow the approach of reverse engineering an architecture model from existing artifacts, such as architecture diagrams [18], source code or documentation [17,22,32], as well as Docker and other configuration files [8,22]. In addition, runtime data such as log files or monitoring data [8,12] is utilized for architecture reconstruction. Especially the methods that focus on source code analysis have to make some compromises regarding the used technology stack and communication protocols to reduce the parsing effort. For example, some works [17,32] focus on Java Spring technologies and HTTP-based REST communication. In contrast, the architecture reconstruction method proposed in this work relies on lightweight, modular, and reusable source code detectors [21] that are not restricted to any specific programming language or framework.

Defining a specific set of metrics to assess the quality of a microservice architecture is also the subject of some studies: Zdun et al. [35] for instance describe metrics covering the decomposition of microservice systems, whereas Selmadji et al. [25] define a metric set for supporting the transformation of a monolithic application into several microservices. A more visual approach is proposed by Engel et al. [5]: In their study, they introduce a graph-based visual representation of their service metrics along with visualizations of metrics and their severity.

3   Static Analysis

3.1   Microservice API Communication Model

To model the communication flow observable at the API level, this paper uses a directed graph-based approach, similar to [23,35]. We define a microservice system as a graph $G = (V, E, F)$ where V is a set of vertexes (nodes) $V = V^{ms} \cup V^{interface} \cup V^{api} \cup V^{con} \cup V^{other}$, with each subset representing one category of vertexes. E are edges of the form (v_i, v_j) with $v_i, v_j \in V$. $F = \{ms, sync, async\}$ represents a set of additional functions and predicates that operate on the graph. The different vertex categories are:

- V^{ms} represents the **Microservices**, i.e. is the set of all microservice root nodes in the system.
- $V^{interface}$ represents the **API Interfaces**. These nodes are part of the public interface of a microservice and provide access to a specific group of (business) functionalities [16]. While they are not technically necessary for modeling the flow of communication in our model, they improve model understandability by adding more structure to the model.
- V^{api} represents the **API Operations** which play a crucial role in our communication model. They are the only direct access points to the underlying microservice functionality, making them the origin of any communication path through the system. API operations can either be synchronous or asynchronous, and have a unique address under which they can be reached, e.g., an HTTP endpoint, a queue/topic name, a specific message type, and so on.
- V^{con} represents the **Connection Operations**. The invocation of an API operation is expressed by connection operation nodes. Each of these nodes represents a technology-specific invocation of an API, e.g. by calling an HTTP endpoint or sending a message via a message broker.
- V^{other} represents any **Other Operations** in the graph which are not covered by the previous sets, such as calls to business services or domain entities.

The Set F provides the following functions and predicates:

- **ms** is a function $v \longrightarrow v^{ms}$ with $v \in V, v^{ms} \in V^{ms}$. It returns the corresponding microservice vertex when given a vertex of an arbitrary type. That is, it returns the microservice the vertex is part of. The boundaries of a microservice end at its connection operations.

- **async** is a predicate of the form $v^{api\_con} \longrightarrow boolean$ with $v^{api\_conn} \in V^{api} \lor v^{api\_conn} \in V^{con}$ that returns $true$ in case the input node uses an asynchronous communication model, otherwise returns $false$.
- **sync**: $v^{api\_con} \longrightarrow boolean$ with $v^{api\_conn} \in V^{api} \lor v^{api\_conn} \in V^{con}$ returns $true$ if the given node uses synchronous communication, otherwise $false$. It can also be defined as $\neg async$.

Figure 1 shows our model as a UML meta-model.

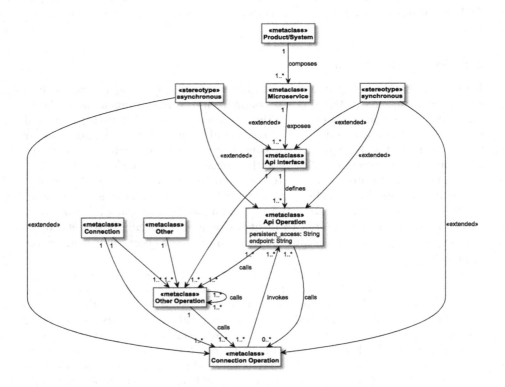

Fig. 1. Meta-model describing communication flow in a microservice system

The following constraints must be met to consider a microservice communication model as sound concerning our definition:

C1 Matching Connection Types: $\forall(v_i, v_j)$ with $v_i \in V^{con}, v_j \in V^{api}$: $(sync(v_i) \iff sync(v_j)) \lor (async(v_i) \iff async(v_j))$. This ensures that an API operation can only be called by a connection operation with a compatible communication model.

C2 A Microservice should not call its own API: $\forall(v_i, v_j)$ with $v_i \in V^{con}, v_j \in V^{api} : ms(v_i) \neq ms(v_j)$. Since our model focuses only on the API perspective, we do not include the case where microservices call themselves as we consider those calls as internal system calls, not API calls, and therefore not relevant for our considerations.

C3 At least one operation per service: Since our model maps the communication on API level, we assume that a service must provide at least one publicly available API to be part of our model.

Compared to other approaches (such as [8,13]) our model has a clear communication-centric focus. Thus, we consider connection operations and the API operations they target as central elements for describing the communication flow.

3.2 Model Reconstruction

Due to the highly polyglot nature of microservices [20], using full-blown language parsers for reconstructing the communication model out of the underlying source code would not be a practical solution. Configuring each parser and keeping it up to date would require a considerable amount of work and a deeper understanding of each language structure. Instead, our approach uses a concept from our earlier research, called modular, reusable *source code detectors* [21]. These lightweight source parsers are based on the Python module *PyParsing*[1] and scan the code for predefined patterns, while at the same time ignoring all other source code artifacts unrelated to the communication model. While these detectors must still be adopted to identify technology-specific patterns, implementing and especially maintaining them requires less effort than comparable approaches.

Figure 2 illustrates the four-phased reconstruction process based on an example microservice taken from the *Lakeside Mutual*[2] project. This open-source project is also used later during the case studies (see Sect. 5). In Phase 1, the detectors isolate all relevant model elements (also called *Hot Spots*) by scanning the source code for concrete keywords and patterns. Phase 2 uses a bottom-up search to establish invocation links between the various hot spots. During this search, the algorithm also identifies additional classes and methods or function calls as part of the invocation paths and adds them to the model as nodes of type V^{other}. Top-down connections between microservices, API interfaces, and their API operations can be created directly since, for them, no bottom-up search is necessary. After the invocation call tree is reconstructed, a path reduction algorithm again removes all non-hotspots from the model in Phase 3. Removing these elements simplifies the model drastically without losing any communication-relevant information. While this step is not necessary from a technical point of view, it significantly improves the human readability of the model. Phase 4 finally connects the isolated microservice sub-graphs by mapping

---

[1] https://github.com/pyparsing/pyparsing/.
[2] https://github.com/Microservice-API-Patterns/LakesideMutual.

the endpoint information stored in the connection operations to the corresponding API operation endpoints. This happens by matching HTTP addresses used for synchronous connections or mapping publishers and subscribers by their message types in asynchronous channels. The latter is the core focus of our work.

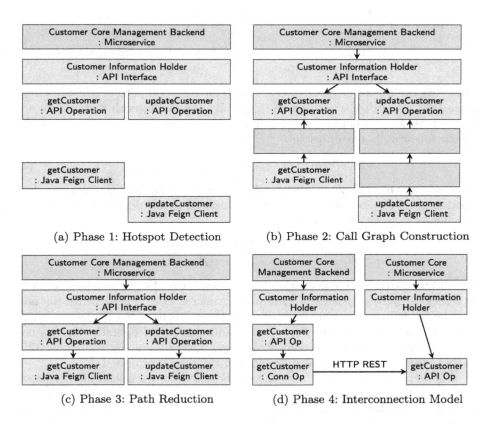

(a) Phase 1: Hotspot Detection   (b) Phase 2: Call Graph Construction

(c) Phase 3: Path Reduction   (d) Phase 4: Interconnection Model

Fig. 2. Process for reconstructing a microservice system communication model

4 Metrics

Based on our formal communication model introduced in Sect. 3.1, we define a set of architectural metrics that allow us to identify and assess cyclic dependencies within a microservice system. Using our definition of a microservice system as a directed graph V, any communication chain through this system can be considered a path $p_{vu} = (v = v_1, v_2, \ldots, v_n = u)$ such that $(v_i, v_{i+1}) \in E$ for $1 \leq i < n$ [10] and $v, u \in V^{api}$. We furthermore specify $P(v)$ as the set of all outgoing communication paths *starting in v*. According to Ma et al. [17], a communication path forms a cycle whenever its start and endpoint are identical or when both endpoints belong to the same microservice. While the first case results in strong cycles, which are viewed as highly problematic, the latter results in weak cycles, which still can negatively affect the deployability of the system [17]. This leads already to the first two boolean metrics that operate on a given communication path $p \in P(v)$:

$$
\begin{aligned}
cyc_{strong}(v, p) &= \begin{cases} true, & \text{if } v_1 = v_n \quad with\, p = (v_1, v_2, \ldots, v_n), p \in P(v) \\ false, & \text{otherwise} \end{cases} \\
cyc_{weak}(v, p) &= \begin{cases} true, & \text{if } ms(v_1) = ms(v_n) \quad with\, p = (v_1, v_2, \ldots, v_n), p \in P(v) \\ false, & \text{otherwise} \end{cases}
\end{aligned}
\tag{1}
$$

These two metrics return *true* in case the communication path is either a strong cycle (cyc_{strong}) or a weak one (cyc_{weak}). By combining both metrics, we are now able to decide whether a given communication path is cyclic at all, expressed by the following boolean metric:

$$
cycle(v, p) = cyc_{strong}(v, p) \vee cyc_{weak}(v, p)
\tag{2}
$$

By applying this metric on all outgoing communication paths of a given API operation v, one can now calculate the ratio of cyclic dependencies for this specific API operation as follows:

$$
cycRatio_{api}(v) = \frac{|\{p \in P(v) : cycle(p)\}|}{|P(v)|}
\tag{3}
$$

Values larger than zero indicate that communication paths initiated by v result in at least one cyclic dependency with another microservice. Further investigation may be needed to determine whether this behavior is intended by design. There exists also a scenario where $P(v) = 0$, meaning that API operation v does not call any other microservices, and accordingly, has no outgoing communication paths. Then the node v is not relevant, and the metric returns 0.

Another essential aspect and one of the main contributions of this paper is the possibility to distinguish the nature of cycles further into technical and domain-based ones. For this, we first define the set of all connection operations within a given path p as $C(p) = \{c \in p : c \in V^{con}\}$. Applying the predicate *async* (see Sect. 3.1) on every element in C, we can determine whether a cycle exists rather on a domain or technical level.

$$
domainCycRatio(p) = \frac{|\{c \in C(p) : async(c)\}|}{|C(p)|}
\tag{4}
$$

Since a communication path p must always have at least one connection operation, this metric is always valid. The counterpart of this metric that measures the ratio of technical connections in the cycle can trivially be expressed by:

$$
techCycRatio(p) = 1 - domainCycRatio(p)
\tag{5}
$$

Specifying which type of cycle is less problematic is challenging to decide: While in the literature, asynchronous techniques are often recommended over synchronous ones [7,33], scenarios with harder time constraints might require a synchronous communication flow [9]. In practice, it might also happen that an unintended cycle contains both synchronous and asynchronous service calls.

The last metric introduced here measures how often a specific API operation is part of a cyclic communication chain without being the actual root of that chain. Nodes through which disproportionately high traffic is routed are also known as hubs and play a central role in a network's topology [1]. Due to their importance, they can also have a significant impact on the creation of cyclic dependencies. Let P_{cyc} denote the set of all cyclic paths in an API model, we can then express this impact of a given vertex v through the *CyclicMembershipRatio* metric as follows:

$$cycMemberRatio(v) = \frac{|\{p = (v_1, v_2, \ldots, v_n) \in P_{cyc} : v \in p \wedge v \neq v_1\}|}{|P_{cyc}|} \quad (6)$$

Calculating this metric for a given API operation can be done by comparing the number of all cyclic paths through the given operation with the total amount of all cyclic paths in the whole microservice system.

Our current implementation calculates all of these metrics as part of a post processing step after the reconstruction process finished the model generation (see Sect. 3.2). Finding outgoing paths and cycles from a given API operation is achieved by using standard depth-first search and a cycle detection algorithm such as the one proposed in [29], modified to detect both strong and weak cycles.

5   Case Studies

To evaluate our approach and test the performance of our metrics, we conducted two case studies with two different open-source microservice architectures, both taken from GitHub (see footnotes below). Based on the guidelines for observational case studies suggested in [24], the source code of the projects was not altered in any way during the observation.

5.1   Case Study 1: Lakeside Mutual

Lakeside Mutual[3] models a sample microservice system that realizes the business process of a fictional insurance company (designed based on real-life insurance systems). Its level of maturity and well-documented architecture makes it a good substitute for a real production system. It is also used in several other research studies [11,22]. The system consists of seven mostly Java Spring technologies-based backend microservices and four client applications – three Web frontends and one Node.js console client. Communication between the various services is mainly performed through synchronous HTTP REST calls and asynchronous messaging. We considered two of the seven backend services as too infrastructure-related [8] and therefore not relevant for our domain-centric approach. A third one, the *RiskManagementServer* was also not incorporated in our communication model as it does not provide any outgoing connections and hence cannot play any role in API-level communication cycles.

---

[3] https://github.com/Microservice-API-Patterns/LakesideMutual.

Our detectors were able to identify 40 API operations in total, split up into 19 API interfaces, with a majority (35) of these operations as being synchronous REST endpoints and only five asynchronous message handlers. From these 40 operations, we removed all that do not initiate a communication path, resulting in a total amount of 13 API operations for further analysis. Most of these communication paths result from the circumstance that many of Lakeside's microservices are designed as *Backend for Frontends* [3] to provide an individual interface to the underlying `Customer Core` service. Because this core service lacks any outgoing connections, none of these paths can be cyclic either.

However, our analysis found one API operation – `respondToInsuranceQuote` – with a $cycRatio_{api}$ of 0.66, meaning two-thirds of its communication chains form a cycle. Figure 3 shows the operation in question and its resulting invocation paths. Each initial invocation of this method leads to a follow-up call to the `receiveCustomerDecision` operation. From there, communication branches out in three different directions: While one path forwards to the `CoreService` and terminates there, the two others route back to the original service, resulting in two cyclic connections (see *Cycle 1* and *Cycle 2* in the diagram). Both can be considered weak cycles as each one addresses a different endpoint than the one from where the cycle started [17]. The *domCycRatio* for each of them reveals in addition that both rely on asynchronous messaging, making them purely domain-based. Resolving these cycles would therefore require a conceptual redesign of the architecture. If such a redesign is desired, the `receiveCustomerDecision` operation could be a possible starting point for further considerations: Its *cycMemberRatio* value of 1 indicates that it plays a central role in creating both cycles.

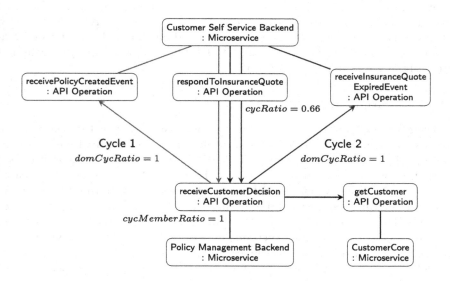

Fig. 3. Communication cycles in the lakeside mutual project

We detected these cyclic relations in the *Spring Term 2020* release from March 2020 of the Lakeside Mutual Project[4], while in the most recent version, a major refactoring happened, which led to a resolution of the cycle. Whether this was intended or just a side effect could not be determined. We checked that our tool correctly identifies in the recent release that the cycle has been removed.

5.2 Case Study 2: eShopOnContainers

The eShopOnContainers[5] repository is Microsoft's reference implementation for microservice applications and, as such, has also been the subject of various research studies [2,31]. It provides several frontend clients for different platforms and four backend microservices plus additional infrastructure-related services. As in the Lakeside Mutual case study, we also focus on the three backend services with the largest share of business-related domain logic. In contrast to the first study, a major difference is that all communication here is handled exclusively via an event bus (configurable to either RabbitMQ[6] or Azure Service Bus[7]). This design decision reduces the technical coupling between services to a minimum but lifts all potential cyclic dependencies to the domain level, making them harder to track. But this event-based characteristic also reflects in the implementation style of the project: The dispatch of domain messages is often decoupled from the actual creation process through event queues or caches, making the creation of an invocation graph a relatively challenging task compared to the previous case study. Our analysis revealed one cyclic dependency in the eShopOnContainers architecture (see Fig. 4). Here, invoking `CheckoutAsync` operation sends a message over the event bus that is handled by the Ordering API, which sends its answer back to the Basket Service, where the responsible event handler processes it. Because of the system's asynchronous nature, these dependencies manifest obviously only on the domain level. Although this is the only cycle originating from this API operation, as can be determined by its *CycRate* metric value of 1, this link would be pretty hard to track manually since the connections between the services are not immediately visible.

6 Discussion

Regarding **RQ1**, the case studies have shown that our approach is very well suited for finding domain-based cycles. We identified this kind of cyclic dependencies in both cases by only analyzing source code artifacts without gathering time-consuming runtime information, with the second example project even using a very implicit communication model. This makes our approach particularly interesting for agile or DevOps processes, as executing our cycle checks

---

[4] Available as a separate branch under https://github.com/Microservice-API-Patterns/LakesideMutual/tree/spring-term-2020, last accessed on August 18, 2021.

[5] https://github.com/dotnet-architecture/eShopOnContainers, commit hash 6012fb... from April 12, 2021.

[6] https://www.rabbitmq.com/.

[7] https://docs.microsoft.com/en-us/azure/service-bus-messaging/.

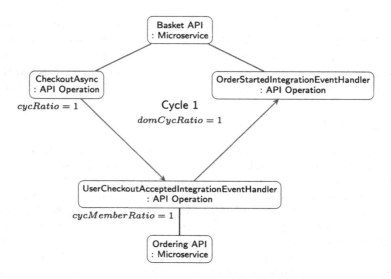

Fig. 4. Communication cycle in eShopOnContainers

could be done as part of the development or continuous integration pipelines. But our case study also revealed that applying our detector approach requires some additional initial effort, like identifying common technologies and coding patterns that are applied during the whole system and writing the relevant detectors to locate these patterns within the code. This upfront workload needs especially to be considered for larger systems. Complex communication scenarios, where service endpoint addresses are constructed during runtime, for example by reading input parameters, would also bring our detector approach to its limits. Here the use of additional heuristics to provide additional guidance would be necessary.

Considering **RQ2**, we could also show that our communication model contains all relevant elements to describe the information flow within a microservice system sufficiently and discover potential cycles. Focusing on API operations as central communication elements allows for a very detailed analysis of various cycle properties. At the time of this writing, we are not aware of any other research that combines so many different cycle characteristics into a single analysis.

Regarding **RQ3**, we showed in the case studies that the metrics we defined in our process provide a broad tool-set for architects to identify and assess potential cycles within a microservice application. This is especially true for domain-based cycles, which are not easily trackable as their structure often is hidden in the underlying message system. Nevertheless, the final judgment, whether a specific cyclic connection is problematic or intended, can only be made by an expert who is familiar with the underlying business domain. However, our tool-set can provide meaningful information to support a qualified decision.

7   Threats to Validity

This section gives a short overview of potential threats to validity (see e.g. [34]) and which mitigation measures we have applied:

Construct Validity expresses to what extent the correct measures were taken to study the phenomenon and how well our abstraction represents the original system. Since we developed our detectors iteratively and compared the generated model successively with the underlying source code, we can assume with a high degree of certainty that our model and the derived metrics are correct with respect to the underlying architecture. While in general possible, it is unlikely that we have missed a cycle or misinterpreted one, or made a substantial mistake in the reconstruction of the two architectures that occurred both in our manual and automatic reconstruction.

Internal Validity plays a role when there might be unknown factors that could affect the conclusions drawn from the study. Since our communication model and, therefore, our derived metrics are based on source code artifacts, all implementation related impacting factors are known at the time when the model is generated. Nevertheless, there might still exist additional artifacts like requirement specifications or specific domain knowledge that could have driven architectural design decisions. Currently, we are not considering these artifacts.

External Validity describes how well the findings could be generalized to a larger problem space and how relevant the results are beyond this specific research. The ongoing discussion about cyclic dependencies in the research community (see, for instance [17, 33] or, for real-world scenarios [6]) underlines the relevance of this problem and the example projects we used for our case studies are both open-source systems, well known to the public and research community, and combine various architectural styles and best practices. While they certainly do not reflect all possible microservice implementations, they provide a representative character to a specific extent. But still, generalization to commercial systems or systems other than enterprise domains might not be possible without adaptation of our approach.

8   Conclusions and Future Work

In this paper, we presented a novel approach for detecting technical and especially domain-based cyclic dependencies in microservice API architectures. Our approach confirms that the detection is possible by relying solely on static source code artifacts, which makes our method ideal to be applied in continuous integration pipelines. To extract our communication model from existing source code repositories, we implemented modular, reusable source code detectors and adjusted them to support different microservice systems. While this requires some upfront implementation work, our case studies revealed that this effort is manageable and can also be reduced by reusing existing detectors where possible. In the next step, we derived a set of metrics from our model, which we then used to detect and classify potential communication cycles in two open-source microservice systems during a case study. The study results show that the applied metrics can detect even inconspicuous domain-based cycles that manifest only on a conceptual level. The information gathered through our cycle analysis provides software experts with a solid foundation for making qualified decisions regarding a microservice system's architecture. While our approach can detect the existence of various types of cycles, it cannot make any assumptions about whether and how often these cycles are actually called during execution or if the deployment of the system is negatively affected through these cycles in practice. Thus, it would be necessary to collect additional runtime data and enrich the communication model with this supplementary information. We have already taken the first steps in this research direction.

Acknowledgments. This work was supported by: FWF (Austrian Science Fund) project API-ACE: I 4268; FWF (Austrian Science Fund) project IAC^2: I 4731-N; FFG (Austrian Research Promotion Agency) project DECO, no. 864707. Our work has received funding from the European Union's Horizon 2020 research and innovation programme under grant agreement No 952647 (AssureMOSS project).

References

1. Al-Mutawa, H.A., Dietrich, J., Marsland, S., McCartin, C.: On the shape of circular dependencies in java programs. In: 2014 23rd Australian Software Engineering Conference, pp. 48–57. IEEE (2014)
2. Assunção, W.K.G., Krüger, J., Mendonça, W.D.F.: Variability management meets microservices: six challenges of re-engineering microservice-based webshops. In: Proceedings of the 24th ACM Conference on Systems and Software Product Line, pp. 1–6. ACM, Montreal Quebec Canada (2020)
3. Brown, K., Woolf, B.: Implementation patterns for microservices architectures. In: Proceedings of the 23rd Conference on Pattern Languages of Programs, pp. 1–35 (2016)
4. Dragoni, N., et al.: Microservices: Yesterday, today, and tomorrow. arXiv:1606.04036 [cs], April 2017
5. Engel, T., Langermeier, M., Bauer, B., Hofmann, A.: Evaluation of microservice architectures: a metric and tool-based approach. In: Mendling, J., Mouratidis, H. (eds.) CAiSE 2018. LNBIP, vol. 317, pp. 74–89. Springer, Cham (2018). https://doi.org/10.1007/978-3-319-92901-9_8
6. Esparrachiari, S., Reilly, T., Rentz, A.: Tracking and controlling microservice dependencies: dependency management is a crucial part of system and software design. Queue **16**(4), 44–65 (2018)
7. Garriga, M.: Towards a taxonomy of microservices architectures. In: Cerone, A., Roveri, M. (eds.) SEFM 2017. LNCS, vol. 10729, pp. 203–218. Springer, Cham (2018). https://doi.org/10.1007/978-3-319-74781-1_15
8. Granchelli, G., Cardarelli, M., Di Francesco, P., Malavolta, I., Iovino, L., Di Salle, A.: Towards recovering the software architecture of microservice-based systems. In: 2017 IEEE International Conference on Software Architecture Workshops (ICSAW), pp. 46–53. IEEE, Gothenburg, April 2017. ISBN 978-1-5090-4793-2

9. Hohpe, G., Woolf, B.: Enterprise Integration Patterns: Designing, Building, and Deploying Messaging Solutions. Addison-Wesley Professional, Boston (2004)

10. Johnson, D.B.: Finding all the elementary circuits of a directed graph. SIAM J. Comput. **4**(1), 77–84 (1975). ISSN 0097–5397, 1095–7111

11. Kapferer, S., Zimmermann, O.: Domain-driven service design-context modeling, model refactoring and contract generation. In: Proceedings of the 14th Advanced Summer School on Service-Oriented Computing (SummerSOC'20) (to appear). Springer CCIS (2020)

12. Kleehaus, M., Uludağ, Ö., Schäfer, P., Matthes, F.: MICROLYZE: a framework for recovering the software architecture in microservice-based environments. In: Mendling, J., Mouratidis, H. (eds.) CAiSE 2018. LNBIP, vol. 317, pp. 148–162. Springer, Cham (2018). https://doi.org/10.1007/978-3-319-92901-9_14

13. Levcovitz, A., Terra, R., Valente, M.T.: Towards a Technique for Extracting Microservices from Monolithic Enterprise Systems. arXiv:1605.03175 [cs], May 2016

14. Lilienthal, C.: Sustainable Software Architecture: Analyze and Reduce Technical Debt. dpunkt. verlag, Heidelberg (2019)

15. Lotz, J., Vogelsang, A., Benderius, O., Berger, C.: Microservice architectures for advanced driver assistance systems: a case-study. In: 2019 IEEE International Conference on Software Architecture Companion (ICSA-C), pp. 45–52. IEEE, Hamburg, Germany (2019). ISBN 978-1-72811-876-

16. Lübke, D., Zimmermann, O., Pautasso, C., Zdun, U., Stocker, M.: Interface evolution patterns: balancing compatibility and extensibility across service life cycles. In: Proceedings of the 24th European Conference on Pattern Languages of Programs - EuroPLop '19, pp. 1–24. ACM Press, Irsee, Germany (2019). ISBN 978-1-4503-6206-1

17. Ma, S.P., Fan, C.Y., Chuang, Y., Liu, I.H., Lan, C.W.: Graph-based and scenario-driven microservice analysis, retrieval, and testing. Future Gener. Comput. Syst. **100**, 724–735 (2019). ISSN 0167739X

18. McZara, J., Kafle, S., Shin, D.: Modeling and analysis of dependencies between microservices in devsecOps. In: 2020 IEEE International Conference on Smart Cloud (SmartCloud), pp. 140–147. IEEE, Washington DC, WA, USA, November 2020. ISBN 978-1-72816-547-9

19. Nadareishvili, I., Mitra, R., McLarty, M., Amundsen, M.: Microservice Architecture: Aligning Principles, Practices, and Culture. "O'Reilly Media, Inc.", Sebastopol (2016)

20. Newman, S.: Building Microservices: Designing Fine-Grained Systems. 1st edn. O'Reilly Media, Beijing Sebastopol (2015). ISBN 978-1-4919-5035-7

21. Ntentos, E., Zdun, U., Plakidas, K., Meixner, S., Geiger, S.: Detector-based component model abstraction for microservice-based systems. Submitted for publication (2020)

22. Rademacher, F., Sachweh, S., Zündorf, A.: A modeling method for systematic architecture reconstruction of microservice-based software systems. In: Nurcan, S., Reinhartz-Berger, I., Soffer, P., Zdravkovic, J. (eds.) BPMDS/EMMSAD -2020. LNBIP, vol. 387, pp. 311–326. Springer, Cham (2020). https://doi.org/10.1007/978-3-030-49418-6_21

23. Ren, Z., et al.: Migrating web applications from monolithic structure to microservices architecture. In: Proceedings of the Tenth Asia-Pacific Symposium on Internetware, pp. 1–10. ACM, Beijing, September 2018. ISBN 978-1-4503-6590-1

24. Runeson, P., Höst, M.: Guidelines for conducting and reporting case study research in software engineering. Empirical Softw. Eng. **14**(2), 131–164 (2009). ISSN 1382–3256, 1573–7616

25. Selmadji, A., Seriai, A.D., Bouziane, H.L., Oumarou Mahamane, R., Zaragoza, P., Dony, C.: From monolithic architecture style to microservice one based on a semi-automatic approach. In: 2020 IEEE International Conference on Software Architecture (ICSA), pp. 157–168. IEEE, Salvador, Brazil, March 2020. ISBN 978-1-72814-659-1

26. Soares de Toledo, S., Martini, A., Przybyszewska, A., Sjoberg, D.I.: Architectural technical debt in microservices: a case study in a large company. In: 2019 IEEE/ACM International Conference on Technical Debt (TechDebt), pp. 78–87. IEEE, Montreal, QC, Canada, May 2019. ISBN 978-1-72813-371-3

27. Taibi, D., Lenarduzzi, V.: On the definition of microservice bad smells. IEEE Softw. **35**(3), 56–62 (2018)

28. Taibi, D., Lenarduzzi, V., Pahl, C.: Architectural patterns for microservices: a systematic mapping study. In: Proceedings of the 8th International Conference on Cloud Computing and Services Science, pp. 221–232. SCITEPRESS - Science and Technology Publications, Funchal, Madeira, Portugal (2018). ISBN 978-989-758-295-0

29. Tarjan, R.: Depth-first search and linear graph algorithms. SIAM J. Comput. **1**(2), 146–160 (1972)

30. Thones, J.: Microservices. IEEE Softw. **32**(1), 116–116 (2015). ISSN 0740–7459

31. Vural, H., Koyuncu, M.: Does domain-driven design lead to finding the optimal modularity of a microservice? IEEE Access **9**, 32721–32733 (2021). ISSN 2169–3536

32. Walker, A., Das, D., Cerny, T.: Automated code-smell detection in microservices through static analysis: a case study. Appl. Sci. **10**(21), 7800 (2020). ISSN 2076–3417

33. Wolff, E.: Microservices: Flexible Software Architecture. Addison-Wesley, Boston (2017). 978-0-13-460241-7

34. Yin, R.K.: Case Study Research and Applications: Design and Methods. 6th edn. SAGE, Los Angeles (2018). 978-1-5063-3616-9

35. Zdun, U., Navarro, E., Leymann, F.: Ensuring and assessing architecture conformance to microservice decomposition patterns. In: Maximilien, M., Vallecillo, A., Wang, J., Oriol, M. (eds.) ICSOC 2017. LNCS, vol. 10601, pp. 411–429. Springer, Cham (2017). https://doi.org/10.1007/978-3-319-69035-3_29

Optimized Dependency Weights in Source Code Clustering

Tobias Olsson$^{(\boxtimes)}$, Morgan Ericsson , and Anna Wingkvist

Department of Computer Science and Media Technology, Linnaeus University,
Kalmar/Växjö, Sweden
{tobias.olsson,morgan.ericsson,anna.wingkvist}@lnu.se

Abstract. Some methods use the dependencies between source code
entities to perform clustering to, e.g., automatically map to an intended
modular architecture or reconstruct the implemented software architecture. However, there are many different ways that source code entities
can depend on each other in an object-oriented system, and it is not
likely that all dependencies are equally useful. We investigate how well
an optimized set of weights for 14 different types of dependencies perform
when automatically mapping source code to modules using an established
mapping technique. The optimized weights were found using genetic optimization. We compare the F1 score of precision and recall to uniform
weights and weights computed by module relation ratio in eight open-
source systems to evaluate performance. Our experiments show that optimized weights significantly outperform the others, especially in systems
that seem not to have been designed using the low coupling, high cohesion principle. We also find that dependencies based on method calls are
not useful for automatic mapping in any of the eight systems.

Keywords: Orphan adoption · Software architecture · Incremental
clustering · Corrective clustering · Source code dependencies

1 Introduction

A fundamental principle for building software systems is to group parts of the
source code with similar responsibilities, for example, a database layer in a layered architecture or a view module in a model-view-controller architecture. To
make it easier to maintain, reuse, or completely exchange such groups (i.e., modules), the modular architecture describes the intended modules, their responsibilities, and dependencies on each other [3]. It is advantageous to have as few
dependencies as possible to and from the outside of a module and keep collaborating entities inside the module to achieve a high degree of modularity. The
module should be as cohesive internally and as loosely coupled to the outside as
possible.

Clustering algorithms can use the assumption of high cohesion and low coupling to either recover the modular architecture (software architecture recovery)

© Springer Nature Switzerland AG 2021
S. Biffl et al. (Eds.): ECSA 2021, LNCS 12857, pp. 223–239, 2021.
https://doi.org/10.1007/978-3-030-86044-8_16

or provide an automatic mapping to a module for a newly introduced source code entity in the system [4,5,13]. Such a mapping is a prerequisite for Static Architecture Conformance Checking (SACC) techniques such as Reflexion modeling [1].

Tzerpos and Holt describe the problem of automatically clustering a source code entity to an existing architectural module [13]. They refer to this problem as orphan adoption, which includes both *incremental clustering* and *corrective clustering*. An orphan is an entity, and incremental clustering is the mapping of a newly introduced orphan to a module (cf. Fig. 1). Software evolution can cause a need for corrective clustering, i.e., remapping an entity to a new module. They identify five criteria that affect the mapping, including the *structure*: using the relations between an orphan and already mapped entities to find a mapping. However, many different types of relations exist, and all relations are likely not equally valuable for clustering purposes.

We use a genetic optimization algorithm [6] to find a possibly optimal set of weights for a rich set of dependency types for eight object-oriented open-source systems, where the ground truth mapping is known. We compare this approach to a simple computation of the module (internal) relation ratio for each type of relation and uniform weights to determine whether these perform well enough. We pose the following questions:

- Will optimized relation weights result in significant F1 score improvements over intuitive weights and/or uniform weights?
- Are there any noticeable patterns in the optimized relation weights?

We find that optimized weights perform significantly better and that the MethodCall dependency type, which is highly valued in related studies, e.g., [4,11,12] is not effective. Our research focuses on using dependency weights in incremental clustering, i.e., orphan adoption, but we hypothesize that the findings could improve, for example, clustering techniques for software architecture recovery.

2   Background

In object-oriented systems, we find rich sets of different types of dependencies between classes. For example, a class can contain an attribute of some other type (class) and call methods defined in another class using this attribute. Most object-oriented languages also have some dependency type between classes, indicating that one class is considered more general and another more special, e.g., inheritance, and allows for overloading operations in such hierarchies. These logical dependencies are directed from one class to another.

Developers often place the source code files in different directories, and this structure of directories can convey important information regarding modularity. In some languages, this structure is also reflected by constructs in the source code, e.g., packages in Java. We divide such physical relations between the source code files of the system into vertical and horizontal relations. Files in the same directory have a horizontal relation, and files in direct parent and child directories have a vertical relation. These two types of relations are not directed and do not imply any dependency between the files per se.

By analyzing the Java Bytecode for a system, we can find the following types of relations:

- *Extends*, a type is inherited.
- *Implements*, an interface is realized.
- *Field*, a type is a member variable definition.
- *Argument*, a type is an argument in an operation.
- *Returns*, a type is used as a return type.
- *LocalVar*, a type is used as a local variable definition.
- *MethodCall*, an operation is called on a type.
- *ConstructorCall*, a type is created.
- *OwnFieldUse*, a type is used by a field in this type.
- *FieldUse*, a type is used by a field in some other type.
- *Throws*, a type is used in the form of an exception.
- *File_Horizontal*, a type is defined in the same directory as this type.
- *File_LevelUp*, a type is defined in a directory above this type.
- *File_LevelDown*, a type is defined in a directory below this type.

HuGMe [4] is a semi-automatic mapping technique that relies on a pre-existing set of mapped entities to perform orphan adoption. HuGMe is applied iteratively, and as the set of mapped entities can grow for each iteration, it can automatically map more orphans. In each iteration, human intervention is also possible using the failed automatic mapping results as a guideline. The automatic mapping is done by calculating the attraction between the orphan and the mapped entities for each module using two attraction functions (CountAttract and MQAttract) based on dependencies in the source code, i.e., the structure criteria. We consider only the CountAttract function as this function has outperformed MQAttract in evaluations.

The CountAttract attraction function [4] in HuGMe uses the relations between an orphan and the already mapped entities to compute an attraction. This attraction is the sum of the relations between the orphan and all mapped entities minus the sum of all relations between the orphan and other entities mapped to other modules. These other entities are divided into two sets based on the intended architecture: allowed relations and violating relations. The sum of the allowed relations is weighted using a parameter, $\phi \in [0, 1]$, where a value of 1 means that the function should strive to map entities to maximize cohesion. In the example illustrated by Fig. 1, setting ϕ to 1 would map StringChange to Logic and setting ϕ to 0 would map it to GUI.

Equations 1, 2, and 3 illustrate the CountAttract function; a formal definition is given and discussed in [4]. An orphan entity is denoted by o, and m is the module to calculate the attraction for. ME is the set of all mapped entities, and e_j is one such mapped entity. R is the set of all implemented relations between entities in the source code. w_{o,e_j} is the weighted sum of all relations between o

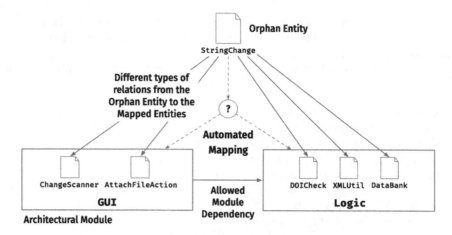

Fig. 1. A mapping example from JabRef. StringChange is an orphan entity to be mapped to either the GUI or the Logic module. The automated mapping can use the dependencies from the orphan to mapped entities, e.g., DOICheck. Allowed module dependencies and dependency weights also need to be taken into account.

and e_j, where the type of dependency decides the weight. Finally, A is the set of allowed dependencies between the architectural modules, and $[m, e'_j]$ denotes a relationship between the module m and the *mapping* of e_j.

$$CountAttract(o, m) = AllRelations(o) - ToOthers(o, m) \qquad (1)$$

$$AllRelations(o) = \sum_{e_j \in ME} \left\{ \begin{array}{l} w_{o,e_j} : [o, e_j] \in R \\ 0 : otherwise \end{array} \right\} \qquad (2)$$

$$ToOthers(o, m) = \sum_{e_j \in ME} \left\{ \begin{array}{l} 0 : e_j \in m \\ \phi \times w_{o,e_j} : [o, e_j] \in R \wedge e_j \notin m \wedge [m, e'_j] \in A \\ w_{o,e_j} : [o, e_j] \in R \wedge e_j \notin m \wedge [m, e'_j] \notin A \end{array} \right\} \qquad (3)$$

By calculating an attraction for every orphan and module, HuGMe can decide if an attraction is considered "valid enough" to map the orphan. The set ME will thus grow and possibly allow for more orphans to be mapped in the next iteration. It could, therefore, be better to wait to map an orphan until some other orphans are mapped. HuGMe uses $\omega \in [0, 1]$ to specify a threshold for the ratio between an orphan's relations to entities in ME and to all entities. For example, if $\omega = 1.0$, then only orphans that only have relations to entities in ME are considered for mapping.

To measure the performance of CountAttract we use the F1 harmonic mean of the precision and recall (cf. Eqs. 4 to 6). In our previous work, we have shown that the F1 score is highly dependent on the size and composition of the initial set of mapped nodes [8,9]. The F1 score gives an overall indication of the performance, i.e., how many entities are mapped (recall) and how well they are mapped (precision). It assumes equal importance of precision and recall, and if this assumption does not hold, e.g., in a practical application, precision and recall need to be judged individually.

$$Precision = \frac{SuccessfullyMappedOrphans}{MappedOrphans} \tag{4}$$

$$Recall = \frac{SuccessfullyMappedOrphans}{SuccessfullyMappedOrphans + UnmappedOrphans} \tag{5}$$

$$F1 = \frac{2 \times Precision \times Recall}{Precision + Recall} \tag{6}$$

We use a rich set of relations, and it is not apparent how such dependencies should be weighed for an attraction function such as CountAttract to perform well. In addition, the relations are likely not independent, i.e., one type of relation can co-exist with and affect the amount of other relations [12]. A first indication of the importance of the relations could be to examine the cohesiveness of the relation. We call this the *module relation ratio*; the number of relations of a particular type between entities within a module divided by the total number of dependencies of that specific type in the module. We consider this an intuitive weighting as it can be roughly known by a system expert or found by inspecting the code. This calculation is also straightforward. We will use such weighting to compare to a more elaborate optimization using a genetic algorithm (GA). Finding an optimal set of weights is challenging as there are many weights expressed as continuous variables, and they may very well affect each other. The effect of the initial set composition and size adds another dimension of complexity. Weights need to perform well overall and not just in a specific case. A GA is typically helpful in finding non-intuitive near-optimal solutions in a wide range of applications and problems where a brute force search is infeasible [6].

3   Related Work

The original work related to HuGMe [4] defines seven types of relations (cf. Table 1). Our rich set of relations cover these and, to some degree, provides a more fine-grained view. However, we do not differentiate between method sets and method uses for variables. They evaluate the CountAttract function in four case studies, of which two are object-oriented systems implemented in Java. Their goals are to evaluate the usefulness of HuGMe in general, compare two attraction functions, and evaluate the effect of the two parameters ω and ϕ on

Table 1. Dependencies and weights from [4]: v is a variable, m is a method or routine, c is class, i is an interface, t is a type (including classes and interfaces).

Type in [4]	Corresponding types	Weight in [4]
m calls m	Method call	2
m uses v	FieldUse, OwnFieldUse	1
m sets v	FieldUse, OwnFieldUse	3
c implements i	Implements	1
v of-type t	Field, LocalVar	1
m has-parameter-of-type t	Argument	1
t inherits t	Extends	1

the clustering results. The weights used are not changed per system but rather seen as universally good enough weights. They mention that varying the weights would be interesting future work.

The weights used in [4] are derived from [11], an investigation of the effect of different call graph construction approaches for object-oriented systems on automatic clustering. Object-oriented languages introduce polymorphism and late binding, so it is not trivial to determine which method that is called as it can be overloaded in a sub-class. While the same effect can be achieved in procedural languages using, e.g., function pointers, it is much more common in object-oriented languages. In [11], it is specifically mentioned that the weights used on edges in their experiments are based on the researchers' judgment. They are thus not empirically validated, and finding optimal values is mentioned as future work. They use a Java-based object-oriented system as their case. To conclude, they find different approaches to generate call graphs results in different clusterings. However, they have no ground truth clustering to compare to and cannot say that one graph is better. Concerning this work, we use the approach described as Naive, i.e., we use what the Java Bytecode states and perform no extra analysis. Table 2 show the relations used in [11] and our corresponding relation. Note that the Inner Class Declaration is inherent in our model as the outermost class contains all inner classes and their respective relations in our model.

The question of what relations and combination of relations work best for architectural reconstruction is investigated in [12]. They define several relations (cf. Table 3) that can be extracted from object-oriented systems and use these in different combinations in their clustering algorithm. The results are compared to ground truth architectures that are generated using all possible relations. They use six object-oriented systems, Apache Ant, Apache Ivy, Apache Maven, jEdit, JHotDraw, and TexMaker, to evaluate their approach. Their findings suggest that at least four combinations of relations are needed and that the Accesses, Calls, and Sets relations should always be included. In addition, they find that it is advantageous to add some of the medium-high relations as defined in Table 3.

Table 2. Dependencies and weights from [11].

Type in [11]	Corresponding type	Weight in [11]
Inheritance	Extends, Implements	low
Inner Class Decl.	inherent	high
Type dependence	Field, ReturnType, LocalVar, Argument	low
Exceptions	Throws	low
Instantiation	ConstructorCall	high
Array Creation	Argument	medium
Field Read	Extends	medium
Static Field Read	FieldUse, OwnFieldUse	low
Field Write	FieldUse, OwnFieldUse	high
Static Field Write	FieldUse, OwnFieldUse	high
Invocation	MethodCall	medium

Table 3. The analyzed object-oriented dependencies and their importance from [12].

Relation in [12]	Corresponding type	Importance
Calls	MethodCall, ConstructorCall	high
Includes	n/a	medium-high
Sets	FieldUse, OwnFieldUse	high
Accesses	Fielduse, OwnFieldUse	high
Class Belongs To File	inherent	medium
Inherits From	Extends, Implements	no-effect
Has Type	Field, Returns, Attribute, Throws	no-effect
Defined In	inherent	medium-high
Declared In	inherent	medium-high
Attribute Belongs To Class	Field	medium
Method Belongs To Class	inherent	medium-high
Uses Type	LocalVar	no-effect

Note that the importance column is our interpretation of their results and analysis, as the importance is not explicitly stated in [11].

4   Method

To answer our questions, we first design and implement a GA to find the optimized weights for our subject systems, run it on each system, and compute the module relation ratio. Second, we use the optimized weights, the intuitive weights calculated by the module relation ratio, and the uniform weights (set to 1.0) when executing several mapping experiments. We perform each experiment several times to account for variations in initial set size, composition, and algorithm parameters (ω and ϕ). The experiments are constructed and executed in our tool suite for mapping experiments [10] and are of the same type as presented in [8]. Data is collected and analyzed using R (v 4.0.0). The source code of our GA and the application used to run the experiments, as well as the analysis scripts and the generated data are available in a replication package[1].

4.1   Data Analysis

A system expert optimally sets the algorithm parameters ω and ϕ, but in our case, we use random values for each experiment. Each data set is filtered to counter random parameter values producing overly poor mappings by computing the upper and lower limits of the ϕ parameter for the 10% best mappings. We do the same for the ω parameter, but in slices of the data based on the initial set size, i.e., the ω parameter depends on the size of the initial set, which is something a human user would know.

After filtering, we perform statistical significance testing to determine whether there is a significant difference in the F1 score and investigate the effect size for every system and weighting schema combination. We test for statistical significance at $p < 0.05$. The data is likely not normally distributed, so we use the Wilcoxon rank-sum test. We report the effect size using r and the median difference. It is also interesting to show whether specific intervals of the initial set sizes are different. A weighting schema may perform well within a particular interval, giving an overall significant difference but perform poorly or similar to the other attraction functions in some intervals. We, therefore, provide visualizations that show the median and distribution of the F1 scores for the entire interval of the initial mapping sizes to complement the significance testing.

4.2   Genetic Algorithm

The following section provides a brief overview of the particulars of the GA used; for specifics, see the replication package (see footnote 1), and for fundamentals see [6]. Our GA uses the weight of each dependency as the genome, and a complete set of weights denote an individual. A generation consists of several individuals that are all evaluated using the same system and initial sets of mapped entities. The initial set sizes range from 1% of the entities to 99%. Our *fitness function* deems that an individual to be more fit than another if it has a better F1 score in a majority of these ten initial sets. We calculate the F1 scores using CountAttract with ϕ set to 1.0 (maximum module cohesion) and ω set to be increasing from 0.1 to 0.75 depending on the initial set size as advised in [4].

---

[1] https://github.com/tobias-dv-lnu/Replication/tree/master/ECSA21.

Using ten initial sets, we optimize for weights that can be considered generally good over a spectrum of initial sets. Note that the composition of the initial set will change for each generation, so the actual F1 scores may be lower in the next generation as the environment has changed. Using several generations for evaluation, we should get a genetic composition that tends to survive multiple compositions. Therefore, it is not likely that the individual with the highest mean F1 score has the best genes since this can be a consequence of the composition of the initial set.

The first generation has its genome seeded by random values from 0 to 1). After that, each generation spawns a new generation via a tournament selection process where a number of individuals are randomly selected from the generation. The two with the highest fitness become the parents of a new individual. The parent genes are combined using *uniform crossover*. We also let the best individual from a generation survive to the next generation, i.e., elitism, capped by maximum age. Finally, a spawned individual has a random chance of *mutation*; if so, one random gene is changed by a random delta value, bound by 0 and 1. We do not expect any weighting schema to produce a perfect mapping for any system, so we run the algorithm for a set number of generations deemed feasible.

4.3 Subject Systems

We use eight open-source systems implemented in Java. Ant[2] is an API and command-line tool for process automation. ArgoUML[3] is a desktop application for UML modeling. Commons Imaging[4] is an image library for reading and writing a variety of image formats developed by the Apache Software Foundation. Jabref[5] is a desktop application for managing bibliographical references. Lucene[6] is an indexing and search library. ProM[7] is an extensible framework that supports a variety of process mining techniques. Sweet Home 3D[8] is an interior design application. Teammates[9] is a web application for handling student peer reviews and feedback.

Table 4 presents the sizes of the systems in Lines of Code, number of Entities, number of Modules, and the number of dependencies. There is a documented software architecture and a mapping from the implementation to this architecture for each system. Jabref, Teammates, and ProM have been the subjects of

---

[2] https://ant.apache.org.
[3] http://argouml.tigris.org.
[4] https://commons.apache.org/proper/commons-imaging/.
[5] https://jabref.org.
[6] https://lucene.apache.org.
[7] http://www.promtools.org.
[8] http://www.sweethome3d.com.
[9] https://teammatesv4.appspot.com.

study at the Software Architecture Erosion and Architectural Consistency Workshop (SAEroCon) 2016, 2017, and 2019 respectively, where a system expert provided both the architecture and the mapping. The architecture documentation and mappings are available in the SAEroCon repository[10]. One of the developers provided the documentation for Commons Imaging as part of the evaluation of our tool suite for mapping experiments [10]. ArgoUML, Ant, and Lucene were studied in [2,7], and the architectures and mappings were extracted from the replication package of [2]. The researchers extracted the ground truth architectures and mappings from the system documentation for these systems.

5   Results

We executed the GA to optimize the weights for each system and found that after 300 generations, the F1 scores seemed relatively stable. We decided to end the optimization at that point for each system. Each generation used 30 individuals, resulting in 720 000 mappings to produce the optimized weights. Table 5 presents the results from computing the internal coupling ratio, i.e., the intuitive weights as well as the optimized weights. Intuitive weight values below 0.5 (marked with *) indicate more instances of the dependency type span over module boundaries than being internal to modules. The compiled versions of Lucene and Sweet Home 3D do not include the local variable information. Note that File_LevelUp and File_LevelDown are the same since each dependency of this type has a counterpart in the opposite direction.

Table 4. Subject systems and versions. *Entities*, *Ent.Dep.*, *Modules*, and *Mod.Dep.* are the number of entities, modules, and dependencies between these. LoC is the Lines of Code in each subject system.

System	Version	LoC	Entities	Ent.Dep.	Modules	Mod.Dep.
Ant	r584500	36 699	515	2 476	16	86
A.UML	r13713	62 392	1 485	8 121	19	79
C Img	v1.0a2	17 803	329	1 485	21	21
Jabref	v3.7	59 235	1 015	5 482	6	15
Lucene	r1075001	35 812	515	2 764	7	16
ProM	v6.9	9 947	261	747	4	5
S H 3D	r002382	34 964	167	1 175	9	29
T.Mates	v5.11	54 904	779	5 841	15	28

---

[10] https://github.com/sebastianherold/SAEroConRepo.

Table 5. The module relation ratio weights, and the optimized weights (in italics).

System	Ant		A.UML		C Img		JabRef		Lucene		ProM		S H 3D		T.Mates	
Extends	0.6	*1.0*	0.9	*1.0*	0.8	*1.0*	1.0	*1.0*	0.9	*1.0*	0.9	*0.0*	0.9	*1.0*	0.9	*1.0*
Implements	0.8	*1.0*	0.8	*0.9*	0.8	*0.9*	0.8	*1.0*	0.8	*1.0*	0.8	*0.0*	0.4*	*0.5*	0.3*	*0.3*
Field	0.5	*0.0*	0.8	*1.0*	0.9	*0.3*	0.8	*0.0*	0.7	*0.2*	0.9	*0.5*	0.7	*0.0*	0.6	*0.0*
Argument	0.6	*0.0*	0.8	*0.6*	0.6	*0.2*	0.6	*0.3*	0.6	*0.1*	0.9	*0.0*	0.4*	*0.0*	0.3*	*0.0*
Returns	0.6	*0.9*	0.9	*0.8*	0.8	*1.0*	0.8	*0.3*	0.8	*1.0*	0.9	*0.0*	0.7	*1.0*	0.4*	*0.5*
LocalVar	0.6	*0.0*	0.8	*0.1*	0.8	*0.3*	0.5	*0.0*	n/a	*0.5*	0.8	*0.0*	n/a	*0.5*	0.1*	*0.0*
MethodCall	0.4*	*0.0*	0.4*	*0.0*	0.5	*0.0*	0.5*	*0.0*	0.7	*0.0*	0.8	*0.0*	0.4*	*0.0*	0.3*	*0.0*
ConstrCall	0.4*	*0.0*	0.9	*0.8*	0.7	*0.0*	0.9	*0.8*	0.9	*1.0*	1.0	*0.5*	0.9	*0.8*	0.5*	*0.4*
OwnFieldUs	0.5*	*0.0*	0.9	*1.0*	1.0	*0.0*	0.8	*0.0*	0.7	*0.0*	0.9	*0.0*	0.5*	*0.0*	0.5*	*0.0*
FieldUse	0.9	*0.3*	0.8	*0.0*	1.0	*1.0*	0.7	*0.1*	0.9	*0.1*	0.8	*0.0*	0.7	*0.0*	0.1*	*0.0*
Throws	0.2*	*0.0*	1.0	*0.9*	0.2*	*0.0*	0.9	*1.0*	0.9	*0.9*	1.0	*0.6*	0.1*	*0.8*	0.0*	*0.0*
File_Horiz	1.0	*0.7*	1.0	*1.0*	1.0	*0.8*	1.0	*1.0*	1.0	*0.6*	1.0	*1.0*	1.0	*1.0*	1.0	*1.0*
File_LvlUp	0.2	*0.0*	0.8	*0.0*	0.7	*0.0*	1.0	*0.1*	1.0	*0.1*	1.0	*1.0*	0.0	*0.7*	1.0	*1.0*
File_LvlDwn	0.2	*0.0*	0.8	*0.1*	0.7	*0.2*	1.0	*0.4**	1.0	*0.1*	1.0	*1.0*	0.0	*0.2*	1.0	*1.0*
All Dep	0.5*		0.6		0.8		0.6		0.7		0.9		0.5		0.3*	
All	0.3*		0.6		0.8		0.7		0.8		0.9		0.5		0.3*	

We used 50 000 mappings per system and weighting scheme (uniform, intuitive, and optimized) for the final experiment, resulting in 1 200 000 mappings with varying initial set size, composition, and algorithm parameters (ω and ϕ). The filtering reduced the number of data points of each system used for analysis (cf. Table 6).

The data analysis revealed that the optimized weights outperform both the intuitive weights and the uniform weights in every case (cf. Fig. 2 and Table 6). This difference is more apparent in systems that show an overall low module relation ratio, i.e., Ant and Teammates, and less in systems that show an overall high cohesion of modules, e.g., ProM. Intuitive weights also outperform uniform weights, but the median difference is less, and in ProM, this difference was not statistically significant (cf. Table 6). Finally, Fig. 3 shows the running median F1 score across initial set sizes, including the 75th and 25th percentiles. The average median precision, recall, and F1 score per weighting schema (uniform, intuitive, optimized) are: precision 0.76, 0.79, and 0.90; recall 0.64, 0.67, and 0.81; and F1 score 0.68, 0.72, and 0.84.

6   Discussion and Threats to Validity

Using intuitive weights seems to suffer because each weight does not consider the impact of other weights. As a result, the intuitive weights have relatively high precision at the cost of a lower recall. The optimized weights are, in that respect, more balanced and thus get a higher score. In some cases, a more precise result may be desirable.

Table 6. The statistical significance testing and effect size for comparing all weighting schemes. All results are statistically significant at $p < 0.05$, except for ProM Int. v.s. Uni (marked with *). The r statistic shows the standardized effect sizes and $\widetilde{diff}$ shows the median difference. A positive $\widetilde{diff}$ indicates that the first schema has a higher F1 score. N1 shows the number of data points for the first schema and N2 for the second schema.

System	Statistic	Opt. vs. Int	Opt. vs. Uni	Int. vs. Uni
Ant	N1	28 867	28 867	28 701
	N2	28 701	28 520	28 520
	r	0.72	0.73	0.27
	Z	171.95	174.36	63.73
	$\widetilde{diff}$	0.30	0.39	0.08
A.UML	N1	15 885	15 885	17 809
	N2	17 809	17 979	17 979
	r	0.61	0.67	0.28
	Z	111.75	123.99	52.76
	$\widetilde{diff}$	0.11	0.16	0.05
C Img	N1	14 966	14 966	16 944
	N2	16 944	16 696	16 696
	r	0.29	0.36	0.08
	Z	51.76	63.31	14.74
	$\widetilde{diff}$	0.06	0.08	0.02
JabRef	N1	25 075	25 075	22 498
	N2	22 498	22 140	22 140
	r	0.37	0.45	0.13
	Z	79.849	98.47	27.30
	$\widetilde{diff}$	0.03	0.04	0.01
Lucene	N1	23 668	23 668	23 415
	N2	23 415	25 009	25 009
	r	0.40	0.46	0.08
	Z	86.34	100.82	17.23
	$\widetilde{diff}$	0.04	0.05	0.01
ProM	N1	31 971	31 971	32 128
	N2	32 128	31 137	31 137
	r	0.27	0.28	0.01*
	Z	69.28	71.36	1.45*
	$\widetilde{diff}$	0.02	0.03	0.00*
S H 3D	N1	28 583	28 583	29 898
	N2	29 898	31 172	31 172
	r	0.63	0.66	0.11
	Z	151.22	160.54	27.682
	$\widetilde{diff}$	0.22	0.25	0.03
T.Mates	N1	19 259	19 259	22 602
	N2	22 602	23 215	23 215
	r	0.77	0.80	0.43
	Z	158.01	165.45	92.65
	$\widetilde{diff}$	0.25	0.35	0.10

Dependency Weights F1 Score Comparisons

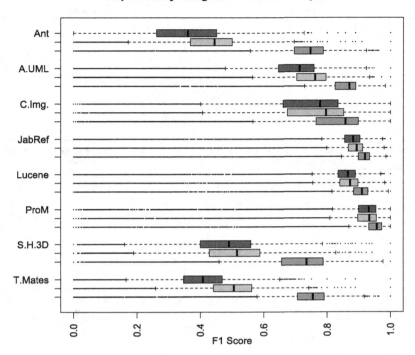

Fig. 2. Comparison of the Uniform (blue), Intuitive (orange), and Optimized (green) relation weights for each system. (Color figure online)

Table 5 shows some interesting findings. Neither Ant nor Teammates seem to be designed with the principle of high cohesion, as their overall cohesion of relations is quite low. This is also possibly true for Sweet Home 3D. In Teammates, only the Extends relation has a high weight together with the file relations, and the optimized weights also reflect this. For these systems, the difference in performance is also the largest, and the uniform and intuitive schemes' performance worsens as the initial set grows (cf. Fig. 3). This is not surprising since the systems violate the assumption of high cohesion and low coupling, which worsens the more data you use.

One fascinating finding is that the MethodCall dependency is not essential in the optimized weights and not a very cohesive relation in any of the systems. This makes some sense as method calls would be a common communication method between entities in general and between entities in different modules in particular. However, this is also in contrast to the related work that seems value weights for this relation from medium to high (cf. Tables 1, 2, and 3). In contrast, previous work appears to downplay inheritance and interface implementations, while our data shows high value these relations, especially the inheritance dependency. In our experience, this makes sense as effective use of inheritance often

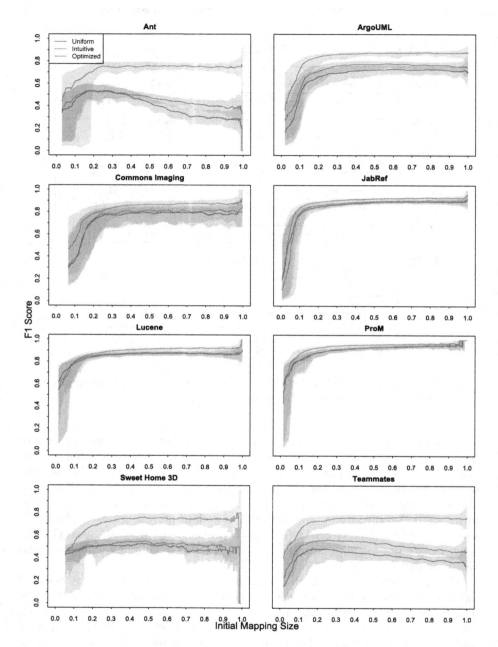

Fig. 3. The running median F1 score (vertical axis) with limits of the 75th and 25th percentiles for each system and relation weight over the interval of initial mapping sizes (horizontal axis).

requires intimate knowledge of parent classes, and these would be more likely to be in the same module. However, this relation does seem to depend on the fundamental design principles used; for example, ProM does not seem to value such relations at all. This discrepancy compared to the related work needs to be investigated further, and a more comparative study would be beneficial, using the same subject systems and the same algorithms.

The dependencies reflected in ConstructorCall and Throws show an interesting pattern. In Table 5, Throws only shows a medium weight (0.59) in ProM, and ConstructorCall shows medium weights (0.52 and 0.40) in ProM and Teammates respectively. These weights could reflect some design decisions related to object construction (for example, using a factory pattern) and error handling.

When looking at the optimized weights, it is essential to note that a weight that does not contribute to a change in performance can be random due to mutation. In general, this means we cannot know if a weight is a contributing factor or just random noise. We can, for example, see this in the LocalVar dependency for Lucene and Sweet Home 3D. These two dependencies are not available, and their values do not matter for the performance. In the optimized weights, we find 0.45 and 0.51 for these weights, respectively; however, as values are more extreme, the likelihood of having an actual impact on the performance increases.

While we could show that it is possible to create a set of optimized weights using a GA, we cannot be sure that the weights presented are optimal, i.e., there may be some other set of weights that produce even better results.

Humans created the ground truth mappings. These are thus affected by the subjectivity of the human performing the mapping. It is not likely that another human would produce the exact mapping for every entity. There are likely some entities that are not typical for a module in any evolving system. Such outliers may be very hard to map and may affect the mapping if they happen to be part of the initial set. While we do think such outliers exist, we are confident that they are the minority of entities.

In Java, the logical organization of classes in packages directly reflects the file structure. This may explain the high usefulness of the file-based relations and may not apply to implementations in other languages.

We treat the intuitive weights as something a human expert could have set. However, it is hard to know how a human would set such weights in practice, and indeed having such a rich set of weights would require some guidance to be usable. Possibly weights could be derived from the initial set, but this would make the technique even more sensitive to the size and composition of the initial set.

7   Conclusion and Future Work

We have shown that weight optimization can significantly improve the performance of the CountAttract attraction function. The improvement is more significant in systems that do not show high overall modularity regarding relations between entities. Optimal dependency weights can thus improve the usefulness of the CountAttract function for a broader set of systems and not be limited to systems created with a strong influence of the low coupling and high cohesion design principle.

Regarding patterns of the optimized weights, high weights for the file-level dependencies (*File_Horizontal*) and the inheritance (*Extends*) are promising when appropriate. It also seems reasonable that a system expert knows the use of inheritance and whether the modular structure reflects the file structure. The use of *ConstructorCall* and Throws relations could be a consequence of design decisions related to object creation and error handling. As such, they seem to be very important in some systems but not at all in others. *FieldUse* and *OwnFieldUse* relations are only valued highly in one system, respectively. We also find that neither the optimal weights nor the intuitive weights favored using *MethodCall* as a valuable relation for mapping. This finding seems to be contrary to related work in architecture reconstruction and clustering. We think performing more comparative studies can shed light on this phenomenon.

Deriving the weights from the initial set, essentially adding a learning step, would be an interesting approach compared to manually setting all weights.

References

1. Ali, N., Baker, S., O'Crowley, R., Herold, S., Buckley, J.: Architecture consistency: state of the practice, challenges and requirements. Empir. Softw. Eng. **23**, 1–35 (2018)
2. Brunet, J., Bittencourt, R.A., Serey, D., Figueiredo, J.: On the evolutionary nature of architectural violations. In: IEEE Working Conference on Reverse Engineering, pp. 257–266 (2012)
3. Buschmann, F., Henney, K., Schmidt, D.C.: Pattern-Oriented Software Architecture, A Pattern Language for Distributed Computing, vol. 4. Wiley, Hoboken (2007)
4. Christl, A., Koschke, R., Storey, M.A.: Automated clustering to support the reflexion method. Inf. Softw. Technol. **49**(3), 255–274 (2007)
5. Garcia, J., Ivkovic, I., Medvidovic, N.: A comparative analysis of software architecture recovery techniques. In: 2013 28th IEEE/ACM International Conference on Automated Software Engineering (ASE), pp. 486–496. IEEE (2013)
6. Haupt, R.L., Haupt, S.E.: Practical Genetic Algorithms. Wiley, Hoboken (2004)
7. Lenhard, J., Blom, M., Herold, S.: Exploring the suitability of source code metrics for indicating architectural inconsistencies. Software Qual. J. **27**(1), 241–274 (2018). https://doi.org/10.1007/s11219-018-9404-z
8. Olsson, T., Ericsson, M., Wingkvist, A.: Towards improved initial mapping in semi automatic clustering. In: Proceedings of the 12th European Conference on Software Architecture: Companion Proceedings. ECSA 2018, pp. 51:1–51:7 (2018)
9. Olsson, T., Ericsson, M., Wingkvist, A.: Semi-automatic mapping of source code using Naive Bayes. In: Proceedings of the 13th European Conference on Software Architecture - Volume 2, pp. 209–216 (2019)
10. Olsson, T., Ericsson, M., Wingkvist, A.: s4rdm3x: a tool suite to explore code to architecture mapping techniques. J. Open Source Softw. **6**(58), 2791 (2021). https://doi.org/10.21105/joss.02791

11. Rayside, D., Reuss, S., Hedges, E., Kontogiannis, K.: The effect of call graph construction algorithms for object-oriented programs on automatic clustering. In: Proceedings IWPC 2000. 8th International Workshop on Program Comprehension, pp. 191–200. IEEE (2000)
12. Stavropoulou, I., Grigoriou, M., Kontogiannis, K.: Case study on which relations to use for clustering-based software architecture recovery. Empir. Softw. Eng. **22**(4), 1717–1762 (2017). https://doi.org/10.1007/s10664-016-9459-z
13. Tzerpos, V., Holt, R.C.: The orphan adoption problem in architecture maintenance. In: Proceedings of the Fourth Working Conference on Reverse Engineering, pp. 76–82. IEEE (1997)

Experiences and Learnings from
Industrial Case Studies

Reliable Event Routing in the Cloud and on the Edge
An Internet-of-Things Solution in the AgeTech Domain

Linus Basig[1,2(✉)], Fabrizio Lazzaretti[1], Reto Aebersold[2],
and Olaf Zimmermann[1]

[1] University of Applied Sciences of Eastern Switzerland (OST),
Oberseestrasse 10, 8640 Rapperswil, Switzerland
{linus.basig,fabrizio.lazzaretti}@lifetime.hsr.ch, olaf.zimmermann@ost.ch
[2] CARU AG, Weberstrasse 3, 8004 Zürich, Switzerland
{linus.basig,reto.aebersold}@caruhome.com

Abstract. The AgeTech domain poses both opportunities and challenges for the architects of Internet of Things (IoT) solutions. Key requirements concern data privacy and cost-efficiency, as well as guaranteed, interoperable delivery of event messages from resource-constrained edge devices to the cloud and consumer applications; public cloud deployments and asynchronous, queue-based messaging are common building blocks of such solutions. This experience report features the conceptual, pattern-oriented design and open source implementation of a custom-built embeddable event router that natively supports the CloudEvents specification from the Cloud Native Computing Foundation. Our CloudEvents Router introduces standardized event routing targeting the software landscape of the AgeTech startup CARU; this landscape reaches from an embedded microcontroller to cloud-scale services running on Amazon Web Services. The report further analyses the message delivery guarantees given in messaging protocol specifications and their implementations (for instance, MQTT libraries) and presents an alternative delivery management approach, implemented and validated in the open sourced Rust microkernel of the CloudEvents router. The report concludes with lessons learned about messaging edge cases and protocol particularities, in MQTT in particular.

Keywords: Asynchronous messaging · Enterprise application integration · Cloud-native computing · Internet of things · Quality of service guarantees

1 Introduction

The AgeTech domain poses both opportunities and challenges for the architects of Internet of Things (IoT) solutions. Key requirements concern data privacy and cost-efficiency, as well as guaranteed, cross-platform delivery of event messages from edge devices to the cloud and applications; asynchronous, queue-based messaging and public cloud deployments are common building blocks of such

S. Biffl et al. (Eds.): ECSA 2021, LNCS 12857, pp. 243–259, 2021.
https://doi.org/10.1007/978-3-030-86044-8_17

solutions. CARU AG is a Swiss startup targeting this domain. One of its main products is a digital flatmate, an IoT device comprising many sensors connected to Amazon Web Services (AWS) cloud offerings and consumer applications.

This experience report features the domain analysis, design, and implementation of the content-based CloudEvents Router, whose main design goal is to provide a unified event plane to route standardized events conveniently and reliably over multiple messaging protocols such as Message Queuing Telemetry Transport (MQTT), Amazon Simple Queue Service (SQS), and Advanced Message Queuing Protocol (AMQP). We evaluated existing solutions, but did not find any solution that can be deployed both to low-power devices and to the cloud while fitting into the overall software architecture of CARU. Our novel CloudEvents Router is written in Rust and open sourced under the Apache 2 license.[1]

The remainder of the paper is structured in the following way: Sect. 2 introduces architecture design challenges in the AgeTech domain, evidenced and exemplified in the business model, products, and software architecture of CARU. Section 3 specifies the CloudEvents router architecture that addresses these challenges; Sect. 4 covers reliability and delivery guarantees and their implementation in Rust and MQTT. Sections 5 and 6 present lessons learned and related work; Sect. 7 summarizes and concludes the paper.

2   Business Context: AgeTech Startup with IoT Device

CARU is an AgeTech startup with the mission to help the elderly live independently for longer by providing a digital flatmate in the form of an IoT device. It aims at increasing the safety of its human users by a) allowing these users to call for help in an emergency, b) facilitating communication with relatives and caretakers, and c) integrating services that foster a comfortable life at home.

When comparing the CARU Device against traditional social care alarm systems, its main differentiator is that the alarm call can be triggered by the embedded voice recognition model. The CARU Device also integrates the relatives into the care process by allowing them to exchange voice messages with the elderly user via the "CARU Family Chat" smartphone app. The device is also equipped with several sensors that support data-driven functionalities like air-quality monitoring, sleep quality analysis or activity detection that can be used by professional caretakers to optimize the care they provide.

2.1   Software Architecture Overview

Figure 1 shows an overview of the current software architecture of CARU. It consists of four main components: (1) the *CARU Device* running embedded Linux, (2) the *CARU Cloud* backend running on AWS, (3) the *myCARU* Web App(lication), and (4) the *CARU Family Chat* smartphone app. The two apps

---

[1] https://github.com/ce-rust/cerk.

communicate with the backend over a GraphQL endpoint managed by AWS AppSync; the MQTT protocol connects the devices and the backend via AWS IoT Core.

The use of a public cloud such as AWS allows CARU to build upon its many managed services and therefore minimize the operational burden on their small DevOps team. AWS IoT Core, in particular, provides many of the building blocks required to successfully manage an IoT device at scale. This includes device identity management (e.g., certificate management), connectivity (e.g., serverless MQTT broker), remote device configuration, and data management. AWS AppSync was chosen because it lets CARU run a fully serverless backend that automatically scales and does not require infrastructure maintenance.

As the CARU Device is a safety-critical device and its users depend on it in case of a fall or another medical issue, measures are built into the architecture to reduce the risk of a device going offline. The main challenge is that the device is deployed in the home of its user and relies on infrastructure outside the control of CARU. Two factors in particular can cause a device to go offline: power outages and issues with the mobile network.

To mitigate the risk of a power outage, the CARU Device is equipped with a battery that allows it to operate normally for a few hours without an active power supply. The main strategy to reduce the risk of mobile network-related issues is the use of a roaming SIM that automatically connects to the best network available at the location of the device. Additionally, the CARU Device is also able to connect to WiFi networks for added redundancy; that said, most users of the CARU Device do not have one installed in their home at present.

Because of the uncontrollable environment of the device, strong emphasis is put on monitoring it from the cloud. If a device goes offline or connectivity issues are recognized, the relatives or caretakers are alerted immediately and provided with instructions how to resolve the issue.

Finally, the safety-critical functionality (emergency call) does not depend on an active Internet connection. The recognition of the keyword to trigger the emergency call runs on the device, and the call itself can be made over the 2G/GSM mobile network as a fallback. The 2G/GSM network has a better coverage (at least for now; in Switzerland some providers started to turn it off) and is able to place calls even if the signal is not strong enough to transport usable Internet traffic. Important events that are generated while the device is offline are stored and sent to the cloud as soon as the device comes back online.

2.2   Vision: Unified Event Plane

The remainder of this experience report focuses on two components of the architecture of CARU: the CARU Device and CARU Cloud (Fig. 1). In the future, the concepts introduced in this paper could be applied to the other architectural components as well.

Because the CARU Device can place calls even if the signal quality is too bad to connect to the Internet, it was decided early on to give the device as much independence from the cloud as possible. To support this decision and because

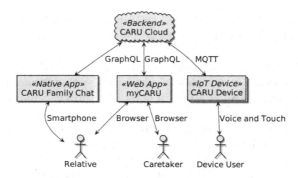

Fig. 1. Architecture overview of the CARU system landscape

of the nature of the data that the device produces (i.e., domain events reporting that something business-relevant has happened), an event-driven architecture was chosen. This design worked well in the beginning; with a growing number of events, several issues arose.

Event Design and Process Mismatches. The first issue arose because only minimal effort was put into the design of the events when CARU started the development. This was great for iterating fast on the product but caused some pain when the number of productive devices grew. This pain was amplified because the events are the only interface between the CARU Device and CARU Cloud, and these two systems have vastly different deployment cycles: while the CARU Cloud is developed with a continuous deployment approach, the deployment cycle of the CARU Device is longer because the cost of each deployment is significantly higher. The higher cost is caused by the more manual testing process, the more involved communication with the elderly device users, and the expensive bandwidth required to bring the update onto the devices.

Routing Intricacies. The second issue was that the event routing patterns in each component turned out to be quite different. Hence, unnecessary friction occurred when a developer switched from working on one system to another: between the CARU Device and CARU Cloud, the topic-based subscription mechanism of the MQTT protocol was used. To keep the design of the CARU Device simple, an in-process message bus with type-based event routing distributed the events. In the CARU Cloud, AWS EventBridge with its content-based subscriptions was responsible for event routing. The mental friction caused by switching from one component to the other slowed down the development because CARU has a small DevOps team that often has to work on different systems in parallel.

Adoption of CloudEvents Specification to the Remedy. To make the content-based event routing in/with AWS EventBridge more convenient, CARU introduced CloudEvents as its standardized event format for events exchanged inside the CARU Cloud. CloudEvents is a specification proposed by the Serverless Working Group of the Cloud Native Computing Foundation (CNCF) [6].

```
{
    "type": "caru.sensor.voice",
    "specversion": "1.0",
    "source": "crn:eu:::device:wvugxd5t",
    "id": "e30dc55b-b872-40dc-b53e-82cddfea454c",
    "contenttype": "text/plain",
    "data": "help"
}
```

Listing 1: A CloudEvent in the JSON Serialization Format

The goal of the specification is to simplify event declaration and delivery across services, platforms, and vendors. To achieve this goal, the specification defines the event fields, different serialization formats, and multiple protocol bindings. The specification has attracted attention and contributions from major cloud providers and Software as a Service (SaaS) companies. Listing 1 shows an example of a CloudEvent in the JavaScript Object Notation (JSON) format.

The introduction of the CloudEvents event format also helped with the management and the safe evolution of the events by encouraging strict definition and versioning of schemas defining the event payload.

The Unified Event Plane. After the successful introduction of CloudEvents in the CARU Cloud, the vision of a *Unified Event Plane* emerged. The *Unified Event Plane* aims at letting events flow with as little friction as possible between the different components of the CARU architecture, which was introduced in Sect. 2.1. This should be achieved by introducing the CloudEvents event format and a content-based event router (CloudEvents Router) in all systems.

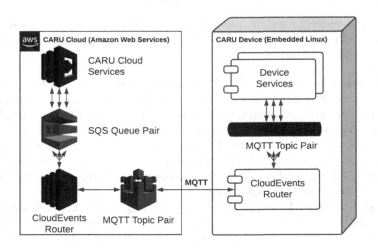

Fig. 2. CARU's unified event plane

Figure 2 shows the envisioned Unified Event Plane. Whenever events are exchanged, they are formatted according to the CloudEvents specification. CloudEvents Router instances appear in the CARU Cloud and the CARU Device systems. The CloudEvents Routers connect to each other as well as to the different services of their respective systems. To keep complexity minimal, the CloudEvents Routers are stateless and use existing services to handle the event transport: on the device, an embedded Eclipse Mosquitto MQTT Broker has this duty; in the cloud, Amazon SQS queues are responsible for reliable event delivery. This also means that the CloudEvents Routers must be able to route messages between the protocols supported by these services reliably and in an interoperable manner. For each CARU Device and CARU Cloud Service, an inbox and an outbox channel pair are used to communicate with the CloudEvents Router. In the cloud, this is implemented by an SQS Queue Pair; on the device and between the device and the cloud, an MQTT Topic Pair is used.

3   Design and Implementation of the CloudEvents Router

This section presents the architecture and implementation of the CloudEvents Router and shows how the design goals in Sect. 2.2 are reached. From the beginning, the project had a focus on a lean and easily extendable architecture as well as a flexible deployment on IoT devices and in the cloud. Later on, the router was extended to provide an *At Least Once* delivery guarantee.

3.1   Technical Constraints and Requirements

Before the decision to design and implement the CloudEvents Router was taken, we evaluated existing solutions. The following non-functional requirements and constraints guided the evaluation:

CloudEvents Support. CARU has already invested in CloudEvents and has gained a positive experience with it so far. The solution must be able to make routing decisions based on the fields defined in the CloudEvents specification.

Reliable Messaging. The CARU Device is a safety-critical device. Therefore the solution must be able to give some delivery guarantees for the events it processes. The current delivery guarantee provided by the used infrastructure (AWS IoT Core) is *At Least Once*. The CloudEvents Router must provide the same or better delivery guarantees.

Support for MQTT 3.1.1. To leverage existing messaging infrastructure on the CARU Device (Eclipse Mosquitto MQTT Broker) and in the cloud (AWS IoT Core), the solution must be able to interact with MQTT 3.1.1 endpoints. This enables a smoother transition from the current state into the direction of the unified event plane.

Runs on the CARU Device. The device has an ARM Cortex-A7 (armv7l) 1 Core CPU clocked at 198 - 528 MHz, 500 MB RAM, and runs a Yocto Linux.

Modularity. The solution should be adaptable to different deployment environments. Additional messaging protocols should be easy to add.

Rust Programming Language (optional). CARU wanted to gain experience with Rust as an alternative to C/C++.

After the evaluation criteria had been defined, ten existing solutions were analyzed.[2] Out of these ten solutions, two (Apache Camel and Node-RED) looked promising. However, both of them do not support CloudEvents out-of-the-box; it is possible to extend them to do so. Unfortunately, their resource requirements were incompatible with the available resources on the CARU Device. As the hardware was already in production and used by customers, upgrading it to satisfy the resource requirements was not an option.

For these reasons, we decided to design and implement a specialized, stateless CloudEvents Router in Rust. Messages are only stored by the incoming and outgoing message channels and never persisted in the CloudEvents Router itself. This eases the deployment of the CloudEvents Router, especially in the cloud; its horizontal scaling is simplified. Furthermore, this design reduces the complexity of the router itself. A negative consequence of this architectural decision is that all important messages have to be persisted before they are processed by the CloudEvents Router, e.g., by an underlying message broker.

3.2 CloudEvents Router Architecture

For our implementation of the CloudEvents Router, we chose the Microkernel architecture [5]. The Microkernel pattern is commonly used as the architectural foundation of modern operating systems. A prominent example is Linux. Our Microkernel defines the interfaces to the four plugin types that implement the bulk of the functionality. The four plugin types are Scheduler, Configuration-Loader, Router, and Protocol-Port.

Besides the four plugin interfaces, the kernel only consists of a small amount of glue code that facilitates the data flow between the plugins. Because the plugins are defined through their interfaces, a specific plugin type can be implemented in different ways. The users can then choose the implementation for each plugin type based on their specific use cases.

One reason for choosing the Microkernel pattern was the ability to adapt the router to different deployment environments easily. In the embedded Linux environment of the CARU Device, for example, the router could use a different Configuration-Loader plugin implementation than in the cloud. On the device, the loader implementation could read the configuration from a file while the loader implementation in the cloud fetches it from a database. The modular system design also allows adding support for new messaging protocols by writing

---

[2] The ten analyzed messaging products are: CloudEvent Router and Gateway, Knative Eventing v0.9, Pacifica Dispatcher v0.2.3, Serverless Event Gateway v0.9.1, Amazon Simple Notification Service, Apache Camel v2.24.2, Crossbar.io v19.10.1, D-Bus v1.12, Node-RED v1.0.1, RabbitMQ v3.8 [2].

plugins that implement the Protocol-Port plugin interface. It also helps to optimize the size of the executable by only including the plugins that are required for a specific use case. In Fig. 2, for example, the CloudEvents Router on the device is only required to communicate with the MQTT protocol, while the CloudEvents Router in the cloud has to support both MQTT and Amazon SQS.

3.3 Implementation: Rust SDK for CloudEvents

When our project started, there was no suitable Rust Software Development Kit (SDK) to work with CloudEvents, so we built our own to implement the open source CloudEvents Router. Later on, we had the opportunity to evolve this SDK and co-design the official CloudEvents Rust SDK[3] in the name of the CNCF Serverless Working Group.

4   Delivery Guarantees and Their Implementations

This section investigates the reliable routing process of the CloudEvents Router and explains why the *At Least Once* delivery guarantee was chosen. Before doing so, we recapitulate how reliability is defined in the context of software engineering in general and messaging systems in particular.

ISO 25010 is a suite of standards defining eight characteristics of quality for software engineering and systems [14]. Reliability is one of these eight system/ software product quality characteristics. Availability is a sub-characteristic of reliability and reflects the degree to which a system is operational and accessible. Reliability requires that an action is completed as intended, while availability just requires that the system is operational and reacts to requests somehow [14,17].

In messaging systems, reliability is often defined as a non-functional property, e.g., in MQTT as Quality of Service (QoS) [1]. QoS, in a broader context, often describes much more than just reliability [12,13,17,19]. In our context, reliability is primarily concerned with not losing messages during transport, and with preserving the order of subsequently sent messages during delivery. Dirty reads or other inconsistencies of messages usually are not in scope.

4.1   Reliable Event Routing with the CloudEvents Router

To address the business requirements in the AgeTech domain (Sect. 2), the CloudEvents Router should be able to route messages between different channels (e.g., MQTT topics, Amazon SQS queues) in a reliable fashion. This means that messages are routed whenever possible (i.e., the configuration is correct, and the destination is ready to accept messages). They are not lost even in case the router crashes.

Figure 3 shows a simplified example in which it is critical that events are not lost. The embedded classifier of the *Voice Recognition Service* detects the

---

[3] https://github.com/cloudevents/sdk-rust.

keyword **Help** and emits the *Keyword Recognized Event* (see Listing 1). The *CloudEvents Router on the Device* then applies its routing rules and forwards the event to the *Call Service* on the device and the *CloudEvents Router in the Cloud*. The router in the cloud applies its routing rules and forwards the event to the *Alarm Receiving Center* (ARC) that assigns the alarm to a call taker and prepares him/her for the incoming call. In the meantime on the device, the *Call Service* initiates a call to the ARC over the cellular network.

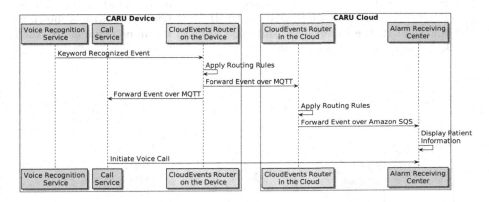

Fig. 3. Example use case that requires reliability

The literature and most protocols define a common set of delivery guarantees: *At Most Once, Exactly Once, At Least Once* [9,11]. A first step towards implementing cross-protocol reliable routing was to select a protocol-independent delivery guarantee. With such a delivery guarantee defined, the CloudEvents Router can route messages between message channels that use the same or different messaging protocols while preserving the delivery guarantee.

Most protocols and messaging systems provide subscription- or publication-based delivery guarantees; on the contrary, we propose a single delivery guarantee on the channel-level. A property called "delivery guarantee" should be defined on the channel to remove any confusion as to what guarantees can be expected from any given channel. This property should be used to specify how reliable a channel is. A declarative specification can be added to the messaging contract to signal what the receiver can expect. A producer then knows how it must publish messages to the channel. However, not all protocols support all options, and so in practice, not all "delivery guarantee" values make sense for each protocol.

4.2   Different Approaches to Reliable Event Routing (Options)

A stateless router such as the CloudEvents Router should be able to forward event messages from an inbound channel to one or more outbound channels

according to predefined routing rules. All three stated delivery guarantees from
Sect. 4.1 should ideally be supported.

The following examples show the case of one incoming and two outgoing
message channels. Message transmission may involve one or more messaging
systems (brokers).

At Most Once. We start with the simplest delivery guarantee: *At Most Once.*
This delivery guarantee does not satisfy the business need of this router, as
the business requires that every message reaches the destination and will be
processed there. The flow for a router with *At Most Once* semantics is shown in
Fig. 4a: **1.** First, the router gets a message from an incoming channel and then
2., 3. publishes it to all subscribers.

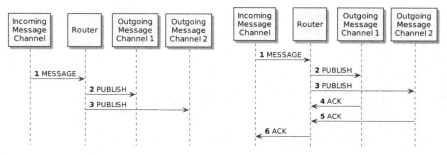

(a) *At Most Once* Delivery
The message is sent in a fire-and-forget
mode; no acknowledgments are sent or
waited for.

(b) *At Least Once* Delivery
The acknowledgment (ACK) has to arrive in
a certain time frame. If this does not happen, the message will be sent again.

Fig. 4. Routing with different delivery guarantees

At Least Once. This flow guarantees that every message is transmitted to the
subscriber at least once; duplicates are permitted. The flow for a router with
At Least Once is shown in Fig. 4b. The steps are: **1.** The incoming messaging
component sends the messages to the router. **2., 3.** The message is then sent
to the subscribers. **4., 5.** The router waits for the acknowledgments from the
subscribers. **6.** After the acknowledgments are received, the router will know
that the message was delivered, enabling it to send the acknowledgment to the
sending component.

If any of the steps is not successful or a service crashes during the processing,
the sender will restart the process after a timeout. The timeout is reached when
the sender does not receive an acknowledgment in the expected time frame. In
this case, the sender will retry to send the message to the receiver, which will

result in a restart of this process. The routing process only ends if the last step, the acknowledgment from the router to the sender (Step 6), was successful. This causes the message to be deleted from the incoming channel, which completes the routing [9].

Exactly Once. This delivery guarantee is hard to achieve, especially when involving different messaging protocols or products. One challenge is to define a point in the transmission process when the transaction of sending a message is completed. In *Exactly Once*, this point has to be coordinated between all participants. If that does not happen (e.g., a participant crashes or does not respond), the message may be submitted multiple times or not at all [9,20,22]. The Two-Phase Commit protocol [23] can help to overcome this challenge. It describes how to persist data on multiple machines with the help of a global system transactions, which comes at a price. The process can still fail for some edge cases and requires a coordinated state that all participants agree upon. This is not feasible in our project and business context. An *Exactly Once* stateless-routing can work for specific protocols, such as Kafka that provide a central coordinator that controls and performs a global commit operation [3,8,18].

4.3 How Common Protocols Implement Delivery Guarantees

We analyzed the messaging protocols for which a protocol binding is defined in the CloudEvents specification. At the time of writing, the specification contained such bindings for MQTT, AMQP, WebHook over HyperText Transfer Protocol (HTTP), Neural Autonomic Transport System (NATS), and Kafka [6]. During the analysis we compared the strategies for providing reliable messaging in these protocols and studied whether it would be possible to combine them in a reliable CloudEvents Router.

We were able to categorize the five protocols into two categories: message-oriented and stream-oriented protocols. Both categories provide similar delivery guarantees, but they take different approaches [3].

Message-Oriented Protocols. Message-oriented protocols provide delivery guarantees on a per-message basis. The receiver sends an acknowledgment for each transferred message (when guaranteeing *At Least Once* delivery). To achieve an *Exactly Once* delivery guarantee, the protocols require the receiver to remember already received messages to prevent duplicates until extra steps are performed to safely remove the message from both the sender and the receiver. MQTT, AMQP, WebHook over HTTP belong to this category of protocols.

Stream-Oriented Protocols. Stream-oriented protocols provide delivery guarantees on a stream of messages where each message can be identified by its position in the stream. The advantage of a stream-oriented protocol is that not every single message must be acknowledged when reading from the stream.

Instead, the receiver can acknowledge its position in the stream from time to time by sending the position of the last successfully processed message. This results in a lower network overhead but requires a central server that manages the stream. For writing to the stream, the same mechanisms as for the message-oriented protocols are used (acknowledgments for *At Least Once* and de-duplication for *Exactly Once*). The Kafka protocol and NATS Streaming protocol, which is built on top of the NATS protocol, fall into this category.

4.4   Selection of *At Least Once* for the CloudEvents Router

As the goal of CARU is to achieve safe message routing so that every message reaches its destination, an *At Most Once* delivery guarantee is not appropriate. So a decision between *At Least Once* and *Exactly Once* had to be taken.

We decided to implement an *At Least Once* delivery guarantee because of the following reasons: (1) The significant complexity of a Two-Phase Commit that is required to achieve an *Exactly Once* delivery guarantee. (2) The lacking support or non-interoperable implementations of *Exactly Once* in the targeted messaging protocols (see Sect. 4.3). (3) The statefulness that *Exactly Once* requires. (4) The possibility to deduplicate an event based on the id field defined in the CloudEvents specification (see next paragraph).

If the solution requirements call for strict *Exactly Once* delivery semantics, messages can be transferred with an *At Least Once* delivery guarantee, ensuring *Exactly Once* processing at the receiver with the help of a stateful Message Filter [11]. Implementing this pattern is straightforward with CloudEvents because these events contain the id field that can be used to detect events that were retransmitted and to prevent their reprocessing [6].

4.5   Implementation and Validation of *At Least Once* Channels

Implementation. Our router is able to route messages from one channel to zero or more channels while providing an *At Least Once* or no delivery guarantee (the latter is called *Best Effort*) for each route.

Implementing the AMQP plugin and upgrading from the *Best Effort* delivery guarantee to the *At Least Once* delivery guarantee in our Microkernel was straightforward. However, the upgrade from the *Best Effort* delivery guarantee to *At Least Once* on the MQTT plugin turned out to be rather challenging (see Sect. 5 for more information).

Validation. Different test methods were applied, from unit tests to integration tests. The main test objective was to gain confidence that the router works as intended and does not loose any messages even under harsh conditions. The most assuring test was an integration and reliability test that we ran both with the *At Least Once* and with the *Best Effort* delivery guarantee. This test setup is visualized in Fig. 5. The setup was an automated script that deploys the CloudEvents Router in a Kubernetes cluster and generates 100'000 events. The router consumes them on Channel A, and publishes them on Channel B. During the test, the single router instance was killed every 10 s by chaoskube and restarted by Kubernetes. chaoskube is a chaos engineering tool that periodically kills random instances in a Kubernetes cluster[4] (in our case, always the router instance). The messages were generated in a 1ms interval during the test so that the test ran for at least 100 s. With the *At Least Once* delivery guarantee, all messages were routed successfully to the output channel. Not a single message was lost. In the *Best Effort* routing mode, an average of 7'000 messages were lost per test run. The results differed widely depending on the used protocol-plugins.

With *At Least Once*, we can be sure that no events get lost while still providing a good balance between reliability and performance. However, "sure" means that no messages were lost in our specific test scenarios. These results give us, CARU, and other potential users confidence that the CloudEvents Router works properly. Still, our test scenarios are not proofs in a mathematical sense.

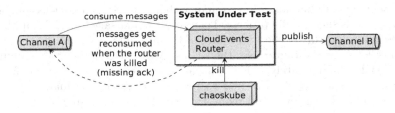

Fig. 5. Integration test setup of the router inside the kubernetes cluster

5   Lessons Learned

The messaging protocols that we worked with handle reliability in slightly different ways. Our router implementation demonstrates that the current design works for MQTT and AMQP; we are confident that it can leverage other messaging protocols as well [2,3]. In this section, we report two of our learnings and findings w.r.t. the delivery guarantees of existing messaging middleware.

Non-transient Error Handling. All error scenarios merely take transient errors into account. Our router design introduces a retry mechanism; however, there are also permanent errors that can not be resolved by just retrying to route a message if its routing failed. This could, for example, be caused by a wrong configuration or a malformed message. In such a case, the message can never be delivered. Such a problem can lead to a crash loop of a receiver, especially when the delivery guarantees are considered: Without taking the delivery guarantee(s) into account, these messages would be dropped; with a delivery guarantee such as *At Least Once*, the message will be resent and re-consumed over and over. In this

---

[4] https://github.com/linki/chaoskube.

scenario, some additional error handling is required; resilience measurements are an important concern. This is crucial when introducing retries to handle failures. Two already applied mechanisms in the CloudEvents Router for that is a Dead Letter Channel [11] and a health-check endpoint to integrate a Watchdog [9].

MQTT Reliability Underspecified and Not Configurable. Our most significant and somewhat surprising lesson learned was that MQTT behaves differently from most other protocols (see Sect. 4.3) when looking at the *At Least Once* and *Exactly Once* delivery guarantees.

In MQTT, the *At Least Once* and *Exactly Once* semantics are not defined as strictly as in most analyzed protocols: MQTT does not define whether a message should be acknowledged before or after the application has processed it.

The specification of the protocol only contains a non-normative example in which the messages are acknowledged before they are processed [1]. As a result, many MQTT libraries acknowledge the messages before they are processed. Even worse, they do not offer an option to change that behavior. Acknowledging a message before it is successfully processed can result in message loss if the application crashes before or during the processing of the message.

The CloudEvents Router uses the Eclipse Mosquitto library to communicate over MQTT. Unfortunately, this library also acknowledges messages before they are processed successfully. We had to fix this issue with a small code change which is currently an open pull request on the Eclipse Mosquitto repository.[5]

6   Related Work

Bernstein and Newcomer describe how client-server communication over queues can be processed with *Exactly Once* semantics in an abstract way [4]. Their examples describe a client that requests some processing via a queue by a server and gets a response in another queue. For this scenario, the possible error states are specified. Later, interactions of queues with other transactional systems that are irreversible are analyzed, and transactional processing is discussed.

Gruener, Koziolek, and Rückert measured resilience of different MQTT brokers under unreliable network conditions and show how a message can get lost [10]. Tai, Mikalsen, Rouvellou, and Sutton describe a way of adding conditions not to the message channel but to the message itself [21]. Application-specific conditions are then handled by the messaging middleware.

Steen and Tanenbaum give a broad overview of many distributed system concepts. For instance, they present concepts for error recovery and fault-tolerance [20]. Lampson, Lynch and, Søgaard-Andersen show proof for two *At Most Once* Message Delivery Protocols with additional order guarantee [16].

In "Exactly Once Delivery and Transactional Messaging in Kafka", the design of Kafka's *Exactly Once* strategy is described [8]. While this work is not protocol-independent it presents relevant general concepts. In the context of

---

[5] https://github.com/eclipse/mosquitto/pull/1932.

Simple Object Access Protocol (SOAP) based Web services, there were multiple attempts to standardize reliability with the standards WS-ReliableMessaging and WS-Reliability [7, 15].

7   Summary and Outlook

In this experience report, we presented the analysis, design, implementation, and validation of a versatile message router that natively supports events structured according to the CloudEvents specification. Our CloudEvents Router introduces standardized event routing targeting the software landscape of the AgeTech startup CARU; this landscape reaches from an embedded microcontroller on the edge to public cloud services from AWS. The introduction of CloudEvents in all systems helps CARU to safely evolve the structure of their events and reduces friction when developers have to work on different components of their system landscape.

In the CloudEvents Router architecture, special attention was paid to modularity, scalability, and reliability. To support flexible deployments while ensuring a minimal footprint, the Microkernel pattern was chosen as architectural foundation. This design makes it possible to select deployment-specific plugins for configuration access and messaging protocol integration to make the executable as small as possible. To ensure scalability and minimize complexity, we decided to leverage existing messaging infrastructure and to keep the Cloud-Events Router stateless by tasking services like Amazon SQS, AWS IoT Core, and Eclipse Mosquitto to store and transport messages reliably. As many events produced by the CARU Device are safety-relevant, providing a delivery guarantee for events entrusted to the router was particularly important. Because of the desired statefulness and the limited protocol interoperability of *Exactly Once*, implementing *At Least Once* was the only feasible option.

When analysing the reliability properties of the messaging protocols in the CloudEvents specification and the implementation of *At Least Once*, we discovered some unexpected properties. MQTT in particular provides rather limited guarantees for *At Least Once* and *Exactly Once*.

The presented CloudEvents Router design and its open source implementation provide a solid foundation for realizing the vision of a unified event plane. To further advance this vision, we have identified three development topics for our future work: (1) Implement the new CloudSubscriptions Discovery API and CloudEvents Subscription API specifications. (2) Integrate the CloudEvents Router into the monitoring solutions from the CNCF. (3) Adopt the asynchronous Application Programming Interface (API) of Rust to lower the resource requirements even further.

References

1. Banks, A., Briggs, E., Borgendale, K., Gupta, R.: MQTT version 5.0 (2019). https://docs.oasis-open.org/mqtt/mqtt/v5.0/os/mqtt-v5.0-os.html
2. Basig, L., Lazzaretti, F.: CloudEvents Router. HSR (2020). https://eprints.ost.ch/id/eprint/832/
3. Basig, L., Lazzaretti, F.: Reliable messaging using the CloudEvents Router (2021). https://eprints.ost.ch/id/eprint/904/
4. Bernstein, P.A., Newcomer, E.: Queued transaction processing. In: Principles of Transaction Processing, pp. 99–119. Elsevier (2009)
5. Buschmann, F., Meunier, R., Rohnert, H., Sommerlad, P., Stal, M.: Pattern-Oriented Software Architecture. Wiley, Hoboken (1996)
6. CloudEvents specification v1.0. GitHub (2019). https://github.com/cloudevents/spec/tree/v1.0
7. Davis, D., Karmarkar, A., Pilz, G., Winkler, S., Yalçinalp, Ü.: Web services reliable messaging (WS-ReliableMessaging) (2009)
8. Exactly once delivery and transactional messaging in Kafka (2017). https://docs.google.com/document/d/11Jqy_GjUGtdXJK94XGsEIKCP1SnQGdp2eF0wSw9ra8
9. Fehling, C., Leymann, F., Retter, R., Schupeck, W., Arbitter, P.: Cloud Computing Patterns. Springer, Vienna (2014). https://doi.org/10.1007/978-3-7091-1568-8
10. Gruener, S., Koziolek, H., Rückert, J.: Towards resilient IoT messaging: an experience report analyzing MQTT brokers. In: IEEE International Conference on Software Architecture (ICSA) (2021)
11. Hohpe, G., Woolf, B.: Enterprise Integration Patterns. Addison Wesley, Boston (2004)
12. Hwang, S.Y., Wang, H., Tang, J., Srivastava, J.: A probabilistic approach to modeling and estimating the QoS of web-services-based workflows. Inf. Sci. **177**(23), 5484–5503 (2007). https://doi.org/10.1016/j.ins.2007.07.011
13. ISO/IEC 13236:1998(E): Information technology - quality of service: Framework
14. ISO/IEC 25010:2011, systems and software engineering – systems and software quality requirements and evaluation (SQuaRE) – system and software quality models (2011). https://www.iso.org/standard/35733.html
15. Iwasa, K., Durand, J., Rutt, T., Peel, M., Kunisetty, S., Bunting, D.: Web Services Reliable Messaging TC WS-Reliability 1.1 (2004)
16. Lampson, B.W., Lynch, N.A., Søgaard-Andersen, J.F.: Correctness of at-most-once message delivery protocols. In: Proceedings of FORTE 1993, Boston, MA, USA (1993)
17. Ming, Z., Yan, M.: A modeling and computational method for QoS in IOT. In: 2012 IEEE International Conference on Computer Science and Automation Engineering. IEEE (2012). https://doi.org/10.1109/icsess.2012.6269459
18. Narkhede, N.: Exactly-once semantics are possible: Here's how Kafka does it (2017). https://www.confluent.io/blog/exactly-once-semantics-are-possible-heres-how-apache-kafka-does-it/
19. Petrova-Antonova, D., Ilieva, S.: Towards a unifying view of QoS-enhanced web service description and discovery approaches. EPTCS (2009). https://doi.org/10.4204/EPTCS.2.8
20. van Steen, M., Tanenbaum, A.: Distributed Systems (2017)

21. Tai, S., Mikalsen, T., Rouvellou, I., Sutton, S.: Conditional messaging: extending reliable messaging with application conditions. In: Proceedings 22nd International Conference on Distributed Computing Systems. EEE Computer Society (2002). https://doi.org/10.1109/icdcs.2002.1022249
22. Treat, T.: You cannot have exactly-once delivery (2015). https://bravenewgeek. com/you-cannot-have-exactly-once-delivery/
23. Distributed transaction processing: The XA specification (1991). http://www. opengroup.org/onlinepubs/009680699/toc.pdf

An Experience Report on Modernizing I/O Configuration Software

Kiana Busch[(✉)], Norman Christopher Böwing, Simon Spinner,
Qais Noorshams, and Michael Grötzner

IBM Deutschland Research & Development GmbH, Böblingen, Germany
kiana.busch@ibm.com, {boewing,sspinner,noorshams,
michael.groetzner}@de.ibm.com

Abstract. When a system evolves, its architecture co-evolves and
becomes more complex. Thus, the development team needs to continuously expend modernizing efforts to reduce the complexity and improve
the maintainability. To this end, software development processes can be
used. However, many processes in their original form are mainly used
for greenfield projects or integrating new requirements. Thus, many processes are not ideally suited to continuously modernize software while
considering the existing requirements. In this paper, we present our experience during the modernization of a long-lived software system. During
the modernization we used a process which is based on the spiral model
and combined it with different agile development principles to continuously modernize a long-lived system in a lightweight manner. Our process
aims at improving quality attributes of a software system while considering existing and changing requirements. This process was applied to the
Hardware Configuration Definition (HCD), which is used on IBM Z for
several decades to define I/O configurations. Using this real-world software system, we present the lessons learned and our experiences during
the modernization.

Keywords: Modernization · Maintainability · Software architecture

1 Introduction

A software system is developed based on a set of initial requirements. During its
life cycle, various change triggers such as new requirements or changing technologies lead to continuous changes in the system (i.e., Lehman's law of continuing
change [15]). Thus, the longer the system is in operation, the more it evolves
and drifts from its initial requirements. During the evolution of the system its
architecture co-evolves and becomes more complex. Further, several factors such
as limited domain knowledge, deadlines, or inappropriate development processes
can increase the technical debt of the system [19]. Thus, changes to the system
are increasingly difficult over time. This results in further maintenance efforts to

© Springer Nature Switzerland AG 2021
S. Biffl et al. (Eds.): ECSA 2021, LNCS 12857, pp. 260–276, 2021.
https://doi.org/10.1007/978-3-030-86044-8_18

reduce the complexity of the system (i.e., Lehman's law of increasing complexity [15]). Over time, the maintenance costs of a long-lived system can become higher than a modernization or even a new development [21].

Compared to the modernization, at once replacement can be considered as a risky task, as a long-lived software system is in operation (see modernization vs. replacement [21]). One possible solution to reduce the risks is an iterative modernization, as introduced by the Strangler Fig Application pattern [6]. It proposes incrementally rewriting the functionalities of a legacy system by introducing new smaller services (e.g., microservices) [6]. Modernizing a system by introducing microservices can also improve the maintainability, as the effects of changes can be reduced (i.e., maintainability definition [10]).

There are several approaches focusing on one modernization aspect (e.g., architecture recovery [2] or testing [24]). In contrast, several approaches consider the holistic process of modernization. This resulted in several categorizations of modernization approaches, for example redevelopment, wrapping, and migration approaches based on the paradigm used [11] or white-box and black-box approaches based on the internals of a system [21]. As the migration of a whole system at once is a risky task [21], we consider the related approaches focusing on an incremental modernization and its application in a real-world software system (e.g., [5,12]). There are further related approaches focusing on the identification of tasks needed to modernize a system (e.g., [4]). But, most approaches focus on the process and neglect the quality attributes of the system during the modernization.

This paper presents our experiences and lessons learned during a real-world software evolution based on the Hardware Configuration Definition (HCD) – a component of the z/OS operating system [8]. HCD is used to define I/O configuration for several decades. Thus, it can be considered as a long-lived system. For the modernization, we defined a quality-driven process, which combines the evolution cycles of the spiral model [3] with different agile development principles [22]. With particular focus on the quality attributes of a software system, the process considers both existing and changing requirements of a long-lived system. Further, we present our experiences by application of this process to HCD and discuss the influence of the application of this process on improving the quality attributes regarding the maintainability and performance.

The remainder of this paper is organized as follows: Sect. 2 describes the background information regarding the IBM Z, firmware, and the spiral model. Our process for modernizing the system is presented in Sect. 3. Section 4 outlines our experience regarding the application of the process to HCD. The lessons learned during the modernization are discussed in Sect. 5. The related work to this paper is given in Sect. 6. Finally, Sect. 7 concludes the paper.

2   Background

This section gives an overview of IBM Z in Sect. 2.1, its firmware in Sect. 2.2, and the spiral model in Sect. 2.3.

2.1 IBM Z

IBM Z is a family of z/Architecture mainframes [25]. Today's mainframes are virtualized systems [25]. To this end, Processor Resource/Systems Manager (PR/SM) hypervisor is used. The PR/SM allows allocating physical resources to logical partitions (LP), which can run different operating systems (e.g., z/OS or Linux) [9]. Mainframes are connected to storage servers in order to enable the I/O operations [9]. Processor and memory hardware are usually organized independently from disks [8].

To isolate the operating systems running on the mainframe each mainframe features an I/O configuration describing the logical connections and physical resources used by those connections for each LP and the operating system running in it (e.g., connections to specific disks of a storage server or a storage area network) [8]. This I/O configuration is usually created and maintained with HCD. HCD is an interactive application, which allows a user to plan, define, validate, maintain, and dynamically update the I/O configuration of an IBM Z server [8]. At the same time HCD is used internally by firmware components of IBM Z to update the I/O configuration of a system dynamically. Thus, this part of HCD can be considered as a firmware service. The process of dynamically updating a running system is called dynamic hardware activation and aims at providing zero downtime for the system. It consists of multiple steps with each step being the configuration of one or more I/O elements such as a disk.

2.2 Firmware

All software that is delivered with the IBM Z system itself is considered firmware. This is in contrast to the operating systems or any middleware and application software that a user installs within LP. The IBM Z firmware includes services to manage the LP and their I/O configuration. As a result, parts of HCD are delivered as firmware services. Firmware services are subject to additional requirements as they operate in a highly restricted environment where users have no access. These requirements are: i) The service runs completely autonomous. It must be able to react to every expected and unexpected situation. There is no operator who is monitoring the service and who could intervene in critical situations. ii) The runtime environment of the service is highly restricted. The service may consume only a fixed amount of resources (CPU and memory). Those resources are shared with other services. The environment provides no resource elasticity to react to spikes on demand. iii) Failure analysis cannot be performed on a production system. Only post-mortem analysis on the collected failure data can be performed. The service needs to collect all required data and attach it to a call-home request (i.e., sending the required data for the debugging process) to the support system. iv) The runtime environment does not provide any storage for long-term persistence of data. v) The service needs to support concurrent updates without having to restart the complete system.

These requirements must be considered during the design of firmware services.

2.3   Spiral Model

The spiral model of software development [3] is a framework to guide the software development of a project. It offers a risk-driven approach to develop a software project. The spiral model describes multiple cycles consisting of four phases: i) *determine objectives*, ii) *evaluate alternatives and resolve risks*, iii) *develop and verify next stage product*, and iv) *plan the next phase*. Each software project may run through any number of cycles and after each cycle all stakeholders will align their objectives for the next phase. The frequent evaluation of alternatives and risks will help in addressing the major risks of a software project first.

3   Applied Process for Modernizing a System

This section presents our process for iteratively modernizing a software system at a high abstraction level. This process is based on the spiral model [3] and combines it with the concept of the Strangler Fig Application pattern [6]. One reason for using the spiral model is that requirements and constraints are given by the existing software system during the modernization. Further, the spiral model was designed to reduce the risks of projects and supports the software evolution using explicit rounds. However, we had to adapt the spiral model to a process which is more suitable to modernize a long-lived software system (in contrast to the development of a new software system). The adaptation of the spiral model to a process resulted from our experiences on real-world software evolution problems in the industry context. In the following sections, we describe the main phases of the process and the relationship between them and the rounds of the spiral model. A summary of this relationship is also presented in Fig. 1.

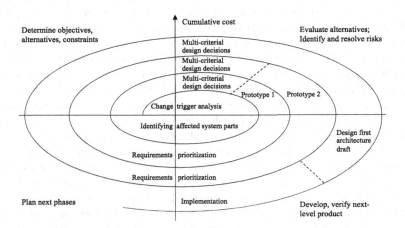

Fig. 1. Adaptation of the spiral model [3] for the modernization process

3.1 Change Trigger Analysis

The first main phase is concerned with the triggers of the modernization in general. These triggers can be considered as change triggers for a system (e.g., changing technologies). This phase of the process together with the next phase (see Sect. 3.2) replaces the first round of the spiral model for the modernization process, as these phases aim at analyzing and reducing the risks in a project. This replacement is due to the specific properties of the modernization, which involves existing requirements and constraints by a given software, the existing hardware environment, and the domain under study (e.g., firmware). Compared to a greenfield project, the software modernization usually starts with a change trigger. But, depending on the specific use case and domain, other parts of the existing spiral model can be considered in this phase of the modernization process.

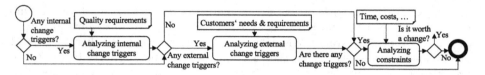

Fig. 2. Overview of the steps for the change trigger analysis

There are several categories of change triggers such as *corrective, adaptive,* or *perfective* changes as proposed by Swanson [23]. This paper uses a more general categorization based on *internal* and *external* change triggers [1], as they affect the modernization process in different ways. Other categories can also be mapped to the internal and external change categories. Figure 2 presents this phase of the modernization process regarding the analysis of change triggers.

A long-lived system might no longer meet all quality requirements due to continuous evolution. Violation of quality requirements is a main cause of internal change triggers leading to the modernization of a system. For example, the performance requirements may not be met due to continuous changes to these systems. Another example is the maintainability, as implementing new functionalities can become a challenging task over years (e.g., due to technical debt). Thus, these factors can be an indicator of internal change triggers.

Change triggers can also be external to an existing system [1]. For example, new customers' needs can result in changing the system. Another example is changing technologies, which the system is based on. The system can also have dependencies to other systems, whose interfaces have evolved.

Both internal and external change triggers are indicators for modernizing a system. If or to which extent a system must be changed, also depends on other constraints such as time and costs of the modernization. There can also be other factors influencing the decision on modernizing a system. For example, external change triggers such as new or changing customers' requirements can rather be considered compared to internal change triggers. Thus, this phase is a complex trade-off decision, which depends on the specific context and cannot be decided in general. The process presented in this paper is concerned with the case, when software architects decide to change and modernize a long-lived system.

3.2 Identifying Affected System Parts

After software architects decided to modernize the system, the next phase is to identify the system components affected by the change. As this phase is concerned with the given change triggers and different requirements and constraints of the existing system, it replaces the first round of the spiral model together with the first phase of the process (see Sect. 3.1).

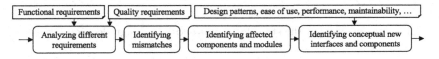

Fig. 3. Overview of the steps for identifying the affected system parts

Figure 3 shows the process steps regarding the identification of the affected system parts. As one main goal of our process is to enhance different quality attributes of a long-lived system, each change request can be used to improve the quality attributes of the system. Thus, the first step is concerned with analyzing the system requirements. As a long-lived system evolves over decades, software architects need to ensure that the system meets all requirements. Thus, analyzing the quality and functional attributes of the system results in two cases. In the first case, the current system meets all requirements. Thus, the system after the modernization has to meet these requirements, too. This can be ensured for example by designing test cases for the functional requirements or scenarios for quality requirements. For quality requirements, software architects have to first measure and analyze different quality attributes of the system such as performance or memory consumption. They can also use models to document the software architecture and extend the models with quality annotations. These models can be used to simulate and estimate different system properties such as performance. In the second case, software architects identify functional requirements, which are not met, or mismatches (e.g., bottlenecks) regarding the quality requirements. For example, the performance of the system can drop for some inputs or some components may be hard to maintain. Addressing these issues during the implementation of change triggers helps to improve the quality attributes of the whole system. Based on the change requests and the analysis of quality requirements and mismatches, the affected system parts have to be identified. Then, the interfaces between these system parts and the existing system have to be determined. This step involves considering different influencing factors such as architecture patterns. Note that the steps of this process and their order can be adapted to the specific project context.

3.3   Multi-criteria Design Decisions

After the affected components were identified, this main phase is concerned with design decisions in order to enable the integration of the modernized components. As this main phase is executed iteratively to find a solution for the modernization, it closely corresponds to all rounds in the spiral model which aim at creating and refining prototypes.

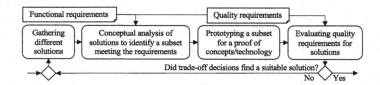

Fig. 4. Overview of the steps for a multi-criteria design decision process

Figure 4 illustrates this phase of the process regarding multi-criteria design decisions. This phase starts with gathering different solutions addressing the change triggers at a conceptual level, as there are different ways to implement a change [20]. These solutions should be reviewed regarding different criteria such as their feasibility in terms of technologies used, time, and costs. Each solution, in its turn, can have different degrees of freedom, which can be on a high abstraction level, such as the application of an architectural pattern or on a low abstraction level, such as the programming language used. Then, software architects need to analyze, to which extent the proposed solutions address different functional requirements and quality requirements identified in the steps before.

After a subset of suitable solutions was identified, a prototype should be provided for the proof of concept and technology. The prototypes can also be used to calibrate simulation models for estimating different quality attributes of the system. Software architects iterate these steps, until they identify at least one suitable solution.

3.4   Requirements Prioritization

This phase corresponds to the requirements plan of the spiral model. However, compared to the spiral model, requirements prioritization should be planned before the implementation phase. This order is mainly important during the modernization, as the requirements of a long-lived system co-evolve. Thus, in addition to the existing requirements given by the long-lived system, obsolete, new, and changing requirements (e.g., due to changing technologies and stakeholders' needs) have to be identified and considered.

One of the main goals of the requirements prioritization is to create a product with minimum functionalities and to enable an iterative integration of requirements. The requirements prioritization is based on the solutions identified in the previous main phase, as different solutions can meet the requirements and constrains in different ways or only partially. Thus, the most suitable solution can be identified based on the requirements and constraints analysis. Further, early stakeholders' feedback regarding the initial solutions helps to have a common understanding of their needs and identifying the most suitable solution.

3.5 Designing a First Architecture Draft

In this phase, software architects need to design the architecture of the identified solution. This phase corresponds to the detailed design in the development and test phase in the last round of the spiral model. Compared to the spiral model, this phase involves the architecture of the whole system in general and the architecture of the affected system parts in particular, as the architecture documentation of a long-lived system is not always available. Further, interfaces between the existing system and the new system parts have to be considered in a modernization process. Compared to the previous phases, the architecture should be specified in a more fine-grained way.

The architecture specification can be considered at two abstraction levels. At a high abstraction level, software architects have to specify the architecture of the whole system including the system parts that have to be modernized. As the architecture of the whole system cannot be changed during a modernization step, this step is concerned with identifying the parts of the existing systems, which communicate with the new system parts, their interfaces, and the data flow. This phase can also involve technical constraints in the long-lived system and the use of architectural patterns.

At a lower abstraction level, the architecture of the new system part must be designed. The approaches addressing this issue can be categorized into top-down approaches, bottom-up approaches, and approaches combining both top-down and bottom-up approaches [18]. While the bottom-up approaches analyze systems' parts and functionalities to identify the components and to extract the architecture, the top-down approaches start with a given architecture. During the modernization, a bottom-up approach can be more suitable, as various constraints are given by the existing system. However, the choice of the approach depends on the specific context and requirements. The architecture resulted from this phase is a first architecture design, which can be refined and extended in the next phases.

3.6 Implementation

The last phase of our process is the implementation phase. This phase corresponds to the development and test in the last round of the spiral model. While the first phases of the process are based on the spiral model, the spiral model in its original form or another software development process (e.g., agile methods [22]) can be used in this phase. This is due to the nature of the modernization in contrast to a greenfield project: The first phases of the process are mainly concerned with analyzing the modernization triggers and identifying the affected software parts, while the requirements, constraints, and environment (i.e., hardware and software) are given by the existing software. After the affected system parts were identified, agile development principles can be used to successively integrate the requirements. Further, iterative approaches enable the continuous monitoring and improvement of functional requirements and quality requirements. Agile approaches, additionally, allow short feedback loops from the stakeholders. In this way, mismatches and errors can be identified in early development phases, which can reduce the costs of errors.

In the following, we present the main steps of the implementation phase regardless of the chosen development process. An important aspect in each iteration is to ensure that the system meets the requirements. While functional requirements can be checked by various types of tests (e.g., unit tests), different input scenarios and monitoring tools can be used for the quality requirements.

In each iteration, playbacks can help to update the stakeholders and involve their feedback early in the development process. Further, different factors may lead to refining the design or the architecture of the solution (e.g., due to stakeholders' feedback). Thus, the development process should be iterative to allow software architects and developers to continuously improve different development artifacts from architecture to code, until the solution is feature complete.

4   Application in a Real-World Project

This section presents the application of the aforementioned process to HCD – a software for defining I/O configurations for IBM Z mainframes. The main focus is on our experience report during the modernization process and a real-world software evolution.

4.1   Change Trigger Analysis

The changes in HCD were triggered both internally and externally, as described in the following.

As mainframes have grown over decades, the use cases and the resulting requirements also continuously evolved. HCD was originally developed to be used via a user interface. However, changing use cases for new mainframes led to increasing sizes of I/O configurations. This led to the need to have more coarse-grained interfaces to define these I/O configurations suitable for batch processing. Further, monitoring different quality attributes of the software system showed changing the functional requirements and the software system can result in changing quality attributes of the software system over time. Thus, the software system has to be changed due to the future quality requirements resulted from changing functional requirements (i.e., the increasing size of I/O configurations). Improving the quality requirements for future scenarios, which are resulted from evolving the functional requirements, led to our internal change triggers.

HCD as a firmware- and operating system-related component uses native code. When the technologies were evolving over decades, the addressing modes also co-evolved. Thus, different addressing modes are an important aspect during the development and the maintenance. This key aspect led to the other change trigger resulting from changing the functional requirements due to changing technologies and was external to the system. In order to be able to provide customers with long-term support, any dependencies to libraries with deprecated addressing modes (e.g., 32-bit libraries) had to be avoided.

The described change triggers resulted in modernizing the system. During the modernization a new component was developed. As a firmware- and operating system-related component, it faced the constraints regarding the hardware usage, especially the memory and CPU consumption (see Sect. 2.2). Although the resources for this component are provided in addition to the customers' resources, one of the main constraints was that the new component should meet all constraints of the existing component. As mainframes are critical to customers' business, the modernization of an existing component must not degrade user experience and workflow. Further, as the existing component meets all functional requirements, the new component resulting from the modernization must also meet all functional requirements and improve upon the quality attributes of the existing component.

4.2   Identifying Affected System Parts

As described previously, there are various constraints and requirements for HCD such as memory and CPU usage. The existing requirements regarding the memory consumption require the new software system to operate on the given memory even for the maximum size of the I/O configuration for the maximum size of mainframes. Another important requirement is the performance of the whole hardware activation (see Sect. 2.1). The performance of these activations includes the time for activating the I/O configuration in addition to the time for creating an I/O configuration and sending it to be activated. Thus, it contains the communication overhead between the involved components.

During the modernization, the described influencing factors regarding the performance were considered and analyzed in different scenarios. The scenarios were chosen with regard to two aspects: i) to be representative of the typical customers' need and ii) to represent a worst-case configuration (e.g., to stress the system). During the analysis we could identify different cases that could be improved during the development. For example, the performance of the whole activation process could be improved by sending only a necessary subset of the I/O configuration regarding the hardware activation. Further, the analysis showed that the performance of the step-by-step creation of an I/O configuration could also be improved by creating a configuration in advance.

HCD provides customers with various services. To identify the affected components by the change, we had to first identify all provided services including the initial services and the services that were integrated over decades. This step also involved excluding all services that are no longer relevant for the current workflows of the customers. Based on the provided services, expert interviews, documentations, and the specification of the existing interfaces, we created a service-based component diagram of the current software system at a high abstraction level. The new components after the modernization should reflect the provided services. Thus, the component diagram does not reflect the code, but is based on the services provided by the existing system. This diagram enabled us to map the change scenarios to the affected services and the corresponding components providing these services. In this way, we could identify the affected system parts at a high abstraction level. These system parts in HCD were already developed as modules, which allowed replacing them by the new components.

4.3 Multi-criteria Design Decisions

Several solutions addressing the change triggers were discussed and analyzed regarding different requirements and constraints.

In the following, we show our approach using two solutions as two examples: i) One solution was to use a wrapper (see the categorization of [11]) to map the dependencies to the 32-bit libraries. ii) Another solution was to replace the functionality of the affected part of the existing software with new components.

For the first solution, an expert team developed a first close-ended prototype, which could be used to analyze different requirements and constraints. Although this solution addressed the changing requirements resulting from evolving address modes, it could lead to more complexity and potential source of errors. Further, using a wrapper could not improve the quality attributes such as performance and maintainability, as it can be considered as a further layer.

For the second solution, we created a close-ended prototype, which allowed us to analyze different dependencies to the existing components and libraries. Further, we could estimate the feasibility of the solution, the time and cost of the development, the long-term support of the software system, and the maintainability. For example, to analyze the maintainability different representative usage scenarios were considered. In order to be able to improve the performance attributes of our software system, we estimated the response times based on the prototype and the performance measurement for a set of representative scenarios. In this way, the performance of the solution could be estimated in advance.

The quality aspects of the solutions were analyzed and compared regarding both short-term and long-term impact. Although the short-term effort of the second solution is higher than the first solution due to the implementation effort, the long-term effort of the first solution could be much higher due to the maintainability aspect. Additionally, for each solution various degrees of freedom were also considered. For example, to improve the maintainability a stateless solution was preferred over a stateful solution. In addition to the described solutions several other solutions were also identified and analyzed. Based on the analysis of different solutions and their quality attributes we decided to develop new components, as our goal was to enhance the quality attributes of the system when implementing the changes.

4.4   Requirements Prioritization

To prioritize the requirements, we organized an architecture design workshop with the development team and the stakeholders. Its goal was to discuss and prioritize the requirements and stakeholders' needs. In the following, the requirements and needs are discussed using examples.

As we developed the new system parts as a modernization project, these parts have to meet all functional requirements of the existing one. One of the functional requirements was concerned with designing a new object model to describe the I/O configurations, as the existing object model co-evolved with the system over years. The object model can be considered as a language (i.e., frame) that can be used to define I/O configurations. The evolution of the object model involves integrating new types of resources or removing the deprecated ones. Designing an object model aims at enabling the existing system parts to communicate with the new system part, as the object model serves as the base for the data flow between the system parts. Thus, it aims at reducing the complexity of the existing object model resulting from evolution and improving the communication overhead between different system parts.

As described previously, we analyzed the quality attributes by designing prototypes and evaluating different usage scenarios. As the new system parts are part of a long-lived system, some quality attributes such as maintainability, serviceability, or testability had to be prioritized highly.

4.5   Designing a First Architecture Draft

As described previously, the architecture of the software system has to be defined at two abstraction levels: i) at a high abstraction level for the whole system and ii) at a low abstraction level for the affected system parts.

At a high abstraction level, the newly developed system parts have to be integrated in the existing software system as new components. Thus, one of the main aspects is the communication (i.e., interfaces) between them and the whole system. As a result, a new object model was used in order to support the data flow, as described in the previous section. Further, new interfaces had to be introduced to support this data flow.

To specify the architecture of the new system parts we used a bottom-up approach, which allowed us to identify the components based on the provided functionalities. In addition to the functionalities, further criteria such as expert knowledge or the ability to reuse the provided features were used. Another important criterion was the testability. To this end, the components were designed to encapsulate the functionalities and to reduce the dependencies to the firmware. This aims at improving the testability of the required components. After identifying the components, a dependency graph was used to visualize the dependencies between the identified components. Using the components and their dependencies, a first architecture draft could be designed based on the architecture patterns.

4.6   Implementation

The implementation phase was based on various agile development principles [22]. In the following, several aspects of the development are highlighted. We used a vertical implementation approach to implement and assemble all components of the new system parts in parallel to create a product with minimum functionalities. In the following iterations, we integrated the features iteratively until the product met all exiting functional requirements. The playbacks at the end of each iteration allowed us to show the current status of the development to the stakeholders. In this way, we received early feedback from the stakeholders that we integrated in the development. To test the functional requirements, the following types of tests were automatically executed in each build: i) Unit tests test individual units of functionalities, ii) integration tests show each I/O operation such as creating a new partition, and iii) acceptance tests are end to end functional tests including a composition of I/O operations. Further, each build checks different development artifacts such as generating and validating the documentation. Additionally, different scenarios were designed and refined to test different quality requirements such as memory consumption and performance. For example, we used maximum I/O configurations to test the memory consumptions for the maximum size of the real hardware supported. To test the performance, the scenarios identified during the bottleneck analysis and a set of representative scenarios were used (see Sect. 4.2). Thus, the new system parts were designed and implemented to improve the performance of the identified scenarios. The described aspects resulted in the architecture refinement of the new system parts and the object model. The goal of various refinements was to address the stakeholders' needs and to improve the quality attributes of the system.

5   Lessons Learned and Discussion

This section emphasizes the most important aspects and lessons learned from the modernization process. The first aspect results from the solutions designed in the early phases of the development. For a subset of them, close-ended prototypes were created and analyzed regarding different requirements and constraints. Using the prototypes, we could estimate the feasibility and costs of the project and consider the first stakeholders' feedback early. Further, the prototypes could be used to analyze and reduce the risks of the project. This led to discarding a prototype and a possible implementation very early on saving time and resources. Additionally, it garnered support to go another direction.

Another important aspect during the development process was the continuous analysis of different quality attributes such as performance and memory consumption. On the one hand, the prototypes and the first measurements enabled the performance estimation of the resulted product. In this way, we could ensure the product can meet the given quality requirements. For example, no degradation of performance has been observed since the conclusion of this modernization.

On the other hand, the analysis of different mismatches (e.g., bottleneck analysis) of the exiting projects allowed us to identify the potential for improvement and address it in the resulting product. By doing so, different quality attributes of the product could be improved during the modernization.

Combining the iterative process of the spiral model and agile development principles during the development is one of the most important aspects, as the resulting process could reduce various risks in the project. Compared to a horizontal implementation, our iterative approach is based on the vertical implementation to create a product with minimal functionalities. This approach was feasible since the complexity of the implementation, in our case, stems from the interaction of all components and does not lie within a single component. Further, it was of great benefit to start with the most difficult possible vertical implementation approach to solve critical issues early on. Based on that and the prioritization of requirements we could then incrementally integrate all features into the product. The iterative process did not only reduce the development risks but also improved the onboarding of new developers by integrating small complete features.

6   Related Work

As the modernization process involves many aspects, the related work to this paper can be divided into two groups: i) approaches focusing on one modernization aspect and ii) approaches with a holistic view on the modernization process. Both groups are described in the following in more detail:

There are several approaches, which mainly focus on one modernization aspect, such as the architecture recovery of a legacy system. One approach addressing this aspect is Micro Service Architecture Recovery (MiSAR) [2]. It aims at identifying the architecture of a microservice software system by providing a metamodel and mapping rules. MicroART [7] is another approach to retrieve the architecture model of a given microservice software system. Another work focusing on the testing aspect during the modernization is described in [24]. There are also further approaches focusing on one or a set of quality requirements during the modernization (e.g., performance simulation [13] or quality of services [17]). However, we introduce a whole modernization process based on quality attributes and show its application to an existing real-world software system.

Compared to the previous work, many approaches consider the overall modernization process. They have been categorized using different criteria (e.g., redevelopment, wrapping, and migration based on the paradigm used [11] or whitebox and black-box approaches based on the availability of the internal system knowledge [21]). However, we consider mainly related approaches, which can also be used incrementally (e.g., by decomposing a legacy system) to reduce the risks. Further, the approaches should have been applied to real-world systems. One of these approaches is a methodology [16], which uses the existing regression test suites of a legacy system to identify its features. Then, the corresponding code to the features has to be identified, which has to be extracted to components. Another approach [5] decomposes a legacy software into their components and assembles them using coordinator modules. The main focus is the transformation of a sequential software to a parallel one. The modernization process of Knoche and Hasselbring [12] introduces service facades to clients and replaces the services with microservices. The approach of Krause et al. [14] decomposes a monolithic software system into microservices by combining a domain analysis, including a familiarization phase, modeling phase to derive an architecture, and partitioning, with static and dynamic analyses. Orthogonal to these approaches, the Architecture Options Workshop (AOWS) [4] aims at identifying the required tasks for modernizing the architecture. To create a roadmap architecture options for a set of scenarios must be combined and prioritized regarding the business goals. However, most approaches mainly focus on the process and neglect the quality attributes of the system during the modernization.

7   Conclusion

This paper presented an iterative process based on the spiral model to modernize long-lived systems. This process resulted from practical case studies in the industry context. As a modernization process is driven by triggers, the process starts with analyzing the change triggers. Additionally, further analyses such as bottleneck analysis lead to identifying the components affected by the change. The analyses aim at both reducing the complexity resulted from the evolution and improving the system regarding various quality requirements. In the next step, various solutions have to be weighed against each other regarding different requirements and constraints. To this end, prototypes can be created and used. During the modernization process, most requirements and constraints are already given by the existing system. Additionally, the previous steps may also identify further requirements. Thus, different requirements have to be prioritized in order to enable an iterative approach. Then, in addition to the affected system parts, the architecture of the whole system must be designed. This architecture is the main artifact for the further development process, which should be iterative to enable further architecture refinement, to analyze different system properties, to integrate stakeholders' feedback, and to reduce various risks.

The process was applied to a real-world software evolution problem, which is in operation over several decades. Our experiences showed that one of the most important aspects during the modernization process was prototyping. The prototypes helped us to estimate the feasibility, to analyze different requirements, to reduce the risks, and to integrate stakeholders' feedback as early as possible. Additionally, continuous analysis of different quality attributes such as performance bottlenecks helped us to continuously improve different quality attributes of not only the affected software parts but also the whole system. Further, our process combines the iterative spiral model and agile development principles during the development to reduce various risks in the project.

For the future, we plan to refine the process and its steps.

References

1. van der Aalst, W., Jablonski, S.: Dealing with workflow change: identification of issues and solutions. Comput. Syst. Sci. Eng. **15**(5), 267–276 (2000)
2. Alshuqayran, N., Ali, N., Evans, R.: Towards micro service architecture recovery: an empirical study. In: IEEE ICSA, pp. 47–4709 (2018)
3. Boehm, B.: A spiral model of software development and enhancement. Computer **21**(5), 61–72 (1988)
4. Ernst, N., et al.: Creating software modernization roadmaps: the architecture options workshop. In: IEEE/IFIP 13th WICSA, pp. 71–80 (2016)
5. Everaars, C., Arbab, F., Koren, B.: Modernizing existing software: a case study. In: SC 2004: Proceedings of the 2004 ACM/IEEE Conference on Supercomputing, p. 3 (2004)
6. Fowler, M.: The strangler fig application (2004). https://martinfowler.com/bliki/StranglerFigApplication.html. Accessed 29 Apr 2019
7. Granchelli, G., et al.: Microart: a software architecture recovery tool for maintaining microservice-based systems. In: ICSA Workshops, pp. 298–302. IEEE Computer Society (2017)
8. IBM: Hardware Configuration Definition User's Guide - z/OS Version 2 Release 4. IBM (2019)
9. IBM: IBM Z - Processor Resource/Systems Manager Planning Guide - SB10-7169-02. IBM (2019)
10. ISO/IEC 25010: ISO/IEC 25010:2011, systems and software engineering – systems and software quality requirements and evaluation (square) – system and software quality models (2011)
11. Jha, M., Maheshwari, P.: Reusing code for modernization of legacy systems. In: 13th IEEE International Workshop on STEP, pp. 102–114 (2005)
12. Knoche, H., Hasselbring, W.: Using microservices for legacy software modernization. IEEE Softw. **35**(3), 44–49 (2018)
13. Knoche, H.: Sustaining runtime performance while incrementally modernizing transactional monolithic software towards microservices. In: Proceedings of 7th ACM/SPEC on ICPE 2016, pp. 121–124. ACM (2016)
14. Krause, A., et al.: Microservice decomposition via static and dynamic analysis of the monolith. In: IEEE ICSA-C, pp. 9–16 (2020)
15. Lehman, M.M.: On understanding laws, evolution, and conservation in the large-program life cycle. J. Syst. Softw. **1**, 213–221 (1984)
16. Mehta, A.: Evolving legacy systems using feature engineering and CBSE. In: Proceedings of 23rd ICSE, pp. 797–798 (2001)
17. O'Brien, L., Brebner, P., Gray, J.: Business transformation to SOA: aspects of the migration and performance and QOS issues. In: Proceedings of 2nd International Workshop on SDSOA Environments, pp. 35–40. ACM (2008)
18. Pizka, M., Bauer, A.: A brief top-down and bottom-up philosophy on software evolution. In: Proceedings of 7th IWPSE, pp. 131–136 (2004)
19. Rios, N., et al.: The most common causes and effects of technical debt: First results from a global family of industrial surveys. In: Proceedings of 12th ACM/IEEE International Symposium on ESEM 2018. ACM (2018)
20. Rostami, K., et al.: Architecture-based assessment and planning of change requests. In: Proceedings of 11th International ACM SIGSOFT Conference on QoSA, pp. 21–30. ACM (2015)

21. Seacord, R., Plakosh, D., Lewis, G.A.: Modernizing Legacy Systems: Software Technologies, Engineering Process and Business Practices. Addison-Wesley Longman Publishing Co., Inc. (2003)
22. Stellman, A., Greene, J.: Learning Agile: Understanding Scrum, XP, Lean, and Kanban. O'Reilly (2014)
23. Swanson, B.: The dimensions of maintenance. In: Proceedings of the 2nd ICSE 1976, pp. 492–497. IEEE Computer Society Press (1976)
24. Wendland, M.F., et al.: Model-based testing in legacy software modernization: an experience report. In: Proceedings of 2013 International Workshop on JAMAICA, pp. 35–40. ACM (2013)
25. White, B., et al.: IBM Z15 Technical Introduction. IBM Redbooks (2020)

Enabling SMEs to Industry 4.0 Using the BaSyx Middleware: A Case Study

Subash Kannoth[1]($\boxtimes$), Jesko Hermann[2], Markus Damm[1], Pascal Rübel[2],
Dimitri Rusin[2], Malte Jacobi[3], Björn Mittelsdorf[3], Thomas Kuhn[1],
and Pablo Oliveira Antonino[1]

[1] Fraunhofer IESE, Kaiserslautern, Germany
{subash.kannoth,markus.damm,thomas.kuhn,
pablo.antonino}@iese.fraunhofer.de
[2] DFKI, Kaiserslautern, Germany
{jesko.hermann,pascal.ruebel,dimitri.rusin}@dfki.de
[3] Odion GmbH, Saarbrücken, Germany
{mj,bm}@odion.de

Abstract. Industry 4.0 (I4.0) concepts evolve the current industrial processes towards directly connecting shopfloor machines to systems from different layers of the Automation Pyramid, such as Enterprise Resource Planning (ERP) or Manufacturing Execution Systems (MES). Companies introducing I4.0 concepts aim at (i) facilitating changeable production systems in order to quickly react to customer inquiries such that even lot-size one becomes feasible and (ii) having a holistic view of the different parameters of a production process. Enabling these calls for accessing the different systems of the Automation Pyramid, which is hard to achieve in traditional production systems without technical changes consuming time, effort and budget, mainly due to the lack of standardization, heterogeneous protocols, and the lack of proper interfaces among the systems of the Automation Pyramid. This challenge is greater in small and medium-size enterprises (SMEs) due to economic reasons or lack access to personnel with a skill set encompassing all the levels of the Automation Pyramid. I4.0-based concepts are built according to the Service-Oriented Architecture principle to enable peer-to-peer communication of systems from each layer of the Automation Pyramid. The service-oriented middleware architecture Eclipse BaSyx 4.0 implements SOA and other I4.0 concepts such as Digital Twins, and has been instantiated in German companies of different sizes. In this paper, we present two use cases focusing on of adoption of Eclipse BaSyx in two German SMEs and show how this enables the adoption of I4.0 concepts with improved time, effort and budget.

Keywords: Industry 4.0 · BaSyx · Case study

1 Introduction

The Fourth Industrial Revolution, also known as Industry 4.0, brings extensive changes in the manufacturing systems where manufacturing sector and

© Springer Nature Switzerland AG 2021
S. Biffl et al. (Eds.): ECSA 2021, LNCS 12857, pp. 277–294, 2021.
https://doi.org/10.1007/978-3-030-86044-8_19

information and communications technologies are brought close together. This enables new and advanced applications in industrial automation, involving e.g., cloud services or AI. The key benefits are improved productivity, reliability, cost-effectiveness, quality and flexibility in the production process [7]. This is achieved through the integration of state of the art technologies such as the Internet of Things (IoT), cyber-physical Systems (CPS), Artificial Intelligence (AI), Cloud technologies, Edge Computing, etc. into a unified ecosystem.

The current architecture in production systems is layered in terms of production system levels, with each layer having its own communication technologies and protocols. The lower layers where programmable logic controllers (PLC) are involved use protocols such as CAN, Profinet, Ethernet, or Modbus. The higher layers use more sophisticated protocols such as HTTP, OPC UA, MQTT etc. Due to this heterogeneity of protocols, end-to-end communication between different communication layers is difficult. However, in changeable production systems, where efficient management of process changes of the production system is required, end-to-end communication is inevitable. This situation is worse in small and medium-size enterprises (SMEs) due to economic reasons or lack of access to personnel with a skill set encompassing all the levels of the Automation Pyramid (See Fig. 1 left side). I4.0-based concepts are built according to the Service-Oriented Architecture principle to enable peer-to-peer communication of systems from each layer of the Automation Pyramid. Service-oriented architectures create strict isolation between the definition and implementation of services. Field devices (PLCs) implement and expose the service interfaces. Instead of the devices themselves, entities called orchestrators invoke the services following the production steps with the relevant information provided by digital twins through the unified interface.

In this paper, we present two use cases focusing on of the adoption of the Eclipse BaSyx [1] middleware in two German SMEs and show how this enables the adoption of industry 4.0 concepts. We share our experiences in instantiating BaSyx in these contexts and provide reusable reference architectures. The paper is structured as follows: Sect. 2 reviews the state of the art and the state of the practice in the I4.0 domain, where we discuss the traditional Automation Pyramid, the concept of Digital Twins followed by a brief introduction to the BaSyx middleware and its capabilities in realizing an I4.0 system. In Sect. 3, we discuss in detail the two industrial use cases and provide a comprehensive overview of our reference architectures. Finally, Sect. 4, documents our experiences in digitalizing production systems and draws conclusions.

2   State of the Art and State of the Practice

2.1   Industry 4.0 and the Automation Pyramid

The traditional Automation Pyramid reference architecture defined in IEC 62264 [4] restricts cross-layer interactions. As shown in Fig. 1, the traditional Automation Pyramid architecture consists of separate layers with defined interaction points. The field level consists of devices such as actuators, sensors, and the associated low-level protocol for accessing and controlling the devices. The control layer is dominated by PLCs, that execute predetermined cyclic tasks that control the field-level entities. The supervisory layer consists of the supervisory control and data acquisition (SCADA) system, which controls and manages several distributed PLCs from a single point. The planning level utilizes the manufacturing execution system (MES), which manages the overall production by controlling the high-level manufacturing steps. The management level uses the enterprise resource planning system (ERP), where the management controls and manages the resources and monitors the various levels of the business including manufacturing, sales, procurement, etc. The cross-layer interaction in the traditional Automation Pyramid is difficult because each layer's interaction is restricted to its upper and lower layers. In the case of changes, the architecture demands modification in all layers. I4.0, on the other hand, proposes a complete change of the traditional automation architecture by enabling cross-layer interaction between participants of different hierarchical levels.

2.2   Asset Administration Shells as Digital Twins

A standardized representation of data is necessary to achieve the cross-layer integration of data between the various entities. This is where the concept of Digital Twins (DT) comes into the picture. Among many existing definitions for DTs, within the context of Industry 4.0 *a digital twin is a formal digital representation of some asset, process or system that captures attributes and behaviours of that entity suitable for communication, storage, interpretation or processing within a certain context* [8]. RAMI 4.0 proposes the Asset Administration Shell (AAS) as the implementation of the Digital Twin [2]. The AAS is the digital representation of an asset, where an asset can be anything valuable to an organization, such as a physical device, a software component, a worker, an entire factory etc. In other words, any relevant asset can be viewed as an object represented by an AAS. The AAS is compliant with a protocol-independent type system and meta-model that defines the syntax. The AAS references sub models (SM) that have services to invoke operations and, access and manipulate the asset's associated data; i.e., SMs encapsulate real properties of an asset, such as the rotational speed of a motor (dynamic), the motor manufacturer (static), etc. Representing various assets digitally through SMs enables identification of these assets easier than before. For example, the simulation model SM (dynamic) of motor which enables to simulate the physics of a motor, technical specification SM (static) provide the user detailed technical insights of the asset, condition monitoring SM (dynamic) exposes various sensor values of the plant. The AAS together with its SMs provides information hiding and a higher level of abstraction for assets [5].

To the best of our knowledge, no previous work has been identified which addresses a similar usecase and the challenges discussed in this paper.

2.3   BaSyx Middleware

The open-source middleware Eclipse BaSyx 4.0 provides the necessary software components to enable Industry 4.0. The BaSyx platform is result of the project BaSys 4.0,[1] which is funded by the German Federal Ministry of Education and Research,[2] the use cases in this paper are stemming from follow up publicly funded projects targeted towards SMEs. It defines reference architectures for production systems to realize Industry 4.0 and also implements core concepts defined by the Platform Industry 4.0 specification [2]. The service-oriented architecture of BaSys acts as an enabler to realize changeable production. A change in the production process is thus not reflected by a change in the PLC programs. The service-based production deploys stateless configurable production steps on PLCs where services are implemented. The orchestrator executes those services, which represent a real production process that essentially follows a recipe that interacts with the PLCs through the offered services.

The realization of the changeable production process requires end-to-end connectivity between all the assets of the plant [5], which is not feasible with the traditional Automation Pyramid architecture explained in Sect. 2.1. BaSys proposes the Virtual Automation Bus (VAB) architecture which solves the problem of end-to-end communication with regard to many heterogeneous communication protocols [6]. The VAB is characterized by a set of communication primitives, namely *create, retrieve, update, delete* and *invoke*, which is an extension of CRUD with the addition of *invoke* for invoking remote operations. In addition to the primitives, VAB also provides a technology implement type system. The VAB thus acts as an intermediate language and as a common layer for heterogeneous protocol interoperability. Figure 1 shows the architecture realized with BaSyx using the VAB. BaSyx thus disrupts the strictly hierarchical classical Automation Pyramid and supports architectures that facilitate DT by enabling cross-layer interaction through VAB.

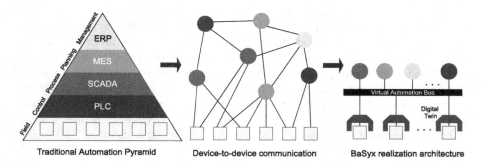

Fig. 1. Transition from traditional Automation Pyramid to cross-layer device-to-device communication and the architecture realized with BaSyx

---

[1] https://www.basys40.de/.
[2] BMBF grant number 01IS16022.

3   Industry Use Cases

To validate the adaptability of the BaSyx middleware, we instantiated BaSyx in two use cases with different objectives. The first use case is about contract manufacturers with small lot sizes and short-term customer requests. The automation of the quotation process via microservices and the implementation of an automated feasibility check enables contract manufacturers to evaluate, schedule and accept production orders with small lot sizes more effectively. To improve the accuracy of the offer, the BaSyx middleware and the concept of Asset Administration Shells were used to determine the tool service life based on real manufacturing data. The second use case concerned data collection and visualization from existing "off-line" machinery. Larger production units usually provide multiple and heterogeneous data sources, as they are often assembled from parts by different manufacturers. Some system parameters or states might have to be read/observed at different places meters apart. By retrofitting such systems with IoT-gateways, all this data is collected and provided via asset administration shells for subsequent visualisation and analysis.

3.1   Use Case 1 - Continuous Optimization of Quotations

The trend towards individualized products leads to a large number of technically different production requests with different lot sizes for contract manufacturers. Especially small and medium-sized enterprises (SMEs) face the difficulty of evaluating and responding to order requests. Often customer inquiries are circulated throughout a company on a paper basis, which leads to delays and, in the worst case, to the loss of the inquiry. For the calculation, expert knowledge is required and surcharges for unknown variables are added, which results in inaccurate quotations. The digitalization of the quotation process and manufacturing equipment holds considerable potential for optimized production planning and associated competitive advantages. Semi-automated feasibility checks of short-term customer inquiries by the company's internal order management provide a significant contribution to a fast and precise offer. Additionally, real manufacturing data of the machines provide information that can be used to improve the accuracy of the quotation. For the use case, the production cell of a contract manufacturer was digitalized and its information provided via OPC UA. The cell consisted of two computer numerical control (CNC) machines and a handling robot. Each cell produced different products and product variants in small lot sizes. Real manufacturing data was used to improve data about the downtime and the calculation of the tool costs by deriving the tool service life of all tools used. The utilization of the BaSyx middleware enabled the processing of the OPC UA variables and provided AASs for the cell and each machine, including the robot. Furthermore, the product and its production plan as well as the tools were described by an AAS. For the modeling of the solution, certain requirements were taken into account concerning the tool service life. The contract manufacturer's internal processes also led to possible simplifications. The underlying requirements and assumptions are listed in Table 1.

Table 1. Requirements and assumptions

Requirement	Description
R1	The system must consider regrinding and re-coating of tools for the calculation of the tool costs
R2	The system must consider that the wear of the tools depends on the material, the machine, as well as on the parameters cutting speed and feed rate
R3	The system must consider that the parameters cutting speed and feed rate are varied depending on different working shifts and machine conditions
R4	The system must consider that standard tools are not uniquely identifiable and just provide information about their tool type
R5	The system must consider that a tool type can be in the machine magazine multiple times and may be used in different ways
R6	The system must allow introducing new tools through an external software system and store the tool information in a persistent way
Assumption	Description
A1	A tool is only used for one type of material
A2	A standard tool is used in the same machine in the same machine magazine until the end of its life

3.1.1 Modeling

The digitalization of the cell included the connection to the programmable logic controller (PLC) of the CNC machines and the handling robot. The following model depends on the available information. For the CNC machines, this information includes the program ID, a part count, total motion time, and last cycle time. The handling robot provides a signal after completing the handling program. The signal is used to derive the time of the whole production process of the cell. However, the PLC does not provide any information about the production process. To reach the objective of improving the calculation of an offer, the relevant information must be modelled. For the integration, the standard of the AAS defined by the Platform Industrie 4.0 is used (Sect. 2.2). There are different aggregation levels for the AASs, with all AASs containing the mandatory submodels (SMs) *AssetIdentification* and *BillOfMaterial*. The *AssetIdentification* SM stores the static information related to the asset and acts as a digital nameplate. Concerning the production equipment, the cell represents the highest aggregation level. It is described by the SMs *ConditionMonitoring*, *CellCosts* and *MachineAssociation*. The *ConditionMonitoring* SM provides the information about which product is manufactured at the moment, the last cycle time, as well as different kinds of downtimes. The *CellCosts* SM provides information about depreciation, interest rates, room costs, operator costs and maintenance costs. The *MachineAssociation* SM provides references to the deployed machines of the cell. This is due to an issue concerning the search of aggregated AASs that are not predefined. Concerning the production equipment, the cell represents the highest aggregation level. It is described by the SMs *ConditionMonitoring*, *CellCosts* and *MachineAssociation*. The *ConditionMonitoring* SM provides the information about which product is manufactured at the moment, the last cycle time, as well as different kinds of downtimes. The *CellCosts* SM provides information about depreciation, interest rates, room costs, operator costs and maintenance costs. The *MachineAssociation* SM provides references to the deployed machines of the cell. This is due to an issue concerning the search of aggregated AASs that are not predefined.

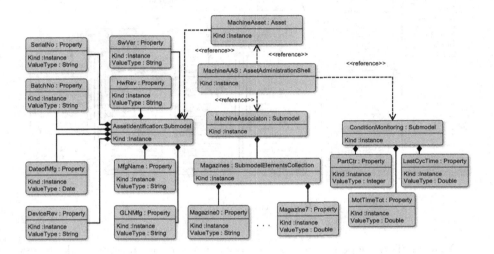

Fig. 2. MachineAAS model

The second aggregation level consists of the machines, including CNC machines and the handling robot (Fig. 2). They are also described by the *ConditionMonitoring* SM. It defines some additional machine-specific information such as the part counter, total motion time, and last cycle time of the machine. The third SM *ToolAssociation* is just provided for the CNC machines. It provides information on which tool is used in which magazine. This information is necessary to update the lifespan information of the currently used tools. On the lowest level is the tool (Fig. 3) that is associated with the CNC machines. In the case of the production equipment, each AAS is of the *assetKind* instance. It contains the SMs *ToolMileage*, *ProductAssociation*, and *ToolCosts*. The *ToolMileage* SM stores mileage-relevant information, such as total mileage and the number of times of grinding and coating of the tool. It also provides information about the reason for the tool's end of life (e.g. wear, crash, or other) and the current state (e.g. new, in use, stored, or other). While the *ProductAssociation* SM defines the material, the machine, the magazine place, and the process parameters (e.g.

cutting speed, feed rate, or other), the SM tool costs defines the purchase price and the price for coating and grinding of the tool. The product, on the other hand, just describes the associated production processes. It provides the necessary information as a map to update the tool lifespan (magazine, mileage per product, or other).

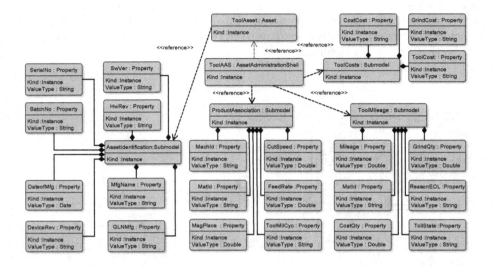

Fig. 3. ToolAAS model

Because of the dependencies of the tools on material, machine and process parameters, they are categorized into specific classes depending on the range of process parameters. This accounts for minimal changes to the process parameters that occur regularly. These classes can then be used to calculate the real lifespan and therefore the costs per usage for a class of tool type. The overview in Table 3 provides the calculations for each product and the product classes. Table 2 defines various terms used for the calculation.

Table 2. Definitions

Term	Description	Term	Description
$T_c \subseteq T_p$	Set of tools belonging to a certain class	C_{tu}	Tool cost per usage
N_c	Number of tools belonging to a certain class	P_p	Purchase price
U_T	Amount of usage per tool	C_g	Grinding cost
LS	Lifespan of tool	N_c	Grinding quantity
LS_{Avg}	Average lifespan of tool	C_c	Coating cost
C_T	Total tool cost	N_c	Coating quantity

Table 3. Calculations

The lifespan LS_t of T_p with an amount of usage U_T	$LS_t = \sum_{\forall u \in U_T} u$
The total costs C_T	$C_T = P_p + C_g * N_g + C_c * N_c$
The average lifespan LS_{Avg} of tools of class T_c	$LS_{Avg} = \frac{\sum_{\forall t \in T_C} LS(t)}{N_c}$
The tool Costs per usage C_{tu} for the tool class T_c	$C_{tu} = \frac{\sum_{\forall t \in T_C} C_T(t)}{\sum_{\forall t \in T_C} LS(t)}$

Table 3 shows the formalization of the various calculations. LS_t is updated with the mileage provided by the product map as a consequence of the Ping event.[3] For a new product inquiry, the features of the products are mapped to different tool classes. The mapping function is provided via the description of the capabilities of a machine. Each capability describes which feature type in which dimension ranges can be produced by which tool at which costs and the corresponding process parameters. In addition tolerances and surface properties are defined to complete the description of the individual capability. The information is updated via the real data of previous products. Using this information a feasibility check service checks if all features of the new product can be provided in terms of dimensions, tolerances and surface properties by one of the cells. It also derives the manufacturing time, verifies the availability and open capacity of the cell, and calculates the corresponding manufacturing costs of the offer.

3.1.2 Architecture

The overall architecture can be divided into office floor, shop floor and BaSyx. Figure 4 outlines the architecture using the C4-model container interaction diagram [3]. The office floor is essential for the automated quotation process. A web portal is designed and implemented to provide the interface for the customer to create new product inquiries. Office and shop floor front ends are written in Angular and Clarity Angular Components. Output is a structured set of data that can be processed. The logic of the quotation process is designed via two BPMN processes that are implemented via two BPMN Engines (Flowable and Camunda). One BPMN process describes the quotation process, the other provides the feasibility check and calculation. Both BPMN Engines incorporate a defined REST API and MySQL database persistence.

To define microservices for each BPMN process, a microservice architecture for the quotation process as feasibility check is created. Each microservice interacts with either the Web portal, the Odion ERP system, or the AASs provided by the BaSyx 4.0 middleware to collect the necessary information. The information is then processed during the quotation process. The details of this process are described in Sect. 3.1.3.

---

[3] A ping event is triggered after the completion of a product and represents the production time of one product in the cell.

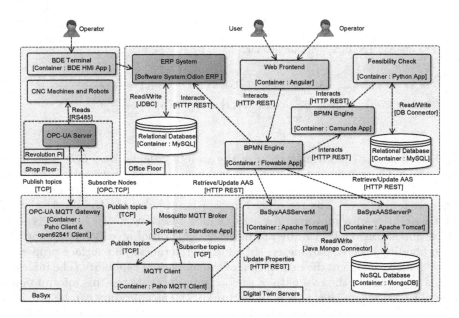

Fig. 4. Overall architecture of use case 1

Since the CNC machine provides an RS485-based interface, an OPC UA server is hosted using a Revolution Pi,[4] an industrial-grade computer, which acts as retrofitting gateway to the BaSyx middleware. The information is polled from the CNC machine to the OPC UA server in regular interval to the corresponding variable nodes in the OPC UA server. During the production process on the shop floor, the BDE terminal acts as the data collection point for the operator who logs various information like idle times, reasons for errors, reasons for machine downtimes, etc. For example, the operator can enter why a particular machine or cell is down. This information is then updated in the corresponding SMs.

We utilized the publish/subscribe mechanism of OPC UA to efficiently detect the events of the OPC UA server. The BaSyx source development kit used in the project is written in Java and the OPC UA stack (open62541[5]) used is based on C language. To avoid the complications from binding C to Java, we introduced the OPUA-MQTT Gateway. In this way, the Java and C implementations are separated which makes it is easy to maintain the software in the long run. The OPUA-MQTT Gateway transforms the OPC UA events to the corresponding MQTT topics and publishes the events to the MQTT Broker. The MQTT client that is subscribed to the topics pushes the data to the corresponding properties of the SMs residing in BaSyxAASServerM. BaSyxAASServerM and BaSyxAASServerP are Apache Tomcat server instances that expose REST APIs for managing and hosting the AAS and the associated SMs. The difference lies

---

[4] https://revolution.kunbus.com/revolution-pi-series/.

[5] https://open62541.org/.

in the lifetime of AASs; i.e., BaSyxAASServerM does not persist the AASs in the database, but BaSyxAASServerP does. BaSyxAASServerP only hosts the ToolAAS (Fig. 3) because (1) all the information related to the tool life-cycle should be preserved for the future since tools are often replaced with the new tools, (2) a maintenance restart of the system should not destroy a tool's life cycle history. Unlike BaSyxAASServerM, BaSyxAASServerP stores all the pieces of information that are static and volatile. For example, the AssetIdentification SM of MachineAAS (Fig. 2), which acts as a digital nameplate, has only static information that will never change unless the machine is changed or some update has happened in the machine hardware or software. The reason for isolating the persisted and non persisted servers into two separate instances is because we want to decouple the frequently used servers with one with the database back end.

3.1.3   Orchestration

The quotation process begins with the customer input via the inquiry web portal. It guides the customer through the process and provides first feedback on whether the input is valid. After the customer has provided all the necessary information a Service Task implements a completeness check of the inquiry. If all required information is provided the process continues, otherwise, a request for the revision of the inquiry is sent indicating the missing or wrong information.

The successfully submitted inquiry is then enriched by the technical experts of the contract manufacturer. While the customer merely provides a drawing of the product, the technical expert enriches the product description with relevant information about the product features that is necessary for manufacturing the product. The combined information of the customer and the technical expert is then transferred to the Service Task feasibility check and the quotation process. Each product is described by quantity, dimensions, and material. The features (e.g. pocket, groove, chamfer, thread) that must be manufactured are defined by their quantity, dimensions, tolerances, and surface property requirements.

On the other hand, each cell is described by its capacity and the corresponding machines. Each machine provides its technical and economic information, such as machine costs and availability, but also tool switch time, swivel time and other information. Each machine has a set of capabilities based on a tool class. This describes the ability to manufacture a certain feature as well as process parameters, possible dimensions, tolerances, surface properties, and costs. Tool costs, tolerances, and surface properties as well as machine availability are calculated based on real manufacturing data of similar products. Thus, continuous optimization of the quotation is possible.

Based on this information the feasibility check searches for capabilities that can provide the demanded product features. This includes the verification of material, product dimensions, form features, surface properties, and tolerances. After checking the feasibility, the Service Task selects those cells that can provide all the necessary features. For each of the cells, production time and costs are calculated by searching for a tool combination with minimal production costs.

Using the corresponding production time, availability is checked and the cell with the lowest costs is chosen as the preferred solution while alternatives are stored as well. All matching process results are documented in a database, which allows analyzing incoming product requests, the matching process, and the reasons for any failed matching. This data can be used to extend the contract manufacturer's business model based on incoming requests.

After the automated feasibility check and the quotation process are finished, an expert checks the results, selects the best option and decides, whether to accept or reject the order. Having the "human in the loop" allows reacting to different scenarios, such as capabilities that are not provided yet or scheduling issues.

3.2   Use Case 2 - Improving the Product Quality Through Continuous Monitoring

Production systems typically have long service life spans, often more than 20 years. Especially larger production systems consist of many parts with diverse functionality by different vendors (e.g. sensors, motors, heating- or cooling elements). This diversity tends to grow over time; certain system parts like motors might have to be replaced by parts from other manufacturers, or might be added for additional functionality. This is especially true for SMEs, where partial upgrades might be preferred over full system replacements out of economic necessity.

This situation presents a challenge regarding data acquisition and presentation. The data from the different system parts might be provided using different digital protocols, or as analog signals. Some data sources might have their own displays, which might reside in different places of the production system, and some data sources might not be used at all.

At the same time, the still ongoing shift to the Industry 4.0 paradigm leads to an ever growing appetite for data. Besides offering support for new business models, a main driver for this hunger is the desire for a more holistic view and understanding of the production process. Predictive maintenance is an example often brought up in this context, but tracing production errors or deficiencies to their root causes through data analysis is an application that is at least as important. Implementing such applications in an environment where it is even difficult to simply present all the relevant data in real time and in a concise manner presents a challenge.

The use case we present here concerns a contract manufacturer specializing in the coating and lamination of technical textiles. The textiles are wound off large coils, and led through a powder-coating system where they are sprinkled with a thermal fusion adhesive and subsequently heat-treated by passing them through a channel with gas burners. After that the material is allowed to cool down and solidify before it is wound back up and tailored for the customer.

This powder-coating system consists of several parts that are relatively independent, like the gas burners and the motors for rotating the coils, each providing data in different formats, either analog or using different digital protocols like

Modbus. To make this data available, the system has been retrofitted with four Arendar IoT gateways[6] that read this data and provide it via OPC UA. While the idea is to install BaSyx on these IoT gateways themselves, this was not possible at the start of the project for technical reasons. Therefore, an asset administration shell was set up on a server that collects the data from the four OPC UA servers, and provides it (possibly after some pre-processing) via a *ConditionMonitoring* SM. It also pushes the data to a database to make it available for later analysis.

3.2.1 Modelling

The AAS for this use case contains two SMs: A *ConditionMonitoring* SM as in the first use case, and a DataMapping SM that describes how to acquire the data and where to put it in the *ConditionMonitoring* SM. That way, it is possible to organize the data in the *ConditionMonitoring* SM independent of the structure of the four OPC UA servers.

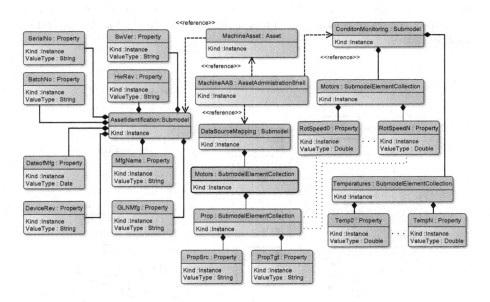

Fig. 5. AAS model for use case 2

The *DataSourceMapping* SM essentially describes for each property what the data source is, where to put it in the *ConditionMonitoring* SM, and possibly how to preprocess it before updating it in the SM. While most of the over 60 properties just use the original OPC UA values, there are two types of values that are preprocessed. The rotational speeds of some motors are given as a continuous

---

[6] https://www.arend-automation.com/arendar.

integer pulse count, where, e.g., 30 pulses correspond to one revolution; these values are converted to float rpm values. Also, a string value is compiled that shows which of the more than 20 error states of the system (e.g., provided by emergency stop switches) is active.

The *DataSourceMapping* SM is static and is provided as a JSON file, which is read by the BaSyx and used to build the *ConditionMonitoring* SM for the AAS. Other than that, the AAS is handled like in use case 1, i.e., it is published with an HTTP server such that it is accessible via the BaSyx REST interface. Apart from the standard SMs *AssetIdentification* and *BillOfMaterial*, the AAS contains no further SMs.

3.2.2 Architecture

The goal of this project is to enable the manufacturers to monitor all relevant parameters of the production process concisely, and to store the data such that it is mapped to specific production runs. Ultimately, the main goal is to find out whether there is any relation between a quality property of a product and the process of its production. So if there is a customer complaint about a product, the data of the corresponding production run can be accessed and analysed for possible causes.

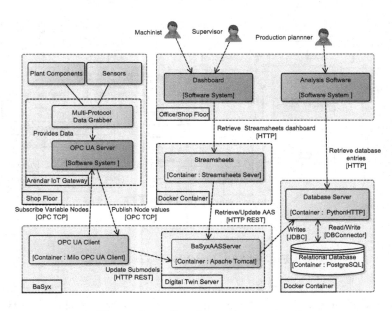

Fig. 6. Overall architecture use case 2

The architecture of our solution is shown in Fig. 6. The core is the Data Collector application built using the BaSyx Java SDK, which runs in a docker container and consists of 3 components:

The BaSyxAASServer provides the *ConditionMonitoring* SM via the BaSyx REST interface. The OPC-UA Client subscribes to and receives the values from the four OPC UA server. The PostgreSQL Database is to persist the received values is set up in a docker container. In use case 1, with persisted AAS servers (Sect. 3.1.2), the AAS structure (serialized JSON) is completely stored in the NoSQL database. In comparison to that, here the database is used to store historical data values for future visualization where a relational database suits better. Therefore the database back end sits separated from BaSyx. Streamsheets[7] is used as the visualization software, which also runs in a docker container. Streamsheets works basically like a spreadsheet application that can also use live data sources, for example data published as JSON via an HTTP REST interface. Since the AAS and SMs in BaSyx are published in this way, it works with BaSyx out of the box. Also, spreadsheets are commonly used in SMEs, so a dashboard realized with it can also be adopted and extended also by personnel with little IT knowledge.

Apart from reading data from the *ConditionMonitoring* SM, Streamsheets can also write to it via HTTP PUT requests to the BaSyx REST interface. This is used to update the ID of the order that is currently being processed inside the *ConditionMonitoring* SM, which is then stored along with the other values such that they can be attributed to the corresponding production run later. To this end, the Streamsheets dashboard contains a field where a worker manually enters the order ID and submits it.

All these components and the four IoT gateways are connected via Ethernet and/or the network component of Docker. The *Data Collector* gets the data from the IoT gateways via OPC UA, while the other components communicate via HTTP REST. The user accesses the Streamsheets dashboard via any Internet browser. The analysis software is not yet specified, but in the simplest case this could be realized by simply retrieving the data entries of a certain production run as a table from the Python HTTP server and analysing it with common spreadsheet software.

4   Experiences and Lessons Learned

With use case 1, one of the main challenges was to evaluate the CAD/CAM models shared by the customer. In most cases, during a customer inquiry, the models are shared in a portable document format, as scanned paper images, or even as text description in emails. Evaluating the dimensions of mechanical parts from such diverse document settings turned out to be out of the scope of this project. For this reason, we had to employ a human/expert in the loop of the evaluation process, which was inevitable. Concerning the scalability of the approach, it needs to be mentioned that each SME has a very unique quotation and production planning process. Therefore it is difficult to design a standardized process that fits all requirements of each individual SME. To realize a scalable

---

[7] https://cedalo.com/products/streamsheets/.

solution, adaptable microservices could be designed and composed into the quotation process based on the requirements of the SME.

Another challenge was the lack of best practices in modeling I4.0 platform digital twins [2]. Associating several AASs and specifying the relationships between them was not straight forward. In other words, it is not clear yet from the (ongoing) I4.0 platform specification how to model the relationship between different AASs. For example the relationships between the AAS for the CNC machine (MachineAAS, Fig. 2) and the tools associated with the machine (ToolAAS, Fig. 3) could not be specified implicitly through the metamodel specified by I4.0 platform. In the case of BaSyPaaS, the entry point for the process was the cell, which allowed optimizing the associations between the different AASs. However, unlike, for example OPC UA, no child-parent relationship is foreseen in the metamodel, which would allow efficient browsing of the AASs and their relationships. Therefore, the implementation contains a cross-association between the associated AASs in both directions. The tool association SM of the machine references the tool while the machine association SM of the tool also references the machine.

Another issue in the context of digitalization is the formalization of expert know-how. For the implementation of the feasibility check, the tool must be modeled, including information such as process parameters, manufacturable dimensions, tolerances, and surface properties. While tool manufacturers provide some abstract information about the tools and the associated parameters, this information is not accurate enough for a company that defines its competitive advantage by differentiation. The knowledge about the process parameters and manufacturing strategies and the associated results such as tolerances and surface properties must therefore be formalized manually. This presents a high initial effort before the automated feasibility check provides a benefit.

Use case 2 was more simple and straightforward than use case 1, yet still presented some challenges in the SME environment. On one had, IT access in SMEs is more difficult. Often there is no in-house IT or electric department, and such services are provided by third parties. This presents a challenge in physically implementing such a project. Setting up servers or installing gateways can typically not be done with in-house resources which makes them time consuming, especially if re-iterations are necessary. Therefore, when planning such a retrofitting project in an SME, these seemingly mundane aspects should not be neglected and need to be considered early on.

Another challenge stemmed from the fact that not all data sources can be used as-is; sometimes some sort of pre-processing is necessary to get the result desired by the user. Such pre-processing may involve simple functions applied to the source values. However, the conversion from continuous pulse counts to revolutions per minute, for example, proved to be very finicky, as it also has to take the timing of the measurements into account.

A positive finding was the usability of the AASs and the BaSyx REST API. As mentioned in Sect. 3.2.2, the Streamsheets software used for the dashboard worked with BaSyx without any alterations being necessary, neither on the side of BaSyx nor on the side of Streamsheets. So the part of the project that followed setting up the data in the AAS submodel actually proved to be the easiest while producing the most visible results.

5 Conclusion

In this paper, we presented two industrial use cases with different objectives and shared our experience in instantiating the Eclipse BaSyx middleware and how it enabled implementing I4.0 concepts. We implemented the use cases in two German SMEs and discussed the proposed solutions and challenges we faced during the implementation. Both use cases have a service-oriented architecture where digital twins have been used to organize data and interface with service providers. Our solutions are deployed in multiple protocol environments and we showed the benefits of using the BaSyx middleware and asset administration shells in conjunction with digital twins to achieve end-to-end communication. Both use cases consisted of retrofitting various assets in the plant and our proposals can be used as solution patterns for similar use cases. The application partners were satisfied with the overall results; a *direct* feedback regarding BaSyx could not be provided though as the end user typically never comes in touch with BaSyx itself.

However, the digitalization of SMEs in general requires experience and know-how. Especially use case 1 - the automated quotation and calculation based on real manufacturing data has the potential to reduce the effort for the SME. However, to implement the approach for all production cells, the workers' expert knowledge must first be formalized. Also, both use cases needed additional IT facilities implemented, which in general is more difficult to do in SMEs. These initial implementation efforts create additional expenditures before yielding any benefit. For SMEs to become part of the fourth industrial revolution, this effort is inevitable, but there are still a lot of companies unwilling to do so or lacking the support to do so.

References

1. Basyx: Eclispe basyx, February 2019. https://www.eclipse.org/basyx/
2. BMBF: Details of the asset administration shell [update], March 2020. https://www.plattform-i40.de/PI40/Redaktion/EN/Downloads/Publikation/vws-in-detail-presentation.pdf
3. Brown, S.: The C4 model for visualising software architecture - context, containers, components, and code, April 2021. https://c4model.com/
4. IEC: IEC 62264-1:2013 - enterprise-control system integration – part 1: models and terminology, February 2019. https://www.iso.org/standard/57308.html
5. Kuhn, T., Antonino, P.O., Schnicke, F.: Industrie 4.0 virtual automation bus architecture. In: Muccini, H., et al. (eds.) ECSA 2020. CCIS, vol. 1269, pp. 477–489. Springer, Cham (2020). https://doi.org/10.1007/978-3-030-59155-7_34
6. Kuhn, T., Sadikow, S., Antonino, P.: A service-based production ecosystem architecture for Industrie 4.0. KI - Künstliche Intelligenz **33**(2), 163–169 (2019). https://doi.org/10.1007/s13218-019-00589-y

7. Mohamed, N., Al-Jaroodi, J., Lazarova-Molnar, S.: Industry 4.0: Opportunities for enhancing energy efficiency in smart factories. In: 2019 IEEE International Systems Conference (SysCon), pp. 1–7 (2019). https://doi.org/10.1109/SYSCON.2019.8836751

8. Schnicke, F., Kuhn, T., Antonino, P.O.: Enabling Industry 4.0 service-oriented architecture through digital twins. In: Muccini, H., et al. (eds.) ECSA 2020. CCIS, vol. 1269, pp. 490–503. Springer, Cham (2020). https://doi.org/10.1007/978-3-030-59155-7_35

Software Architectures for Edge Analytics: A Survey

Marie Platenius-Mohr[✉][iD], Hadil Abukwaik, Jan Schlake, and Michael Vach

ABB Corporate Research Center Germany, Ladenburg, Germany
{marie.platenius-mohr,hadil.abukwaik,jan-christoph.schlake,
michael.vach}@de.abb.com

Abstract. Traditionally, industrial and IoT data analytics applications run in the cloud, leveraging its power regarding big data processing capabilities. With edge computing, opportunities for moving data processing from the cloud to the edge has emerged, i.e., compute nodes become close to where data is generated and to where the processed results are consumed. When running analytics on the edge, lag time is minimal, such that real-time data can be considered and insights can be delivered faster, which leads to improving both the effectiveness and efficiency in online decision-making.

From a software architecture perspective, it is still a challenge to design systems for edge analytics as it raises many architecture-related questions. However, this architectural perspective on edge analytics has not been consolidated in literature so far. Therefore, in this paper, we first give an overview of the edge analytics topic from the perspective of our own experience from industrial projects, before we survey a subset of existing approaches for edge analytics and review them from a software architecture point of view. We investigate the differences among the surveyed architectures in order to shed some light on the covered architectural aspects of edge analytics architectures, which will be useful for future academic and industrial projects incorporating edge analytics.

Keywords: Edge computing · Data analytics · Software architecture

1 Introduction

Nowadays, software systems have to process a tremendous amount of data generated by the increasing number (billions) of Internet of Things (IoT) devices, like mobile devices or sensors. While cloud computing was the answer to deal with this challenge in the past decade, in the last years, both industry and academic research show an increasing interest in edge computing [17,26]. In edge computing, computing nodes are placed "at the internet's edge" in close proximity to the devices. It enables more data processing tasks to be moved from the cloud to the edges that are close to where data is generated and where the processed results are consumed. Only filtered and/or aggregated information then

© Springer Nature Switzerland AG 2021
S. Biffl et al. (Eds.): ECSA 2021, LNCS 12857, pp. 295–311, 2021.
https://doi.org/10.1007/978-3-030-86044-8_20

must be transmitted to the cloud. Further typical advantages of edge computing compared to cloud computing include improved security, lower costs, and higher availability [26].

Various data-intensive applications can be found in the areas of artificial intelligence (e.g., machine learning (ml)), and data analytics in general. Such analytics applications already play a big role in many industries and there are numerous sources about the expected growth of their importance (e.g., [11,23]). Traditionally, industrial and IoT analytics applications run in the cloud, leveraging its power regarding big data processing capabilities [25]. Meanwhile, the edge can only consume a small part of the data that might be processed on the cloud. However, the advantages that edge computing comes with are beneficial for many analytics applications. Especially the edge's benefits regarding low latency, i.e., the ability to process real-time data is essential: Since lag time is minimal, real-time data can be considered and insights can be delivered faster not only to the users and operators, but also to the devices. Thereby, improved and accelerated decision-making increases efficiency and productivity [25]. Use cases for edge analytics can be found in various business domains, e.g., smart cities and smart transportation, public safety, and process automation. One typical use case for edge analytics in the process industries domain is anomaly detection as support for alarm management in process plants.

Designing systems for edge analytics is not only an analytics or a networking issue, but also a challenge from the perspective of software architecture. It raises many architecture-related questions and challenges: Which layers and components should be part of the edge analytics systems? How are they connected and how they should interact? Which functionality should be deployed where? Which other factors should influence the architectural decisions for edge analytics systems? Are there any reoccurring architectural patterns?

There are recent surveys and position papers on the intersection of software architecture and analytics (e.g., [4,22]) and there are also surveys on edge computing (e.g., [17,31]). However, the software architecture perspective for analytics in the area of edge computing has not been consolidated so far, even though there are thousands of publications in this area.

In this paper, we give an overview of the edge analytics topic from the perspective of our own experience from industrial projects, and we review a subset of existing (academic) approaches for edge analytics and (informally) compare them from a software architecture point of view. There is a common three layer architecture that most approaches share, but there are many variants and solutions to special challenges when looking into the concrete architectures. We investigate what exactly differs among the architectures and why, which will be useful for future academic and industrial projects incorporating edge analytics. We also identify open questions in this area.

All in all, this paper provides an overview of the state of research in edge analytics from a software architecture point of view, which is both relevant for academia and industry and addresses various domains and use cases.

In the next section, we give an overview of the edge analytics topic and discuss an example use case. In Sect. 3, we describe our research questions and our survey method. In Sect. 4, we introduce the investigated approaches, which are then compared in Sect. 5, followed by a discussion of the most interesting findings. Section 6 draws conclusions and outlines future work.

2   Edge Analytics

In this section, we give an overview of general edge analytics concepts and illustrate an example use case. This overview is based on our experiences within industrial projects and serves as a basis for the survey reported in the later sections of this paper.

2.1   Edge Analytics Foundations

First of all, there are different understandings of the notion "Edge". In edge analytics, the edge usually serves both as a gateway to the cloud and as a processing node itself, performing not only simple data filtering and aggregation tasks, but also more advanced analytics applications. The edge can be represented by one or also by a multitude of (networked) compute nodes. In some systems, the edge nodes are rather tiny, very resource-limited devices, in others, they can be rather powerful compute nodes. Most often, edge nodes are viewed as additional processing nodes, representing mediators between the devices and the cloud. But sometimes, the edge is referred to as the "edge of the internet" and comprising also the IoT devices themselves.

The typical benefits industrial projects expect from edge analytics are usually these (extended list based on [26]):

- The physical proximity to the devices makes it easier to achieve low latency and high bandwidth.
- The possibility to process data on the edge allows to reduce traffic towards the cloud as only filtered/aggregated information needs to be transmitted.
- In line with the previous items, scalability of analytics deployments improves as well.
- On the edge, it is easier to enforce privacy and security policies, as data is processed on-site, before releasing (parts of) it to the cloud.
- The edge can operate even if cloud services are unavailable (e.g., due to network or cloud failures or also on purpose for privacy/security reasons) and therefore it improves availability and reliability for many services.

On a high level, the typical edge analytics architecture (see Fig. 1) consists of three layers: the devices layer (or gathering layer or data input layer), the edge layer, and the cloud (or data center). The devices layer includes the field sensors and controllers. The edge layer includes edge node(s) that serve as a gateway to the cloud and it hosts analytics-related components. The cloud layer usually includes analytics model management and dashboards for visualizing

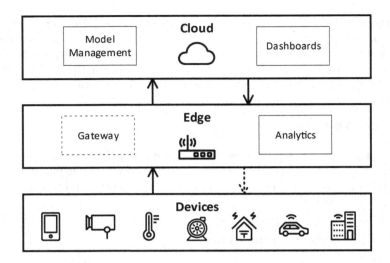

Fig. 1. High-level architecture of a typical edge analytics solution

the results. The data flows from the devices layer to the edge and (most often in filtered/aggregated form) from the edge to the cloud. Depending on the use case, the results of data processing are returned back to the devices or are only accessed in the cloud, e.g., via a dashboard.

Depending on the use case, the devices producing the data and those consuming the results—which can be but are not necessarily the same—could be either stationary or mobile. The devices' data may also be collected and (pre)processed by an intermediate system, like a control system, before it is sent to the edge. The data that is collected and processed can be manifold, structured or unstructured data, and any kind of data types, e.g., time-series/telemetry, events, audio, or video. Usually, the produced data by the devices is received at the edge as streams of real-time data, although there are also use cases and solutions for batch processing.

As common in many IoT systems, communication is usually message-based, via the MQTT protocol, where multiple technologies for MQTT brokers with different advantages and disadvantages exist [13]. The components are often deployed as Docker containers.

Of course, there are many more concrete instances and variants of such an architecture. This section highlighted only some points of variations. Later in this paper, we show further variation aspects based on our investigation of the different surveyed approaches.

2.2   Example Use Case

Typical use cases for edge analytics are from the industrial domain but also from public domain, like smart cities, including intelligent transportation services (where edge nodes are deployed on moving vehicles) and public safety applications. As mentioned before, data that is analyzed can be anything ranging from simple sensor data, e.g., in forms of time series, to large video streams.

One relevant application for edge analytics in the process industries domain is anomaly detection as part of asset (device) condition monitoring, e.g., for monitoring plant equipment like valves, pumps, or compressors. Traditionally, process plant operators use an alarm management system to monitor the condition of single assets, aggregated sub systems to whole plant systems. A good alarm management system follows procedures defined by the standardization body ANSI/ISA [1]. Technically, the operator creates simple alarm rules that determine under which conditions different kinds of alarms should be raised (e.g., signal crosses a specified threshold). In order to avoid too many unnecessary false alarms, more advanced systems can also take the current state of system into account. The quality of these rules depends on the expertise of the engineer creating them; there are many examples of wrongly configured alarm management systems causing major incidents [12].

Today, these operators can be supported by machine learning algorithms, usually running in the cloud. Since an edge device can be used to collect and store historical data from the process plant, the edge storage is also a good source for learning models using supervised learning. Instead of creating the alarm rule directly, the operator creates labels for the historical data indicating the rare event. Then, data-driven anomaly detection algorithms (e.g., [24]) can be used to learn a model, mapping the raw data to the label which can then be implemented in the edge calculation engine.

Deploying anomaly detection apps on the edge rather than on the cloud allows for leveraging the usual edge analytics advantages, especially the fast responses due to low-latency. Especially for asset condition monitoring or process function monitoring cases, the advantage of low latency and reliability is essential as this is a continuous process often operating at max. 1 s latency.

3   Survey Method

This survey is supposed to be an (informal) review of academic literature. In this section, we introduce the research questions which drive our research and explain the method we used for this survey.

3.1   Research Questions

Our main research question is: How do software architectures for edge analytics look like?

This question includes many subquestions, e.g.: Which components are deployed where? How are they connected and how to they interact? Which data is processed where? Why is the architecture designed as it is? Which factors influence the architectural decisions for edge analytics systems? Are there any reoccurring architectural patterns or best practices?

Not all questions are answered in all of the sources that we investigated within the scope of this survey, but we watched out for as many responses as possible and focused on exploring the design space.

3.2 Search Method

We searched for academic papers on approaches to run analytics on the edge. We used "Edge Analytics" as a search string in Google Scholar. The search time frame was February–March 2021.

There are quite many search results for this search string (Google Scholar says "about 2.670 results"), so there was the need to narrow down the scope. We went through the top hits on Google Scholar and manually excluded all papers that do not discuss the software architecture but mainly address other aspects of edge analytics, e.g., algorithms. We iterated through the results as ranked by Google Scholar[1] until we had a decent number we could use to get first answers to our research questions. Following this process, we excluded 20 papers and selected 10.

4 Overview of Edge Analytics Approaches

All selected approaches have in common that they apply analytics based on real-time data and involve components deployed on the edge. In most of the approaches, the edge is understood as a node with processing power, which also represents a gateway to the cloud.

In the following, we briefly introduce each selected approach and highlight interesting solutions.

Xu et al. (EAaaS), 2017 [30] present EAaaS, a service for real-time edge analytics. Amongst others, the service is supposed to address the work of the user creating edge analytics applications involving a lot of manual development and deployment tasks. Thus, EAaaS comes with a unified rule-based analytics model that aims to ease the user's programming efforts for applications based on rule-based analytics. The analytics model is extensible wrt. data selection, transformation, and rule conditions.

A light-weight high performance edge engine is developed to serve as the analytics runtime on the edge and to apply the rule-based analytics. The engine handles not only the incoming device data streams, but also model activation and deactivation requests in real-time.

In the cloud, EAaaS provides dashboards as well as a RESTful API for edge analytics management and composition with external services. Using the APIs or the dashboards allows the end-user to remotely enable and monitor the analytics execution on connected gateways.

---

[1] Relying on the Google Scholar ranking to some extent seemed promising as they already apply reasonable ranking criteria, described here: https://scholar.google.com/intl/de/scholar/about.html (accessed: June 2021).

Lujic et al., 2017/18 [18,19] focus on edge analytics use cases in the domain of smart buildings. They address the problem of analyzing incomplete datasets leading to inaccurate results and imprecise decisions. To this end, they propose a semi-automatic mechanism for recovery of incomplete datasets on the edge.

They describe the typical architecture with three layers: the devices ("gathering") layer, the edge layer, and the cloud layer. There are analytics components deployed on the edge as well as on the cloud. However, they argue that recovery of incomplete datasets for analytics on the cloud is often infeasible, due to the limited bandwidth available and the strict latency constraints of IoT applications. Thus, there is an extra component for the recovery of incomplete data as part of the data processing on the edge, closer to the source of data, promising a better efficiency.

Cheng et al. (GeeLytics), 2015/16 [7,8] designed an edge analytics platform called GeeLytics. As many edge analytics solutions, GeeLytics is designed to support easy and dynamic closed-control loops among sensors, edge analytics, and actuators. This means, the goal is to achieve fast and automated reactions based on low latency analytics results derived from real-time stream data.

In GeeLytics, a network of edge nodes is considered, where each edge node comes with a built-in stream processing engine that can perform on-demand IoT stream data analytics. The system takes into account node characteristics and workload in order to achieve low latency analytics results while minimizing the edge-to-cloud bandwidth consumption. Especially the nodes' locations and topology are taken into account. The data streams generated by data producers can be fetched push-based or pull-based and uses a registry based on ElasticSearch.

Chen et al., 2019 [6] present an edge analytics system for power meters in smart homes. Also in this system, the edge serves as a gateway between the devices and the cloud and it is responsible for executing the analytics. On cloud-level, the system deploys user interfaces and provides interfaces to third-party services.

Furthermore, this is one of the few papers addressing also the training phase as part of the analytics approach. It points out repeatedly that the training is done in the cloud, while the trained model is deployed on the edge or even on an IoT end device.

Chowdhery et al. (Urban IoT edge analytics) [9] contend an edge-assisted architecture, in which edge computing is a key component for enabling urban IoT analytics in smart cities. It aims at tackling especially the requirement for an enormous amount of bandwidth and centralized real-time processing of such data volume. This architectural solution is based on having edge devices in a hierarchy alongside the existing cloud-based architecture to improve the overall system performance by offering a strong interconnection between information acquisition, data communication, and processing across the many geographical and system scales.

The layered architecture maximizes the efficiency of data communication through edge devices that are based on the notion of context- and computation-aware data selection and compression. These devices also enable content- and process-aware networking protocols for resource allocation and interference control. With maintained semantic structures, information searchability with improved availability is argued to be facilitated by this architecture.

Cao et al., 2018 [5] propose an edge computing platform for transportation transit systems producing data streams by the Internet of Mobile Things. It supports descriptive analytics at a mobile edge node and generates actionable information for transit managers. It utilizes mobile edge nodes that are physical devices deployed on a vehicle (e.g., a transit bus) where descriptive analytics is used to uncover meaningful patterns from real-time transit data streams.

The mobile edge node performs pre-processing for the online stream data to remove errors and inconsistencies. It is also responsible for three descriptive analytical tasks that aim at reducing the burden on the data hub as well as avoid bottlenecks due to lower network bandwidth. These tasks annotate data (i.e., vehicle moving or not), aggregate periods of the vehicle's trips, send it periodically to the hub, and give a summary on average trip times. Data sent to the hub is used for further pattern analysis and actions.

Wen et al. (ApproxIoT), 2018 [29] present an approach that uses approximate computing in order to enable real-time stream analytics with a focus on resource-efficiency. The main idea is to do the analytics over a representative sample instead of the entire input dataset and, thereby, address the trade-off between output accuracy and computational efficiency.

The network of edge nodes collecting data from the IoT devices performs a weighted hierarchical sampling algorithm. The goal is to parallelize the sampling process and, thereby, to make the system highly scalable. The degree of sampling is adjusted by the system based on resource constraints of the nodes. The actual processing of the samples, i.e., the analytics computation, is done in a central data center (e.g., the cloud). The implementation is based on Apache Kafka and Kafka Streams.

Ferdowsi et al., 2019 [10] provide an architecture for edge analytics within the context of intelligent transportation systems with the goal of achieving low latency and high reliability. They collect a heterogeneous mix of sensor data and combine and process it using deep learning techniques deployed on mobile edge nodes. The mobile edge nodes can be deployed at the vehicles or they can also be mobile phones of the passengers. The training of the utilized neural networks can be done offline. However, a less time-consuming training is mentioned as challenge yet to be solved.

Harth et al., 2017/18 [14, 15] execute predictive analytics on edge nodes. Their system determines locally whether to disseminate data in the edge network or not and also re-construct undelivered data in order to minimize the required communication.

For their predictions, Harth et al. do not only "push intelligence" to specific edge nodes but also to the devices (sensors and actuators) themselves. For the sake of improving the efficiency, they accept a reduction of the quality of analytics, but they argue that they are able to significantly decrease the communication overhead by tolerating a "relatively low" error.

Ukil et al., 2019: [28] present a system in the domain of healthcare that deploys a machine-learning-based system for evaluating cardiac health signals on the edge devices (here mainly smartphones). The data is provided by wearable sensors. Not only the analytics, but also the training of the ml model is supposed to be performed on the edge. The analytics results are accessed via an analytics platform portal.

Ukil et al.'s approach keeps it open to also involve the cloud for model development or for deploying the analytics. However, due to their domain, one main concern of their solution is controlled data privacy protection, which is an additional motivation for keeping the processing of the data on the edge. Their approach also involves obfuscation and elimination of sensitive data, based on configurable requirements.

5   Comparison and Discussion

In this section, we compare the reviewed approaches and discuss the differences.

5.1   Overview of Edge Analytics Features and Variants

Figure 2 shows the key results of our survey. It provides an overview of the features and their variants that we collected while reviewing the selected publications. We already addressed some parts of the feature space in Sect. 2, but here, we present a consolidated view based on the investigated publications. Please note that we do not claim that this overview is complete and shows all edge analytics features in general. It rather gives a first idea of the design space and of the variety of solutions that have been published on the architectural solutions for edge analytics. It is supposed to shed some light on the different design decisions that edge solution architects need to take into their consideration.

The first level of the feature diagram separates four subtrees: the data processed by the edge analytics solutions, the edge layer, the cloud layer, and the quality properties considered in the selected publications. The data subtree is further characterized by the different kinds of input providers and output consumers, the types of the data being processed, and the data mode. The edge subtree informs about the different roles of the edge, the multiplicity, and the functionalities/components hosted on the edge. The cloud subtree focuses on the different functionalities/components hosted on the cloud. For space reasons, some features have been aggregated. For example, "raw data processing" may include data buffering, filtering, aggregation, and optimization, while "data cleansing" may include detection/correction of incomplete/noisy data sets.

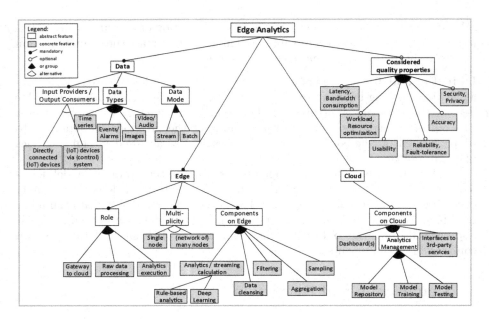

Fig. 2. Edge analytics features and variants

The considered quality properties include network-related qualities like latency and bandwidth consumption, but also workload and general resource optimization. Futhermore, software-related qualities like usability, reliability, fault-tolerance, security, and privacy play a role. Last but not least, also data-related qualities like accuracy are considered.

As software architectures usually depend on the use cases and the requirements derived from these use cases, in Table 1, we collected the domains, use cases, as well as the data types and modes they come with. As we can see, there are some approaches that are not developed for a specific domain or use case, however, many are. Especially the area of smart home/buildings/cities appears a lot. Some of the approaches state also the beneficiary stakeholders of their solutions. For example, in Xu et al. (EAaaS) [30], Cao et al. [5], and Chowdhery et al. [9], the end-user of the analytics solution is the advantage receiver like a transit manager, while in Wen et al. [29], it is the data analyst.

The table also confirms that most edge analytics approaches process real-time (online) data streams except for one approach serving batches [18,19]. Most of the selected approaches process time series of telemetry data collected from sensors, but some mention also other data types, e.g., video. Video processing is actually often called the "killer app" for edge analytics [3]. In our selection, we have this use case only once but there is a large body of literature on this topic as well.

Table 1. Comparison of use cases and input data

	Domain or use case	Processed data types	Data mode
Xu et al. (EAaaS), 2017 [30]	Power meter monitoring	time series	stream
Lujic et al., 2017/18 [18,19]	smart buildings, energy managem.	time series	batch
Cheng et al. (Geelytics), 2015/16 [7,8]	geo-distributed IoT systems	various	stream
Chen et al., 2019 [6]	power meters, smart home	time series	stream
Wen et al., 2018 [29]	general IoT	time series	stream
Ferdowsi et al., 2019 [10]	smart cities, transport. systems	various	stream
Harth et al., 2017/18 [14,15]	general IoT	time series	stream
Cao et al., 2017 [5]	transportation systems	time series	stream
Chowdhery et al., 2018 [9]	smart city, video processing	video	stream
Ukil et al., 2019 [28]	healthcare	time series	stream

Table 2 gives an overview of the deployment of components that are part of the selected edge analytics solutions to the edge and the cloud layer. Typical architectures involve both edge and cloud, but each approach comes with a different idea of which components to deploy where and why. A common pattern is that data is processed and analyzed on the edge but then forwarded to the cloud for presentation in dashboards or provided for access via APIs to 3rd party services. Sometimes, there are analytics components both on cloud and on edge, especially, when the edge is represented by a network of nodes and the cloud is needed to provide a consolidated view on multiple edge nodes. Some approaches are flexible regarding deployment to edge or cloud, e.g. [7,8]. There are also solutions with no cloud involved at all [5]. But in general, it is not always the case that the cloud plays a secondary role in edge analytics compared to the edge; but the preprocessing of data at the edge reduces the data that has to be analyzed on cloud level.

5.2 Highlighted Subjects for Further Discussion

In addition to the tables, we discuss some further topics addressed by the surveyed approaches the following. Many of the discussed topics include a lot of potential future research opportunities.

Table 2. Comparison of deployment to layers

	Components deployed on edge	Components deployed on cloud
Xu et al. (EAaaS), 2017 [30]	gateway controller, rule-based analytics engine, device adapter	data management, model management, interf. to 3rd-party services
Lujic et al., 2017/18 [18, 19]	monitoring, local analytics, data preparation, recovery of incomplete data, data storage, mediator	historial data repository, big data analytics
Cheng et al. (Geelytics), 2015/16 [7, 8]	controller nodes, compute nodes, master nodes	controller nodes, compute nodes, master nodes, dashboard
Chen et al., 2019 [6]	edge analytics, controller, gateway	interface to 3rd-party services, analytics, training, UI
Wen et al., 2018 [29]	sampling, pub/sub modules, computation, stream processing	query-based analytics
Ferdowsi et al., 2019 [10]	deep-learning based analytics	results collection, profiles storage for unpredictable situations
Harth et al., 2017/18 [14, 15]	data reconstr., training, context prediction, delivery decision-making	aggregation and predictive analytics
Cao et al., 2017 [5]	preprocessing, aggregation, analytics	–
Chowdhery et al., 2018 [9]	data selection, filtering, compression	analytics
Ukil et al., 2019 [28]	analytics, privacy protection control	interf. to 3rd-p.s, analytics portal

Maturity and Industrial Participation: Most of the surveyed approaches were published between 2015 and 2019 and they stem from academia, while some have been co-authored by industrial partners and describe industrial case studies. For example, Wen et al. [29] collaborate with Nokia Bell labs, Ferdowsi et al. with Ericsson, and Cao et al. [5] with Codiac Transit. For Xu et al. (EAaaS), [30] and Cheng et al. [7, 8], they stem from industry, namely from IBM Research and NEC laboratories respectively. It is also worth mentioning that all described systems seem to be prototypes, with no published product or sources mentioned. Still, some of them have been evaluated through industrial case studies with customers or partners [5, 19, 30].

However, going beyond the academic work, edge analytics is also seeing an increasing amount attention by well-known software companies, who now have related products in their portfolio. Microsoft enables its Azure Machine Learning Solution to be deployed as an IoT Edge module [21], Amazon has its AWS IoT Greengrass [2] solution, then there is Cisco which is working together with IBM to integrate IBM Watson into Cisco Edge Analytics [16], just to name a few. Furthermore, well-known companies that offer industrial control solutions, e.g., Siemens, ABB, Honeywell etc., all offer their own industrial edge analytics products, often relying on services from large cloud services providers such as Microsoft Azure or Amazon AWS in their implementation.

Network of Edges: Some of the investigated papers deal with a network of edge nodes (e.g., [7,9,15,29]). Others focus on what happens on one edge node [6,19,30]—which does not mean that their approaches cannot be applied or extended to edge networks as well. Also Harth et al. [15] distinguish between distributed analytics and group-based centralized analytics. In distributed analytics, there is a network of edge nodes collaborating in executing or training the analytics model. This can improve robustness and scalability but comes with the expense of additional communication overhead. In group-based centralized analytics, the focus is on one edge node, which may be more efficient with respect to communication but the scalability is limited and a single-point of failure is introduced. In general, the typical advantages and disadvantages of distributed vs. centralized systems play a role here and need to be evaluated and balanced when designing an edge analytics system.

Transfer of the Analytics Results: Most approaches aim at displaying the analytics results in a dashboard. However, edge analytics provides much more possibilities, as the analytics results are already close to the devices. This enables, for example, closed-loop control, where the analytics results are directly transferred back to the devices such that they can adjust accordingly. In our selection of approaches, only GeeLytics [7] mentions closed-loop control.

Dealing with Incomplete/Noisy Data: A common issue in analytics systems is the availability and quality of input data. In the real world, we usually deal with imperfect data, including incomplete, noisy, and imprecise data. This is even more usually the case, when dealing with a stream of data in real-time. This issue is only rarely discussed in the papers that we investigated. Only [19] has an additional component on the edge for incomplete dataset recovery, which seems to be a promising approach for many use cases.

Trade-Off: Efficiency vs. Accuracy: In contrast to inevitably dealing with imperfect input data, when processing data on the edge, there can be the need to intentionally produce a decrease of data quality for the sake of a better efficiency in terms of bandwidth reduction or general performance. Also efficiency with respect to computational power is a topic, especially for small edge devices or in cases where the IoT end devices (e.g., sensors) themselves are used for computation. In edge analytics, there are multiple flavors of the trade-off between efficiency and accuracy.

There are some papers especially interested in minimizing required communication/bandwidth by reducing the amount of data [15,29] or by compressing the data [9] going from devices to edge to cloud. In edge analytics, compression and filtering is often needed and can be essential for the scalability of the whole system. In the machine learning community it is common sense: We often do not need the perfect data, it just needs to be "good enough" for the current situation. However, determining "how good is good enough" and how to achieve this when designing the system is often tricky. As always, this trade-off needs to be addressed with regard to the underlying use case.

Models Training and Retraining: Interestingly, only few papers also mention how the training phase works in their system even though this is an important aspect for any ML/analytics-based system. In Chen et al.'s approach [6], training is done in the cloud, while the trained model is deployment on the edge, such that the analytics can run on the edge. This makes sense as training is often a expensive task in terms of resources and the benefits of executing analytics on the edge can still be leveraged when separating the training phase and the execution phase. However, there are many open questions on how to deal with this. For example, how does retraining work, in cases where the machine learning model does not perform well anymore? Model degradation necessarily happens to ML models over time, which leads to a need for (self-)adaptation opportunities within the software system [22]. In such cases, there needs to be additional interaction triggering a redeployment of the model from the cloud to the edge. Here, the topic of continuous delivery for analytics (AIOps/MLOps [20,27]) comes into play. However, we did not find any discussion on this topic in the papers that we considered as part of the survey.

Technologies: In the papers selected for this study, there are many technologies mentioned for edge, cloud, messaging, and AI/ML systems. However, none of them were reoccurring in more than two papers, except for the very basic technologies (REST, MQTT, Docker). Thus, it looks like, at least in the academic approaches, there is no very dominant technology yet, or at least there was none in the last years.

We would have expected a broader usage of the usual cloud provider solutions, like Azure IoT Edge, or of more advanced streaming frameworks, e.g., Kafka (as also used in [29]). We also wondered, why none of the described architectures touched upon 5G technology, which is expected to play an important role in industrial systems, also in the area of edge computing.

Further Subjects: For space reasons, we only discuss a selection of relevant subjects in the paper. Further relevant topics are security in edge analytics solutions, legal questions regarding the usage of platforms and AI/ML models in general, including IP protection of the models, and further quality properties like reliability and robustness, and many more.

Furthermore, please note that focusing on academic papers, while only marginally considering the industrial work on this topic, is a threat to the validity of this study. We take this point up again in the final section.

All in all, we conclude, that—even with the increasing interest seen in both industry and academia in the last years—the field of edge analytics is still forming and provides a lot of open challenges both in research, industrial application, and from a tooling perspective.

6 Conclusions

In this paper, we compared systems from academic literature dealing with edge analytics from a software architecture point of view. We presented the collected features and variants in the form of a feature model, compared the considered approaches, and discussed open challenges.

There are many aspects to consider when designing an edge analytics system in all devices, edge, and cloud layers, and concerning various quality characteristics. All in all, edge analytics is a rather novel topic but already gains a lot of interest in both academia and industry. Although there is a lot of literature already, there are still a lot of open challenges, especially from the perspective of software architecture.

In the future, we plan to extend our analysis to further approaches. In this paper, we only considered academic sources, however, as mentioned, there are many companies offering edge analytics solutions as well, ranging from the big IT companies over automation companies also to a variety of start ups with an AI focus. Thus, to get a complete picture, the industrial sources need to be taken into account as well. Based on an extended state-of-the-art analysis, next steps would then be a more detailed investigation of architectural alternatives and patterns for systems dealing with edge analytics and their advantages and disadvantages with respect to different use cases using real industrial systems.

References

1. Management of alarm systems for the process industries, ansi/isa-18.2-2016 (2016)
2. Amazon Web Services: AWS IoT Greengrass (2021). https://aws.amazon.com/greengrass/
3. Ananthanarayanan, G., et al.: Real-time video analytics: the killer app for edge computing. Computer **50**(10), 58–67 (2017)
4. Bosch, J., Olsson, H.H., Crnkovic, I.: Engineering AI systems: a research agenda. In: Artificial Intelligence Paradigms for Smart Cyber-Physical Systems, pp. 1–19. IGI Global (2021)
5. Cao, H., Wachowicz, M., Cha, S.: Developing an edge computing platform for real-time descriptive analytics. In: 2017 IEEE International Conference on Big Data (Big Data), pp. 4546–4554. IEEE (2017)
6. Chen, Y.Y., Lin, Y.H., Kung, C.C., Chung, M.H., Yen, I., et al.: Design and implementation of cloud analytics-assisted smart power meters considering advanced artificial intelligence as edge analytics in demand-side management for smart homes. Sensors **19**(9), 2047 (2019)
7. Cheng, B., Papageorgiou, A., Bauer, M.: Geelytics: enabling on-demand edge analytics over scoped data sources. In: International Congress on Big Data (BigData Congress), pp. 101–108. IEEE (2016)

8. Cheng, B., Papageorgiou, A., Cirillo, F., Kovacs, E.: Geelytics: geo-distributed edge analytics for large scale IoT systems based on dynamic topology. In: 2nd World Forum on Internet of Things (WF-IoT), pp. 565–570. IEEE (2015)

9. Chowdhery, A., Levorato, M., Burago, I., Baidya, S.: Urban IoT edge analytics. In: Rahmani, A.M., Liljeberg, P., Preden, J.-S., Jantsch, A. (eds.) Fog Computing in the Internet of Things, pp. 101–120. Springer, Cham (2018). https://doi.org/10.1007/978-3-319-57639-8_6

10. Ferdowsi, A., Challita, U., Saad, W.: Deep learning for reliable mobile edge analytics in intelligent transportation systems: an overview. IEEE Veh. Technol. Mag. **14**(1), 62–70 (2019)

11. Gartner: Gartner predicts the future of AI technologies (2019). https://www.gartner.com/smarterwithgartner/gartner-predicts-the-future-of-ai-technologies/

12. Goel, P., Datta, A., Mannan, M.S.: Industrial alarm systems: challenges and opportunities. J. Loss Prev. Process Ind. **50**, 23–36 (2017)

13. Gruener, S., Koziolek, H., Rueckert, J.: Towards resilient IoT messaging: an experience report analyzing MQTT brokers. In: 2021 IEEE International Conference on Software Architecture (ICSA). IEEE (2021)

14. Harth, N., Anagnostopoulos, C.: Quality-aware aggregation & predictive analytics at the edge. In: 2017 IEEE International Conference on Big Data (Big Data), pp. 17–26. IEEE (2017)

15. Harth, N., Anagnostopoulos, C., Pezaros, D.: Predictive intelligence to the edge: impact on edge analytics. Evol. Syst. **9**(2), 95–118 (2018)

16. Internet of Business, Cambridge Innovation Institute: Cisco and IBM team up to drive edge analytics for IoT (2021). https://internetofbusiness.com/cisco-ibm-team-drive-edge-analytics/

17. Khan, W.Z., Ahmed, E., Hakak, S., Yaqoob, I., Ahmed, A.: Edge computing: a survey. Futur. Gener. Comput. Syst. **97**, 219–235 (2019)

18. Lujic, I., De Maio, V., Brandic, I.: Efficient edge storage management based on near real-time forecasts. In: 2017 IEEE 1st International Conference on Fog and Edge Computing (ICFEC), pp. 21–30. IEEE (2017)

19. Lujic, I., De Maio, V., Brandic, I.: Adaptive recovery of incomplete datasets for edge analytics. In: 2nd International Conference on Fog and Edge Computing (ICFEC). pp. 1–10. IEEE (2018)

20. Masood, A., Hashmi, A.: AIOps: predictive analytics & machine learning in operations. In: Cognitive Computing Recipes, pp. 359–382. Apress, Berkeley, CA (2019). https://doi.org/10.1007/978-1-4842-4106-6_7

21. Microsoft: Azure IoT Edge (2021). https://azure.microsoft.com/en-us/services/iot-edge/

22. Muccini, H., Vaidhyanathan, K.: Software architecture for ml-based systems: what exists and what lies ahead. arXiv preprint arXiv:2103.07950 (2021)

23. Ng, A.: Why AI Is the New Electricity (2017). https://www.gsb.stanford.edu/insights/andrew-ng-why-ai-new-electricity

24. Niggemann, O., Frey, C.: Data-driven anomaly detection in cyber-physical production systems. at-Automatisierungstechnik **63**(10), 821–832 (2015)

25. Perino, J., Littlefield, M., Murugesan, V.: Living on the edge - edge computing in the new OT ecosystem. LNS Research (2020). https://resource.stratus.com/whitepaper/edge-computing-in-the-new-ot-ecosystem/

26. Satyanarayanan, M.: The emergence of edge computing. Computer **50**(1), 30–39 (2017)

27. Tamburri, D.A.: Sustainable MLOps: trends and challenges. In: 22nd Int. Symposium on Symbolic and Numeric Algorithms for Scientific Computing (SYNASC), pp. 17–23. IEEE (2020)
28. Ukil, A., Jara, A.J., Marin, L.: Data-driven automated cardiac health management with robust edge analytics and de-risking. Sensors **19**(12), 2733 (2019)
29. Wen, Z., Bhatotia, P., Chen, R., Lee, M., et al.: ApproxIoT: approximate analytics for edge computing. In: 2018 IEEE 38th Int. Conf. on Distributed Computing Systems (ICDCS), pp. 411–421. IEEE (2018)
30. Xu, X., Huang, S., Feagan, L., Chen, Y., Qiu, Y., Wang, Y.: EAaaS: edge analytics as a service. In: International Conference on Web Services (ICWS 2017), pp. 349–356. IEEE (2017)
31. Yu, W., et al.: A survey on the edge computing for the internet of things. IEEE Access **6**, 6900–6919 (2017)

How Software Architects Focus Their Attention

Eoin Woods[(✉)] [iD] and Rabih Bashroush [iD]

University of East London, University Way, London 16 2RD, UK
{eoin.woods,rabih.bashroush}@uel.ac.uk

Abstract. As part of our software architecture research and practice we have found that a common difficulty for new architects is knowing where to focus their attention to maximise their effectiveness. This led us to wonder whether successful experienced architects have any common techniques or heuristics that they use to help them achieve this. In an earlier study where, having interviewed experienced architects, we found that in fact there were some common heuristics that they use, we created a simple model based on an analysis of their advice. In this paper we explain how we validated that model with a wider survey of experienced enterprise and software architects and, from the findings of that study, extended the model with an additional dimension. This resulted in our model having four primary guidelines, which are: focus on stakeholder needs and priorities, prioritise time according to risks, delegate as much as possible, and ensure team effectiveness.

Keywords: Software architecture · Software architecture decision making · Software architect effectiveness

1 Introduction

In our research and practice in the field of software architecture, we have noticed and experienced that it is difficult for software architects to focus their attention. The software architect's responsibilities are broad and in principle they can be involved in almost any technical aspect of a project from requirements to operational concerns.

However, we also observe that successful software architects appear to be very good at focusing their attention effectively, which led us to wonder how they achieve this. They may use time management techniques (like [2]) but we wondered whether there are common role-specific heuristics which could be taught to new architects.

In a previous study [15], we decided to investigate this via a questionnaire-based study of a group of experienced architects. We discovered that there are common heuristics which experienced architects use to focus their attention and we created a model to capture and relate them.

In this paper we explain how, in a second study, we then validated the model with a much wider group of software and enterprise architects, via an online questionnaire, and refined the model based on their input.

In the next section of this paper we present the refined model and, in the rest of the paper, we briefly summarise the earlier work and then explain how we went about validating the original model and identifying that an extension to it was required.

© Springer Nature Switzerland AG 2021
S. Biffl et al. (Eds.): ECSA 2021, LNCS 12857, pp. 312–326, 2021.
https://doi.org/10.1007/978-3-030-86044-8_21

The contribution of our work is not the heuristics in our model, as most of them are quite familiar to experienced practitioners. Our contribution is to capture them clearly in a simple, coherent model, and to validate their value to experienced practitioners. Our work makes the implicit knowledge held in the heads of experienced architects explicit and accessible. We believe that this makes the model a useful reminder for experienced practitioners and an effective teaching aid for new architects.

2   A Model for Focusing Architectural Attention

Our experience-based model to guide architects where to focus their attention in order to maximise their effectiveness is shown in Fig. 1.

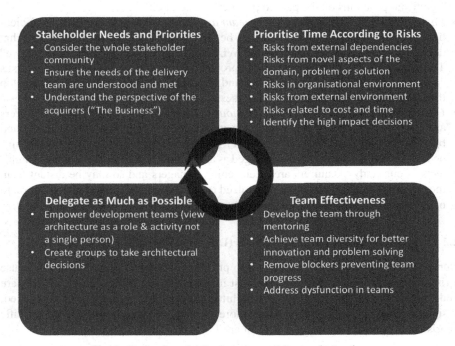

Stakeholder Needs and Priorities
- Consider the whole stakeholder community
- Ensure the needs of the delivery team are understood and met
- Understand the perspective of the acquirers ("The Business")

Prioritise Time According to Risks
- Risks from external dependencies
- Risks from novel aspects of the domain, problem or solution
- Risks in organisational environment
- Risks from external environment
- Risks related to cost and time
- Identify the high impact decisions

Delegate as Much as Possible
- Empower development teams (view architecture as a role & activity not a single person)
- Create groups to take architectural decisions

Team Effectiveness
- Develop the team through mentoring
- Achieve team diversity for better innovation and problem solving
- Remove blockers preventing team progress
- Address dysfunction in teams

Fig. 1. Refined model for focusing architectural attention

The model is comprised of 4 aspects: Stakeholder Needs and Priorities, Prioritise Time According to Risks, Delegate as Much as Possible and Team Effectiveness. It provides a guide, or an aide memoir, on how to prioritise architectural work to maximise its effectiveness. Each of these aspects is explained in the subsections below.

2.1   Stakeholder Needs and Priorities

The first theme which emerged strongly in our study was to focus on the needs and priorities of the stakeholders involved in the situation. The principle that architecture work involves working closely with stakeholders is widely agreed [3, 13] and this theme reinforces that.

Architects need to focus significant effort to make sure that stakeholder needs and priorities are understood, in order to maximise focus on the critical success factors for a project and maximise the chances of its success. Three specific heuristics to achieve this which emerged from the study are:

- *Consider the whole stakeholder community.* Spend time understanding the different groups in the stakeholder community and avoid the mistake of just considering obvious stakeholder groups like end-users, acquirers and the development team. As the architecture methods referenced above note, ignoring important stakeholders (like operational staff or auditors) can prevent the project meeting its goals and cause significant problems on the path to production operation.
- *Ensure that the needs of the delivery team are understood and met.* Spend sufficient time to ensure that the delivery team can be effective. What is the team good at? What does it know? What does it not know? What skill and knowledge gaps does it have? These areas need attention early in the project so that architecture work avoids risks caused by the capabilities of the team and that time is taken to support and develop the team to address significant weaknesses.
- *Understand the perspective and perceptions of the acquirers of the system.* Acquirers are a key stakeholder group who judge its success and usually have strategic and budgetary control, so can halt the project if they are unhappy. Addressing this group's needs, perceptions and concerns emerged as an important factor for experienced architects in our study. Acquirers are often senior managers and so may be distant from the day-to-day reality of a project and need regular, targeted, clear communication to understand their concerns and ensure that they have a realistic view of the project.

2.2 Prioritise Time According to Risks (Driven by Impact × Probability)

During a project, an effective approach to prioritising architectural attention is to use a risk driven approach to identify the most important tasks. If the significant risks are understood and mitigated, then enough architecture work has probably been completed. If significant risks are unmitigated, then more architecture work is needed. The specific heuristics to consider for risk assessment are:

- *Risks from external dependencies.* Understand your external dependencies because you have little control over them, and they need architectural attention early in the project and whenever things change.
- *Risks from novel aspects of the domain, problem, or solution.* Another useful heuristic, from the experience of our study participants, is to focus on novelty in your project. What is unfamiliar? What problems have you not solved before? Which technology is unproven? The answers to these questions highlight risks and the participants in our study used them to direct their effort to the most important risks to address.
- *Risks in the organisational environment.* Each organisation is different and there are nearly always risks specific to an environment such as the internal political situation, what is possible in the organisational culture, and the maturity of the organisation

with respect to architecture, change and risk. Different organisations have different cultures and capabilities for change, which can create risks. The speed which different sorts of risk can be addressed can also be affected by organisational factors and so may cause you to change where you focus attention. Participants in our study noted the importance of "situational awareness" [14] to allow risks specific to the organisational environment to be identified and addressed.

- *Risks from the external environment.* Nearly all organisations exist in a complex ecosystem of interacting partners, customers, regulators, competitors and other actors and they can be a source of risk for many systems. So can general trends and changes in the industry that the organisation exists within (such as a changing regulatory environment, or industry wide pressures such as reducing margins on products or services).
- *Risks related to cost and time.* Most architects will report that they are often expected to achieve challenging goals in unrealistic timescales or with unrealistic cost estimates. Many of our study participants reported that they needed to focus significant attention on risks resulting from cost and time.
- *Identify the high impact decisions.* Prioritise architecture work that will help to mitigate risks where many people would be affected by a problem (e.g. problems with the development environment or problems that will prevent effective operation) or where the risk could endanger the programme (e.g. missing regulatory constraints).

2.3   Delegate as Much as Possible

Delegation was an unexpected theme that emerged from our study. The architects who mentioned this theme viewed themselves as a potential bottleneck in a project and focusing attention on the delegation and empowerment of others was a way to minimize this. Delegation was also seen as a way of freeing the architect to focus on the most important aspects of the project.

The general message of this theme is to delegate as much architecture work as possible to the person or group best suited to perform it. This prevents individuals becoming project bottlenecks, allowed architects to spend more time on risk identification and mitigation, and spreads architectural knowledge through the organisation. The heuristics that were identified to help achieve this are:

- *Empower the development teams.* To allow delegation and work sharing, architects need to empower (and trust) the teams that they work with. This allows governance to become a shared responsibility and architecture to be viewed as an activity rather than something that is only performed by one person or a small group. This causes architectural knowledge, effort, and accountability to be spread across the organisation, creates shared ownership, reduces the load on any one individual and prevents a single individual from delaying progress.
- *Create groups to take architectural responsibilities.* A related heuristic is to formalise delegation and create groups of people to be accountable for specific aspects of architectural work. For example, in a large development programme, an architecture review board can be created to review and approve significant architectural decisions. Such a group can involve a wide range of expertise from across the programme and beyond,

so freeing a lead architect from much of the effort involved in gathering and under-standing the details of key decisions, while maintaining effective oversight to allow risks to be controlled and technical coherence maintained. Similarly, a specific group of individuals could be responsible for resilience and disaster recovery for a large programme, allowing them to specialise and focus on this complex area, and allowing a lead architect to confidently delegate to them, knowing that they will have the focus and expertise to address this aspect of the architecture.

2.4 Team Effectiveness

A theme that emerged when we validated our initial model with a wider group was the need to spend time making sure that the development team was as effective as possible. The participants who highlighted this factor were concerned with developing the individuals in the team and ensuring that the team was as diverse as possible, to provide it with a range of skills and perspectives.

Other aspects of this theme were the importance of architecture work being used to quickly unblock the team when it hit difficulties and the importance of technical leaders, like the architect, to step in when needed to make sure that the team was functioning well and to address any dysfunctional behaviour observed.

The heuristics identified as being important for achieving team effectiveness were:

- *Develop the team through mentoring.* Every team should be on a collective journey towards improvement and hopefully every individual in a team is on a similar personal journey to be the best that they can be. People doing architecture work tend to be experienced, so a valuable area to focus attention is developing the individuals and the team as a whole, through thoughtful, intentional mentoring.
- *Achieve team diversity for better innovation and problem solving.* To innovate and identify good solutions to problems, it is valuable to have a range of experience, perspectives and skills in the team. Our study participants indicated that a valuable use of time is building diverse teams that can achieve this.
- *Remove blockers preventing team progress.* Development and support teams often end up blocked by technical or organisational factors, so spending time resolving these problems is a valuable focus for many architects.
- *Address dysfunction in teams.* Sometimes teams don't work well, and it requires someone who is close to the team, and respected by them, but outside the team structure, to identify the problem and suggest solutions. People doing architecture work are often close to the teams but outside their structure, and have the respect, soft-skills and experience to resolve team problems. This use of architectural time can have huge benefits when dysfunctional behaviour is observed in teams.

2.5 Summary

This model provides a simple guide to focusing architectural attention during a project. It is comprised of 4 aspects: Stakeholder Needs and Priorities, Prioritise Time According to Risks, Delegate as Much as Possible and Team Effectiveness. We believe that it can be an effective guide or reminder on the best ways to focus architecture work during a project.

In common with any set of heuristics, the model is only a starting point and must be considered, interpreted, and applied in a context specific way by the architects and teams who use it. However, as we explain later in the paper, it has validated well against a reasonably broad survey of experienced, practicing architects and so we believe that it is a useful guide upon which to build a personal approach for prioritisation.

3   Related Work

When we started investigating this topic, we were primarily interested in how practitioners really worked. However, we also performed a literature search to find related work from the research community.

We did not find any studies investigating the specific topic we are interested in, but an architectural method which helps architects to focus their attention is Risk and Cost Driven Architecture (RCDA) [11]. This method transforms the architect's approach from defining architectural structures early in a project, to providing a stream of decisions throughout it, prioritising their work using the risk and cost of open decisions. This guides the architect to focus on the important architectural decisions to work on at any point in time but does not provide any guidance beyond that aspect of their work. So, while valuable, it is quite narrow in this regard. Also, while a recognised approach, it isn't very widely used in the industry, so we were interested how the practitioners who don't use RCDA prioritise their attention.

We also found some very specific advice from a very experienced architect and researcher [9] that architects should spend 50% of their time on architecting, 25% on inbound communication and 25% on outbound communication. However, this is anecdotal advice based on personal experience, so we don't know how many (if any) practitioners follow this advice.

In the research domain we found a research on the prioritisation of requirements [4, 6] and a literature review of this area as of 2014 [1]. Prioritising requirements is related to focusing architectural attention, but it is only one factor from a large possible set, so this research was not very relevant to our investigation.

Finally, there is a large amount of mainstream business literature on time management (such as [1, 8]) however we were interested in providing more specific advice for software architects rather than this sort of more general advice.

4   Research Method

When planning this research, we selected a qualitative research approach because we wanted to explore the "lived-experiences" of expert practitioners by asking them questions to encourage reflection and insight [12] rather than assessing performance or alignment with specific practices via quantitative means.

The process was organised into four distinct stages.

- Stage 1: gathering primary data using semi-structured interviews with practitioners.

- Stage 2: analysis of the primary data and creation of a preliminary model.
- Stage 3: validation of the preliminary model via a structured online questionnaire, completed by practitioners in relevant architecture roles (primarily software, solution, and enterprise architects).
- Stage 4: analysis of the validation data and refinement of the preliminary model into a final, validated model.

The first two stages were reported in [15] but we will briefly explain the whole process here for the sake of clarity.

We chose to gather our primary data using semi-structured interviews, providing interviewees with a written introduction to the question we wanted to answer and some questions to start them thinking. The content of the interviews was analysed through iterative thematic coding and, as suggested in [12], the process of collection and analysis was iterative and exploratory rather than a rigid linear one.

This exercise produced a set of heuristics that the architects use with themes to classify them. A heuristic had to be mentioned by at least three of the participants (a third of them) for us to consider it significant enough to be included in the model. We combined the themes and heuristics to form a simple model (the "preliminary model") of how experienced architects go about prioritizing their effort.

Once we had the preliminary model we published it at a research conference [15] and via a LinkedIn post[1] and created an online questionnaire to allow architecture practitioners to evaluate and comment on the usefulness of the model. We publicised the survey via LinkedIn, Twitter and email to our network of architects.

We received 84 responses to the survey that answered our closed-ended questions, of which 50 contained answers to the open-ended questions. We used the closed-ended questions to evaluate the usefulness of the model and analysed the open-ended responses to identify themes missing from the model.

The model was validated strongly across respondents from different locations, with varying amounts of experience, and from different architectural specialisations. A small number of suggestions for improvement emerged from the answers to the open-ended questions. These suggestions were used to revise and extend the model, creating an improved final version, that reflected the input from the respondents.

A description of the four stages of the research method is presented in the following sections of the paper.

5   Stages 1 and 2: The Initial Study

Our primary data gathering was performed using a semi-structured, face-to-face survey of 8 experienced software architecture practitioners in 4 countries. As Stages 1 and 2 were previously reported in [15] we just summarise the work here.

We found the participants by approaching suitable individuals from our professional networks. We were looking for practitioners who had a minimum of 10 years' professional experience and who worked as architects in the information systems domain (rather than architects from – for example – embedded systems).

---

[1] https://www.linkedin.com/pulse/focusing-software-architects-attention-eoin-woods.

We focused on the information systems domain because we know from experience that working practices differ between professional domains like information systems and embedded systems. Hence, we thought it more likely that we could create a useful model if we limited ourselves to one broad domain, at least initially.

Our preliminary model for focusing architectural attention is shown in Fig. 2.

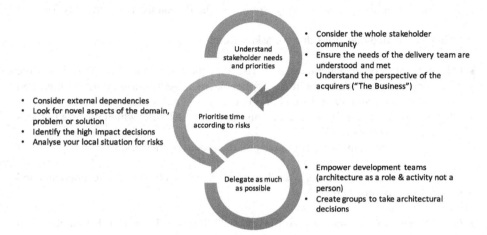

Fig. 2. Preliminary model for focusing architectural attention

The three categories of heuristic that the study revealed were: the need to focus on stakeholder needs, the importance of considering risks when deciding on where to focus attention, and finally the importance of spending time to achieve effective delegation of responsibilities. These categories form the structure of our model and remind the architect of the general ways in which they should focus their attention. The categories and heuristics are explained in [15] and Sect. 2 of this paper.

6   Stage 3: Validating the Preliminary Model

6.1   The Questionnaire

Once we had a preliminary model, we wanted to validate its usefulness with a much larger group of experienced practitioners using a structured online questionnaire.

The questionnaire asked the respondents to read the model and then comment on its credibility and usefulness. We asked both closed questions, that asked respondents to rate the model on 5-point scales, and open-ended questions that allowed the respondents to consider whether there were aspects of focusing attention that we had missed and to collect general comments on the model. Finally, we asked some closed classification questions to allow us to understand who had completed the survey, while preserving their anonymity if desired.

We asked three closed-ended questions to find out whether the respondent thought that the model was credible and useful. These questions and possible responses were:

- Q1. "Is this model similar to how you focus architectural attention in your work already?" Not at all similar/Not Very Similar/Somewhat Similar/Quite Similar/Very Similar
- Q2. "Would you find this model helpful in guiding architectural attention for maximum benefit?" Definitely Not/Probably Not/Possibly/Probably Yes/Definitely Yes
- Q3. "Are the areas of risk mentioned in the "Prioritise time according to risks" activity valuable?" Definitely Not/Probably Not/Somewhat/Probably Yes/Definitely Yes

The open-ended questions that we asked were:

- Q4. "Are there other general areas of risk that should be added to "Prioritise time according to risks" that would be applicable to most (information) systems and environments? If so please list and briefly explain them."
- Q5. "Are there any significant factors missing from the model which you use to focus your architectural work?"
- Q6. "Do you have any other comments on the model or the survey"

The closed-ended questions we asked to allow us to classify the respondents and their possible answers were:

- Q7. "What environment do you work in?" Industry/Industrial Research/ Academic/Other (please specify)
- Q8. How many years of post-graduation experience do you have? 1–5 years/5–10 years/10–15 years/15–20 years/More than 20 years
- Q9. What is your main job role? Software Architect/Enterprise Architect/Software Designer/Researcher/Other (please specify)
- Q10. Where in the world are you based? North America/South America/Europe (inc. UK) / Middle-East and Africa/Asia-Pacific/Other (please specify)

Having trialled the questionnaire ourselves, and with two other individuals, we expected most respondents to take 10 – 15 min to complete it.

6.2 The Respondents

To use the questionnaire to validate the model, we needed to find a suitable set of architects who could read it and complete the survey for us. We found our initial respondents via a LinkedIn post (https://www.linkedin.com/pulse/focusing-software-architects-attention-eoin-woods/) that appeared in the LinkedIn news feed of practitioners, which resulted in 23 people completing the survey successfully.

To gain more responses to the survey, we sent a targeted email to practicing software, solution and enterprise architects in our professional network, which resulted in 61 more responses to the survey, making a total of 84 completed surveys.

About a third of the respondents identified themselves as software architects, about a quarter as enterprise architects, about 12% as software designers, 10% as solution architects, and 5% as technical architects. Four respondents didn't complete this answer and four had other job titles (a risk assessor, a technical manager and systems engineer, a project manager and a strategy consultant).

We asked the respondents to classify their work environment as Industry, Industrial Research or Academic and a few respondents self-identified as working in the public sector. 78 respondents (~90%) were from industry or building systems in the public sector (several of whom identified as both "Industry" and "Industry Research"), one was from an academic work environment and 5 (~6%) did not answer this question.

We then asked respondents where they worked geographically, and 55% of respondents identified themselves as from Europe, 30% from the Americas and only 7% from Asia-Pacific and a single correspondent from the Middle East and Africa.

We discuss the possible impact of geographical location when we consider threats to validity, but we think that we achieved good cross-geographic participation, but still ended up with a strong bias to Western Europe and North America.

The final classification we asked our respondents for was the number of years of experience that they had. Over half of them (55%) had at least 20 years of post-graduation experience, 17% had 15–20 years of experience, 15% had 10–15 years of experience 7% had 5–10 years if experience and only one respondent had less than 5 years of experience. Four of our correspondents did not answer this question.

6.3   The Closed-Ended Responses

As mentioned earlier, we structured the questionnaire into two parts, the closed-ended questions that asked people to rate the usefulness of the model and the open-ended questions that asked whether we had missed anything important from it. In this section, we review and analyse the responses for the closed-ended questions.

The first question we asked was to find out if the model was similar to how experienced architects already focused their attention, to assess the basic credibility of the model for experienced architects. 75% of respondents indicated that it was "very similar" or "quite similar" to their existing approach for focusing their attention, 20% said it was "somewhat similar", 5% said it was "not very similar" to how they worked, and no respondents replied that it was "not at all similar". These responses suggest that the model validates strongly against the participants' existing practice.

The second question attempted to establish, whether the respondents thought that model would be useful in practice. 27% responded that it was "definitely useful", 43% that it was "probably useful", 26% said "possibly useful" and 3 respondents (4%) said "probably not". These responses suggest that most of the participants see probable value in the model (i.e., 70% see it as definitely or probably useful).

Finally, we wanted to check that the areas of risk we had identified as important within the "prioritise time according to risks" heuristic were valuable to a practicing architect. 43% of respondents indicated "definitely yes", 37% indicated "probably yes", 15% responded "somewhat", 4% as "probably not" and a single respondent indicated "definitely not". The single individual who indicated "definitely not" was an enterprise architect in the 10 – 15 years of experience group, who commented in the open-ended questions that he did not believe that it was possible to define general software development risks in a useful way.

From this response, 80% of respondents believe that the areas of risk were "definitely" or "probably" valuable, suggesting that this aspect of the model should be of value to many practitioners.

In summary, having analysed the answers to the closed-ended answers in our survey, we conclude that our model is likely to be credible and useful for the architects who responded to our survey and broadly aligns with the prioritization approach used by many experienced architects.

We interpret these results as a successful validation of the model, but we were also interested in how the model could be improved and so we used the responses to the open-ended questions in the survey to find themes that we might have missed.

6.4   The Open-Ended Responses

As explained earlier, we asked two open-ended, questions, Q4, to identify missing risk factors from the "prioritise time according to risks" heuristic (*"are there other general areas of risk that should be added to "prioritise time according to risks" that would be applicable to most (information) systems and environments?"*) and Q5, to ask whether we had missed any aspects of the model (*"are there any significant factors missing from the model which you use to focus your architectural work?"*). We had 44 responses to Q4, about missing risk factors, and 51 responses to Q5, about missing areas of risk.

Given the nature of these responses, we again used a simple thematic coding analysis to analyse them, coding each one initially using straightforward, descriptive labels, reflecting the language in the response, then refining this with further coding steps, to identify higher-level categories to group the responses into.

For the first question, Q4, we initially coded the responses to 37 distinct categories, plus two null categories for the initial coding of "None" and "General Comment". The responses suggested a diverse range of possible risk areas, and when we refined the coding to find common concepts, this resulted in 24 higher level categories.

We attempted to refine this further but did not find further meaningful refinements as we tried further rounds of coding and ended up with a very long "tail" of risk areas with only a single mention in the responses. We ended up with 5 categories that had 4 responses or more: Organisational Environment (11 occurrences), Stakeholders (6 occurrences), Cost (6 occurrences), Time (4 occurrences) and External Environment (4 occurrences). We chose to focus on categories with at least 4 occurrences as this represents approximately 5% of the total respondents to the survey and we judged this to be high enough to include as risk areas for the "prioritising time according to risks" element, in the refined version of the model, presented in Sect. 2.

For the second open-ended question, Q5, on missing aspects of the model, we initially coded the responses into 43 distinct categories and continued with the process of refining the coding further, ending up with 26 higher level categories. As with the responses to Q4, many of the categories were only mentioned once and only four were mentioned 4 times or more: Team Effectiveness (10), Benefits (7), Stakeholders (6) and Time (5). Of these factors, "Stakeholders" are already a significant factor in the model and the comments provided in these cases were suggesting a particular emphasis on certain stakeholders or method of dealing with stakeholders, suggesting that a new element was not needed in the model.

Adding a completely new aspect to the model is a significant step and so we only wanted to consider this for aspects which had been identified as important by a significant number of respondents to the survey. Hence we decided to add a new element to the model to reflect the "Team Effectiveness" theme as it was the only additional aspect that at least 10% of the respondents had identified as important.

Finally, we also received 51 general comments in the open-ended questions which we thematically coded into 23 groups, most of which had one or two comments in them. However, there were 14 "Positive Comments", 6 about "How the Architect Should Work" and 5 on the "Presentation of the Model".

These comments were interesting but only the five comments on the presentation of the model suggested the need to change the model. These comments consistently suggested that our graphical presentation indicated a linear process, whereas we actually meant to communicate a continuous process throughout the project lifecycle, so this was an indicator that we needed a better graphical representation for the mode.

7 Stage 4: The Refined Model

We took the results of the open-ended question analysis described in Sect. 6.4 and used them to add missing features to the model, improve the list of risks to suggest for time prioritisation and improve the model using the advice provided in the general comment responses to the survey. The result of this work is the model that was presented in Sect. 2.

As can be seen, if you compare the final model in Sect. 2 with the preliminary model in Sect. 5, three significant changes have been made:

1. An additional feature, "Team Effectiveness", has been added to the final model, because this theme was noted as an important missing feature of the model by more than 10% of the respondents to the survey.
2. The list of risks to use to guide time prioritisation has been extended and refined based on common suggestions made from question 4 in the survey.
3. In response to comments in the survey' open-ended questions, the graphical presentation of the model has been altered to try to emphasise that it is not a linear "process" but a set of activities to be performed throughout the project lifecycle.

The result is a model that guides an architect where to focus their attention during a project, focusing on four themes: Stakeholder Needs and Priorities, Prioritise Time According to Risks, Delegate as Much as Possible and Team Effectiveness.

In common with any set of heuristics, the model must be considered, interpreted, and applied in a context specific way, but it validated well against a reasonably broad survey of experienced, practicing architects and so we believe that it should be a useful guide for many practitioners.

We did not ask participants in the study whether they had a particular architectural domain specialisation (such as web-based systems, data analytics systems, embedded systems and so on) however we didn't target any specific group as we did in the preliminary study (where we limited ourselves to information systems architects) and we didn't get any comments about applicability to specific domains in the open-ended answers to the survey. This leads us to have reasonable confidence that the lessons captured in the model are quite widely applicable.

8   Threats to Validity

Specific steps we took to ensure the integrity of this work included focusing on the practitioner community (the intended users of the model), focusing on experienced respondents who have the experience to evaluate the model, finding a reasonably large, geographically distributed group to validate it for us, structuring the questionnaire to allow disagreement as well as confirmation, and analysing the results in a careful, structured manner to allow the data to lead us to the conclusions, to avoid unconscious bias. However, we acknowledge that there are potential limitations to any qualitative study, which could threaten our study's validity.

There are four main types of threat to the validity of a study like this, namely construct, internal, external and conclusion validity as defined in [10].

Construct validity is concerned with the relationship between theory and observation. Common threats when using questionnaires are the phrasing of the questions and using too many closed-ended questions. We kept the questions brief and refined the questionnaire wording after testing it. We provided open-ended questions for the participants to explain, expand or clarify their answers.

Internal validity is concerned with the validity of the causality relationship between the observations and the outcomes of the study. We addressed this by using very straightforward analysis so the threats to the correctness of the analysis we performed are minor. We also reviewed each respondent's responses for coherence.

External validity is concerned with the generalisability of the results of the study. In our case the key risk is an unrepresentative respondent population. We mitigated this risk through a geographically distributed, relatively large respondent population. However, a residual risk is the lack of representation from Asia. We mitigated concerns about experience and competence by targeting experienced architects. We know a significant percentage of the respondents at least slightly and have confidence in their ability to validate the model. This leaves us with a residual risk that our participants may share more common opinions than a random sample, but anecdotally we believe that they are similar to most practitioners we have met over the years.

Conclusion validity is concerned with the validity of the relationship between the data obtained in the study and the conclusions that have been drawn from it. We mitigated the possibility of asking the wrong questions by using a semi-structured interview in the first stage and providing extensive opportunity for open-ended responses in the third stage. We mitigated risks of analytical mistakes by reviewing and cross checking our work and using a simple, repeatable process. We avoided unconscious bias by using a structured coding process for open-ended question analysis, to allow us to be led by the data.

In summary, we designed and executed the study carefully but acknowledge that there are some threats to its validity which could threaten the generalizability of our results. The most significant is the lack of Asian participation, however a model useful in Europe and America would still be a valuable outcome.

9 Future Work

The refined model is now ready for dissemination to the practitioner community to see if it proves as useful in practice as our survey of the preliminary model suggests. We have already published the refined model in a less formal style via LinkedIn[2], resulting in a number of positive comments. We will also try to publish a summary of it in practitioner-oriented publications and publicise it through practitioner conferences, if it proves to be of interest to programme selection committees.

We could also run a further study to establish if there are useful elements missing from the model, such as those related to design, implementation, modelling and other more general and technical aspects of architecture work. These may not have been mentioned by the experienced practitioners because they have largely been internalised due to their level of expertise. Or it is possible that they are not all that useful for prioritisation of architectural attention.

Finally, another possible area of study is the validation of Philippe Kruchten's insight [9] that they should spend 50% of their time on architecting, 25% on inbound communication and 25% on outbound communication.

10 Conclusion

Our experience and informal discussion with architects over many years suggested that they find it difficult to decide how to focus their attention to maximise their effectiveness. We were interested in how experienced practitioners solved this problem and whether there were commonly used heuristics. To investigate this, we used a four-step process of investigation.

We started with a semi-structured interview process with eight experienced practitioners and concluded that there are some shared heuristics which practitioners use, but that practicing architects are not aware that the heuristics are common and shared. We found that the heuristics clustered into three groups: focus the architects attention on stakeholders, use their time to address specific risks and delegate as much as possible, in order to give them as much time for architecture work as possible.

We then created a simple structured model to capture and explain the heuristics that emerged from the initial study and we published this via social media channels. In the next step, we asked practitioners to complete a survey to comment on the usefulness of the model and whether anything had been missed. 84 responses were received to the survey, mainly from European and North American software, solution and enterprise architects with over 10 years of professional experience.

When we analysed the survey responses we found that the model validated well, as 70% of the respondents think it would probably or definitely be useful, but we found that we had missed several important risk factors which are commonly used for prioritisation and we had missed an element of focusing attention, which is the need to ensure overall team effectiveness. We added these missing elements to the model.

These findings are not completely unexpected and many of the heuristics in the model are familiar. However, neither the participants or ourselves knew that these were

---

[2] https://www.linkedin.com/pulse/revisiting-how-people-prioritise-software-work-eoin-woods.

the important, shared heuristics before we undertook the study, so we believe that the model that we have created will have value as a teaching aid and as an aide memoir for experienced practitioners.

We have started to publicise the model via social media and plan to continue this by incorporating it into practitioner-oriented articles and conference talks. If the model gains some acceptance over a period of time, there would be value in a future survey of its users to review the model's usefulness after experience of using it.

References

1. Achimugu, P., Selamat, A., Ibrahim, R., Mahrin, M.: A systematic literature review of software requirements prioritization research. Inf. Softw. Technol. **56**(6), 568–585 (2014)
2. Allen, D.: Getting Things Done: The Art of Stress-free Productivity, 2nd edn. Piatkus, Piatkus (2015)
3. Bass, L., Clements, P., Kazman, R.: Software architecture in practice, 3rd edn. Addison Wesley, Upper Saddle River (2012)
4. Berander, P., Andrews, A.: Requirements prioritization. In: Aurum, A., Wohlin, C. (eds.) Engineering and Managing Software Requirements, pp. 69–94. Springer, Heidelberg (2005). https://doi.org/10.1007/3-540-28244-0_4
5. Harindran A., Chandra V.: Research Methodology. Pearson, London (2017).
6. Herrmann, A., Daneva, M.: Requirements prioritization based on benefit and cost prediction: an agenda for future research. In: Tetsuo, T. (ed.) 2008 16th IEEE International Requirements Engineering RE 2008. IEEE (2008)
7. Karlsson, J., Ryan, K.: A cost-value approach for prioritizing requirements. IEEE Softw. **14**(5), 67–74 (1997)
8. Koch, K.: The 80/20 Principle: The Secret of Achieving More with Less. Nicholas Brearley Publishing Boston (2007)
9. Kruchten, P.: What do software architects really do? J. Syst. Softw. **81**(12), 2413–2416 (2008)
10. Matt, G.E., Cook, T.D.: Threats to the validity of research synthesis. In: Cooper, H., Hedges, L.V. (eds.) The Handbook of Research Synthesis, pp. 503–520. Russell Sage Foundation, New York (1994)
11. Poort, E.R., van Vliet, H.: RCDA: architecting as a risk-and cost management discipline. J. Syst. Softw. **85**(9), 1995–2013 (2012)
12. Reimer, F.J., Quartaroli, M.T., Lapan, S.D.: Qualitative Research: An Introduction to Methods and Designs. Wiley, London (2012)
13. Rozanski, N., Woods, E.: Software Systems Architecture, Working with Stakeholders Using Viewpoints and Perspectives, 2nd edn. Addison Wesley, Upper Saddle River (2011)
14. Wikipedia: Situational Awareness. https://en.wikipedia.org/wiki/Situation_awareness. Accessed 10 Apr 2017
15. Woods, E., Bashroush, R.: A model for prioritization of software architecture effort. In: Lopes, A., de Lemos, R. (eds.) ECSA 2017. LNCS, vol. 10475, pp. 183–190. Springer, Cham (2017). https://doi.org/10.1007/978-3-319-65831-5_13

Author Index

Printed in the United States
by Baker & Taylor Publisher Services